Language through Culture, Culture through Language:
A Framework for K—8 Mandarin Curriculum

教汉语教文化
美国幼儿园至八年级汉语及中国文化课程设计

〔美〕柯雪润　主编
〔美〕柯雪润　田凤英　郑莉玲　著
王海颖　〔美〕柯雪润　赵文娟　译

Chief Editor: Sharon A. Carstens
Authors: Sharon A. Carstens, Tien Whyte, Li-Ling Cheng
Translators: Haiying Wang, Sharon A. Carstens, Wenjuan Zhao

北京大学出版社
PEKING UNIVERSITY PRESS

图书在版编目(CIP)数据

教汉语,教文化:美国幼儿园至八年级汉语及中国文化课程设计/(美)柯雪润(Carstens,S.)主编;(美)柯雪润,田凤英,郑莉玲;王海颖,(美)柯雪润,赵文娟译.—北京:北京大学出版社,2013.5
ISBN 978-7-301-22494-6

Ⅰ.①教… Ⅱ.①柯…②田…③郑…④王…⑤赵… Ⅲ.①汉语—对外汉语教学—课堂教学—课程设计 Ⅳ.①H195.3

中国版本图书馆 CIP 数据核字(2013)第 092341 号

书　　　名：教汉语,教文化:美国幼儿园至八年级汉语及中国文化课程设计
著作责任者：〔美〕柯雪润　主编
　　　　　　〔美〕柯雪润　田凤英　郑莉玲　著
　　　　　　王海颖　〔美〕柯雪润　赵文娟　译
责 任 编 辑：刘　飞
标 准 书 号：ISBN 978-7-301-22494-6/H·3305
出 版 发 行：北京大学出版社
地　　　址：北京市海淀区成府路 205 号　100871
网　　　址：http://www.pup.cn　新浪官方微博:@北京大学出版社
电 子 信 箱：zpup@pup.cn
电　　　话：邮购部 62752015　发行部 62750672
　　　　　　编辑部 62752028　出版部 62754962
印　刷　者：北京京华虎彩印刷有限公司
经　销　者：新华书店
　　　　　　650 毫米×980 毫米　16 开本　27.75 印张　482 千字
　　　　　　2013 年 5 月第 1 版　2017 年 12 月第 2 次印刷
定　　　价：58.00 元

未经许可,不得以任何方式复制或抄袭本书之部分或全部内容。
版权所有,侵权必究
举报电话: 010—62752024　电子信箱: fd@pup.pku.edu.cn

序

本书的目标是鼓励并帮助幼儿园至八年级（K—8）的中文教师与中文课程研发人员改进课程模式，设计出语言教学与文化教学相结合的课程。书中提供的课程框架主要针对北美沉浸式、半沉浸式或双语项目中以汉语作为第二语言的学生而设计，理想的课时设置为每日两课时，课时较少（每周五个课时或更少）的项目也可根需要适当调整后使用。本书也适用于教师培训，例如北美各孔子学院组织的教师培训课程及时下广受欢迎的"星谈计划"（STARTALK）培训课程。

以低龄学生为主要研究对象是本书的一大特点。低龄学生的认知能力和心理发展水平与高中生及大学生完全不同，这为第二语言教学带来了新的课题。本书的另一贡献是为低龄学生提供语言与文化相结合的教学理念与教学模式，这是本领域前所未有的尝试。这些理念、模式是在对数个不同的幼儿园至八年级双语课程进行广泛的实地考察，并在波特兰市进行为期两年的教学实验后总结出来的。参与教学实验的人员包括四位当地的幼儿园至八年级的中文教师，他们在不同年级教授各种中文课程，为本书的编写提供了丰富的教学经验与教学智慧。

最为优秀、高效的课程模式常常是根据具体的学校、课程以及学生情况量身定做的。因此，本书并没有试图提供可使教师一劳永逸的综合性课程模式，而是为保持学生的学习兴趣，提升学习效果提供一个可供参照的教学范式。现代信息日新月异，本书提供的教学资料与网络信息可能很快就会过时。我们期望使用本书的教学人员在理解我们的思路、宗旨之后，能够自行收集更多教学资源与教学材料。

如此规模的研究计划，其实施与成功得益于许多人士的辛勤付出和赞助单位的耐心支持。感谢富布赖特·海斯项目的国外教学研究基金为我 2004 至 2005 年在北京与香港的研究提供经济支持。感谢波特兰州立大学的两项教学发展奖金，为我 2006 年在加拿大埃德蒙顿学校的研究及 2011 年中的英文翻译工作提供资助。感谢波特兰州立大学孔子学院慷慨赞助了我与四位波特兰当地的幼儿园至八年级的中文教师 2009 至 2011 年的合作项目。同样感谢北京、香港、旧金山、埃德蒙顿等处许多敬业的中文教师与课程研发人员为我们的研究大开方便之门,无私提供他们的经验与卓见。四位幼儿园至八年级的教师,我的合作者——田凤英、郑莉玲、萧月华、郭文球——以巨大的热情和耐心不断给我鼓励,和我一起在这片未开垦的研究领域进行了诸多尝试,并就中国文化教学和以学生为中心的教学提出了诸多新见。没有他们的支持,我们的这项研究无法结出硕果。感谢波特兰州立大学的同事刘美如,她给本项目提供了至关重要的支持、建议和鼓励。我还要感谢我的朋友Mary Erbaugh,在过去的三年里她一直给予我坚定的支持和有益的建议。此外,Mary还为我联系了她以前的学生王海颖,把我的英语翻译成流畅的中文。

我愿将这本书献给我的女儿Laura Nausieda:她从幼儿园时期开始学习中文,今年已经高中毕业,准备去南京继续深造。Laura在中文沉浸式课程中的经历激发了我对这个课题的研究热情。我坚信我们可以探索出更多优质、高效的方式来帮助孩子们学习中文。我愿为之不断努力。

柯雪润
2012年8月4日

Preface

Our goal with this volume is to encourage and assist Chinese teachers and curriculum development staff in developing curricular models and lessons that integrate language and culture instruction for K—8 students. This curricular framework is primarily aimed at students of Chinese as a foreign language in immersion, partial immersion, or bilingual programs in North America, with an ideal time frame of two class periods per day. However, these ideas can also be modified for students with more limited language instruction (5 or less hours per week). The book should be especially useful in teacher training sessions, including those organized by the different Confucius Institutes throughout North America and the currently popular STARTALK programs.

One of the most important contributions of this book is its focus on younger learners, who bring to second language study a unique set of cognitive and psychological skills and interests that differ significantly from older students in high school and university settings. This is also the first volume to offer a systematic framework and rationale for integrating Chinese language and cultural instruction for younger students. The ideas presented are the product of both extensive research on existing K—8 Mandarin bilingual programs in multiple settings and a two year Portland based team project that has drawn on the knowledge and experience of four local K—8 Chinese teachers who have taught Mandarin to younger American students in a variety of programs.

Effective curriculum works best when designed to meet the specific needs of particular programs, schools, and students. Therefore, the results of this project, rather than providing a comprehensive curriculum for programs in general, are meant to be illustrative of the type of curriculum that we believe is necessary for sustained student achievement and motivation. We realize that recommendations for specific instructional resources and websites can become quickly outdated, so urge teachers and others who use this volume to accept these suggestions in the spirit offered, and then to continue their own ongoing searches for resources and materials as they are increasingly available.

Large scale projects such as this can only be undertaken and completed through the hard work, patience, and support of numerous people and funding agencies. In particular, I am pleased to thank and acknowledge a Fulbright Hays Faculty Research Abroad Grant, which funded my 2004—2005 research in Beijing and Hong Kong; two Portland State University Faculty Enhancement Grants, which supported research in Edmonton, Canada in 2006 and English/Chinese translation expenses in 2011; and a PSU Confucius Institute grant, which generously supported my collaboration with a team of four Portland based K—8 Chinese teachers from 2009—2011. Special thanks are due to the many dedicated Chinese teachers and administrators in Beijing, Hong Kong, San Francisco, and Edmonton who graciously shared their insights and experiences, and to the administrators who opened their programs to this research. My four K—8 teaching colleagues, Tien Whyte, Li-Ling Cheng, Lily Tsang, and Wen-Chyou Guo consistently inspired me with their enthusiasm, their patience in working through different approaches in unchartered territory, and their creative ideas about Chinese culture and student centered learning. Without their support and belief in this project, it would never have come to fruition. I would also like to thank my good friend, Mary Erbaugh, who has been an unfailing source of encouragement and productive comments during the past three years, and my PSU colleague, Meiru Liu, whose support, advice, and encouragement have been central to this project. Mary also put me in touch with her former student Haiying Wang, who has done an admirable job of decoding my English prose into a nicely readable Chinese translation.

I would like to dedicate this volume to my daughter, Laura

Nausieda, a recent high school graduate who plans to spend the coming year in Nanjing continuing the Mandarin language study that she began in kindergarten. Laura's experiences in Mandarin immersion classes inspired my questions and interest in this topic, and my conviction that there must be better ways to teach Mandarin to young children.

Sharon A. Carstens
August 4, 2012

目 录
Contents

第一章
　针对幼儿园至八年级（K—8）学生的
　中国语言及多元文化教学 …………………………………… 1

第二章
　面向儿童及青少年的文化教学 …………………………… 19

第三章
　善用求知欲：幼儿园至二年级阶段的教学 ……………… 34

第四章
　启发创造力：三至四年级阶段的教学 …………………… 57

第五章
　提升学习力：五至六年级阶段的教学 …………………… 86

第六章
　建立成就感：七至八年级阶段的教学 …………………… 114

第七章
　更多探讨：关于教材选择、
　学生评估和教师培训 ……………………………………… 144

Chapter One
　Mandarin and Chinese Culture Instruction
　in Diverse K—8 Programs …………………………………… 151

Chapter Two
　Conceptualizing and Teaching
　Culture to Young Students ………………………………… 178

Chapter Three

    Guiding Curiosity: Kindergarten to Grade 2 ·············· 200

Chapter Four

    Inspiring Creativity: Grades 3 to 4 ························ 235

Chapter Five

    Promoting Learning Ability: Grades 5 to 6 ················ 281

Chapter Six

    Establishing a Sense of

    Achievement: Grades 7 to 8 ····························· 327

Chapter Seven

    Ongoing Challenges: Materials,

    Real World Assessments, Teacher Training ·············· 374

附录：文化主题总表

Appendix: Master Thematic Table ························· 385

参考文献

References ··· 431

第一章　针对幼儿园至八年级(K—8)学生的中国语言及多元文化教学

引　言

在全球化进程日益加快的今天,能够与来自不同文化、使用不同语言的人沟通和交流,是人们为追求事业成功、生活美满所必备的一项重要技能。在跨文化交际中,即使沟通双方使用的是同一种语言,也可能由于文化的差异而造成误解。由此而设立的跨文化交际课程会专门教导学生如何注意并处理交际中的这些问题。而对有志于更深入持久地研究跨文化交际的人来说,学习另一种语言则是至关重要的。纵观美国的教育史,大多数学生直到高中才开始学习外语,在大学阶段通常也只修读两年的外语课程即可满足人文学科专业的毕业要求。这样培养出来的学生的外语能力普遍处于初级水平,学生缺少提升语言能力和加深文化领悟的实践机会,无法进行有效的跨文化交际。

近年来,有研究表明儿童更易学习外语,因而各中小学纷纷开始设立各种外语课程。这些课程设计形式不一,有的学校每周设数小时课程,有的采用所谓的"沉浸式教学"方式,每天至少半天时间都以外语进行教学。这些课程大多处于初级阶段,课程的设计和教学资源的开发尚未完善。以教材而言,以往的外语教材大都是为高中生与大学生设计的,这些学生的认知能力和兴趣与低年级学生完全不同。因此,如何设计和评定适合低龄学生学习的语言文化教材或读物是目前儿童外语教学界面临的最大挑战。本书正是从这一基点出发,为幼儿园至八年级的学生设计出了一个将语言教学和文化教学结合在一起的课程框架。

  本书的编写受 1998 年美国俄勒冈州波特兰市一个全美较早的汉语普通话沉浸项目的启发。在此之前,波特兰市的公立学校开设的日语和西班牙语沉浸式课程颇有成效,进而扩展开发汉语沉浸式课程。伍德斯托克小学(Woodstock Elementary)被选为试点,该校希望以此提高学校的吸引力,扩充生源。该项目直到 1998 年暮春才正式得到批准,教师、课程、教材、招生的安排也都是仓促决定的。我是少数几名能说汉语并对中国的教育、文化与社会有所了解的家长之一[①],我女儿进入这门课程的实验班,我便也参与了课程的策划工作。一位来自中国的语文教师受聘教授这个由 26 名幼儿园和小学一年级学生组成的混合班。学生们来自各种不同的家庭背景:有以说粤语为主的美籍华人,有美国家庭收养的中国儿童,有白种人后代,还有亚裔混血儿。课程安排仿效其他学区的沉浸式项目:半天采用汉语教学,课程包括语文、数学和科学,另外半天为英文和社会学课程。汉语教材选用了新加坡课本,因为新加坡的小学汉语教材是为汉、英双语的小学生设计的,大部分课程用英语进行教学,其难度和教学进度都很适合我们的学生。在此后的两年里,课程开发委员会[②]研制出一套从幼儿园至五年级的汉语课程大纲,包括汉语(听、说、读、写)、文化、科学、卫生健康与数学等课程内容。其中数学、科学及卫生健康方面的内容大致与一般的英语教材相仿;随着学生年级的提升,对汉语听、说、读、写各方面的要求更趋详尽,难度也逐级加深;文化主题的设定则都

---

  ① 我的汉语学习背景包括:修习大学汉语课程六年;从 20 世纪 70 年代早期到 80 年代中期在台湾地区陆续学习台湾"国语"与客家话,累计约三年;从 70 年代到 90 年代在马来西亚与新加坡研究华人社群,累计亦三年;1985 年曾在上海复旦大学交流学习一学期。

  ② 委员会由波特兰公立学校语言沉浸式项目教学协调员、三位小学汉语教师、一位在中国生活过的伍德斯多托克幼儿园教师和两位会说汉语的家长组成。

很宽泛。①

像任何一个新兴事物的产生一样,实验班最初的教学令人振奋,却发展不均衡。大部分家长是特意让孩子选修汉语课的,大家为孩子有机会学习一门新的、(对大多数人来说)十分特殊的语言而骄傲,所以对教学非常支持。热心的家长会在课堂中做志愿者,在课外安排中国民族舞和传统珠算等兴趣小组活动,还组织汉语夏令营,集资购买教辅材料。但升入高年级后,学生对汉语的学习热情大为减退。学生感到用汉语学习数学和科学相当吃力,汉语水平也落后于同龄的新加坡学生,五年级学生还在读新加坡三年级学生的汉语课本,文化课程也仅限于反复庆祝中国的传统节日和讲解几个选定的艺术项目。这一问题的症结在于缺少难度更大、文化意义更强的授课内容,无法提高学生的汉语运用能力和学习热情。实验班进入第五年时,全班只剩下九名学生,并且,除了一个学生以外,其他所有学生填报中学志愿时都选择了没有汉语课程的学校。学生人数的缩减可以部分归因于学区内的汉语教学实力不强,区委也不很重视,家长们缺少信心;但更为主要的原因是,经过五年的语言强化学习,学生的汉语水平令人非常失望。

我作为家长和课程最初的顾问之一,不得不开始思索是否有更好的、更适合我们学生的教学模式。如果用英语学习数学、科学及卫生健康课程效果更佳的话,何必非得用汉语教授这些内容?为什么不多教一些中国历史、文化及社会知识来丰富教学内容、促进学生的学习热情?作为大学人类学专业的教师,我在中国社会及文化理论课程方面的教学经验应该如何应用于对低龄学生的汉语教学呢?

为了解决这些问题,我阅读了大量资料,既有如何在外语教学中融合文化教学的概括性讨论,也有如何在汉语教学中融合中国文化教育的具体论述。尽管学术界对这个课题的兴趣与日俱增(Kramsch, 1993; Heusinkveld, 1997; Lange and Paige, 2003),但大部分讨论都仍停留在理论层面,关于具体操作的实证研究和实践性探讨屈指可数(Paige et. al., 1999)。另外,我很快发现,大部分研究都是针对高中生与大学生的,

---

① 例如,幼儿园至一年级学生学习中国与美国的家庭、职业、见面问候语及礼仪。幼儿园至三年级学生的文化主题包括儿歌、游戏、手工、民间故事、文学以及中国传统节日。二、三年级学生要"了解中国过去及现在的生活"。四、五年级的文化课程教学目标为一句话:"教师须设计包含当代、历史、环境和/或艺术等不同视角的文化课程。"

这些研究成果是否适用于处在不同发展阶段的低龄学生？这个问题仍有待讨论。①

既然学术文献的指导有限，我的下一步计划便是调查现有幼儿园至八年级如何在汉英双语课程中结合中国文化进行教学。我相信任何一个行之有效的课程案例都带有地方特色，同时我也想考察不同地区的幼儿园至八年级的语言和文化课程各自具备哪些重要的变量。因此，我做了一项规模庞大的调查：我从中国和北美各处（如中国北京、香港、美国旧金山市、加拿大埃德蒙顿市）选择了 11 所背景殊异的学校，综合考察它们的课程结构设计和教学方式。我的目的是双重的：一是忠实记录不同地区、不同学校在汉语教学和文化教学相结合方面的实际操作；二是从中总结出一套适用于低龄学生的汉语课程，并借此为越来越多的美国幼儿园至八年级学生设计一个有效结合语言和文化教学的课程框架。

本章以下内容来自对不同学校的详细考察记录，并着重对教学手段的异同和学生的学习效果进行对比。后面的章节，我们总结了研究所得的经验教训，并与波特兰市其他四位汉语教师合作，共同设计了一个针对幼儿园至八年级学生的行之有效的汉语与中国文化相结合的课程框架。

不同国家和地区的幼儿园至八年级双语课程②

如前所述，由于幼儿园至八年级双语教学中对文化教学课题的研究甚少，我的考察具备一定探索性质：本考察以传统人类学的调查方式为主，包括对课堂参与者的观察，正式与非正式的采访以及对教学提纲、教材和学生作业等相关文本的研究。我假设学生学习语言和了解文化的过程受到以下几个因素的影响：家庭背景、课外的语言和文化环境、课内的语言与文化学习时间、教学材料和教学方式以及其他有待发掘的可能因素。被考察的学校都经过精心选择，以突出以上几项变量的差异所引发的不同效果。这些学校包括：中国北京的三所建制各异的国际学校，中国香港的两所国际学校，美国旧金山的一所开设汉语沉浸式教学项目的私立学校，加拿大埃德蒙顿市的一所开设汉语沉浸式教学项目的公立学校。

---

① 关于"文化教学作为汉语教学一部分"的讨论，详见 Bonin (1982), Myers (2000), Teng (2001) 及 Xing & Janet Zhiqun(2006) 的著作。

② 以下部分段落摘自 Carstens (2008)。

北京与香港都有中国文化环境的优势,又存在较大的语言和社会差异。旧金山和埃德蒙顿虽然缺乏课堂之外的语言与文化环境,但大部分学生——尤其是埃德蒙顿——来自中国家庭,因此得以通过其他途径弥补这一缺陷。

在美国教育部提供的富布赖特基金的赞助下,我于2004年8月至2005年6月间携家人造访中国,期间主要居住在北京,并在各节假日走访各个历史和文化景点。我的女儿在北京芳草地小学就读。芳草地小学是一所中等规模的国际学校,采用中国普通公立学校的课程,大部分学生来自中国和亚洲裔家庭。芳草地小学的教学与我调查的其他三所北京的双语学校(北京耀中国际学校、北京协力国际学校和北京京西学校)完全不同。此外,2005年4月,我前往香港考察香港耀中国际学校及汉基国际学校;2005年12月我考察了旧金山中美国际学校;2006年6月考察加拿大埃德蒙顿公立学校的汉语教学。我在各个学校的调查过程是:先采访学校的行政人员和课程协调人员,然后在他们的安排下旁听若干语言与文化课并采访这些课程的教师。采访主要依照一套标准的问卷进行[1],另外也会讨论一些听课过程中发现的问题。在对11所学校的7种不同课程的调查中,我一共采访了17位行政人员,旁听了44堂课,采访了23位汉语教师(其中19位用英语进行采访,7位用汉语进行采访)。

采访中发现,这些学校的双语课程的开设情况受学校的地理位置与学生的家庭背景的影响很大[2]。北京协力国际学校完全采用双语教学,半天教汉语,半天教英语;耀中国际学校安排了30%的汉语和70%的英语课程;北京京西学校则每天安排一定的汉语学习时间。因为北京的国际学校不招收本地的中国学生,而流动性强的国际学生可以在任何年级入学,所以校方必须为同一年级的学生提供不同的汉语课程,方便学生选择。语言课程的强度越大,数量越多,越难实现这个目标。在北京协力国际学校,英汉双语班的低年级学生不断减少,转而接收大量韩国学生,最后整个班几乎都是韩国人。耀中和京西学校有更多的生源,教学灵活程度也更高。耀中国际学校的大部分学生来自中国家庭(60%)或亚裔混血家庭,学校对汉语为母

---

[1] 问卷内容包括被采访者的个人信息及受教育背景、教学与管理经验、在中文课程中如何教授中国文化以及在教授中国文化的过程中遇到过怎样的困难等。

[2] 详见表1的各项课程对照,后面的章节对此有更详细的讨论。

语的学生和汉语为第二语言的学生分组授课;每组学生又按语言能力和先前的学习分为三个级别,分别授课。京西学校的大部分学生来自非亚裔家庭,他们被按照不同的语言背景和兴趣分入三个不同的班级。

各校文化课的设置方式为:协力国际学校的中国文化课融合在汉语语言课和社会课中;耀中国际学校有独立的中国文化课程,每周两次,多数用汉语教授;① 京西学校不同年级学生的汉语水平参差不齐,所以中国文化课用英语教授,并且融合在各门课程中,各科的英语老师都必须讲授相关的中国文化主题。

表1:各校双语课程开设情况(2004—2006年)

北京协力国际学校

学生	课程结构	语言教材
全部是国际学生,80%为韩国学生。学生可在任何年级入学。	幼儿园—6年级 双语教学:半天用英语授课,半天用汉语授课。 7—9年级 每日设有汉语课程。	中国内地常规教材。

北京耀中国际学校

学生	课程结构	语言教材
全部是国际学生,60%为中国学生,大部分来自说汉语的家庭;其余多来自亚裔家庭。学生可在任何年级入学。	幼儿园—6年级 70%英语,30%汉语。 每日设有汉语课程,按学生能力分级授课。每周设一次中国文化课。 7—9年级 每日设有汉语课程。	汉语为母语的学生使用耀中自编教材和新加坡的教材;以汉语为第二语言的学生使用耀中自编教材。

---

① 因为文化课程按不同年级授课,每个年级学生的汉语水平参差不齐,所以教师须采取各种手段授课,有时会用英语讲授。

北京京西学校

学生	课程结构	语言教材
全部是国际学生,40%为欧洲学生,25%为北美学生,20%为亚洲学生。学生可在任何年级入学。	幼儿园—5年级 每日设有汉语课程(40分钟),中国文化教学包含在英语课程中。 6—8年级 每日设有汉语课程。	按学生的不同能力或学习经历分为三组授课,分别使用中国内地常规教材、新加坡教材和中国出版的以汉语作为第二语言的教材。

香港耀中国际学校

学生	课程结构	语言教材
全部是香港本地学生。85%说广东话(粤语),10%说普通话。大部分在幼儿园/1年级或7年级时入学。	幼儿园—6年级 70%英语,30%汉语。每周设8课时汉语课。每周设一次中国文化课。 7—9年级 每日设有汉语课程。	使用耀中自编教材(为汉语为母语的学生编写)。学生到3年级时须认识1500个汉字,5年级时须能阅读中文报纸。

香港汉基国际学校

学生	课程结构	语言教材
全部是国际学生,且为长期居住的香港居民。90%为中国学生,70%来自说汉语的家庭,大部分学生说粤语。大部分在幼儿园/1年级或7年级时入学。	幼儿园—6年级 每周设8课时汉语课,2课时艺术课(汉语授课)。每学年中,一学期设中国音乐课,一学期设中文图书馆课。 7—9年级 每日设有不同级别的汉语课程。	幼儿园—6年级 使用香港常规教材。 7—9年级 A级:《今日汉语》 　　(香港教材) B级:《汉语》 　　(澳大利亚教材)

教汉语,教文化:美国幼儿园至八年级汉语及中国文化课程设计

旧金山中美国际学校

学生	课程结构	语言教材
全部是本地学生。50%为亚裔,23%为混血,27%属于其他情况。20%的学生来自说汉语的家庭,其中10%说普通话,10%说粤语。大部分在幼儿园/1年级时入学。	幼儿园—5年级 双语教学:半天用英语授课,半天用汉语授课。 6—8年级 每天设两课时的汉语语言课和社会课,用汉语授课。	幼儿园—5年级 使用台湾地区常规教材(修订后使用)。 6—8年级 使用旧金山中美国际学校自编汉语教材。

埃德蒙顿中英双语学校

学生	课程结构	语言教材
全部是本地学生。90%为华裔,85%来自说汉语的家庭,大部分说粤语。大部分在幼儿园/1年级时入学。	幼儿园—6年级 双语教学:半天用英语授课,半天用汉语授课。 7—9年级 每周设3课时的汉语语言、文化课程。	幼儿园—6年级 使用针对海外学生设计的台湾地区教材。 7—9年级 教师自选或自编教材。

由上表可见,在香港,虽然香港耀中国际学校和香港汉基国际学校都属于私立国际学校,但学生大部分为在幼儿园或1年级就入学的香港本地居民。这使学校语言课和文化课的课程内容及目标更为明确、统一。它们不像北京的国际学校那样要为插班的学生提供不同程度的语言课[1],对学生的语言能力的要求也更高[2]。香港耀中国际学校与北京耀中国际学校一样采用30%汉语和70%英语进行教学,每周设有一次用汉语讲授的中国文化课。香港汉基国际学校的教学模式与之相似,每周设8课时的语言课,另有两次以汉语授课的中国艺术与社会课。这些学校的中国文化课程都着重于中国历史、文学、艺术和传统,每个年级有指定的

---

[1] 香港汉基国际学校近期决定扩招插班生并为他们提供单独的汉语课程,但在我的调查进行期间尚未实行。

[2] 例如,香港耀中国际学校的三年级学生须掌握1500个汉字,五年级学生须能阅读中文报纸。

话题内容。

与香港的学校一样,旧金山和埃德蒙顿的学校中,语言课的学生也是从幼儿园入学,连续读至八年级。两校的学生以往都来自华裔家庭,不过,旧金山中美国际学校现在招收的学生背景更为复杂,不像埃德蒙顿的学生大部分在家能说中文。另外,两校虽然都采用半天教汉语,半天教英语的模式,但旧金山中美国际学校作为私立学校,每个班级的学生更少,课程灵活性更大:旧金山中美国际学校同时用汉语和英语教数学和社会课,如此可以强化语言习得效果。此外,该校每个年级的社会课里都有指定的有关中国文化的内容。埃德蒙顿公立学校的教学内容必须遵循本省的教学大纲,以前用汉语教授的社会、卫生健康和艺术课都须按照经过翻译的课程内容进行。最近,根据该省新颁布的社会课程大纲,该校的课程协调人员已把汉语教学从社会课中撤出,转到数学课里。在所有接受调查的学校中,唯有埃德蒙顿的学校没有专门针对中国文化课的课程要求,由语言课的老师自行决定是否教授文化内容。

除了课程结构的设置之外,这些学校的地理位置对学生的语言和文化学习又有怎样的影响?在此之前,我想当然地以为北京和香港的语言环境会给学生带来很大便利,但实际情况却复杂得多。在北京,"协力"和"耀中"两所学校的学生以亚裔居多,这些学生能很快地适应当地社会。但京西学校的学生以非亚裔居多,他们大都住在北京郊区的外国人社区,除了与家中雇佣的女佣和司机接触之外,缺少和其他中国人的交流。京西学校的教职人员反复提到,一些学生由于受生活环境的影响,对中国人和中国社会产生了负面的情绪[1]。现在想来,学生们对中国文化的不同反应也在情理之中。有研究表明,移民对新的语言与文化环境的适应程度各有差异(Klafehn, Banerjee and Chiu, 2008)。因此,我们也无法要求所有的年轻人在接触中国社会与文化时都有积极、正面的反应。

香港学生在中国文化的问题上因特定环境而有不同的反应。港人的

---

[1] 京西学校的一位中学教师在回答"在中国文化教学中有哪些特殊的难题"时说:"设身处地地替学生想一想,他们没有机会看到中国文化美好的一面,就无法喜欢这个文化。他们看到中国人随地吐痰和其他不文明的举止会很反感,难以对这个文化、这个国家产生尊重。"(摘自2005年6月9日的采访)

自我定位是以粤语为基础的中国文化,这与以普通话为基础的中国文化有一定差别。一位耀中学校八年级的教师说,她的很多香港学生更喜欢日本和西方文化①。对于这些香港学生而言,他们更认同的是以粤语为基础的香港版混合型中国文化。

文化教学与学生的反应

尽管被调查的幼儿园至八年级的汉语课程结构和学生背景各异,在文化教学方面却有些共同的特征。最普遍的三个共同点是:(1)设有专门的文化课程,有具体的教学纲领。(2)通过语言课来进行文化内容的教学与练习。(3)以汉语为母语的教师将其自身的文化视角引入课堂。

专门的文化课程/明确的文化课教学大纲

每个年级的文化课教学大纲都有指定的课题内容,不过教师未必严格执行,尤其当文化教学被包含在其他课程里时更难执行。香港汉基国际学校和北京耀中国际学校及香港耀中国际学校都设有专门的文化课,每个年级文化课的具体内容都尽可能地考虑到了学生的不同认知能力和兴趣(Carstens,2008:61—63)。小学低年级课程注重让学生参与与民间故事、神话传说、传统节日等话题相关的活动;高年级的文化课内容则更抽象、复杂。这种教学理念在耀中国际学校体现得最为显著,该校的文化课教学原则是"从情到理,从具体到抽象,从现象到本质"②循序渐进。耀中的汉语课程着重于中国传统文化,而香港汉基国际学校更着重于中国现代社会。无论重心如何不同,两个学校强调的都是文化(而非风俗习惯),尤以历史、文学和艺术为主。香港耀中国际学校的汉语教学负责人吕教授认为,这也部分体现出了被香港学校在英属时期忽略的中国文化教育的复兴。

文化课的教师们根据这些教学大纲来备课,齐心协力地搜集多种教

---

① 耀中的学生在五年级时去西安交流,六年级去澳大利亚,初中与高中阶段去其他亚洲和西方国家,这使他们可以接触与比较东西方的多元文化。

② 耀中国际学校中国文化课教学大纲提到:"小学课程比较偏重于学生对中国文化具体现象的认识,所掌握的内容属于文化现象层面,强调情感上的熏陶;中学课程则比较偏重于对抽象事理的认识,深入到对文化本质的探讨,强调理性的认知。"

学材料并共同使用①。在我旁听的大部分课堂上,教师都尽力用各种方法,把课本教学、多媒体教学和学生的自主探究活动结合起来,使课堂更吸引人,文化更生动鲜活。例如,三年级学生在学习"北京颐和园"这一主题时,教师先安排实地参观,然后在课堂上讲授颐和园的地理及艺术特征,最后由学生自行在网上查阅相关材料②;另一位北京的五年级教师在讲解完中国四大发明(指南针、印刷术、造纸术、火药)之后,让学生尝试自己造纸。香港汉基国际学校的五年级学生在学习北京的传统建筑时,要先在课堂上展示各种图片并用普通话讲解,然后在网上搜索相关材料。香港耀中国际学校的六年级学生在学习有关毛泽东的课程时,先听了一首歌颂毛主席的时代歌曲,又看了一小段录像,体会其中的时代感。

学校不提供如何教授文化课的特殊培训,许多教师坦言文化课的备课最难、最耗时。香港耀中国际学校小学部校长唐美兰称,该校的文化课教材至今仍在不断地进行更新、改进:"最初的教学大纲是由吕教授和其他老师尽力搜集资料,再经学生的反馈而修改制定的。每个老师都有不同的见解,每一年的学生情况也不一样,去年的教材未必适合今年的学生,所以教材很难保持不变,每年都需要改进。中国文化内容庞杂,很难在不同内容之间建立起联系,所以教材编写一直是个难题。"③

吕教授认为香港在英属时期教育体制的缺陷也是如今文化课教学困境的成因之一:"这就是我们现在面临的问题,英属时期香港的学校不教授中国文化课,我们现有的汉语教师没有受过这方面的训练,没有中国文化的意识。现在他们必须教授文化课,可他们缺乏相关背景知识,没有受过专门的培训,也缺乏文化意识。"④为了帮助老师开发文化课程,耀中学校委员会正在策划出版有关中国文化的教学材料,包括为教师提供的参考资料,为有兴趣深入研究的学生提供的带有背景知识和补充阅读材料

---

① 例如,北京耀中国际学校的专用教学材料储存柜里有中国风筝、面具、游戏和书法材料等,还有分门别类的中国文化教育系列书籍,包括地理、历史、北京景点、生活方式(33)、民间传说、风水、民间信仰、宗教(12)、书法、绘画、剪纸、手工等艺术门类(30)、古代中国文化(26)、饮食、茶文化(18)、童话、成语故事、舞蹈(27)、配有教师录音的神话故事类儿童读物(51),其他语言教材和课堂可以直接使用的其他内容的书籍(58)。

② 需要补充的是,虽然学生都很乐于使用电脑,但大部分的互联网站是为成人开发设计的,学生——尤其是三年级学生——能够从中获取的信息比较有限。

③ 采访于2005年4月21日。

④ 采访于2005年4月22日。

教汉语,教文化:美国幼儿园至八年级汉语及中国文化课程设计

的学习资料。①

有些学校并不开设专门的中国文化课,但大都在教学大纲中为不同年级、不同语言水平的学生指定了相关的文化教学内容,这些内容有时包含在汉语语言课里(如北京京西学校),有时包含在社会课里(如北京协力国际学校、香港汉基国际学校)。不管教师们是否将其付诸实施,大纲都对教学目标与教学内容做了明确规定。比如,北京京西学校对以汉语为第二语言的学生要求较低,只教授节日故事和一些地理知识,而对母语为汉语的学生则要求学习唐诗、中国民间故事、谚语、著名科学家及其他主题。北京协力国际学校幼儿园至三年级的社会课包括民间传说、手工制作和节假日等内容;四至八年级学生的社会课则包括儒家思想、丝绸之路、君主与农民、中国地理等知识。现有的社科类中文材料多是针对母语者设计的,对学生来说难度较大,所以协力国际学校的中文老师们选择利用学校图书馆,共同开发出自编的课程。美国加州旧金山中美国际学校的文化教学内容也列在社会课里,教师们也使用了相似的策略,搜集各种教学资源来备课。

学生对独立的中国文化课大都反响热烈,部分原因是在这些课中有很多要求学生动手参与的活动,课堂气氛比较轻松。学生的成绩主要由他们的努力程度和学习态度决定,而不取决于考试。这一点深受学生欢迎,但同时也意味着文化课不如其他课重要。随着年级的提升,高年级的教学主题更趋抽象,据课堂观察和教师反映,有些学生的兴趣明显下降。一位香港耀中国际学校六年级的汉语老师说,学生对中国传统文化缺乏兴趣,尤其当学到18世纪的中国名著《红楼梦》时,常有人抱怨所学内容与现在的生活和经历相差太大。一位北京耀中国际学校的教师认为,文化课的选题多半是成年人认为重要的东西,更好的处理方式或许应该是选择孩子们更感兴趣的话题,施教者应从小培养学生对中国文化的热爱,这样他们长大以后才会进行主动的学习和深入的探索。

语言教材中的文化内容

文化课中的第二个重要资源是语言教材。各种教材中文化知识内容

---

① 此外,耀中国际学校也开始通过每年一度的汉语教师研讨会着手解决教师培训的问题。耀中国际学校所有校区的老师都参加了2006年和2007年分别在北京和黄山举办的汉语教师研讨会。

相差很大,每个老师从课本中挖掘出的文化角度和层次深浅也不同。汉语语言教材不仅包括为中国内地、香港、台湾地区、新加坡等处的以汉语为母语的学生设计的"真实文本"①,也包括为以汉语为第二语言的学生设计的课本(见表1)。一些开设多种语言班的学校给以母语为汉语的学生(以及一小部分学习认真或成绩优秀的学生)用"真实文本",给其他学生用种类各异的第二语言教材。选择"真实文本"旨在复制各地的"本土"学生所受的教育,是一种实现"文化融入"的方式。但这些为中国内地、香港、台湾地区的学生设计的课本并不适用于那些生活在其他语言和文化环境下的、以汉语为第二语言的学生。如果教师采用了这些教材,他们的使用也具有"选择性",他们会有选择地使用这些文本,避免其中的一些内容,并在必要时修改一些词汇。使用"真实文本"的另一个问题是,读到小学高年级的学生往往跟不上当地学生的语言水平,只能学习那些低年级的课本,而低年级的课本内容又与他们的认知能力和兴趣不协调。

为以汉语为第二语言的学生设计的语言教材大致有三种,一种是中国内地或台湾地区的教师为海外的中国学生编写的课本,一种是国际学校的教师自编的教材,还有一种是面向低龄的学生的商业教材。这些第二语言入门教材通常注重实用性语言,重在教学生如何用汉语表达他们通常用母语交流的内容。一位参与教材编写的耀中国际学校的教师说,学生对如何用语言讲述日常生活最有兴趣②。更高级的课本则常收入一些中国民间故事,传达更明确的文化寓意。总之,第二语言教材中的文化内容差别很大,有些教材在第二、三册里仍以实用性语言为主③,另一些则更偏重于展示、挖掘丰富的文化与历史内涵(如暨南大学为海外中国学生编写的教材)。

相较于常规的语言教材,埃德蒙顿的小学高年级教师更喜欢被他们称为"小说系列"的中国台湾地区的教材,因为这些教材里的故事篇幅更长、情节更丰富,比常规教材里的短故事更具吸引力。但老师们同时也称,要找到学生感兴趣的故事主题并非易事。除了语言课上使用的教材

---

① "真实文本"在这里实际上是名词误用,因为该词的本意是"与课本中预先设计好的人工语言和教学式对话相反的……非教学的、自然交流中运用的语言"(Kramsch,1993:177)。由此而言,"真实文本"不可能存在。

② 采访于2005年5月19日。

③ 例如上海耀中国际学校的教师为以汉语为第二语言的学生编写的《愉快学汉语》(世界图书出版公司出版)。

之外，每个学校还为学生们提供各种补充阅读材料，不过每个学校甚至同一学校不同课程的阅读内容都互不相同。

那些从低年级就开始学习汉语的学生，升入中学后很少再使用常规教材，而是用教师自编的或经过选择和修改的，适合学生能力的各种材料，以提高学习兴趣。例如，旧金山中美国际学校的老师让八年级的学生自选一段本地中文报纸上的新闻（之前先阅读英文报纸上的相关报道），用汉语进行书面和口头的概括。这个阶段的汉语学习时间大都缩减为每天一个课时，老师和其他人员都觉得很多中学生的汉语水平停滞不前甚至退步，因为与其他课程相比，汉语课已退居为最不重要的课。

中国本土教师在文化方面的言传身教

文化教学的第三种常规方式是雇用中国本土教师。这些教师不仅可以在语言和文化专项课上教授文化，同时也会在课堂中隐性地成为学生心目中的"文化代言人"。所有接受采访的老师都是华裔，除了一位之外，其他都在中国内地、香港或台湾地区出生、成长。有研究表明，在沉浸式教学课堂中，本土教师通过"言传身教"进行的文化传导能帮助学生更正确地使用语言，培养其正面、积极的态度（Falsgraf, 1994）。此类现象经常出现在我所调查的这些汉语班中。① 中国式的教学和课堂管理都比较严格，强调尊敬师长，遵守纪律。这种教学方式通常受到家长和管理人员的欢迎，但其中也有一些内容受到了质疑。例如，一些学校的汉语课程协调人员指出，中国本土教师习惯于采用"以教师为中心"的教学方式，他们正是在这样的方式中受教育的。但很多人认为这种方式显然不适用于今天的学生。还有很多中国教师要求学生必须记住很多生词，由此引发了不少关于"死记硬背"是否有效的争论。另外，在汉字学习方面，老师们对华裔学生和非华裔学生的期望值也不同，总认为后者一般跟不上前者的学习进度。② 这些"文化形成性态度"表明言传身教式的文化传导也可能是一把有利有弊的双刃剑。不过，这方面的文化在学生的学习内容中只占很小的一部分。

---

① 详情请见旧金山中美国际学校 2005—2006 年度秋季简报，其中重点介绍了该校的文化教学中中国本土教师"言传身教"的重要影响（Anon, 2006）。

② 我对这类评论常感不安，它们似有种族主义之嫌。但换一种角度来看，老师们也有他们的道理，他们接触的中国家长都会督促孩子做作业，对孩子的学习要求也更严格。

相当多的即兴课堂教学是更直接地产生的。老师们在回答关于课堂文化教学的问题时,通常都会津津乐道于一些具体传输中国传统价值观的具体课程。比如"孔融让梨"讲述了弟弟孔融把大梨让给哥哥,把小梨留给自己的故事,体现了中国讲究"谦虚礼让"和"长幼尊卑"的传统家庭观念。一位老师说她的美国学生难以理解这个故事,因为西方的家庭观念与之不同。另一位老师教学生如何用中文写信封:要把国家名写在最前面,收信者的个人姓名写在最后——这样的书写顺序也反映了"国家高于个人"的价值观,这又与西方的观念相悖。课堂上的文化教学还很注重问候礼仪,这比课文内容更为实用。北京京西学校的一位老师说,当他的学生用中国传统的问候方式"吃了吗"向他问好时,他感到非常高兴。

中国教师有能力把丰富的文化体验带入课堂教学,但带入的程度和方式受到多种因素影响。一是时间因素,尤其在像埃德蒙顿那样的双语课程中,有地方政府指定的教学内容,教师能掌控的教学时间和教学范围较少。此外,教师的个人背景也会带来不同效果。从我的观察结果来看,有些教师缺乏在中国内地/香港之外的地区的生活经历和受教育背景,这些人对中国文化的理解相对狭隘和保守一些,更固守中国古典文学、艺术和历史观。一些土生土长的北京/香港学校的老师很难接受人类学上认为的"文化就是人们的日常生活习惯和观念"这一观点。用北京协力国际学校校长 Jon Zatkin 的话来说,这些内容(即日常生活习惯和观念)像母乳一样,已经成为人们生活中的一大部分,大家对此已经熟视无睹了。[1]这样的老师常常看不到中国文化的多样性。比如,一个从没离开过中国的北京老师认为,中国人一旦出了国,就不再像中国人了。[2] 而经历更丰富的老师则更鼓励学生讨论中国习俗的多样性,经常让一些从其他地方来的华裔学生阐述自己的观点。有些老师还把"海外华人群体"列为必学内容。还有一些老师质疑是否有必要向身处现代社会的学生教授中国历史、传统习俗。一位成长于泰国华裔家庭的旧金山中美国际学校的老师谈到同一文化的地域性差异时说:"文化教育当然很重要,但文化一直在变化,比如我们现在正在旧金山发展自己的文化。我们的文化和中国本土的文化并不相同,比如我们庆祝新年的方式就不同。我们自己的文化

---

[1] 采访于 2004 年 11 月 16 日。
[2] 采访于 2005 年 1 月 19 日。

也在不断发展之中。"①

总而言之,不管采用何种方式,文化教学在质量和数量上的差异都远甚于语言教学,因为它的进行并不依赖于专业的教材和有系统的教师培训,更多地取决于教师本身的素质。因此,教师的不同背景和观念在很大程度上决定了文化课的传授方式。

经验和教训

综上所述,这项调查深入研究了各个国家和地区的幼儿园至八年级汉语和中国文化教学。每个学校的课程结构、教材、教师安排和教学方式都取决于学生的家庭背景、学校所在地域、教学资源和公立/私立学校不同的课程灵活度这些关键变量。每个学校都有自己的长处与局限,这些不同的教学方法和实践也充分展现了低龄儿童汉语教学中的各种利弊,为改进美国学校的汉语课程提供了宝贵的经验。

所有被调查学校的一个共同优势是教师的投入。汉语教师们一般都很乐意与学生们分享他们对中国语言、文化的了解和热爱。这在课堂旁听和课后与教职人员的谈话中都有明显表现。我总结了四条汉语和中国文化教学的实践经验,希望可对培养学生兴趣、提升语言技能有积极的作用。

1. 根据学生的年龄和家庭背景采取不同的教学方式。例如,耀中国际学校为不同年级设计了从具体到抽象的文化课程内容,大部分学校给以汉语为母语和以汉语作为第二语言的学生分别提供不同的教材和教学方法。又如耀中国际学校和香港汉基国际学校为大部分中国学生提供内容丰富的文化专项课。

2. 以多种教学媒介来激发学生的兴趣。教师可以调用的媒体/手段包括视听教材、课堂表演、歌曲、谜语、网络和实地考察。这在强调文化教学的课堂中尤为重要。

3. 重复、巩固学生在英语课堂中学到的内容。比如用维恩图表(Venn Diagrams)进行比较和对比,为深入阅读提供系列小说读物,以及用英汉双语进行数学教学。许多教师都认为这些技能的培养大大提高了学生的认知能力。

---

① 采访于2005年12月14日。

4. 为各年级学生提供课本之外的补充阅读材料。这一措施在不同学校的实施程度不一,但得到了老师们的一致好评。这样的独立阅读即使对学习有困难的学生也十分有效,能帮助他们巩固课内知识,并加强对自身能力的信心。

此外这些学校课程中的一个共同缺陷是缺乏一个真正完善、统一的语言和文化相结合的教学大纲。即使是设有文化专项课的学校,其教授的文化也只是一系列现象的罗列,而不是完整地结合在语言和交流中。没有文化专项课或指定文化教学大纲的学校虽然没有完全忽视文化教育,但都是依靠教师个人和一些指定的语言课本来传授文化,必然导致学生知识覆盖面的不均衡,学生的知识和理解能力也无法在后续教学中得到连续性的发展。学生评估目标与教师培训的缺乏也进一步体现了现阶段对文化教学的忽视。

公立学校中的沉浸式教学项目对文化教育的忽视最为明显。受政府规定的限制,学校必须用英汉两种语言教授相应学科。尽管学生的汉语水平与母语水平差距日增,但仍必须用汉语学习同年级的数学、科学或社会学课。这些课的课堂时间有限,教师没有余暇引导学生在规定的教学内容范围之外探讨文化主题。而且,使用经过翻译的数学、科学和社会学课本,似乎本身就在表明,在知识的获取和理解过程中,"文化"的作用无足轻重:无论用汉语还是英语进行学习,效果都一样。语言和文化的联系就这样被完全切断了。

目前所有学校面临的最大挑战就是小学高年级学生对汉语学习的兴趣减弱,到初中时本现象更为明显。学生态度发生变化的原因无疑是多种多样的。汉语与其他学科一样(也许更甚),随着年级的提升,学生语言水平的差距日益加大,老师们即使调整课程也很难吸引所有的学生。学生似乎也对他们有限的汉语表达能力感到失望,甚至因此完全放弃学习:即使是最简单的低年级词汇,他们也宁可退而转用母语进行表达。

课堂考察和教师的反馈都表明,这种趋势出现在所有被调查的学校和课程中。我女儿的中文课堂里出现的学生兴趣衰退的问题并非特例,而是普遍存在的现象。这个研究结果更表明,我们急须对目前的幼儿园至八年级汉语课程进行反思,应该为各个年级的学生提供能促进其知识、技能的发展且极具吸引力的内容。要达到这一目标,关键是要从低年级起,把语言教学系统与文化教学系统有机地结合起来,向学生们传授在英语课堂里学不到的思想与思维方式,以循序渐进的教学手段鼓励、维持学生学习汉语的兴趣。下一章将讨论外语教学中语言与文化的关系,列举出一些有创意的观点,并指出低龄学生的语言与文化教育中存在的一些关键问题。随后的章节将具体论述我和四位波特兰市幼儿园至八年级的中文教师组成的研究小组如何寻找合适的文化主题,共同设计语言和文化相结合的课程框架。

柯雪润　著

第二章　面向儿童及青少年的文化教学

如何建立语言与文化的联系

要制订一个能实现语言教学与文化教学有机结合的课程框架,首先必须明确语言教学中的"语言"和"文化"的多重关系。我所采访的教职人员大都认为文化知识对语言学习十分重要,语言和文化是自然结合、密不可分的。关于这一点,北京京西学校的一位中学老师说得很生动:

> 文化与语言一样重要。懂语言而不懂文化等于什么都不懂。这两者是不可分的。语言学得越多,需要的相应的文化知识也越多,否则……就像有些机器人一样,他们可以说话,但不能理解所说的内容,这时语言只是一种机械的工具。当你去一个国家时,能够使用这种工具是不够的,你是作为一个人去参与当地的生活,要带着感情和人打交道。所以,语言和文化是不可分的。①

但也有部分教师(包括前一章提到的旧金山市的教师)对中国文化和学生的具体语言文化处境之间的矛盾有更深的体会。加拿大埃德蒙顿市的一位二年级的中文教师说:

---

① 采访于 2005 年 6 月 9 日。

教汉语,教文化:美国幼儿园至八年级汉语及中国文化课程设计

文化的确是我们中文课程中的一个重要组成部分,但有时如何教文化也很让我头疼。我不知道你说的文化是指传统文化还是现代的全球性文化。在交通和交流如此发达的今天,文化越来越具有共通性,中国文化已不仅仅是传统意义上的中国文化了。我们教文化时既教语言,也教艺术,这些内容和我们的生活习俗和传统相结合。但现在很多文化也具有了"全球性"——各地的人所做的事都差不多。如果要教传统意义的文化,比如儒家、道家等等,学生会觉得很遥远,会觉得这些内容与他们的生活毫不相关。而我们教中国新年时,这却是每个中国家庭的生活内容。所以,我们究竟应该教古老的传统文化,还是现代中国家庭中仍在沿袭的文化?即便是后者,现在的中国内地和香港的民俗文化又和我们以前的完全不同。①

这些教师对语言和文化的复杂关系有更深的认识,正如 Karen Risager 等语言学家所指出的,在日益全球化的今天,"各种语言渗入各种文化,各种文化也渗入各种语言。"(2006:2)这个观点尤其适用于以英语为代表的强势语言的全球化扩张,也同样适用于中国语言文化在中国及中国以外地区的普及。汉语普通话并非只局限于某个单一的文化信仰、习俗。事实上,它在中国内地、香港、台湾地区、新加坡,甚至这些国家和地区内部的不同人群中都有不同的地位。

我们的学生将会在各种不同的文化情境中使用汉语,因此我们必须仔细考虑什么样的文化内容对他们最有用。我认为有三种基本的文化常识和技能是最需要掌握的,即行为学角度的知识、阐释学角度知识和文化内容型的知识。

从行为学角度而言,学生要学会在不同的社交场合中使用得体的语言。这要求学生掌握基本的礼仪规则,知道如何与各社会阶层中各种身分的人应酬交际。当面对处于不同年龄阶段的交流对象(如成年人和同龄人)时,学生们应该知道哪些语言是适宜的,也要知道在不同的场合中分别应该交流哪些信息,应该采取怎样的姿态。例如,在什么情况下可以打听对方的年龄?怎样不失礼貌地婉拒别人给你添菜加酒?对熟人和陌生人应如何用不同方式表达感谢?对低龄学生来说,这方面的知识主要靠背诵相关词汇来获取,不过,当他们逐渐长大成熟,就该学会如何在不

---

① 采访 2006 年 5 月 31 日。

同场合调整自己的说话方式。

　　从阐释学角度而言,学生还要学会读取或听取语言中潜在的社会和文化信息。不同的交流方式如何体现作者或说话人的不同动机？从语言中如何判断使用者的社会地位和交流双方相互间的社会关系？为什么"农村人"与"城里人"在说话和书写方面都存在不同？中国父母一般不当面表扬孩子,这是否意味着他们不为孩子感到骄傲？让学生从不同的交流方式中体会其中隐含的意义的做法可以包含在低年级的教学材料中,随着学生年龄的增长,这将引起更直接的关注。

　　在文化内容方面,学生要对交流对象的历史、地理和文化背景有基本的了解。中国地大物博,历史悠久,文化灿烂,即使穷尽一生心力也难以研究完全,学生们须了解一些基本常识以建构与中国人对话的基础。他们不仅要了解中国的历史传统和当代文化的某些基本内容,随着年龄的增长和学习的深入,也要了解中国、新加坡及海外华人地区等几大主要汉语使用区的不同政治和社会情况。

　　我们目前的研究课题是如何将这三种文化层次上的教学融入到语言课程中。在回答这个问题之前,让我们先来了解一下一般语言教学中最常用的文化教学模式。文化(Culture)通常被分为两类:一类在英文中被称为"大写的 C"(Big C),包括艺术、文学、历史等;另一类为"小写的 c"(Little C),包括日常生活、风俗习惯等。汉语里的"文化"这个词也有相应的两个分支:一方面指文明、艺术、历史、文学等,而日常民俗通常被称为"风俗习惯"。我最初研究和采访双语课程的教职人员时也使用过这种分类,但逐渐发现另一些与语言文化教学联系更紧密的模式对课程开发更为有效,尤其是哈默利(Hammerly)1982年的著作及1999年的著作《21世纪外语学习标准》(Standards for Foreign Language Learning in the 21st Century)中的观点。[①]

　　哈默利在 Synthesis in Language Teaching(1982)一书中把文化分为三种类型:成就文化（Achievement Culture）、信息文化（Informational Culture）和行为文化（Behavioral Culture）。成就文化包括艺术、文学、音乐甚至科技等领域的杰出成就。信息文化指普通人对自己国家的地理、历史、自然资源、政治等主要领域所具备的常识。行为文化包括为大众广

[①] 这两种模式在 Li Yu 的文章 Where is Culture: Culture Instruction and the Foreign Language Textbook(2009)里有精彩的概括和评论。

泛接受的语言和身体行为，以及该文化体系对这些行为的价值判断。前两个类型中涉及的各类文化常识是我调查过的中国文化课中普遍的教学内容。行为文化较少被提及，但其实同样重要：它不仅可以帮助人们在现实中实现有效交流，理解对话中的文化内涵，并且有助于提升对文学、音乐、艺术等其他文化形式的了解。

美国的外语教师更熟悉的文化教学模式是20世纪90年代后期制定的《美国国家外语学习目标大纲》(*National Standards for Foreign Language*, Phillips, 2003)，其中的部分内容后为《幼儿园至高中的中文学习课程标准》(*K—12 Chinese Standards Project*, 1998)所采用。"文化"在此被定义为外语学习内容的五个"C"之一，其余四个分别为交流（Communication）、贯连（Connections）、比较（Comparisons）和社区（Communities）。文化教学的目标被定义为三个"P"，即文化观念（Perspectives，包括含义、态度、价值、观点等方面内容）、文化习俗（Practices，即社会交往的各种形式）和文化产物（Products，如书籍、工具、食物、法律等）之间的联系。

表2：语言与文化的关系模式

哈默利		《美国国家外语学习目标大纲》	
成就文化	艺术、音乐、文学、科技等	文化产物	书籍、工具、食物、法律等
信息文化	地理、历史、资源、政治、社会组织等领域相关知识		
行为文化	为大众所广泛接受的语言和身体行为	文化习俗	社会交往的各种形式
	关于这些语言和身体行为的价值判断	文化观念	含义、态度、价值、观点等

《美国国家外语学习目标大纲》里的"文化产物"包含了哈默利所说的"成就文化"和"信息文化"，但后者提到的"地理"和"政治"这两方面内容似乎无法归类到"文化产物"中去。《美国国家外语学习目标大纲》里的"文化习俗"与哈默利的"行为文化"相似，但不包括后者中提到的价值判

断,而是与"文化观念"这个独立类别相对应,与"文化产物"和"文化习俗"互相结合并起决定性作用(Li Yu,2009:82)。除了分类不同,这两种模式对文化学习的重点也有不同的强调:《美国国家外语学习目标大纲》对三个"P"(文化产物、文化习俗、文化观念)一视同仁,不分主次;哈默利则认为"行为文化"比另两类更重要,更倾向于语言文化的实践性学习[①]。两种模式各有利弊,学者们也各有所好。而对我们这些课程设计者来说,第一步要做的就是综合各不同模式中提到的文化内容,然后将它们系统有序地融入语言教学中。以下将详细描述我们所做的一个尝试。

针对儿童及青少年的语言与文化教学法

幼儿园至八年级阶段的汉语教学的第二个关键是了解学生认知和情感的发展如何影响语言学习。认知学的研究表明,儿童的认知发展过程是从最初的对具体事物的认知逐渐发展到形成超越个人经验的抽象概念。儿童不断(并且凌乱无章地)将新信息和他们的已有经验进行对比,以这种"假设评估"来学习抽象知识。因此,对他们来说,最好的学习方式是在教师的指导下积极广泛地获取各种信息,不断产生新的"假设"。这种把知识个人化和内在化的发现式学习(Discovery Learning)要与通过系统地指导帮助学生发现问题的"指导式"教学结合起来(Langford,1989)。

不少外语教学研究者注意到了成人和儿童学习语言的不同能力和不同效果,针对这些现象做过许多比较研究(Griffiths,2008)。大脑研究领域中的相关成果表明,人类在儿童时代有一段语言学习突飞猛进的关键时期,过了这段时间后学习语言的能力将有所降低。按照这些理论,外语学习应该从小学生抓起。但事实情况与理论并不完全一致。课堂调查显示,低龄儿童在教室里学习新语言的能力不如年龄稍大的学生和成人,后者具备的更成熟的认知能力能帮助他们更好地理解语言及掌握语言结构。然而,儿童学外语的优势是发音比成人更加地道,更接近母语者。儿童的另一个优势在于他们比成人更敢于尝试使用语言,不过他们进入青春期后常会改变

[①] 这种实践性强的语言文化教学模式为 Walker & Noda(2000)、Christensen & Warnick(2006)进一步发展,他们主张即使在教室里也应该采取与现实结合更为紧密的实践型教学。Tang(2006)等持批判观点的人则认为过分强调实践会忽略产生这种实践行为的文化背景。

态度。除此之外，不同年龄的学生的语言学习差异还取决于其他种种因素，比如学习和使用第二语言的环境、教学强度和学习动机等（Munoz,2006）。学生如果有经常使用第二语言的环境，那么他们的练习机会和学习动力都远比那些在教室之外不太使用该语言的学生大得多。

对于北美幼儿园至初中阶段中的那些以英语为母语的学生来说，即使每天的中文教学时间与英语相同，他们在中文口语、书面语和理解力等方面能达到的水平与母语仍是不可同日而语的。任何第二语言都是如此，也许中文尤甚。以英语为母语者通常选择西班牙语、法语等作为第二语言，因为其字母、语法、词汇都与英语相似。而中文则与这些语言完全不同，经常要学习者付出比其他语言的学习多四五倍的时间才能掌握。①课堂之外学生练习中文的机会也不多。即使在华裔人口众多的几个北美大城市里，因为历史原因，最常用的汉语口语一直是广东话（粤语），而不是普通话。在幼儿园至八年级阶段，学生越学到后期，英语与汉语的能力差距越以几何倍数增长。学生的英语能力通常应该从"学习阅读"发展到"从阅读中学习"，他们要学会通过自己的阅读理解更复杂深刻的知识。而他们相对薄弱的中文能力无法实现这样的效果，学生们会因此觉得中文对他们没有很大用处。

两种语言间的能力差距造成小学高年级学生和中学生的中文学习热情大减，这是幼儿园至八年级阶段外语项目中普遍存在的趋势（Tragant,2006:239）。产生这种现象的关键因素之一是第二语言与学生的学习目的之间关系的变化。有研究表明，儿童对外语学习的兴趣直接与他们对课堂教学的满意程度相关，而年龄大一点的学生更关注语言在当前和将来的实用性（Tragant,2006:240）。这就要求中文教师不断改进和调整教学模式和材料，不仅要以创造性的方式把语言与学生当下的兴趣联系起来，而且要逐步提高学生的语言能力。尤其对小学高年级学生和中学生而言，要让他们有能力阅读认知程度较高、与现实世界息息相关的材料。

从理论到实践：以团队为中心的课程开发

我们现在须在课堂教学和课程设计的实践中对上文提到的各项发现

---

① 参见 *Languages Learning Difficulty*（http://www.foreignlanguagesweb.com/essentials/difficulty-1.htm）。

加以检验，这对我们的项目至关重要。我决定挑选一些经验丰富并且喜欢了解孩子的中文教师一起合作。根据我在不同学校对不同的教师的观察及与他们交谈的经验，一个好老师不仅要知识丰富，能够同情、理解学生，并且要有集体协作的精神，善于分享观点、调动情绪。波特兰州立大学孔子学院慷慨地为我提供了经济赞助和后勤资源，并且提供了条件适宜的候选教师名单。2009年夏末，我开始和四位在波特兰教授幼儿园至八年级中文课程的教师一起投入这项为时一年的计划，为北美幼儿园至八年级的学生设计一个实现语言与文化有机结合的课程框架。

本章将在以下部分详述我们是如何将本书中提及的文化主题、教学内容和教学策略付诸实施的。希望我们的实践过程对其他教师和课程设计者能起到借鉴作用，使大家在设计课程目标或具体教学计划、设置适合本地学生的课程时，可以遵循相似（未必相同）的步骤。每个学校的学生及其家庭背景不同，公立、私立学校的课程情况和财政预算不同，各地文化背景也不同，课程设计应该因地制宜。另外，让教师（甚至还可以包括学生和家长）参与课程设计的好处是，这样不仅可以让他们明白自己要教（或者学习）什么，也可以理解为什么要以这些特殊的方式进行教学（或者学习）。

最初，我与四位中文教师分别见了面，简要讲述了我在双语课程方面所做的研究，以及设计一个语言与文化相结合的课程框架的目标。我也承认自己对此并无完全把握：幼儿园至八年级阶段的语言与文化相结合的课程框架设计是无先例的，我的课程设计经验也仅局限在大学层次的人类学课程方面。老师们都承担着全日制教学工作，我们初步商定每个月见一次面，就某一既定话题分享各自收集的材料并进行讨论。九月份的第一次小组会议上，我向大家介绍了研究中总结出的语言文化教学的几个关键问题，然后大家集思广益，讨论了我们的目标是什么，要从哪里入手，如何实施我们的教学计划。大家一致认为最有效的入手方式是逆向设计：先确定从幼儿园开始学习中文课程的学生在八年级时应该达到怎样的语言及中国文化理解水平，然后逐步确定每个年级的教学内容，以帮助学生达到这个水平。这是小组成员的第一项"家庭作业"。

在十月的小组会议上，我们讨论了第一次的"家庭作业"，即各自设计的八年级学生应达到的语言和文化能力目标。每个人的设想形式不一，内容迥异，有非常具体的识字量标准（这个标准又相差很大，从600至2500字不等），有更概括抽象的对学生听、说、读、写各项能力的要求，还有与历史、地理、食物、节日、中药、传统手工艺、民谣、成语等内容相关的文化主题。我们讨论了各种标准之间的差异,在讨论到关于词汇量的问题时,我们想到学生能理解的书面语和口语的词汇量要大于他们能在书面语和口语中主动使用的词汇量,所以应该设立两种不同的标准。此外,有一位小组成员建议以《国际汉语教学通用课程大纲》(*International Curriculum for Chinese Language Education*, OCLCI, 2009)里的五个阶段的文化主题与学习目标作为参照建设我们的框架,不过我们很快发现这些主题和目标更适用于年龄较大的学生及成人学习者。

在讨论具体的文化主题时,我们不断回到同一个问题:为什么北美的孩子会对这些事物感兴趣,尤其是那些抽象的话题?向孩子教授这些内容时应该使用哪些材料?这次会议中提出的两个建议在我们以后的月会上被反复提及:一是把成语教学[①]和每年重复教授的文化主题结合起来(而不是作为单独的课题);二是把文化主题与英语课程中的社会课的教学大纲结合起来。

十一月的会议留给大家的"家庭作业"是:为我们列出的文化主题找出相应的幼儿园至八年级阶段可用的教学材料,并尽可能提供实例。我在整个研究过程中十分注意搜集各种适合幼儿园至八年级学生的语言、文化教学材料(比如在书店里、图书馆或网络上,但常常没有收获),我期望其他小组成员能提供新的资料。不过,结果不出所料,虽然大家提供了各种各样的材料,但大部分不是针对年龄很小的孩子(比如很多彩色图画书),就是针对认知和语言能力较强的年龄较大的学生。这种情况和我的调查结果基本一致。另一个普遍的问题是,缺乏较好的关于中国文化(传统及节日)的初级读物。同时我们怀疑,一些文化内涵复杂,却与中国历史和文化相对脱节的课本内容对北美学生是否合适。大家一致推荐了两个较为有用的网站,一个来自中国台湾[②],另一个来自北京[③]。两个网站都有语言和文化课程,还包括展现当代中国社会的短小视频。有些为海外中国学生设计的课本也包含文化内容,但教科书式的语言和分散的主题使得它们用途有限。我们本来也没有期待能找到理想的、系统的教学

[①] 成语的理解及正确使用是体现中国人受教育程度和文化层次的标志。成语在中国人的日常交流中的重要性比英语谚语在英语交流中的重要性大得多,两者在各自语言中的地位不同。如何向北美学生教授成语是一个具有挑战性的难题。

[②] http://edu.ocac.gov.tw/home_htm

[③] http://www.myechinese.org

材料,这次的研究更证实了我们之前的预想,即无法从现有的材料中确定要教授的文化主题。下一步我们便把小组成员分入四个年级组:幼儿园至二年级,三至四年级,五至六年级,七至八年级。每个年级组的教师要自行设计适合该年级组的语言与文化主题。

我们在一月份再次集会,每人汇报了各自设计的语言及文化主题。每个成员都为此倾注了很多心血与精力,提议中有经典的地理、食物、节日、历史、民俗等话题,也有围绕着诸如丝绸之路、四大发明、孙悟空等主题展开的系列话题,还有和学生的学习成果直接相连的话题,比如让学生比较中美具体文化实践的差异。在会议中,我们再次讨论了怎样让美国学生对这些话题感兴趣。

我注意到大家提出的大部分话题都属于哈默利模式中的信息文化和成就文化,但几乎没有涉及行为文化。如果我们的学生要掌握正确的文化交流方式,那么行为文化的学习是至关重要的。于是,我们开始讨论行为文化的具体内容,从而发现大部分语言教师都没有留意过这个方面,常常把它当作日常生活、交流的基础环节而忽视。我们便兴致勃勃地提出了适合各个年级学生的行为文化方面的话题,现列举如下:

一至二年级:
见面问候:交流个人信息
谜语、绕口令、游戏
如何应对别人的赞扬
日常生活习惯

三至四年级:
姓氏
买糖/购物
日常杂务
与新朋友见面
拜访朋友的家
家庭旅游:中国人的常用交通方式/旅游目的地

五至六年级(初一):
用餐礼仪:在餐馆进餐、在家里进餐、和朋友一起进餐、筷子的使用

上菜/食物分享、食物的象征意义、各类食物
写信、写电子邮件、留言
电话礼仪
应对赞扬/侮辱：表示谦虚、表示自信
关于兄弟姐妹关系的经典故事
如何称呼朋友的家人

七至八年级（初二至初三）：
约会：如何提出邀请、化妆与穿着
公共场合的行为规范、文化禁忌
品牌/时尚与个人创造性
各种游乐场所、娱乐项目
俚语

　　下一步我们决定继续收集适合各个年级学生的行为文化方面的话题和课程内容，尤其是对美国学生有吸引力的内容。此外，我又让大家思考如何教授成语。我们通常会从成语背后的故事开始教，但这些成语怎样在日常口语与写作中使用？中国孩子是怎样将成语学以致用的？有没有较具实践性的应用？我们也考虑了普通话课程的时间长度，一致认为每天两小时的中文课和社会课最为合理，因为即使采用中文沉浸式教学，仍要教授数学、科学、卫生健康等其他课程。

　　二月的会议伊始，小组成员们汇报了各自准备的行为文化方面的课堂主题和课程设计，并提出了各种改进教学的建议。不过，因为主题与教学设计又呈现出较大的差异，我们再一次面临同样的问题：如何组织一个文化主题系列，循序渐进地从低年级向高年级发展？大家一致认为，最理想的办法是在这个文化主题系列中的每个大主题下设计若干个具体小主题。于是我们再一次集思广益，合作草拟了一个文化主题系列，其中的大主题为：家庭(Family)、食物(Food)、节日(Festivals)、朋友与娱乐(Friends & Fun)、时尚(Fashion)、情感(Feeling)、名人(Famous People)、名胜(Famous Places)。然后，我们为每个大主题添加了适合不同年级的具体小主题，并把它们归类到哈默利模式里的行为文化、信息文化和成就文化中。

　　在三月的会议上，小组成员们带来了各自准备的围绕上述八个大主题展开的小主题列表，及其在行为文化、信息文化和成就文化中的归类。

不过,这次会议没有具体讨论这些列表。美国旧金山中美国际学校将于四月份在旧金山市举行中文教学大会,我们决定选择一个文化主题着重讨论,形成我们的参会报告。我们的目标是围绕一个有趣的、便于循序渐进的文化主题设计出一套语言与文化相结合的教学计划,随着年级的提升逐步扩展教学内容并加深难度。我们没有选择诸如食物、节日这些中文教师最常用的主题,而是选择了"情感"这个主题。我们讨论了中国人有哪些不同的情感表达方式,教师应怎样把它们结合到课堂教学中。一位小组成员对这个主题的选择有所怀疑,因为中国学生普遍接受的教育是把自己的情感隐藏起来。不过我们觉得从低年级开始教授适宜的表达情感的词汇是可行的,孩子们也可以很容易地把这些与自己的情感和经历联系起来。等他们逐渐长大后,便可将教学重点放在中西方在情感表达方面的文化差异上。我们集体讨论了情感主题下的适合各个年级的语言与文化内容,最后决定结合"5C"标准,采用逆向设计方式来制定我们的教学计划。每个老师先确定最终的教学目的、阶段性教学目标以及教学评估手段,然后再确定课程内容和学生活动。

接下来的几周非常忙碌,每个小组成员精心准备各自的幻灯片演示,经过几轮的讨论与修改形成定稿。我们于四月份的第二周在旧金山市的会议上作了小组报告。我们的题为《为幼儿园至八年级的中文学习者设计的语言与文化相结合的课程框架》的报告得到了一致好评。参加这次大会不仅使我们接触到了更多的观点和研究视角,而且在准备报告的过程中大大提高了团队合作的热情。不过事后看来,我们的最大收益是学会了更谨慎地组织语言,表达我们的观点。我还参加了由 Jennifer Eddy 博士主持的为期一天的"单元主题的设计与评估"研讨会,从而更坚定地拥护"文化教学是语言教学的核心"这一观念。Eddy 博士认为,语言学习的最终目标是顺利地把在一个环境中学到的知识和技能灵活地转换到另一个新的、陌生的环境中。学生应该尽早、尽可能多地练习这种转换并尽可能接触具有代表性的、地道的目的语文化材料(Eddy, 2010)。研讨会还介绍了如何围绕一个中心问题设计出包含互动、阐释、演示活动在内的教学框架。

旧金山会议之后,大家在我们的小组会议上再次明确了本项目的最终目标,并回到三月份起草的八个文化主题:家庭、食物、节日、朋友与娱乐、时尚、情感、名人及名胜。我们从"家庭"这一主题开始,详细讨论了各个年级应该教授的内容,并再次提及行为文化、信息文化和成就文化。不过在讨论中,我们将这三种类型合并为"行为文化"和"信息/成就文化"这两类。我们反复强调课堂话题要符合学生年龄,不能要求年龄小的孩子理解太抽象的或者无法与他们的自身经历联系起来的事物。因此,成就文化类知识不适合低年级的小学生。对于这些学生,教师应多采取促进学生主动学习的教学策略,教授容易被理解、吸收的行为文化知识。此外,也可以辅以少量信息文化,培养学生对文化差异和不同文化视角的初步认知。讨论"家庭"主题时,我们发现孩子们经常从自己的家庭出发了解世界万象,比如讨论父母的职业,城市与农村家庭的差异,中国人经常对陌生人使用亲属称谓语等话题。我们重新审视了之前列出的八个主题,觉得有些可以合并。所以,我们最后删除了"名人"这一主题,又把"名胜"与"地理"合并成一个主题。在其后的几次会议中,我们不断修改与充实各阶段的文化主题。我们发现一起合作讨论时的效率最高,于是决定延长每次会议的时间,以达到我们的研究目的。

五月底,我们开始讨论"食品"与"节日",决定围绕两个核心设计各个年级的课程内容:一是强调信息文化,二是包含行为文化内容。例如:

1. **中国人喜欢吃什么?为什么?(信息文化)**
   - 日常饮食(早餐、午餐、晚餐、点心)
   - 进餐的时间/场合(生日、餐馆等)
   - 节日餐饮(是否留到"节日"主题中教授?)
   - 地方小吃(北方、南方等)、食物的象征意义、卫生健康

2. **不同场合的进餐方式(信息文化与行为文化)**
   - 正式与非正式场合(餐桌礼仪)
   - 圆桌与分餐制
   - 筷子
   - 外出吃点心(宵夜等)

这些问题能帮助学生了解各种食品的差异和不同场合下的饮食习惯。每个年级不一定要教授所有内容,教师要根据学生的年龄与认知发展水平来选择他们感兴趣的内容。学生可以从故事、诗歌、艺术、音乐及自己动手烹饪和品尝中国食品等活动中学习中国食物的象征意义和饮食习惯等。关于节日,我们原来计划专设一个单元,后来觉得应该在学期中每遇到一个节日时就带领学生庆祝并学习,内容包括中国的农历和黄历中的"吉日"与"忌日"等。我们为这个主题设计了三个核心问题(中国人

如何组织一年的活动？如何庆祝节假日？这些庆祝有什么意义？），并制作了一个图表，列出了各个年级的适用话题：

表3：中国节庆活动表（分散在各学期中的"节日"主题教学内容）

幼儿园至二年级	三至四年级	五至六年级（初一）	七至八年级（初二至初三）
*教师节：九月十日	*教师节：九月十日	*教师节：九月十日	*教师节：九月十日
*秋季：当令诗歌、音乐、艺术	*秋季：当令诗歌、音乐、艺术	*秋季：当令诗歌、音乐、艺术	*秋季：当令诗歌、音乐、艺术
		*中国农历	*中国农历和历书
*中秋节：月饼、赏月	*中秋节：月饼、传说、诗歌	*中秋节：月饼、传说、诗歌	*中秋节：月饼、传说、诗歌、成双成对的公园散步者（台湾地区）
*国庆节：十月一日	*国庆节：十月一日	*国庆节：十月一日	*国庆节：十月一日
		*万圣节与鬼节	*万圣节与鬼节
*冬季：当令诗歌、音乐、艺术	*冬季：当令诗歌、音乐、艺术	*冬季：当令诗歌、音乐、艺术	*冬季：当令诗歌、音乐、艺术
*中国新年：习俗、生肖、剪纸与装饰、音乐▲	*中国新年：习俗、传说、舞狮、吉祥物、音乐	*中国新年：习俗、吉祥物、禁忌、各地区不同风俗、春节期间的旅游、中国中央电视台的春节晚会	*中国新年：习俗、灶神与门神、春节期间的旅游、海外唐人街的庆祝活动
*元宵节：元宵（汤圆）、灯会	*元宵节：元宵（汤圆）、灯笼与灯谜	*元宵节：传说、灯谜、庙会	*元宵节：灯会、灯谜
		*情人节与七夕的传说	*情人节与庙会

(续表)

幼儿园至二年级	三至四年级	五至六年级(初一)	七至八年级(初二至初三)
*春季：当令诗歌、音乐、艺术	*春季：当令诗歌、音乐、艺术	*春季：当令诗歌、音乐、艺术	*春季：当令诗歌、音乐、艺术
		*劳动节：五月一日	*劳动节：五月一日
*儿童节：六月一日	*儿童节：六月一日	*儿童节：六月一日	*五四青年节(五四运动)
*端午节：粽子、五毒帽	*端午节：粽子、龙舟的传说	*端午节：粽子的不同种类、龙舟的传说	*端午节：屈原的诗歌和历史

▲ 每年的中国春节期间，学生都会有一系列活动：打扫教室、写对联、吃团圆饭和饺子、子夜时分放鞭炮、送红包、说吉祥话、走亲访友等。

在夏天直至秋天的小组会议上，小组成员不断给每个文化主题添加适合各个年级的话题，并设计了不同的核心问题，比如"为什么家庭很重要？如何重要？"这样的问题适用于所有幼儿园至八年级学生，而"为什么家族荣誉很重要？"这样的问题只适用于五至八年级的学生。有了这些核心问题后，每个老师再围绕问题设计各自负责的年级的课程内容(见文化主题总表)。我们还讨论了本项目的最终目标：以出版物的形式与更多的人分享我们的探索实践。我们想写的既不是教科书，也不是一个尽善尽美的幼儿园至八年级的语言、文化课程框架，而是一个指导性的纲领，促使人们思考为什么要将文化教学与语言教学结合起来、该怎样结合、用什么方式结合、结合效果如何等问题。关于这些问题，这本书里没有现成的答案，每个老师最终仍须根据自身情况设计适合自己学生的教案。我们小组成员按各自负责的年级组各写一章，阐述自己的语言与文化相结合的教学方法，展开说明文化主题总表(我们一直在不断充实和扩展这个表)中自己年级对应的主题与课程内容，最终以中文教学大会上汇报过的"情感"主题的课程设计结尾。

我建议每位老师在每章的开头简要说明该阶段学生的社交、情感和认知能力发展情况，以及这些内容对语言技能和教学策略的影响。我原以为这些资料唾手可得。我们阅读并讨论了 Peter Langford 的

Children's Thinking and Learning in Elementary School 的第一章，又浏览了一些有关儿童成长的教科书中的图表，大家很快发现，关于社交、心理与认知发展阶段的论述大都十分抽象与理论化。我于是鼓励各位老师从自己丰富的教学经验出发，介绍面对各个成长阶段的学生时可能出现的教学难题和可能实现的教学目标。我们希望这样的模式能给其他老师带来一些启发，让他们为自己的学生设计教案时也能积极主动地考虑到学生的社交、情感和认知能力发展问题。

以下四章分别由我们四位小组成员中的两位撰写[①]，分别阐述了适用于四个不同年级组的文化与语言相结合的教学方法，为八个文化主题提供了具体的教学建议，并以充分讨论过的"情感"主题教学方案结尾。每个老师撰写自己负责的章节，必然带有鲜明的个性色彩和不同的视角。这和实际教学一样，老师们会把自己独特的个性和经历带入教学之中。这四章皆以中文写作，由我翻译成英语，并设计了双语的文化主题总表（附录），对四个不同年级组的八个主题进行了概括。

柯雪润　著

[①] 另两位小组成员——郭文球老师与萧月华老师——起初分别负责幼儿园至二年级和三至四年级的内容并在小组讨论中作出很多贡献，可惜后来没有足够的时间进行写作。幸有曾经教过幼儿园至四年级的田凤英老师和郑莉玲老师接替，结合她们的教学经验与小组会议中提出的种种建议，负责撰写了相关章节。

第三章 善用求知欲：
幼儿园至二年级阶段的教学

引 言

儿童的身心是随着年龄的递增而迅速发展的，每个阶段的成长都有一定的规律和特点。比方说，四岁幼儿通过语言和动作进行表达的欲望非常强烈：他们不仅爱说话、爱问为什么，也爱自己动手组合东西；在没有家人参与的情况之下，可以自己一个人安安静静地玩，也很容易和其他的孩子愉快地玩在一块儿，并且能从团体游戏和与玩伴的互动中学习一些简单的游戏规则。到了五岁时，儿童的理解力提高了，好奇心也逐渐增强，看到什么事情都喜欢刨根问底。这一时期的儿童特别喜爱用自己的方式尝试探索各种新事物，却不喜欢别人告诉他们怎么做，开始有自我表现的意识。六岁儿童的睡眠时间比幼儿稍短，精神更加充沛，活动能力更强，他们的学习兴致很高，开始看重自己在群体中的地位，会表达个人意见，也会开始与他人争论。因此，教导这个年龄段学生的教师必须对低龄儿童的成长变化有一定的理解并采用适宜的教学引导方式。

五至七岁的儿童在认知方面，对于形象视觉和音律的敏感度高，同时也已具有了数量的概念。这个阶段也是口语词汇发展以及品德形成的重要阶段。教师在课程设计中应注意：(1)利用丰富多彩的视觉形象来呈现教学内容。（2）结合教学内容，设计带有音乐伴奏的肢体活动。（3）随时教导学生注意课堂规范和同学之间的相处礼节。（4）多鼓励学生开口说话，培养其语言表达能力。

从幼儿园到一、二年级，儿童从以游戏活动为主的幼儿园进入到以正规学习为主的学校班级。对于这之间的环境转变和角色转换，儿童在心理方面仍处于适应期，他们的情绪很容易焦躁，行为也常有失控。在面对这种情况时，教师必须营造出有安全感的学习环境，以稳定学生的学习情绪。比方说，每天早上，当学生走进教室时，教师一定要主动跟学生打招呼并随时保持愉悦的情绪，这样会让学生的一天有一个好的开始，可以帮助他们忘记离开妈妈的难过。尤其是对幼儿园的学生，温柔的拥抱常能安抚学生紧张的心情。有的时候，教师可以跟学生说好时间，允许学生和妈妈说一会儿话，但要求学生说完话后按时回到教室，鼓励学生做个"大孩子"。孩子们都喜欢有机会表现自己成熟的一面，这样的方法常能取得较好的效果。

低年级学生在社交方面尚处于探索阶段，仍在学习怎样交朋友，如何与朋友相处。这个年龄的孩子最怕别人排斥他们，同时又怕别人不听他们说的话。因此，同理心的培养和沟通方式的学习都是非常重要的。改变孩子一切以自我为中心的行为习惯，让他们学会关心别人，学会分享，这真不是件容易的事。教师得一步一步地引导，时时以生活中大大小小的事情作为范例，让学生形成说好话的习惯，形成以帮助他人为乐的生活态度。

幼儿园到二年级学生的文化学习内容着重于行为文化方面，包括师生礼仪、学校及课堂中的规矩要求、爱护幼小、尊敬长辈、孝顺父母、用碗筷吃中国饭、中国节庆活动、位置方向的说法等，这些都是在每天的生活中表现出来的。本阶段的总教学目标是使学生能在日常生活中适时表现出应有的礼仪。我们特别建议老师们在低年级阶段多利用寓言故事和成语故事增强学生的文化意识。

生活文化方面的学习需要一定的词汇和句型基础，因此培养语言能力是针对本阶段学生的教学重点。本阶段语言学习中的主题多与"我"的生活密切相关，如家庭、朋友和学校；课程目标则是培养学生的口语交际能力，让学生能听懂与个人或日常生活相关的简短话语，能简单地介绍自己和他人的基本情况，能就日常生活中的常见话题与他人沟通（数字、时间和地点）。对于成语或诗句的教授，我认为图像说明法和情境模拟表演是最容易让学生理解的方式。教师只要在课前多设计些视觉辅助道具，学生就能很快进入学习状态并且理解成语使用的情境。

我们建议在幼儿园、低年级的语言教学活动中多以汉字与图片对照的卡片进行认读练习，同时配合各种视觉、听觉刺激以及肢体动作来加深学生对词语的印象。此外，教师也可以用多阅读短篇故事的方式提升学生的语言理解能力。教师在阅读故事的过程中，千万不要一人从头说到尾，可分成小段落进行讲述并以不同的声音模拟故事中的人物，甚至用声响营造故事里的气氛，尽量将故事里抽象的内容具体化。每一次有人物出现时，教师可指派一位学生想象、模仿。尤其是对话部分，在教师示范之后，可安排学生两两演练，完成对话。在讲完整篇故事后，学生会对表演故事产生很高的兴致，教师要在学生表演时引导学生运用句型进行对话。几次演练和互相观摩之后，学生就能简单讲述故事情节了。

除上述方式外，教师也可以通过儿歌、童谣、教学带动唱进行教学，一方面可锻炼学生的发音和口语速度，一方面也可以增强活动的乐趣。当然，游戏也是很好的教学手段，不论是静态的纸牌配对、宾果游戏或是大风吹、踢毽子、丢手绢、木头人、丢卡片等动态游戏，只要教师先设定好一些简单的规矩，要求学生在玩游戏时必须有一定的口语交流，都能和语言学习相得益彰。

幼儿园的学生对什么事物都很好奇，只要觉得有趣都很愿意跟着做。由于学生年龄稍小，肌肉协调能力和组织观念仍在起步，需要多方面的指导和操练，因此，教师必须多花心思做好课前需要的准备工作。低年级的学生好问、好学，好奇心强烈。他们就像海绵一样，不论教师教什么，都会迫不及待地吸收，但是他们的注意力无法持续太久。因此，教师在一堂课里必须有五种以上不同形态的教学活动，以维持学生的学习动力。我建议老师们将周彦卓、舒一兵的《游戏学中文》(北京语言大学出版社出版)作为游戏活动设计的参考。

另外，针对这一阶段学生的文化教学的主要目的在于"打基础"，在于"熏陶"。因此，在选择有关中国传统文化观念的故事书时，应尽量避免采用老套写作形式或是有复杂历史背景的书籍，应多选用表达形式比较现代的绘本。

最后我想说的是，低年级的教师一定要随时保持一颗童心，这样才能体会孩子们天马行空的创作想象；更要能随时放下身段，蹲下来从孩子的视角出发，感受他们学习上的挫折，理解他们面对的学习上的挑战。如此，您在教学上一定能如鱼得水，学生们也更能享受到中文课的乐趣。

主题说明

（一）主题单元一：家庭

低年级学生的生活重心仍然围绕着家人、朋友和学校，因此"家庭"是个很容易引发学生热烈讨论的话题。本单元的教学目标是让学生理解中国人的孝顺之道，了解家庭成员之间不同的称谓和关系，特别是手足间的关系。

中国家庭成员之间的称谓比美国的复杂得多。称呼不同，代表的关系也不同。笔者认为，幼儿园的学生只要学习"爸爸、妈妈、哥哥、姐姐、弟弟、妹妹"就足够了；一、二年级的学生可以增加"爷爷、奶奶、叔叔、伯伯、姑姑、舅舅、阿姨"。为了使学生能很快记住家人称谓，教室内一定要有家庭成员的挂图展示。如果学生每天都有机会看到这些内容，就能产生印象记忆效果。

实际的手工操作对这个年龄的学生非常重要，因为手部的触觉可以刺激眼睛和脑部的记忆，使之具体化。幼儿园学生对手部小肌肉的使用能力还在发展中，所以笔者建议让学生剪贴形状，组合家庭成员展示图（剪贴对手部小肌肉的运用训练很有帮助）。至于一、二年级的学生，可以使用布料、毛线、粘土、回收玻璃瓶等多种材料，制作布娃娃或是瓶子娃娃。教师在每堂课中可要求学生完成两个家庭成员的制作，同时配合童谣，学习成员关系。比方说，今天做的是爷爷、奶奶，教师就把"爸爸的爸爸是爷爷，爸爸的妈妈是奶奶"这两句童谣写在白板上，要求学生一边做一边念。当所有娃娃完成后，学生对童谣已经能说唱自如，同时也明白了家庭成员之间的关系。之后，教师可以每天选择两位学生展示自己的娃娃，介绍每一个家庭成员，例如"这是爷爷，是爸爸的爸爸。这是奶奶，是爸爸的妈妈。"此外，还可以请学生带一张自己最喜爱的全家照片到课堂上来，让大家认识自己的家人。

当教师带读童谣时，可以请每一个学生扮成不同的家庭成员，教师念到哪一个成员，那个学生就得带领大家做一个动作。比如说到"爷爷"时，学生得模仿爷爷的样子走路或跳舞；教师也可以不直接呼叫称谓，而改说"爸爸的哥哥"，那么，"伯伯"就得出来跳舞了。此活动不但复习了词语，也同时复习了家人关系。同时，也可配合图画卡片，以"Go Fish（钓鱼）"的方式让学生分组玩配对游戏。

本主题中建议引入的儿歌/童谣有：《家族歌》、《世上只有妈妈好》、《宝贝女儿好妈妈》、《咱们从小讲礼貌》。建议引入的成语/谚语有：母子连心、虎父无犬子、孟母三迁、知子莫若父/知女莫若母。此外，也可引入古诗《静夜思》（针对一、二年级学生）。

在选择阅读材料时，给幼儿园学生应尽量选择文字简单、以图片为主的故事书，只要是关于亲子关系的都可以；为低年级的学生，可以选择古代的二十四孝的故事①和现代的家庭亲子故事。讲述故事时，教师应该适时强调中国的孝顺观念以及"兄友弟恭"的相处礼仪。故事学习的重点是让学生从生活表现方式中形成对文化差异的基本认识。教师可以指定学生到图书馆借一本有关子女孝顺父母的故事书，一本有关兄弟姐妹间的友爱的故事书（中英文皆可），带到课堂中来并轮流讲故事。这个作业的目的是让学生在选择故事书的过程中，有机会思考"孝顺""友爱"的意思。之所以不一定要中文的故事书是因为考虑到学生对英文故事书阅读得比较多，容易找到符合要求的书。而且，此阶段的学习重点是培养学生的语言表达能力，采用学生熟悉的读物比较容易引发他们说话的欲望，进入教学主题。

最后，教师可发给学生九大张卡片，让他们画三张图表达孝顺，三张图表达友爱，三张图表达礼貌。在学生完成之后，要互相猜猜其他人的图画表达的意思，然后把所有图画贴挂在教室中的展览板上。此外，建议教师组织学生欣赏儿童动画《大耳朵图图》②，这是很适合低年级学生观赏的家庭影片。

本阶段的学生很容易被带动，只要教师的教学活动变化多样，多给学生说话和表演的机会，学生总会乐此不疲。

（二）主题单元二：食物与中药

低年级学生对食物的兴趣非常高，他们正处在爱吃的年龄阶段。这个单元的文化教学目标是让学生认识中国人常吃的食物，学习有关味道的基本词语，学习筷子的用法和饭桌上的基本礼仪。

---

① http://www.icpcc.cn/edu/student/leyuan/200612/972.html
② http://www.tom61.com/ertongyingyuan/ertongdonghuapian/2010-09-19/2538.html

认识食物不妨从早餐、午餐和晚餐开始。教师可以让学生从超级市场的广告中剪下一系列图片，分别贴到代表三餐的三个纸盘上，然后向大家说明自己每日三餐的食物内容。随后，教师再以图片展示中国人常吃的食物，例如早餐中的包子、豆浆、烧饼、油条、稀饭/粥，午餐和晚餐中的米饭、面条、饺子、炒青菜等。当然，教师若是能在亚洲超市买到几样食物，带到课堂中让学生实际观看和品尝，学生的学习情绪会更活跃，同时也能学习表示食物味道的词语（酸、甜、苦、辣）。

　　做葱油饼、包饺子一直都是很受欢迎的学习活动，若是学校有厨房，教师应该为学生安排机会进行实际操作，加深学生对中国食物的认识和喜爱。即便没有厨房设备，也可以安排学生用面粉团捏出自己喜爱的中国食物模型。教师可以设计几份不同的由中国食物图形排列而成的宾果游戏纸，帮助学生加深印象，也可参考《游戏学中文》中的"闻味道"（第81页）这个游戏。

　　教师还可以指派学生带不同形状、大小的点心到课堂上来，准备好筷子，让学生进行夹点心比赛：将点心分别装在不同的碗里，然后将学生分成两组进行比赛，每组每次派一人出战，限时一分钟，在限时之内夹到较多的点心即可胜出。比赛结束后，累计成绩较好的一组为获胜组，组员可一起分享夹到的点心。筷子游戏有许多不同的玩法，教师可以变换夹取物品，像夹面条、丸子等。此活动的目的是帮助学生了解中国人的餐具并训练他们使用筷子。同时，教师应该分别展示中西方餐具及用餐场景的图片，让学生对照比较两者的差别。

　　在学习用餐场景时，可将桌子组合成几个大桌，请学生练习摆放碗筷。学生可抽签扮演家庭中不同的成员。这一活动可让学生练习就位的先后次序以及吃饭时碗筷的拿法。学生在此时可自由发挥，表演就餐过程，教师须在旁指点，一旦教师指出了表演中的错误，学生必须进行修正。反复重复几次后，学生就会自然明白如何摆放碗筷、如何按次序就坐、如何拿碗筷吃饭。这一切都是学生的自发演练，所以能达到非常好的学习效果。

　　吃饭时不合时宜的行为有哪些？学习此项内容时，可让学生制作禁止标志图：教师分给学生一人一张圆形卡纸，请学生设计餐馆里专用的禁止标志图，完成后将其张贴在教室里的展示板上，简单说明图像的意义。

　　学习完所有内容后，可安排学生分组以"到中国朋友家吃饭"为题表演短剧，教师须提前说明表演要求：表演中情节和语言的设计应综合体现出之前所学各项内容。当某组进行表演后,其他各组应予以评价并给出分数。在评分之前,每一组都有机会对剧情和表现的方式进行说明。这对低年级的学生来说很有挑战性,但是千万别小看学生的能力,只要教师说明清楚对表演内容的要求,学生是绝对可以高水平发挥的。

关于食物的中文歌曲非常少见,笔者建议教师选用学生熟悉的中、英文歌曲或韵律来改编。一、二年级的学生特别喜爱这样的创作活动,老师们不妨多加利用。在课程的学习过程中也不妨穿插范晓萱的《健康歌》,来个带动唱,活跃课堂气氛。其他建议引入的内容有:儿歌《饭前要洗手》、《吃饭歌》、《大米饭》,唐诗《悯农》。教师可将《悯农》当成每日午餐前的开饭令,这样学生就能在不知不觉中记住诗句,并且很快明白珍惜食物的深意。

(三) 主题单元三:节庆活动

节日和庆祝活动是低年级学生最期盼的学习内容。说到节庆总离不开吃喝玩乐,不同的中国节日也都有各种不同的庆祝方式和特别的节庆食物。虽然年年庆祝,然而学生随着年龄的增长,领悟力和学习能力都相对提高,即使教师组织的活动年年不变,学生却能对此不断有更深的理解,所以,教师应该保持此项教学传统。学生经过幼儿园和一年级阶段的学习后,应该对中国传统节日的意义和庆祝活动有了基本的认识。

本单元的文化教学目标是让学生对中国传统节日的由来及其庆祝方式和传统节庆食物(饺子、月饼、粽子)有基本的认识与了解。教师一定要把握好学生的认知水平和生理机能,特别是设计手工活动时,必须依照学生的实际操作能力来进行安排。低年级学生对许多新知识的学习必须经历手动、眼看、脑部思考进而形成记忆的过程。每个孩子都会有不同的记忆方式。对于节庆的神话传说,可以让学生在听完故事后,用画漫画的方式来表现他们对故事的理解。经过这样的一个思考、绘图的过程,学生可对故事进行再一次消化并且达到记忆的效果。

幼儿园的学生需要多方面的体能辅导训练。手工制作材料应该在课前事先都准备好,在制作过程中,教师必须一步一步地引导,慢慢说明、示范。一、二年级学生的肌肉发育得较发达,组织能力也比较成熟。在这个阶段的手工活动中,教师可以将材料的准备工作适当地分派给学生,让学生有机会参与、表现(但对制作过程仍然得循序渐进地展示、说明)。

本单元的教学内容应该包括节日名称、配合图片的节庆神话故事、节庆音乐/歌曲、手工制作及节庆的配合活动。剪贴窗花、制作小灯笼、装饰鞭炮、描红纸写春联、包饺子、做月饼、画孔子像、舞狮舞龙、包粽子、龙船折纸、节庆表演道具制作、观赏节庆动画片或者表演等内容都可引入教学。此外，也可参考《游戏学中文》中的"猜灯谜"（第33页）及"我最喜欢的节日"（第37页）。

笔者相信，老师们为节庆准备的教学内容一定是包罗万象，就不在此多说了。我想提醒老师们的是，节庆活动都有一定的时间节点，因此要选择好时机。比如春节的庆祝时间长，课程内容比较丰富，教学时间可以延伸到两个星期，其他节日最好不超过三天。如此比较能让学生感受当下的节庆气氛，也不会觉得冗长，失去兴趣。就像圣诞节的礼物收过了以后，孩子们就会很快开始期待新年的到来，然后再盼望下一个节日。教师的设计应让学生对中国的节庆一直怀有期待的心情。

最后别忘了设计一堂说话课（Show and Tell），让学生们有机会说说自己喜爱的美国节日和中国节日并展示收集的物品。此处的教学设计可参考《游戏学中文》中的"我最喜欢的节日"（第37页）。

（四）主题单元四：地理与旅游

"地理与旅游"这个单元的学习重点是培养学生对时间、方向、位置的概念，训练学生说明地点的能力，帮助他们认识交通工具和旅行的方式。

首先，学生应该先了解位置的说法，也就是"前面、后面、里面、外面、上面、下面、中间"这些基本概念及其说明方式。此时，"藏东西"是个很好的热身游戏，可以让学生从游戏中学会怎么表示物品的位置，同时也能达到理解位置的目的。为了加深理解，教师可先展示事先准备好的大型图片并提问，让学生轮流说出某物的位置。之后，给学生一人发一块小白板，教师说句子，要求学生画出某物的位置。几次演练以后，学生差不多就能掌握位置的说法了。

教师还可以在大白板上画上房子、树、公园、车子、狗、猫等，然后请学生轮流在白板上把"自己"画在喜欢的位置上（人物必须有动作、形象，比方说画一个在吃东西的"自己"）。每个人都画完之后，大家可以看着图互相猜猜"谁在哪里做什么"。在这个游戏中，学生可随意创作，图画得越是滑稽、夸张（比方说把自己画在狗的肚子里面睡觉），学生越有兴致。绘画游戏之后，再来个"我说你做"活动，再一次复习所学内容，同时也可以提高课堂娱乐性，保证教学中笑声不断。

接下来，教师可让学生画一张教室里的桌椅、物品摆放位置图，注意应依照学生的能力来要求图片上要呈现的物品的详细程度。然后，将所有的图都收集在一块儿。幼儿园的学生可以抽图并看图说话；一、二年级的学生，除了看图说话，还可以看图写句子。如有可能，也可以把学生带出教室画地图：画地图以前，教师先领着学生沿着校园周围走一圈（教师决定范围的大小），让学生有机会认识自己的校园。教师可以在参观校园时说明每个东西的位置，或是以提问方式让学生练习说明，如此能帮助学生在画地图之前建立基本的方位概念。对低年级的学生来说，这是一项大工程，不过也是个有趣的挑战。教师要切记，不必评论学生画的图是否与实物相像，只要能将位置表现出来即可，这个阶段的孩子最怕被"笑话"，所以教师要多发挥自己的想象力去理解学生的艺术创作。同时可以请学生画一张"我家"的地图作为家庭作业，将其住家前、后、左、右四个方位的景色画出，带到课堂上来说明、展示。在课堂上玩游戏时也可以配合《我的朋友在哪里》这首儿歌进行练习：演唱时将"在这里"改唱为"在上面""在里面"或是"在后面"等，帮助学生复习词语。

学会了画地图，学生就有了看地图的基本能力了。接下来，教师可以展示一张配合图片说明的社区地图，让学生学习怎么从 A 地到 B 地，这时可以带入交通工具词语。学习新词语时，最好用以图片为主、文字为辅的卡片帮助学生认读。之后，组织学生玩个有关旅行的游戏，学习如何指引方向（如左传/右转/一直走/停）：两个学生去旅行，选择两个地点（A 和 B）和交通工具，第三个学生负责指引方向。去旅行的学生必须模仿乘坐所选择的交通工具进行表演。若是能到户外以校园实际的场景和地点进行演练，学生的学习过程会更有真实感。教师也可以参照《游戏学中文》中的"好司机"（第 19 页）、"旗手"（第 27 页）、"搭错车"（第 42 页）、"闭着眼睛走"（第 136 页）等有关方向和交通的游戏组织活动。此时建议引入的童谣/儿歌有：《红绿灯》、《交通秩序歌》、《造飞机》、《火车快飞》、《碰碰车，车碰碰》。

学生有了有关地理位置的基本概念后，教师可以展示世界地图，教学生认识中国与美国的位置。低年级的学生应该学习认识地图上的七大洲和四大洋的名称。此时，让学生用不同颜色的粘土做立体世界地图可取得较好的教学效果。

学习"时间"时，幼儿园的学生得先有数字概念，即先学数数，再学看电子数字钟。教师可以带学生做体操，边做边数数，也可以用儿歌、童谣进行演练。一、二年级的学生则应该学说日期、看数字钟（点、分、秒）。教师可以把时间概念带入之前的旅行活动：每一次旅行中，学生都必须说明日期（抽日期卡片）和时间（配合时钟所标示的时间）。

最后，请幼儿园的学生带一件和家人旅行时买的纪念品到课堂上来，说说自己去了什么地方、是和谁去的、带了什么东西去、是怎么去的、去了多久、做了些什么。一、二年级的学生还可以做个简单的计划表。教师得事先设计好计划表格，其中应包括日期、地点、交通方式、时间/活动等内容。学生还应按照自己的喜好设计一份假期旅游计划表并就此作出口头报告。

本主题中建议引入的成语有：风景如画、走马观花、人山人海、一路顺风、一路平安；建议引入诗歌《山村咏怀》（一去二三里，烟村四五家。亭台六七座，八九十枝花）。教师可以让学生以自己的理解力和想象力，用画图画的方式来表现这首诗。学生在创作过程中都会有自己的想法，每幅作品都是充满童趣的水墨写意画。

（五）主题单元五：历史、政治与宗教

低年级的学生对历史、政治与宗教还没有具体的概念，甚至连这些词语本身的意义也无法理解。此时，讲故事是最好的启蒙方式。幼儿园的学生还没有时间的观念，只知道"很久以前"和"现在"；一、二年级的学生已经对年、月、日、星期有了字面上的理解，不过说到今天、明天、昨天、上个星期或者去年时，学生就很容易混乱了。因此，这个主题中，低年级的教学仅以学校生活、教育为主，教师应帮助学生了解学校的功能、基本的尊师重教精神。孔子的故事、学校规矩、师生之间的关系都是本主题中的教学内容。

如何以有趣的方法来进入这些主题，引起学生的兴趣呢？可以请学生上台当一分钟教师。学生可自由选择一个主题，如认字、数学、画图、歌曲，然后实施教学。在这个活动中，可以先让学生自己感受并且分别说说"教"与"学"的乐趣和困难，然后由他们来主导这堂课的讨论。教师则须顺着学生的话题把学习重点引入讨论，比方说，问学生一些关于"为什么"的问题（如为什么要上学？为什么要学写字？为什么要认字读书？为什么要考试？为什么要有功课？）。教师可在白板上写下、在展览板上贴上这些问题，让学生找伙伴进行讨论。等有了结果以后，请学生一个一个地上台说明，同时可以把学生的答案都写下来，贴在展览板上的问题旁边，

表示学生解答了此问题。教师也可以用"为什么不……"的方式来提问，也能达到良好的效果。活动结束后，千万别忘了奖励学生，因为他们解决了教师不懂的问题。这项活动旨在藉由学生的讨论使之了解学校的功能和教育的重要性。教师在总结学生的讨论结果时，一定要联系与他们生活相关的事物。此时建议使用的儿歌/童谣为：《上学歌》、《小二郎》、《拍手歌》、《做早操》。

讨论活动后，可以安排学生观赏蔡志忠动画系列之《孔子说》，看看孔子如何教导学生以及学生与教师之间如何相待。[①] 对幼儿园的学生来说，此动画片仍然太难，教师可另选故事书来介绍孔子。但是对于一、二年级的学生，只要教师随时配合解说，学生基本上可以理解动画片中的故事内容。由于本片各片段时间都很短，学生不会因听不懂而有挫折感。此外，还有一部纪录片叫《请选我》，记录了2007年中国武汉市常青第一小学三年级一班的一次班长选举过程。教师可以选择其中的片段，展示中国学校的实际情形，如班级座位的安排、学校的操场、上下课的礼仪、学生的服装、同学之间的关系等。此时亦可参考北京大学出版社出版的《中美国别文化比较教程》，作者舒一兵先生在这本书里谈到了许多中美生活中的文化差异，并用图片进行了对照说明。教师可进行选择，配合学生程度，简化相关内容，将其作为辅助教学材料。

教师在课堂上的规矩、要求，与学生的互动关系都是存在于生活中的教学内容，学生应该在实际的生活中将其表现出来，比如看见教师应该先问好，进入教室要先"报告"，上课说话或离座必须经过教师同意，上课不吃东西、不趴在课桌上……进行这个单元时，不妨特别强调纪律的遵守，让学生来个"守纪律"的比赛；教师每天发给学生一张一百分的点数卡，学生犯规一次应画掉两个点，表现好则可增加特定点数。在一个时限后，教师结算学生的点数。教师得事先设计好点数的获取标准及奖励措施，这样在比赛时学生才有动力，为了奖品学生通常都会很努力地表现。这个活动可以让学生在不知不觉中适应纪律，养成讲礼貌的习惯。

在这个单元中，可将表示职业的词语（如医生、教师、消防员、图书馆员、商人、厨师、警察）带入教学，以"打苍蝇"的游戏来帮助学生熟悉词语：教师将写有词语的卡片全都贴在白板上或是墙上，每次选两位学生互相对抗。学生听教师说词语并用苍蝇拍击打卡片，谁先打到正确的卡片谁

---

① 可参考网页 http://www.tudou.com/playlist/id/10435985/。

就得分。熟悉词语后，还可以玩"长大以后要做什么"的游戏，互相猜猜同学的志愿；学生轮流出来介绍自己的长处（以 5 个句子为限），比方说"我会看书写字""我有礼貌""我爱朋友""我会唱歌跳舞""我是好学生"。其他的学生从教师准备好的"职业"卡片中为其选出一项适合的职业，说："你要当……"，看看是否与该生的志愿相同。

以此活动作为单元教学的尾声，目的是让学生了解到学校学习与将来的工作有重要的关系。建议教师将故事"铁杵磨成针"作为低年级的文化补充教材，鼓励学生培养勤学的态度。① 本主题可引入的诗句/谚语有：一日为师，终身为父；少壮不努力，老大徒伤悲；一寸光阴一寸金，寸金难买寸光阴。可引入的成语有：光阴似箭、有教无类、努力不懈、勤学苦练。

（六）主题单元六：朋友、娱乐与时尚

"朋友"在这个阶段代表着孩子人际关系发展的第一步。幼儿园的孩子特别需要玩伴，只要能一块儿做游戏、唱歌就是朋友；而低年级儿童对朋友的要求是，除了可以与之共同活动之外，必须与其有某些方面的共同喜好，比方说喜欢同一种颜色、吃一样的糖果或是都会踢足球、跳舞等。本单元的学习目标是引导学生感受到"你怎样对待别人，别人就会怎样对待你"，同时引导其在活动中学习、实践"交朋友"的基本方法和技巧。文化教学目标是帮助学生认识中国儿童的游戏方式和玩具。

"镜中我"是个很能引发学生的参与热情的游戏：两人一组，甲学生为镜外人，做动作；乙学生为镜中人，模仿动作。活动后可请甲谈谈"你看到了什么？"，再请乙说说模仿甲的时候心里的想法。学生在活动的过程中可以学习感受镜子内外的关系，了解朋友之间的相处之道。另一个"你了解我多少？"的活动是给每一位学生发小白板，随机选择一位学生为主角"我"，教师提出一些有关个人嗜好、习惯和情景的问题，所有学生都必须写出主角"我"会选择的答案，对照主角和其他学生的答案之后，看看谁最了解"我"。低年级学生总是乐此不疲。游戏的重点是教师对于问题的设计：必须选择学生感兴趣的话题或生活中可能遇到的需要"脑筋急转弯"的情况。比方说：如果上厕所的时候，没有卫生纸了，你怎么办？（A）叫

---

① 可参考大纪元中国文化课教案（六）（http://www.epochtimes.com/b5/3/10/27/n401012.htm）。

人;(B)不用卫生纸;(C)坐在马桶上等人来。这个游戏活动不但可以拉近学生之间的距离,同时也让学生有机会看到每个人另一面的幽默,互相建立好感。

看图听故事也是很好的游戏方式:教师选择一两个与交朋友相关的故事(如《狮子交朋友》)[①]、不同类别的中国寓言故事,[②]针对故事内容,引出问题要求学生相互问答,帮助学生了解故事寓意,培养其基本社交技能。此外,也可以先让学生分组,各组一同阅读故事,先试着理解内容大意,然后再让学生自己选择搭档,以表演方式来表现故事。教师应鼓励低年级的学生改换不同的角色,多次进行表演,因为戏剧中的模拟最能让学生记忆深刻。表演之后,可将学生分成两组,一组就情节提问题,另一组则回答问题。由此教师可以了解学生对故事的理解程度。

故事结束之后大家可以轻松一下,来玩个音乐游戏——找朋友:一个学生开始一边唱一边"找朋友",找到朋友后就将双手搭在新朋友的肩膀上,两人一前一后,像火车车厢一样搭连起来。然后两人再开始去找另一个新朋友,直到全班的学生都找到朋友,加入队伍。此处建议使用儿歌《找朋友》,活动设计可以参考《游戏学中文》中的"找朋友"(第9页)。

接下来,教师可以在卡片上写出各种情景及该情景中的问题(也可让学生来写),比如说:班上来了一位新同学,你会怎么和新同学交朋友呢?朋友受伤了,你会做什么呢?想和朋友一起分享玩具或是糖果时,你会怎么做?万一你的要求被拒绝,你怎么办?……这是刺激学生进一步思考的好方法。教师可请学生到台前抽卡片,大声念出问题,由学生选出举手最快的学生来回答问题,读问题的学生可以决定回答的学生的得分。教师应事先准备好两张得分卡,一张是微笑的表情图,代表三分;一张是开口大笑的表情图,代表四分。只要参与回答的学生都应有机会得分(得分最好不要相差太大)。教师也可以准备各种不同的物品,将学生分组后,请学生就物品数量将其平均分配给同组的伙伴。这个活动可以让学生练习如何与他人分享,如何"将心比心"。

接下来可进行采访活动"你喜欢和朋友一起做什么":教师设计好一份简单的调查表,让学生互相采访并且将结果记录下来(幼儿园的学生可用图画方式记录)。采访结束后,教师统计结果并将其写在白板上,如玩

[①] 参考网页:http://www.wretch.cc/blog/misseshome/5789975
[②] 参考网页:http://www.vastman.com/fable/traditional/index.htm

游戏——6人，做功课——4人，踢足球——5人。

　　最后可选一个学生喜爱的游戏作为结束活动，借此机会把中国的儿童玩具带入教学。教学生制作中国毽子、沙包、风筝可以增强文化学习氛围，也可让学生有机会比较中国孩子和美国孩子玩的游戏。当然，学生最爱的生日会也是很好的教学机会。教师可帮班上的学生办一场集体生日庆祝会。在那一天，每一个学生都必须为自己的朋友做三件好事。活动中应鼓励学生们身体力行，亲手准备礼物，不可花钱买礼物，让学生体会"友情贵在真诚"。

　　本处建议引入成语有：将心比心、和睦相处、情同手足、一言为定、相亲相爱、不分彼此。在学习活动中，学生已经在体会成语的意义，教师一定要把握机会，运用成语来形容、说明当时的情景，使学生在自然的学习环境中实现对成语的理解。

（七）主题单元七：艺术与科学创造

　　针对低年级学生进行"艺术与科学创造"的教学时，应该先用文字、书法、音乐来引导学习。教师要营造真实的学习环境，使学生在其中耳濡目染，可以亲自操作、实践。这个单元的文化教学目标是帮助学生认识中国音乐中常见的传统乐器，欣赏中国音乐；使学生对中国象形文字有基本概念；学习吟唱唐诗。

　　在认识汉字时，教师可以引导学生们从简易的图画形式开始了解文字的演变。[1] 笔者自己特别偏爱这个教学法，它的效果非常好。如果以书法的形式来介绍中国文字，会更有艺术趣味：学生不但可以学习文字的变化，同时也学习了中国的文房四宝及毛笔的使用方法。教师可以让学生将自己书写的文字简单地裱成一幅中国式的字画，悬挂在教室内欣赏，并轮流就自己的作品说说对文字变化的认识。画山水、花鸟、写"春"字、"福"字或是临摹一首短诗都是很好的演练活动。另外，也可以先展示几个简单的象形字，例如日、月、山、水、木，将字体变化成图像来介绍象形字与自然景观的共同点；之后，再展示几个代表动物的象形字，让学生通过自己的想象将象形字转化为动物图样。如此可加深学生对汉字的基本了解并提高课堂上文字教学的趣味性。

---

　　[1] 本处可参考《文字的故事》，http://v.youku.com/v_show/id_XMTAwMTQ1OTk2.html。

学生对象形文字有了基本了解之后，教师可以将已经学过的汉字做成繁体和简体两种字卡，让学生在竞赛游戏中找出同一汉字的两种形式；或利用繁体字的绘本故事书玩认读游戏，看谁能念出较多的繁体汉字，并能同时从简体字卡中找出该字。笔者的学生常常在念完一本小故事后，对自己对繁体字的认读能力感到惊讶。这个活动能显示出繁体、简体字的差别，使学生对汉字更有兴趣，因此亦提高了汉字书写的学习效果。现推荐给老师们一本由知名画家、诗人、作家蒋勋所著的《汉字书法之美》。该书中有四个主题：汉字演变、书法美学、感知教育、汉字与现代。其中，感知教育部分对于汉字元素的讲解很生动。笔者个人非常喜爱这本书。这本书不但提升了我在汉字美学方面的修养，更丰富了我对中国汉字历史文化层面知识的认识，也因此提高了教学质量。

"中国音乐"也是本主题中的教学内容。介绍中国乐曲之前，可以先来个歌曲接唱的热身游戏，这样一方面可以复习之前学过的中国儿歌，一方面可引导学生了解歌曲中的韵律。接下来，让学生各自选择各种可以发出声音的物品，跟着歌曲的节奏进行敲打。这个结合了肢体动作和声响的活动很能鼓舞学生。笔者通常会让学生自己找伙伴组成一个小乐团，选一首最喜爱的歌曲，配合韵律进行敲打、表演。表演结束后，可轮流播放美国和中国的音乐，让学生聆听，引导其发现各种不同乐器的声音。在听后的讨论中可以请学生说出听到的乐器声音像什么，并模拟发出类似的声音，同时也可以让他们在教室里的大白板上画出自己想象中的乐器样式。从听觉到视觉，学生可以先建构出声音和乐器形状之间的联系，再从乐器的图片中学习分辨中、西乐器的异同。

此时如配合中国乐器的手工制作，可使学生对古筝、横笛、二胡、琵琶、锣有具体、形象的认识。笔者曾经利用学校午餐所剩的纸盒裁剪成乐器的形状，配合在校园内收集的树枝和橡皮圈，让学生利用这些回收资源来制作乐器。完成乐器手工制作，每个学生都有了自己的中国乐器后，教师可以选播几首"女子十二乐坊"的作品，学生要手持乐器，组成一个乐团，听到什么乐器声，手拿那个乐器的学生就必须做表演动作。反复几次以后，学生很快就能辨认中国乐器的音色。教师千万别一开始就播放快节奏的乐曲，因为如果学生没有足够的时间分辨清楚乐声，就无法表演动作。所以，建议教师由慢节奏开始，逐步加快乐曲速度，播放到最后一首快节奏乐曲时，尽管学生仍会手忙脚乱，但是一定会玩得很过瘾。最后，教师可以安排一场小型表演：有的学生跳舞，有的学生唱歌，有的学生吹奏乐器（口技模仿），结束这个热闹的单元。此外,也可利用游戏"Musical Chairs"再做一次复习演练活动:活动时可播放各种不同节奏的中国音乐/儿歌,没抢到椅子的学生必须说出音乐中的一种乐器名称,不然就被淘汰。

本单元中建议引入一些与音乐/声音相关的中国成语故事,如"滥竽充数""五音不全""对牛弹琴""不声不响""不闻不问"等。

(八) 主题单元八:情绪与情感表达

表情是一种独特的情绪语言,是人与人之间交流感情,互相理解的一种方式。学会识别他人的表情,才能准确理解对方表达、传递的信息。因此教师应该利用各种机会引导低年级学生观察周围朋友的各种表情,了解与人的喜、怒、哀、乐等情绪相对应的面部表情,学会正确表达对人和事物的态度和情感。低年级的学生对于情感的理解,仍然以"我"的感受为中心,表达方式停留在较为基础的层面。针对此年龄阶段学生的教学重点是培养学生对表情的识别能力。

第一周的教学不妨先由观察不同的表情开始:利用表情图片让学生说说自己看到了什么,觉得图片中的人高兴还是难过;然后再引导学生看不同的脸部表情,比较不同表情中的五官有什么不一样,如眉毛怎么样,眼睛又是如何的等等;最后,让学生照镜子,做各种表情。这样可让学生从大概的印象进步到对个别地方的细致观察,从而感受到不同的人物表情代表的不同情感。

接下来可以让学生感受喜、怒、哀、乐对应的不同表情。此时可让学生回忆:当你画的画得到大家的夸奖时,你的表情是怎么样的?(眉开眼笑)人家拒绝和你一起玩游戏的时候,你又有什么样的表情?(难过沮丧)你的朋友吃完午餐后要出去玩时,你却还没有吃完午餐,你脸上的表情是怎么样的?(着急的)受到老师批评时,你脸上又会有怎样的表情?(不好意思,难受)

此后,可以让学生学习用各种不同的方式来表现不同的情绪。例如,教师可以组织"画脸游戏",请学生画出代表心情的各种脸部表情,也可以请学生在白板上自由创作一张表情图像,说说图像表达的情感。这是通过平面的视觉图像进行的心情表达方式。教师也可以引导学生以肢体动作进行心情表达:选用类似"如果你很高兴你就拍拍手"的儿歌,让学生边唱边动,学习脸部表情和肢体动作的配合。另外,教师应多利用绘本进行教学。对于低年级学生来说,多彩生动的图片和儿歌能给他们带来直观、形象的感受,帮助他们更好地理解故事内容或歌词的趣味性。(老师们可以去"中国儿童资源网"寻找教学材料,这里有一定的儿童动画、有声故事、电影、图书等资源,可以作为辅助教学的资料库。)

最后,发给学生每人8张卡片,请学生把自己的生活中曾经发生过的心情小故事画出来,形成一本个人的心情小册。

在第二周的教学中可以进行卡片配对活动、苍蝇拍游戏,复习第一周所学的词语和句型:将图片或词语投影在白板上,教师说词语,两个学生分别以苍蝇拍拍打听见的词语,看谁的速度快或准确率高。接下来,播放几种不同节奏、韵律的音乐,请学生用肢体动作表达自己对音乐的感受。比方说,播放节奏轻快的音乐时,学生会拍手或跳动,表达一种轻松愉快的心情。但是,并不是每个学生对同一支曲子都会有相同的感受。当学生们呈现出不同的肢体动作时,教师可以引导学生谈谈为什么有这样的差别,让学生认识到每个人都有自己独特的感觉和看法,每一个人对同样的事物都有可能有不同的情绪反应。此后,可以要求学生听/读一篇故事,谈谈故事中人物的对话和心情表现方式,说说故事中自己最喜爱的人物和最不喜爱的人物,讨论其中的原因,了解故事中人物之间互相的情绪影响。最后进行模拟表演,表现故事的情节。

如果条件允许,教师可以组织学生观赏动画片《大头儿子小头爸爸》:事先发给每一个学生一张心情记录卡片,要求他们一边看动画片一边在卡片上画下自己看到的各种表情并注明有此表情的人物。影片结束后,先以提问的方式了解学生对故事内容的理解程度,训练学生的口头回答能力;之后,再请学生轮流展示自己所画的心情记录卡,用不同颜色的笔区别出"好"心情和"坏"心情,说明归类的标准。

笔者希望学生能养成多说"好话"的习惯,喜欢以"情景模拟"的方式来组织练习:让学生练习遇到问题或是纠纷时,应该如何避免负面情绪,以正面、积极的表达方式与同学沟通,也就是不使用批评、控诉他人的词语,以不伤害同学感受的交流方式来表达自己的情绪。此活动也可训练学生学习如何控制自己的愤怒、害怕、紧张等负面情绪。

第三周的教学目标是使学生明白自己的情绪会影响自己和朋友的关系,学习用较适当的方式表达自己的情感,和朋友融洽相处。

在复习过有关表情和心情的词语、句型之后,教师将写好的事件说明卡片放入一个纸箱中,请每个学生都抽一张卡片并表现卡片上的事件会引发的情绪。然后,请甲学生对乙学生表现一种情绪,乙学生说明自己对此的感受和想法。每一个学生都应有机会表现情绪,表达个人的心情感受。学生从这个活动中将学习到事件会如何影响个人的心情,而个人的情绪对他人又会有何影响。

接着,教师把四张分别标示着"喜""怒""哀""乐"的海报纸贴在教室中四个不同方位的墙上,请每一个学生分别在提前准备好的小袋内抽出"喜""怒""哀""乐"卡,依照不同情绪分为四组。每一组成员之间要互相分享自己最高兴、伤心、生气的小故事,并且在心情海报上写出可能导致本组情绪的事情/情况,画出本组所代表的心情图标。分享、记录都完成后,每组轮流展示心情海报并进行说明,同时区别"好"与"坏"的情绪表现。针对学生举出的"坏"心情,教师可引导学生分享自己对付坏情绪的办法,也可以展示情绪疏解挂图,按照其中的建议带动学生演练,配合音乐的播放,让学生随着音律放松,体会心情的转变。

教师也可以设计某些纠纷,请甲、乙两学生表演事件发生时的情绪和有效沟通方式。比如说,午餐时,甲为了尽快取走自己的餐盒而无意打翻了乙正在喝的果汁,乙很生气,但必须用正面的态度向甲说明他/她给自己带来的负面感受,让甲明白自己对别人的影响。此后,甲应该为自己的粗心道歉,乙则因为果汁被打翻而情绪低落,必须选择一种疏解方式来调结情绪。又比如说,甲因为没做功课被妈妈惩罚,不能玩自己最喜欢的玩具,到学校以后教师也不让甲出去玩。甲把不愉快的心情向乙发泄,乙得理解甲的情绪反应,学用温和的表达方式告知甲自己的感受,甲则练习用呼吸吐气的方式改变自己的情绪。这个活动听起来似乎有点挑战性,但在实际操练上并没有太大的难度,只要教师一步一步地引导,组织不同组合的学生多次模拟,很快学生就能明白整个活动的重点(尤其是一、二年级的学生)。如果面对的是幼儿园的学生,必须设计最基本的情况来组织练习,教学目标则着重在培养学生的情绪识别能力,帮助他们养成多说话少动手的沟通习惯。

在本单元教学结束之前,可以再给学生听一篇心情故事,要求他们重新安排故事中人物的对话方式,改变故事的结局。也可配合音乐让学生进行讨论、表演。最后,再组织一个带动唱(如果你很高兴你就……),一定能取得很好的教学效果。

单元主题：情绪与情感表达
（幼儿园中文班，三个星期）

引导问题

核心问题	焦点问题
1. 我们如何了解情绪和感受？	1. 你知道高兴、生气、伤心和害怕的感觉有什么不一样吗？
2. 我们如何表达个人情感？	2. 什么样的事情会让你高兴、生气、伤心或害怕呢？为什么？
3. 情感的表达方式如何影响人际关系？	3. 当你高兴、生气、伤心或害怕时你会做什么？
	4. 你怎么让别人知道你生气了？
	5. 你为什么会和朋友吵架？怎么和朋友和好？

学习目标与技能

- 学生能运用有关情绪的不同词语和句型进行口头表达和书面报告
- 学生能用口述或书写方式说明影片或文章所表达的大意
- 学生能将汉语知识与其他学科知识连结，强化中文学习效果

学习评估

a) 过程评估：

- 绘制情绪图卡并分辨好/坏心情
- 能用肢体动作/脸部表情表现不同情绪
- 辨认情绪图片并说明引发情绪的原因
- 回答情景中的问题

b) 组别合作项目：

- 画图说故事：学生画出自己的喜怒哀乐，形成故事书并将故事讲给大家听
- 短剧表演：模拟故事情景，表达不同情感

每周教学计划

第一周	
教学目标	• 学生能认读表达心情的基本词语 • 学生能运用有关情绪的词汇和句型来表达个人感受
课程内容	• 有关情绪的词语和句型 • 情绪及对应表情 • 情绪与对应的身体动作 • 情绪产生的原因 • 歌曲、童谣(高兴的时候拍拍手,生气的时候跺跺脚,伤心的时候眼泪流,害怕的时候会发抖。)
教学材料	• 汉字、拼音卡片 • 表情挂图 • 情绪图标游戏卡①(每一个表情图标有两张卡片,教师须事先准备)。 • 各种生活照片/图片/卡通/漫画 • 小镜子 • 童谣、情绪歌② • 小白板、马克笔 • 硬纸卡、彩色笔
演练活动	• 展示表情挂图,学习有关情绪的词汇和句型。 • 将学生分组,发情绪图标卡片,以"Go Fish"玩法配对。 • 要求学生观察照片/图片/卡通/漫画,说明图片内容和人物的情绪。 • 学生分析情绪图标上不同情绪中五官的变化和差别,照镜子演练表情变化,以童谣带动肢体表现情绪。 • 组织学生看表情图标,在小白板上画出引起该情绪的情景。 • 学生制作自己的心情小册。
过程评估	卡片配对、看图说话、情景绘图

---

① 可参考 http://www.icosky.com/iconset/emotions-2s-icons/。
② 可参考 http://www.erge100.com/erge/cn/1539.html。

	第二周
教学目标	• 学生能分辨正面和负面情绪的不同 • 使学生理解个人的情绪表现会影响他人的感受 • 学生能以恰当的方式对同学表达情感
课程内容	• 有关情绪的词语和句型 • 正面情绪和负面情绪的区别 • 个人情绪的表达方式及其对他人的影响 • 恰当的情感表达方式 • 亲子动漫《大头儿子小头爸爸》
教学材料	• 心情图表 • 苍蝇拍 • 心情图标卡片 • 配乐 • 心情故事集：Mr. Happy + Mr. Grumpy • 动漫影碟：《大头儿子小头爸爸》 • 硬纸卡片（教师设计好格子）、彩色笔 • 情景说明游戏卡片（教师事先写好）
演练活动	• 以卡片/苍蝇拍游戏复习词汇和句型。 • 看汉字词汇，练习画对应的心情图/看心情图片，写出对应的词语。 • 播放音乐，要求学生用肢体动作表达心情，使其理解由同一事物可能引发不同情绪。 • 请学生听故事，谈谈故事中人物的对话方式和心情表现方式。然后模拟表演，说说故事中最喜爱的人物和最不喜爱的人物，讨论其中的原因，了解故事中人物相互间的情绪影响。 • 看《大头儿子小头爸爸》，请学生一边看一边在格子卡片上画下所看到的各种表情。影片结束后，以提问方式确认学生的理解程度并训练其口语表达能力。再请学生轮流展示所画的心情记录卡，用不同颜色的色笔区分出"好心情"和"坏心情"。 • 抽情景卡片进行演练，让学生练习遇到问题或纠纷时，如何以好的表达方式向同学表达自己的感受。
过程评估	故事模拟表演、短片欣赏和心情记录、情景对话

	第三周
教学目标	• 了解负面情绪的表现及其对朋友的影响 • 了解如何控制自己的负面情绪 • 了解如何以积极、正面的方式表达情绪
课程内容	• 有关情绪的词语与句型 • 事件与心情的相互影响 • 负面情绪的疏解办法和对应活动 • 表达和沟通的方式
教学材料	• 产生负面情绪的"原因"卡片（教师事先准备） • 喜怒哀乐图卡 • 四大张海报纸、马克笔、胶带 • 情绪疏解挂图 • 疏解情绪的音乐 • 一篇心情故事
演练活动	• 每一个学生都抽一张卡片，并表现卡片上的事件引发的情绪反应。请甲学生对乙学生表现一种情绪，乙学生说明自己的感受和想法。每一个学生都有机会表现情绪，表达个人的心情感受。 • 将四大张海报纸贴在教室四个不同方位的墙上。学生分别抽出喜、怒、哀、乐卡，依照抽到的不同情绪分为四组，每一组讨论并分享自己的小故事，在所属的心情海报上写出影响心情的事情/情况，画出本组所代表的心情图标。 • 每组轮流展示、说明本组心情海报，对本组情绪进行归类。 • 学生分享自己对坏情绪的疏解办法。 • 展示情绪疏解挂图，按照建议方式带动学生演练。 • 播放音乐，让学生随着音律放松自己，体会心情转变。 • 回到第一个演练活动，请学生甲再一次表现情绪，乙必须以正面的态度向甲说明甲对乙造成的负面感受。 • 请学生听一篇心情故事，重新安排故事中人物的对话方式，改变故事的结局，配合音乐播放让学生进行讨论。 • 结束活动带动唱（如果你很高兴你就……）。
过程评估	说明影响情绪的因素、心情海报图、如何正面表达负面情绪、改编心情故事中的对话

教学建议

单元问题设置：针对单元主题设计的引导问题，应该以教学中使用的材料内容为基础。为了提高学生的学习兴趣,设计问题时应尽量以"什么""谁""为什么""如何"的形式来提问,连结整个教学过程中的内容。以下是针对本单元主题设计的一些问题:

1. 什么事情会让你高兴/伤心/生气/难过/害怕?
2. 高兴/伤心/生气/难过/害怕的时候,你的身体会有什么样的感觉和反应?
3. 你怎么表达自己的心情?
4. 你心情好的时候喜欢做些什么事?你喜欢和谁一起做?
5. 你心情不好的时候,会做什么?为什么?
6. 你怎么了解自己心情?
7. 什么是"好"心情?
8. 什么是"坏"心情?
9. "好"心情对你的朋友有什么影响?为什么?
10. "坏"心情对你的朋友有什么影响?为什么?
11. 你怎么让自己的"坏"心情变成"好"心情?
12. 我们可以用什么方法表达自己的"坏"心情而不伤害到别人的"好"心情?

词语与句型:词语及句型的设置应以教师在设计课程时准备的阅读材料及与主题相关的生词、语法为基础,依照学生的语言能力斟情处理。以下是与本单元相关的一些词汇和句型:

◆ 词语
喜、怒、哀、乐、高兴、快乐、幸福、生气、伤心、难过、害怕、紧张、看见、听见、想到、摸到、微笑、大笑、哭、流眼泪、尖叫、发抖、拍手、跺脚、如果、可以/不可以、会/不会、喜欢/不喜欢、客气、不礼貌

◆ 句型
一……就……;……的时候,会……;因为……所以……;虽然……可是……;有的时候……

◆ 成语
唉声叹气、泪流满面、大惊小怪、兴奋不已、欢天喜地、得意洋洋

田凤英　著

第四章 启发创造力：
三至四年级阶段的教学

引　言

　　三、四年级的学生大多为八九岁的儿童，他们正处于童年中期，生理、社会心理、认知、情感等各方面仍在持续稳定地成长。与一、二年级学生相比较，他们的持续注意力增加了，自制力提高了，自我照顾能力渐趋成熟，也更能适应学校生活。因此，一般学校中，本阶段学生的学习任务、学业难度都会增加/提高，学生也会日益重视自己的学业表现和学习成绩。

　　虽然一些发育较快的女孩会于此时期迎接青春期的到来，但就生理成长的"量"来讲，绝大多数的儿童不会有类似青春期时的快速发育；就成长的"质"而言，此阶段儿童则会在精细动作（Fine Motor）和大动作（Gross Motor）发展两方面有很明显的进步。精细动作里的速度（Speed）和平稳度（Smoothness）两方面成熟度提高，所以本阶段学生握笔写字、拿剪刀沿线剪纸、涂画粘贴都较低年级时更为驾轻就熟，做起来更加愉快。所以教师应从本阶段开始着力培养学生的汉字书写能力，进行美工制作的能力以及在课堂中独立完成任务的能力。

　　与手部精细动作相比，腿部肌肉群的大动作发展更胜一筹，特别是在平衡感、协调度等方面。有趣的是，当儿童意识到自身体能上的发展和动作能力的增强时,会开始喜欢自我挑战和彼此较量,也会做出大胆的尝试,例如翻筋斗、倒立、竞跑、玩丢接球或是其他团队运动。此阶段的儿童,往往高估自身体能,他们仍欠缺前瞻性的高层次思维技巧(Higher Order Thinking),无法事先预测事件的可能后果,更无力考虑应对策略,所以经常会有突发状况出现。在笔者早期的教学生涯里,就曾经有学生坚持按照他们的方式进行游戏,并极力保证绝对不会摔倒或伤到彼此。为了让学生感到被信任,我同意依照他们的方式进行活动,结果当然出现了意外。此处的结论是:当面对这个年龄段的儿童时,教师应多信赖自己的直觉;当儿童到了七、八年级时,则可考虑多放手、多信赖、赋予学生较多的自主权。最后,有必要再度强调一下:当利用游戏、比赛来激发三、四年级学生的学习动机时,教师应该考虑环境、教具、活动流程等多方面因素,面面俱到,一切以安全为前提。

此年龄段的儿童的另一个特色是:精力特别旺盛,不懂得调整节奏,常常会一路玩到精疲力竭。所以在设计活动时,教师应尽量安排动态活动与静态活动互相穿插,让学生学习如何在一段时间的学习后沉淀身心,休息加油后再出发。笔者经常利用音乐网站(如 www.pandora.com)中的慢节奏古典音乐来舒缓学生的情绪,提高注意力。

由于儿童之间的体形大小及体能表现会在这个阶段里逐渐出现明显的个别差异,这些差异会进一步影响儿童对自我的观感、对自我体能的自信度以及与他人交往的模式。教师在安排活动、进行分组时,如果能够注意这些,多给体能稍居弱势的儿童正面、积极的信息,这对他们自信心、自尊心的培养会十分有利。同时,也应注意引导体能占优势的儿童学会如何利用自身的特点对同伴伸出援手,在团队活动中互相帮助,这样不仅可以提升课堂中的祥和气氛,还可减少欺凌行为(Bullying)的产生。

学校是这个年龄段儿童社会心理发展的基地,因为学校是儿童由家庭过渡到社会的一个中介点,学生在类似小型社会的学校里学习行为规范;面对家人以外的长辈,学习应对礼仪;与年纪相当的同伴朝夕相处,培养团队精神、同理心以及社交谈判技巧。三、四年级的儿童虽然渴望友谊,希望获得同伴的接受和认可,但他们依旧希望取得成人的肯定。换言之,教师这一角色对这一时期的儿童而言仍具有高度的影响力和号召力,因此教师可以对此特性善加利用,来增进教学成效。三、四年级的学生懂得团队合作,也喜欢彼此竞赛,所以,具有比赛性质的团队游戏会很受欢迎。不过,需要注意的是,三、四年级的儿童可能不喜欢和异性同组同工,教师在安排分组活动时,必须顾及学生的好恶,以求良好的团体动力(Group Dynamics)。

如何增进男生的学习动机,提升他们的学习效果一直是许多专家极力探讨的主题。根据笔者的经验,具有比赛性质的小组活动经常可以引起男生的共鸣。八、九岁学生的注意力一般可以持续10—15分钟,所以应尽量缩短学生被动听课的时长,因为静态活动时间一旦超过其可接受之极限,学生势必烦躁难耐,课堂管理问题就会随之而生。还有,教师在言语中应避免以男女生互比来激励学生,必要时可多尝试利用手势等非语言的沟通渠道来减少师生间的"权力斗争"(Power Struggle)。

三、四年级儿童的创造能力提高了,独立性也有所增强,在认知发展方面,正处于皮亚杰所谓的具体操作期(Concrete Operational Stage):思维依赖于具体形象,常会以尝试错误(Trial and Error)的方式,或是通过对实际物品、形象的直接体验、感知来理解事物,获取知识和技能。在教学上,教师最好避开抽象概念,因为本阶段儿童的具体思维尚占据主导地位,对现实与幻想的分界有时还不是很清楚。建议教师们多设计形式多样、操作性强、需要身体动作参与的活动,给儿童机会,让他们去摸索实践,进而得出结论。这个阶段儿童的书面语表达能力有大幅度的提升,他们学会了用文字记载自己的思维,所以除了在语言、文化教学上逐渐提升内容深度,在课堂中利用深入浅出的"头脑风暴"(Brainstorming)方式来探讨议题以外,教师也可试着培养孩子的反思能力,为将来需要更多高层次思维方式的学习铺路。这一阶段的儿童也特别喜欢读冒险故事、幻想小说,教师可尽量提供机会让儿童利用读故事书、戏剧表演等方式来学习语言、文化。

总之,三、四年级的学生,在身体、心理、情绪和认知方面均有较快发展,本阶段教师的中心任务是培养学生的学习能力,帮助学生取得学习成绩,使其成为一位优秀的学生。在中文课堂中,除了持续低年级时的文化熏陶外,加强语言能力训练的重要性不言而喻。

主题说明

(一) 主题单元一:家庭

  传授知识时,较为事半功倍的手段是以学生的自身经验为出发点和催化剂,进而引介新的概念、知识,最后作跨文化、跨语言的比较。因此,在谈到"家庭"这个主题时,无法避免谈到学生的家庭状况。没有人可以挑选自己的血亲,三、四年级的学生更不可能改变自己的生活环境,况且在当今多元化的社会里,家庭的形态逐渐趋向多样,家庭的定义也不断丰富。所以,笔者建议教师在课前先对学生的家庭背景作一定了解,包括其族裔背景、家庭成员、住宿安排等。如此做的益处良多,但最重要的是当教师须要利用学生的生活经历或背景引申时,可慎选题材,顾及学生的感受,尊重学生隐私,或是引起学生共鸣。

  提及教学目标,本单元将承续与一、二年级一致的核心问题并对中国孝道、家庭教育、性别角色与职责作更进一步的探讨。三、四年级学生的创造力较强,本单元可以以"一个三代同堂家庭的冒险故事"为题组织头脑风暴,利用故事创作的方式来激发学生的兴趣和动机。之所以挑选三代同堂的故事,原因是多重的:首先可以复习一、二年级时所学的家庭成员称谓;其次,大多数学生都来自二代核心家庭,对三代同堂的概念仍感新奇;最后,大家庭的成员增加时,每个家庭分子的职责就必须更明确,此项目的难度也就提高了。

  三、四年级学生的思维仍比较具体,教师必须给学生提供明确的指示或标准。在撰写此故事时,教师可以规定情节中必须提及家规、冲突、人物的角色职责等。为了提升学生的语言水平,除复习一、二年级的亲属称谓外,此阶段可加入家庭成员间的关系词语,例如儿子、女儿、孙子、孙女、侄子等。在描述家庭时,可要求学生同时介绍房子格局、各房间名称、家具陈设等。这样一来,这个单元的教学就会有"一气呵成"的感觉。

  为了培养学生的团队合作能力,此活动建议分组进行,让儿童有学习如何与同伴合作、交流的机会。在活动中,儿童以头脑风暴的方式来决定他们的家庭成员、成员的角色分配和各自承担的职责、成员的房间分布(谁住哪儿和为什么)。学生要发挥他们的想象力来编写冒险故事的情节,设想各家庭成员在故事中如何贡献自己的力量,解决危机或冲突。学生可选择借鉴连环画或绘本的制作方法，以手绘或剪贴等方式来完成任务。当学生完成任务，在课堂中分享成果时，教师可利用故事中的情节和人物来提问，激发学生思考，例如：家庭对故事中的人物而言有何重要性？对你而言呢？为什么？各家庭成员有哪些不同的工作、职责？你的职责是什么？在提问的过程中，由于此阶段儿童的专注力有限，对于问题的解答点到为止即可，不必要求详尽冗长，因为需要分享的故事不止一个，在分享的时候同样的概念可以在不同的时间、地点中重复出现，学生可进行多次学习、体会。

当学生分享完他们的故事后，教师可以让大家利用投票选举的方式，挑选出最受欢迎的作品，改以舞台剧的方式来呈现。在投票之前，可以让各参选小组进行"政见发表"，制作宣传海报，这也是一个小小的民主示范活动。

由故事书到舞台剧是一个由书面转口语的过程，可以借此培养学生的口语表达能力。舞台剧的创作需要不同的道具及声光效果，甚至包括舞蹈、歌唱环节，这些都有利于教师进行多元智能（Multiple Intelligence）教学。当进行舞台剧排演时，家庭成员的关系、各成员职责将表现得十分鲜明，教师可以在舞台剧演练的过程中引入中国文化中的"尊老敬贤""父子有亲""长幼有序""男女有别"等行为文化，让学生可以在戏剧表演中实际体验。在此强调的是学生通过表演进行的亲身体验。中文教师的使命不是将学生改造成中国人，改变其文化行为，而是要教导学生学会因时因地进行语码转换（Code Switching），因此应让学生对文化行为多加体验，耳濡目染，在表演中尝试不同的文化角色扮演。这样一来，当他们自身有意愿时，能够因地随时进行转码。

当告知学生大部分的中国人不把宠物算作家人时，学生经常会发出惊讶、抗议之声。这表现了语言、文化双方面的差异。教师可以利用"宠物算是家人吗？"这个话题来探讨"什么是家？""谁是家人？""谁可以是家庭的一份子？""家庭有哪些不同的形态？"等问题。学生可以利用绘画或文字，列举电视、电影或是故事书里所提到的家庭种类、家庭成员，之后再总结。探讨这几个问题时，不一定要给学生所谓"正确答案"，只要学生能认识到家庭的形态会随文化的不同而不同即可，这是培养国际公民观（Global Citizenship）的重要环节。

在美国，中文教师可能会接触到来自同性家庭或领养家庭的孩子，正如前面所提到的，儿童无法选择他们的家人或家庭，而家庭没有"好"或

"不好"的形态，只有好的或不好的机能。如果身为教师的我们能了解此点，包容、尊重、疼爱来自不同家庭背景的儿童，不形成偏见或让偏见影响教学，就能为学生树立一个典范。

（二）主题单元二：食物与中药

谈到"吃"这个主题，相信绝大多数的人都会精神为之一振，兴致高昂。"吃"已从单纯的求生行为升华到具有多重社会文化意义的复杂行为，然而这个转变也给"吃"带来了许多复杂的社会规范。所以谈到"食物"这个主题时，能探讨的范围也就扩展了不少。

一、二年级的学生对中国人常吃的食物名称、味道、餐具摆设和使用，以及不恰当的餐桌行为已有了基本的认识。在三、四年级的课程设计中，除了巩固学生已有的知识、技能外，更可扩展主题的深度和广度。此外，由于学生的身心发展水平、自我照顾能力的成熟度较低年级时更上层楼，教师可考虑将学生带入社区，实际体验、印证之前所了解的内容。

在深入探讨中国人的三餐饮食这个主题时，笔者喜欢选择"早餐"作比较深入的介绍。此时可让学生分享他们早餐饮食的种类，为了添加趣味，也可邀请家长参与，将学生吃早餐的情景录像之后带到班上分享。在分享的过程中，学生可以作个简单的口头报告，内容包括早餐中食品的名称、数量（复习量词的使用）、口味。若班上有少数民族族裔学生且其保有本民族饮食传统，为达多元文化教学的目标，教师应该特意予以介绍。

建议教师趁此机会录制一部题为《老师的早餐》的影片，配乐可由《猴子穿新衣》这首童谣改编而成："星期一老师吃锅贴、蛋饼，配米粥；星期二老师吃烧饼、油条加饭团；星期三吃馒头、包子，配豆浆；星期四老师喝牛奶，配三明治；星期五老师吃稀饭，配酱豆腐；星期六老师吃猪肉炒饭；星期天老师去茶楼饮茶。"若以教师自家或餐厅当作影片摄制的背景，更能引起学生的兴趣。教师可以利用此影片说明，由于中国的多元文化和重视早餐的传统，所以中国人的早餐有很多选择。笔者曾将为教学所制作的录像上传到YouTube，除了作为自己课堂的教材外，还可与其他中文教师分享。

学生在观赏完教师拍摄的影片后，相信会有兴趣亲手制作早餐并亲口品尝一番。在中式杂货店中购得豆浆、馒头、包子甚至油条的半成品并不难，教师可利用电锅将其蒸熟或用烤箱烘烤，马上就可让学生大饱口福。若要和学生一起亲手制作某食物，建议组织学生包饭团：教师事先将材料备齐，让学生动手即可。此外，任何的烹饪活动都是学习"把字句"（把/Ba Constructions）的好机会，学生可以一边动手做一边讲解步骤。建议教师在进行烹饪教学前，依各州规定取得食物处理牌照（Food Handling License），了解学生们是否有食物耐受不良（Food Intolerance）或过敏病史，以及其他基于宗教或个人嗜好的饮食禁忌。

八九岁的学生适合在社区中学习，所以在和学生探讨中式餐馆和一般餐馆有何不同时，最理想的教学方式是先带领他们到中餐馆吃顿饭，让学生在餐馆里当"沉默的侦探"，用眼、耳、心去观察中餐馆。建议教师事先和餐馆工作人员沟通，说明社区教学的目的，提出希望对方配合的事项。到餐馆吃饭前，学生应具备基本的点菜能力和应对进退的礼仪。如此，社区教学才能成为学生身体力行、学以致用的机会。在社区教学结束之后，回到课堂中教师应该马上组织学生进行讨论，让学生分组用图表（如 Venn Diagram）作总结。中餐馆之行的教学重点在于巩固和印证学生低年级时所学习到的包括餐具和食物的摆设、进食礼仪等内容。

三、四年级的学生使用筷子时的手眼协调能力应比低年级时更胜一筹，建议在此阶段利用身体力行的方式再度强调使用餐具的礼仪。午餐时教师可安排学生在中文教室里进餐。让学生用西方的刀叉、杯盘和餐巾摆设餐桌后再进食。在这个过程中，教师可以邀请学生示范正确的与不正确的餐桌礼仪。教师再挑选另一个机会，在课堂中规定不可以用手，让学生改以中式餐具吃午饭。学生势必会面临一些难题，譬如："怎么用筷子吃三明治？"此时教师可以很有技巧地引导学生了解"因为中国人不用刀叉，所以餐桌上几乎所有的食物都会事先进行切块处理"。教师可以记录学生们所提出的疑问或取得的收获，并让学生比较两次进餐时使用西式和中式餐具的体验，让学生从思考"使用刀叉进食时什么是不合礼仪的行为"延伸到碗筷的使用礼仪上，猜猜碗筷的错误使用方式是什么，然后，教师再归纳重点，补充学生未能认识到的要点。

最后，教师可以用"猜猜看"游戏让学生比较中国人的筷子和其它也用筷子的亚洲国家（如韩国、日本）所用的筷子有何不同，说一说原因。建议教师收集来自不同国家、地区的各式不同的筷子，在探讨筷子的使用礼仪时，即可让学生用筷子进行不同体验，体会正确的及不正确的使用方式。如此亲身体验式的教学法，不仅有趣，也更能让学生记牢筷子的使用礼仪。平时，学生表现优良时，教师也可以让学生玩"看谁夹得快"的游戏，稍作奖励。

对于喜庆活动与食物这个主题,可用生日庆祝会来切入。学生设计自己生日会的菜单(包括食物、饮料);教师则在养老院或社区中心中找一位华人长辈,让学生先熟悉这位长辈,认其为中文班爷爷或奶奶。在学生为自己设计生日会菜单的同时,教师也得为这位长辈的生日设计寿宴菜单。当学生设计好他们的菜单时,可以让学生先两两分享,之后再进行全班分享(Think—Pair—Share)。全班分享时,学生须在报告中提及准备了什么以及为什么这样准备。在学生结束分享后,教师再分享自己设计的菜单。这时,教师可以让学生们进行头脑风暴,猜猜教师选择某些食品(如寿面、鸡蛋、长年菜)的理由。教师最后总结时,可以简要说明中国人利用食物的颜色、特性或名称等方式来表示吉祥、祈求福气的传统由来已久,例如新年吃年糕,取"年年高升"的意义;石榴果表"多子多孙",适合送给新婚夫妇;设计寿宴时,所挑选的食品必须有"长寿"的象征意义等。

接着,教师可以考虑再安排一次社区教学活动,挑选一个生意较为清淡的时段带领学生到中式杂货店为中文班爷爷/奶奶的寿宴购物。教师可事先安排学生根据之前已学习过的食物象征(Food Symbolism)原则去挑选他们认为合适的生日会食物,学生可以利用相机或简易录像机(如Flip Video)拍下影像,带回教室。这样做的好处是可免除不必要的购物花费,而所拍的影像稍后也可作为教材使用。教师购回生日会所需的杂货、果蔬后,可挑选适合学生能力的食材,组织学生在教室里完成制作(如包汤圆),使学生有参与感。

在生日会当天,教师应邀请中文班爷爷/奶奶到教室中担任寿星,利用这个机会示范对长者表示尊重的言行举止,并提供机会让学生也得以模仿。这个生日会可以同时针对餐桌摆设、食物的象征意义、敬老传统等多项内容取得多种示范教学效果。

此单元可以探讨的主题林林总总,可以采用的教学手段不胜枚举,在此仅简略地提出以上方式抛砖引玉。中国饮食文化博大精深,让我们好好加以利用,成功地带动海外中文教育。

(三) 主题单元三:节庆活动

人人都喜欢过节时欢乐的气氛,特别是对无忧无虑的儿童来讲,过节时有的吃、有的喝又有的玩,难怪他们总是对节日的到来憧憬不已。然而对大多数的海外华人而言,不论是儿童或成人,在海外过中国节总少了那么点儿节日气氛,加上中国节日在海外并不是法定假日,庆祝活动的进行也只是点到为止，意思一下而已。所以，在节庆活动教学中最不容易突破的难点是如何营造节日的气氛来激发学生的学习热情。要突破这个难点，比较有效的策略是加强节庆活动的深度和广度：深度是指提升对传统节日的认识，引入有关节日的典故传说、传统食物和庆祝方式的地域差异等内容；而广度则是指将节日庆祝活动从教室带入校园、社区。

为了提高学生的参与度，教师可让学生在不偏离传统意义的原则下，拥有最大的决策空间，让他们集体讨论节日庆祝的方式。还有，为了增强学生的文化比较能力，在庆祝本地主流节日的同时，也可以让学生试着拿主流节日与同一时间中中国人在过的中国当代节日作比较。很多中国当代的节日是受西方文化的影响而出现的，所以学生可以就节日庆祝方式、意义等来进行对比。在庆祝中国传统节日时，也可以很自然地让学生通过头脑风暴寻找可与之配对的本地主流节日或学生所处文化中传承（Heritage）的节日，如犹太灯节（Hanukkah）和中国闹花灯的元宵节。

本单元的教学目标主要是提高学生对中国传统节日的由来、庆祝方式、传统节庆食物等的认识。笔者相信老师们对于传统节庆教学的点子一定很多，以下仅以中秋节为例进行分享。

中秋节是中国三大传统节日之一，也是秋季开学后首先到来的中国传统节日。学年开始时，教师可以将各节日的阴历与阳历日期公示在教室明显处，让尚欠缺抽象时间概念的学生可以具体地"看到"节日的逐渐到来。学生每晚的作业是观察并画下月亮的形状，翌日将前晚画出的月亮改画在阴历日期附近。如此一来，学生即可通过月亮形变的视觉形象逐渐了解阴历与月亮的关系。庆祝中秋节的教案设计时间可长可短，笔者曾在一项为期三周的教案中，纳入了"烤月饼"活动。让学生从认识中国各地月饼的种类开始，了解月饼制作的材料、过程，直到最后亲手烤出月饼。三、四年级学生喜欢故事，也具备了足够的语言能力，教师可编排有关中秋节三个传说故事（嫦娥奔月、吴刚伐桂、玉兔捣药）的节目，并让学生尝试在全校师生前演出。此举可将节庆气氛带入校园。之前烤好的月饼也可以在中秋节当天与其他师生分享。中秋节晚上，教师还可让学生为家人朗诵与明月有关的诗词（如苏轼的《水调歌头》，李白的《关山月》），或唱与明月有关的歌曲（如王菲的《明月几时有》），把学习带出校园，使之进入家庭、社区。

在探讨"美国人和中国人庆祝节日的差异"这个主题时，建议教师先让学生在学年初整理出一年当中美国的主流节日表（从年初的新年至年终的圣诞节)。学生可以利用图画或颜色来呈现各个节日,如红色代表情人节,橙色、黑色代表万圣节,红色、绿色代表圣诞节。在表格整理结束后,教师可以让学生分组进行头脑风暴,分享节日的庆祝方式和理由。之后再让学生进行益智猜谜游戏:中国人是不是也过圣诞节?中国有没有情人节?教师可以一边提出问题一边解答,并在黑板上整理出一份中美节日对照表,将结果记录于教室中的日历上。在以后的学习中,教师可以利用此日历来介绍中国的节日和中国人庆祝该节日的方式。若班上有少数民族族裔的学生,建议腾出特别的时间段,让他们分享该民族庆祝特有的传统节日或当代节日的方式。如此可扩大学生的视野,增强其对异族文化的认识及尊重。

美国的主流节日中并没有与月亮有关的节日,但根据维基百科,在美洲的神话、民间传说中,每个满月都有一个特定的名称。作中秋节的文化比较时,教师可组织学生寻找属于自己出生月的满月名字。此外,印度、菲律宾、越南、新加坡等国都有他们独特的庆祝月亮节日的方式,教师可以用讲故事的形式来介绍,让学生边听故事边画幻灯片(Film strips),然后根据画出的图画,在小组内复述故事,进行口语练习。此外,传统节日的庆祝一定少不了食物,在进行节庆文化比较时,建议教师特别引入传统食物的种类和象征意义,和上个单元的主题"食物"贯连。

如果教学重点包括节日词汇,教师可以让学生分组,利用"比手画脚(Charade)"的方式来演示各个节日。学生在此过程中必须寻找出该节日中最具代表性的动作,为此学生得仔细思考节日的意义,这是学生自主学习的起步。还有,如前所述,在美国过中国传统节日欠缺节庆气氛,若谈及中国人独特的当代节日庆祝方式(如教师节、儿童节),学生虽感新奇,却难以拿自身经验做跳板,因为他们在这些方面的经验可能是零。此时,建议教师利用网络资源、视频、图片来介绍,若有中国的友谊学校,可利用网络电话(如Skype)作视频访问;或以"你认为美国也应该有教师节/儿童节吗?"之类的问题来培养"思辨"这一高层次思维能力。

由于节庆活动有其时间性限制,建议教师在设计课程时,尽量在节日当天举行庆祝活动,若不可行则应提前庆祝,如此学生或可在节日当天与家人同庆,或是参与社区的庆祝活动。此外,由于三、四年级的学生对多种族文化的认识还在建立阶段,建议教师多以学生自身的经验为出发点,再引介其他不同族群的文化,以培养学生的国际公民观。最后,建议多利用社区资源,把教室带入社区,把社区带入教室,让节庆"活"起来、"火"起来。

（四）主题单元四：地理与旅游

本单元的教学目标包括：帮助学生了解时间的意义；明白可使用方位、地图来理解时间和空间的关系；了解旅游对增进个人文化、历史、风俗知识的好处；熟悉旅游的交通工具以及认识美国的华人社区。一、二年级的学生对时间、空间（包括方向和位置的描述）已具备了基本知识和语言描述技能，在三、四年级的课程当中，除继续巩固该知识、技能外，可考虑发展技能的多样性，让学生拥有较多应变能力。例如，学生在一、二年级时会看电子钟，到此阶段应该学习看要动用计算能力的传统钟。多数学区在三年级的课程中将社会学科（如人文、历史）作为评估的一环，建议教师考虑与其他科目教师联系，进行课程贯联，将人文、历史内容加入课程中。

学生在一、二年级时，已经尝试过先画校园、住家附近的地图，再用所绘的平面地图来指路或描述建筑物的位置关系。到了三年级时，可以再加入方向的表达。东、西、南、北四个基本方向（Cardinal Directions）是依据地球与太阳的关系来确定的；而前、后、左、右、上、下等相对方向（Relative Directions）则完全依照沟通者位置的改变而改变，容易让人们混淆。但是，东、西、南、北的方向虽然不变，但因为所采用的参考点（Reference Point）不是学生本身，而且在学生的一般用语中较少出现，所以可能要多花时间介绍。此处的教学建议从认识地球开始（三年级的社会学课的主题之一）：利用气球或纸浆做一个地球，然后上色，随后标示赤道、本初子午线（Prime Meridian）、北半球、南半球、东半球、西半球、南极、北极等。此外，学生也可再标明七大洲、四大洋及美国、中国或任何学生有兴趣的国家位置。这种学习方位的方式可以让学生了解到，方位的描述可用平面（一、二年级时学过的）以及立体两种形式进行。赤道是根据地球自转轴而定的南北半球分割线。本初子午线可以标示东、西两个方向。这两个方向的概念易懂，但是本初子午线的位置没有特殊物理意义，完全由人类硬性规定，如果有学生问及，如此带过即可。顺地球自转为朝东，逆地球自转轴则定为西边的概念可以通过纸浆地球来解说。此外，太阳的东升西落是很重要的基本概念，因为学生可根据此知识来粗略判定基本方向。教师可以趁早晨日渐东升之时，带领学生到校园或操场上，教学生平伸双臂，右臂指向太阳升起的方向，即"东"，左臂自然指向"西"，脸朝"北"，背向"南"，这样学生就很容易记住这四个基本方向。（注：中国古人习惯称东边为左,但为了不让学生将其与地图通用的标示混淆,故用右臂表示东)如果早上不易进行此活动,也可在下午太阳西落时组织。重点是尽量让学生调用肢体动作及多重感官经验来学习和记忆。

此外,在操场或空间合适的任何地点,教师可给学生一个多数中国学生在学校中经历过的"整队"体验,来加强学生对相对方向的记忆;教学生报数并依身高排成数行,练习"立正""向前看齐""向左看""向右看""向后转""齐步走""稍息"等军训指令动作。对方向还不是很清楚的学生出错时,常常面面相觑,势必会引起一片笑声,很有意思。

接下来的学习重点是让学生能够熟练运用基本方向和相对方向。学生可在校园中用基本方向词玩寻宝游戏。在进行游戏之前,教师可以让学生制作一个简易的指南针,学生寻宝时可以使用自制指南针和教师所给的寻宝指示。此外,在教室大楼中练习用相对方向词来藏糖找糖也是一个有趣的游戏。玩找糖游戏时,教师可直接给出口头指令,也可以将指令写在纸条上,交由学生来读出;或是将负责找糖学生的双眼蒙住,由其他学生给予口语指示。本活动可进行分组竞赛,能以最短时间,安全地找到糖的队伍胜出。玩此游戏时,一定要强调安全规则,以免学生绊倒或撞伤,乐极生悲。

当学生熟悉"指路"后,便可以让学生设计题为"校园问路"的小品剧(前提是学生很清楚校园中各建筑的名称和位置)。此时可让学生演出有关问路的情景短剧并用简便摄影器材录像。学生对这个项目的兴致一定很高。此外,也可以让学生试着录制一段校园简介,在短片中用不同的基本方位词及相对方位词介绍学校。中文教师可联合同校的其他外语教师,让学生们用不同的语言来合制校园简介,其成果可作为将来社会交际中使用的礼物送与来访外宾、友谊学校,或仅仅是作为推广外语教育的工具使用。

在进行"时间"教学时,由于三、四年级的学生手眼协调能力较高,可以让学生制作日晷,在日晷上标注相关内容,从而了解古代中国人计时的方式(一天分十二个时辰,采用地支作为各时辰名称)。校准日晷的难度颇高,此活动旨在介绍计时方式的多样化以及古代和现代计时法的异同。扩展此主题时,教师可让学生比较不同的计时方式,探讨时间的意义:"看时间的工具消失了,是好事还是坏事?没有太阳也没有计时工具时可以怎样计时?"

三年级的学习发展了学生地理旅游方面的基本技能。到了四年级,教师可以考虑整合学生所有的技能，设计一个模拟的"北京之旅"。教师可以和学生共同撰写游记，全班每位学生都必须在此游记中扮演一个角色。如果学校有吉祥物（Mascot），也可以考虑带去，让学生在旅途中学着照顾吉祥物。此时的教学重点包括：出发前的筹备工作，从家到机场时所使用的交通工具，每个人制作一本护照，使用现金买机票以及在机场报到、看时刻表、取登机牌、托运行李、过安检、找登机门位置、找座位等。此外，设计一些在飞机上发生的趣事，如遭遇乱流、晕机、病倒、点餐，都可以提升游记的趣味性。学生们有的扮演送行家长、地勤人员、旅客，有的扮演机长、空乘人员、医生。教师可以重新安排桌椅位置，由学生进行布置，让整个教室看起来犹如机舱。当学生"在飞机上"时，教师可以展示中国的卫星地图，介绍中国主要地形（山川河流、边界国家等），把地理知识融入旅游学习。当学生"抵达北京"时，教师则可以播放旅游录像，介绍不同的历史文物、著名景点、北京市景、胡同变迁等，尽量制造逼真的效果。教师还可以特别强调北京人说话多用儿化音等特色，让学生也学上几句北京话，看看京剧，大家热热闹闹地结束此次的北京之旅。

以上是关于地理与旅游的一些教学建议。虽然三、四年级的学生较少有随校出国旅游的机会，但是通过灵活的教学设计，教师仍然可以带给学生许多有趣又实用的学习经历。当我们无法带学生环游世界时，让我们把世界带进教室吧！

（五）主题单元五：历史、政治与宗教

给三、四年级的学生谈历史、政治或宗教这样的主题，难免令人担心学生会缺乏兴趣，因为这些主题对学生来说可能过于乏味。然而，如果利用学生爱听故事的特质，加上以学生的切身经验为基础切入主题，相信比较容易解决上述问题。此单元的教学重点不在于扩展知识层面的广度，毕竟五千年的历史不是用一两个月的时间就可以彻底说明白的。再说大多数的美国学生对自己国家的历史都还一知半解，期待学生了解中国历史的来龙去脉，未免要求过高。所以，建议教师们单点击入，以《西游记》中的故事来介绍中国的历史与宗教，或以秦始皇与长城为出发点来讲述早期中国的政治形态和历史。

在探讨宗教问题之前，建议教师事先与家长取得联系，让家长了解教学目的并和学生在家里讨论其所信仰的宗教，以及参与宗教活动的形式和目的。如果学生家长没有特别的宗教信仰，可以改为讨论如何保持心

灵健康。这种让家长事前参与准备工作的方式不仅可以降低家长对此主题的排斥程度,取得他们的配合及协助,此外,由于学生和家人事先讨论过与宗教信仰、心灵健康有关的话题,学生也比较容易在随后的教学活动中快速进入状况。

学生与家人讨论后,接下来可以让学生在课堂上分享自己与家人讨论后学习到的内容。教师可以建议学生通过绘画呈现以下内容:宗教场合中有哪些主要人物?在这些场所可举办的活动种类有哪些?宗教建筑的设计特点在哪儿?宗教仪式如何进行?学生完成画作后,教师可以按照学生的不同信仰将其分组,同信仰者同组。在小组中,学生可以互相分享绘画,整合他们对自己宗教的认知。分享中学生必须在自己的图画上添加获得的新信息。之后,教师可要求各同信仰小组推派组员,组成"宗教联合国",向大家介绍该组总结出来的宗教信仰知识。无特别宗教信仰的学生,也必须在"宗教联合国"中分享对于"如何保持心灵健康"这一问题的看法。这个活动是个以学生为资源的范例,实现了"利用学生教学生"的效果。应强调的是,在"宗教联合国"的分享过程里,教师应协助学生了解:人们虽有不同的宗教信仰,但不同宗教可能会有相同的功能。即使没有特殊宗教信仰,人们还是可以通过一些理念来追求心灵健康。

如果教师本身有不同于学生们的宗教信仰,我们鼓励教师与学生进行分享。在分享的过程中,最好让学生看到有关该宗教的实际信仰执行过程,例如祷告、宗教仪式以及仪式中所需之特别道具、服装等。如果某家长有非主流的宗教信仰,教师可以考虑邀请该家长到班上与学生分享。在此活动告一段落后,建议让学生挑选他/她感兴趣的一个或两个其他宗教的信仰活动,将其和自己所信宗教的活动进行对比,并以二环或三环维恩图表呈现对比结果。

最后,教师可以安排一次校外教学,带学生参观佛教的庙宇。让学生带着硬夹板、画纸、彩笔,静静地坐在庙宇的一角,担任"沉默的侦探":用眼观,用耳听,用鼻嗅,用手写画,用心揣测。为了让学生收集到完整的资料,教师可以事先分配给学生不同的观察重点,例如人物及活动、庙宇外部建筑、内部陈设等。返校后,教师可以收集成果,在教室外同时展示"宗教联合国"完成的作品与学生在此次校外教学中创作的画作。这样,全校师生都可受益。

参观庙宇后,可以开始讲"美猴王"的故事。很多美国学生都知道中国有个猴王(Monkey King),但不见得知道唐三藏到印度取经的史实。三、四年级的学生特别喜欢读冒险故事、幻想小说,所以《西游记》正适合这个年龄段的学生。建议教师利用故事书或相关视频(可自 www.youku.com 实现观看),挑选经典段落作为教学重点。教学中可根据唐僧与悟空之间既是师徒、又似父子的关系切入文化内容,强调中国传统中的伦理关系。在知识层面上,学生可以通过《西游记》的故事来了解印度和中国的地理关系、中国与西方国家的早期接触,以及佛教是由印度传入中国等知识。为了提升学生的学习兴趣,教师可以让学生们制作孙悟空的头箍,或者到建筑材料行(如 Home Depot)买来棍子,制作金箍棒。接下来,还可以邀请校外华人社区中懂得中国舞蹈或拳术的专家来校教学生"金箍棒功夫舞",让学生模拟孙悟空的猴形猴状,配以中国传统锣鼓,好不热闹!

　　三、四年级的学生多少都知道中国有"皇帝"(Emperor),但不一定知道那已成为历史。而美国学生对"长城"的了解,就仿佛其对熊猫的认识一样:只知道它是属于中国的。所以,在谈论历史和政治时,建议以长城为主题来介绍中国的第一个皇帝和中国早期的政治形态。

　　主题的切入可以为期一周,用一个虚拟故事来进行:两国相争,急需长城以防外敌入侵,长城必须盖在遥远的边境高山上。由于地形险要,唯有步行才可抵达边境。两个国家的皇帝的治国方式完全相反,一个是集权专制的暴君,另一个是仁慈爱民的英主。教师可以把全班分成两个国家(可用战国七雄中之任意二国命名)。因不是民主时代,皇帝皆由教师指派。两位帝王必须根据教师所规定的治理特色,召集人民在最短时间内盖好长城。教师在这个项目中必须时刻给学生提供协助,使各国的政治形态得以维持。学生在项目开始之前要一起决定施行暴政、仁政的君主是如何治理国家的。而担任平民的学生在答应皇帝参与长城的建设后,应该从家中带一个装牛奶的空纸盒或瓶子到校"筑长城"。教师应该规定好长城共需几个牛奶盒才算完成。在这个模拟的政治环境中,学生可以体验不同的施政方式,了解不同政治形态,隐约地意识到秦始皇的治国方式;而担任皇帝的学生必须学会谈判、交涉,或根本不必使用这些手段,下命令即可。当某国的长城盖完后,教师可让学生总结学习心得。最后教师可顺势带入秦始皇的故事和他带给中国历史的正反两方面影响。总结时,教师可以使用图片或视频介绍长城,结束这个单元。

　　总之,与三、四年级的学生探讨中国的历史、政治或宗教时,由于涉及颇多信息文化及成就文化范畴的内容,教学不该以增加学生的知识为重点。选定几个学生感兴趣的主题,采用好玩、带劲的团体小组活动,绝对能提高学生的学习兴趣。只要学生愿意继续学习中文,教师也就不必担心五千年的悠久历史讲不完啦!

(六) 主题单元六:朋友、娱乐与时尚

三、四年级时,学生对朋友的重视程度较低年级时提高许多,受同伴的影响也加大了。在一、二年级时,本主题的学习着重于培养学生的同理心和交友的技巧,以及对中国玩具、游戏的认识。到了本阶段,除了继续探讨朋友的意义、友情表达的方式和调剂生活的娱乐活动外,我们还可进一步了解时尚、流行语对学生交友、生活的影响,因为三、四年级学生对流行和时尚的兴趣和敏锐度正逐渐增强。

在笔者工作的学校,每年春天都有一个"宠物日"(Pet Day)。当天,学生可以把自己的宠物带到学校,供其他学生观赏、逗弄或进行各种竞赛。这个活动不只让学生有机会接触到不同的宠物,还可以扩展每个人对宠物的定义——因为有些学生会把蛇、蜥蜴、乌龟等宠物带到学校来。

"宠物"这个主题可以当作探讨"友情"的题材,因为一般儿童对动物都有股热情,势必积极参与。教师可以先让学生把自己或亲友所饲养的宠物照片带到教室中,作个口头介绍。然后,视学区规定以及宠物的体积大小、性情、安全等因素,决定是否允许学生把宠物带到教室里,若可以,势必在全班引起轰动。家中不饲养宠物的学生可以利用网络资源搜索图像,由教师协助制成PPT后在班上作报告。

接着,教师可以以"宠物可不可以当朋友?为什么?"为题让学生进行一场小型辩论。三、四年级的学生可能对辩论一事尚无经验,教师可进行简单引导。此外,建议教师设置"陪审团",让"陪审员"听取正反双方的论述后,作出决议,共同决定宠物可不可以算是朋友。辩论过程中所持的论据,可以在辩论前让正反方在组内通过头脑风暴集思广益。教师必须视情况帮助学生,将论据稍作整理,在辩论时学生才可以侃侃而谈。利用这个活动,可以训练学生的口头表达(Presentational)能力,当"陪审员"的学生则可锻炼诠释理解(Interpretive)的能力。辩论结果并不是重点,对学生而言,了解友谊的真谛才是这个活动的主要目标,因为正反双方在辩论的准备和竞赛过程中一定会对"朋友"的定义有深入的了解和探讨。

为了让这个辩论活动在结尾时达到高潮,教师可以让学生画出他们理想中的"动物好朋友":它长什么样子?具有哪些当好朋友的特质?同时想一想,自身该如何爱护"动物好朋友"才不会让"动物好朋友"讨厌自

己？学生可以自由发挥想象力、创造力，如果理想中的朋友四不像也无所谓。之所以让学生挑自己想要的"动物朋友"，是为了避免学生在大庭广众下指名道姓说："我要某某当我的好朋友。"这个活动通过学生尚介于幻想和现实之间的认知水平，使用无伤大雅的主题来研究朋友的意义以及什么是维系友谊最重要的因素。若学生对这个主题有进一步探讨的意愿，也可用前述的问题访问全校的学生。

接下来，教师可利用三、四年级学生爱听故事的特性，讲讲有关友情的中国历史故事，如司马光砸缸救友、管宁与华歆割席断交等①。在分享故事时，我认为为师者不宜利用故事来讲道说教，企图替学生下结论或是将自己的观点强加于学生。因为这么做时，我们可能剥夺了学生独立思考的机会。所以较理想的方式应该是用引导问题（Guided Questions）来鼓励学生思考，如：如果你是管宁，你会怎么做？为什么？朋友有困难时，为什么要帮他？

和朋友在一起时，共同的话题常常是如何寻找乐趣。这个单元是介绍大量有关娱乐、爱好的词汇和句型的好时机。教师可以利用图像式思考辅助工具（Graphic Organizer，如 KWL）来收集学生们想要学习的词汇，再归类整理。在词汇的教学中，笔者发现学生很喜欢"比手画脚"游戏。三、四年级的学生在小组组织及与组员合作方面尚处于学习阶段，教师必须很有耐心，一步一步地指导学生，必要时为其提供协助。由于自制力尚不足，学生难免耍小脾气、无理取闹，教师可以通过团体压力给予适度仲裁或变更该学生的小组职务/角色。此外，利用冲突事件本身来诠释友谊的意义，也是机会教育的良好范例。当然，并不是每个冲突都可以当成机会教育的题材。

大多数的美国学生，每天都会花不少时间坐在电视机前观赏节目，中国学生也难免如此。教师可以让学生票选出他们认为最好、最受欢迎的几个电视节目，并让学生解释这些节目受欢迎的原因。同时，教师也须收集时下中国内地、香港及台湾地区最受欢迎的节目，了解其受欢迎的原因。在课堂上，教师可以截取部分节目片段让学生观赏：一方面作为语言教学的工具，一方面作为文化比较的工具。教师可以提问："这个节目有趣吗？为什么？"由于不同文化对于"有趣"的定义可能有很大的差异，也很难彼此欣赏，所以，如果学生无法理解该电视节目的有趣之处，教师可

---

① 以上故事，教师可在小学语文教学（www.vastman.com）或百度（www.baidu.com）等网站用关键词搜索。

以利用这个机会引导学生思考:"为什么中国学生喜欢的节目,我们却不喜欢呢?"通过分享和讨论的过程,希望学生可以领悟到:中美文化对"有趣"可能有不同的认识,而这些不同可能受到文化本身价值观的影响。教师不必进一步解释或分析文化差异的形成原因,因为这对学生而言意义不大,只要学生明白"对同一事物,人们可能会有不同的看法(Perspectives)",埋下一粒理解的种子就足够了。

(七)主题单元七:艺术与科学创造

在"艺术与科学创造"这个主题中,低年级的学生对文字、书法和音乐已经有了粗浅的认识。在三、四年级的课程中,我们会引入中国的四大发明,为五、六年级的课程作铺垫。此外,我们还会继续探讨民俗艺术、中国乐曲和中国语言文字等话题,以巩固学生既有的和新增的知识。

在美国的"世界文明史"的课程中,只要提到中国,大多会涉及中国的四大发明:指南针推动了南宋航海业的发展;造纸术、活字印刷术的发明为中国经典著作的保留提供了不可磨灭的贡献;火药的发明引发了唐末火枪、火筒的出现。四大发明同样推动了西方文明的快速发展。与三、四年级的学生谈四大发明,在知识层面上,只须让学生知道何为四大发明,了解四大发明对中国造成了哪些影响即可。建议老师们在课堂上让学生多花点时间"动手"学习四大发明。

建议教师先让学生看与四大发明有关的图片,然后让学生猜"这是中国的什么?有什么作用?"教师可用"中国四大发明"作为关键词进行网络搜索,获取相关图片。YouTube上也有有关"中国古代四大发明"的系列中文影片可供观看。关于造纸术,维基百科中有斩竹漂塘、煮楻足火、荡料入帘、覆帘压纸、透火焙干这些造纸步骤的图示,教师可以下载打印后分发给学生,让他们试着排列出造纸的正确程序。若是学校附近有造纸厂,更可以试着安排一次校外教学。

让学生"动手"学四大发明,具体的教学方法是让学生当"现代蔡伦"或"现代毕升",在教室里学着造纸或进行活字印刷。教师若对制作纸张的实际操作方法有疑问,可以在YouTube上搜索影片进行自学或请美术教师到教室内协助教学。要注意的是,让学生学习简单的活字印刷术,用到的方法和材料必须稍作更改。

教师可以和学生一起进行头脑风暴,共同设计一份传单或邀请函,例如邀请家长到校参观中文项目的年终成果展。在确定传单或邀请函的内容之后，教师可以分配制作活字的任务，即哪个学生负责版刻哪些字。利用"安全方块"（Safety Block）加上简易的版刻刀，学生即可进行版刻。在学生开始活动前，教师势必要强调工具使用的安全规则。当学生们都完成自己所负责的字版时，教师可收集字版，然后让学生"排版"。在这个过程中，可以再度复习相关词汇。教师甚至可以利用排版来进行小组竞赛，看哪组最先完成。当排版结束后，学生即可在教师的协助下，把油墨刷在排好的字版上，用学生自制的纸来印刷传单、邀请函。当然，印刷成果的品质很难保证，但是学生自己亲手制作、学习体验的过程应高于一切。至于指南针，教师可以在探讨"地理与旅游"这个单元主题时让学生动手制作。火药则因为涉及法规，不宜在教室中动手制作。

笔者不建议设立单一主题介绍民俗艺术和乐曲对中国人的日常生活有何影响，比较理想的方式是把这些与其他单元主题贯联在一起。例如在庆祝传统节日或特殊日子时，可选用极富传统色彩的经典乐曲或民俗艺术来增添节庆气氛，这是介绍传统民俗艺术或曲乐的大好时机。在中国，有新年剪纸、贴窗花的传统，教师可以在庆祝新年时，特别安排剪纸课程，介绍剪纸的材料、工具、技巧，各地剪纸的特色，剪纸的用途等等。讲课结束时，学生可亲手剪纸，布置教室。如此一来，学生就比较容易了解此类民俗艺术适用的场合及时机。

在乐曲方面，上一阶段的教学重点较偏重于对乐器名称、特性的认识，学生在低年级时已经对中国的传统乐器稍有了解，甚至能辨认音色。三、四年级时，建议教师可以与引介民俗艺术一样，多利用机会教育的方式，让学生形成多重贯连。例如，过年过节所用的传统乐曲中常出现的乐器有哪些？这些乐器是否在西洋乐器中有对应的伙伴（比如胡琴可对提琴、扬琴可对钟琴、梆笛可对竖笛）？接着，教师可以让学习西方乐器的学生试着演奏中国的传统曲调，之后再与用传统乐器所演奏的传统曲调作比较。这种"张冠李戴"的活动不仅可以提高学生的好奇心和学习兴趣，还可以让学生对中国乐曲有较深刻的印象，对自身文化里的音乐特色有进一步的体会。

最后是"中国语言文字"这个主题。在探讨这个主题时，低年级的教学重点在于学习、认识、比较象形文字和简体、繁体字；到了三、四年级，由于学生面对的汉字不再局限于象形字或指事字，建议教师把重点逐渐转移到会意字和占汉字数量高达90％以上的形声字上。教师可以系统性地整理常见的部首，例如提手旁、秃宝盖、单人旁之类，将其当成一个主题来介绍。鼓励学生利用联想、画图的方式来将这些部首与其所对应之象形字进行贯联，例如"手"与"提手旁"，"心"与"竖心旁"。学生若学会了这些偏旁、部首，他们识字的能力会有很大的提高。

若要安排这个年纪的学生比较中英文，不能将我们的学生当大学生教，课堂的形式绝对不能像大学讲座一般，因为本阶段学生的认知层次尚浅。笔者认为，必须等到学生八年级后才可作初步系统性的介绍。举语法一例，三、四年级的学生可能还不明白英文中基本句型结构的相关术语，教师不必急于让三、四年级的学生体会中文和英文的异同。当学生的认知足够成熟时，他们会自动提出问题或是他们的新发现。除了汉字，汉语最大的特色就是声调。在语言教学方面，倒是可以尽量让三、四年级的学生在声调的掌握上做扎实的基础工作。因为根据语言学专家的研究，学习第二语言的儿童在进入青春期后，辨析声调的精准度会逐渐降低。教师在语言教学的过程中，可多利用肢体动作、手势来特意强调声调。以歌唱教学时，建议先用童谣的方式，将歌词抑扬顿挫地朗诵几遍，或是利用歌词编个小品剧，最后再教唱。因为唱歌时所有的声调都是第一声，除非是唱嘻哈（Hip-Hop），这于音调教学是不利的。

（八）主题单元八：情绪与情感表达

探讨这一主题时，很重要的一点是，教师必须对学生情绪发展的特点、情绪识别和调控能力有所认识，这样才能设计出比较合理并具有实用价值的教学目标及活动。还有，教师千万别尝试扮演心理咨询师的角色，企图为学生解决所有情绪上的难题。一来，这不是中文教师的教学领域；二来，中文教师基本上没有接受过这方面的训练，不具备这种能力。所以，如果教师发现某学生似乎有情绪障碍或困扰时，应视情况启动教学小组的集体优势，做必要的转介辅导。因此，在探讨情绪这个主题时，教师应把教学重点放在语言、文化比较上。以下是一个适用于四年级的为期三周的教案设计。

一、二年级的课程较偏重于有关基本情绪（Basic Emotions，包括快乐、生气、伤心及害怕等）的词汇、句型。本阶段可再加入其它基本情绪词汇，包括"厌恶"（Disgust）、"感兴趣"（Interest）、"惊讶"（Surprise），以及所谓的"自觉情绪"（Self-conscious Emotions）。低年级时的另一个教学重点是培养学生对表情的识别能力；表情是外显的、可以用肉眼观察到的，对于年幼的低年级学生而言，研究表情是个又恰当又有趣的题材。到了三、四年级，学生已知道多种情绪可以同时存在，他们学会了推测引发情绪的原因，还会试着遵守有关情绪表达的一些社会规范。当他们了解了表现情绪的一些基本规范后，也会试着去隐藏自己的情绪。

依据上述情绪发展特点，第一周的教学可先与低年级内容贯连。既然三、四年级的学生已经懂得隐藏情绪，教师可以组织学生进一步探讨表达情绪的诸多方式，特别是不必通过话语进行的非语言沟通：除了表情外，还有什么线索可以帮助我们了解自己的或他人的情绪？教师可先利用问题带领学生进行头脑风暴："除了表情，人们还可以用什么方法让别人了解他/她心底的感受或情绪？"再将眼神、手势、肢体动作、语气等非语言情绪表达方式带入课程中。所以，第一周的教学重点可着眼于学习基本情绪的相关词汇、句型，引介除了语言和表情外，可用来表达情绪的其它非语言方式。

在实际教学中，教师可以将学生男女夹杂分组，讨论若只用肢体动作及手势而不用面部表情，该如何表达情绪。学生必须想出最有效的情绪表达方式。男女夹杂分组的目的是希望学生在讨论的过程中，试着思考男女在肢体动作、手势使用上是否有差异。接下来可以组织类似猜字谜的游戏——比手画脚：甲组派一名代表，带上只露出眼睛的面具，依据教师所示的情绪词，做出符合该情绪的肢体动作或手势，让乙组队员猜测。需要注意的是，胜负的判定方式必须在比赛结束时宣布：若乙组得最高分，则甲组获胜——这表示甲组使用的肢体动作及手势最具沟通效果。教师在游戏后可让学生思考："光用手势和肢体动作表达情绪，效果理想吗？"

教师也可以给全班一个简单的、不带情绪色彩的短句，例如："我要去买苹果"，让学生练习带着不同情绪说这句话。练习结束后，挑一位"志愿者"上台，背朝全班，使用带有不同情绪色彩的语气来呈现同一句话，让全班猜猜说话的人是快乐、伤心、生气还是厌恶、惊讶。然后，表演者再说相同的短句，但这次可面向全班，同时使用表情、手势、眼神或肢体动作等不同组合来演示。通过这个活动，学生会很容易明白：情绪的表达，除了用表情外，还可以使用不同的语气、手势、肢体动作、眼神来加强。其中，以表情配合语气的效果可能是最理想的。

如果还有时间，可以让学生根据不同的情绪词汇，在硬卡纸上画出眉毛、眼睛、嘴巴可能出现的不同形状。画好后，将其着色、剪下，重新组合。此时学生可根据新组合出的表情试着描述不同情绪，例如："眉毛朝下，嘴角也朝下，眼睛看起来没有光彩，这个人可能很难过。"教师也可以发给学生描述情绪的四字成语，让学生依据成语内容，用图卡排出呈现该情绪的面部表情图。

在训练学生的口语能力时，可以考虑使用 Super Duper Publications 出版的维伯像卡（Webber Photo Cards）。维伯像卡是一套 264 张，含各种情绪表情的图卡。教师可事先抽出希望学生熟悉的情绪图卡放在桌子中间（所有图卡正面朝下），让学生轮流抽取一张卡片，如果图片中显示的是愉快的表情，学生必须用符合该情绪的语气讲述让自己感到愉快的某事。这个活动不含竞争性质，所以学生们可以充分利用时间来思考其想表达的内容。教师也可让学生二或三人一组，给每组学生九张维伯像卡，玩"井"字游戏，在从词到短语，再到完整句子的过程中训练学生的口头表达能力。

在进行文化教学时，教师可以让学生看一些显示学龄儿童在公共场合大吵大闹、无理取闹的图片或影片，询问学生："如果你是那个小朋友的爸爸（或妈妈），你会觉得怎么样？你会怎么办？为什么？"学生可以两人一组讨论，之后进行全班分享，教师则归纳各组观点。接着，展示几张中国儿童大哭大闹的图片，再次问学生："你认为中国小朋友的爸爸妈妈会有不同的反应吗？"让学生猜测、讨论。此时，建议教师把中国人的"面子"观念带入教学，解释中国儿童在公共场所尤其要注意行为举止，以免让父母亲没面子——"丢脸"。如果学生无法了解也无所谓，因为只要在这个年龄段撒下了种子，在下个阶段收获的机率就会提高。总而言之，在三、四年级阶段，文化教学的重点是让学生开始体会到，在中国人的社会里有"面子"的观念。到了五、六年级时，再强调面子的重要性，进行表达情绪、情感的文化差异对比即可。

在八岁前，除了基本情绪外，儿童也能感受到所谓的"自觉情绪"，包括羞愧、尴尬、内疚、嫉妒、骄傲等。在第二周教学中，建议加入与这些情绪相关的词汇、句型，为加强学生表达情感的口语能力，做进一步的工作。教师可以将"自觉情绪"和前一周的"情绪表达方式"贯连，组织学生思考这些情绪的表达方式与之前所学的情绪表达是否有不同之处。例如：光靠表情可以看出这些情绪吗？哪些情绪可以隐藏？内心有这些感受时，还可能有其他情绪的存在吗？

关于词汇的介绍和学习，建议教师采用"多元智能"的教学设计理念，融合动作、图画、文字、小组合作的形式来进行。教师可以先让学生在低年级时做的心情小册里加入新的情绪表达词语，并利用绘画加以阐释。在认读词语时，教师可以将描述情绪的词语写在报事贴（Post-it Note）上

（一张写一个词），然后贴在学生的额头上。被贴的学生不能事先看到报事贴上的词语，他/她必须在教室中来走去，询问其他同学，例如："我感到尴尬吗？""我感到嫉妒吗？"被询问的学生必须能够认读提问学生额头上的词语，才能进行回答。学生在确定正确答案三次后，便可把报事贴取下。为了让学生明白活动如何进行，教师应该自己先示范，将一张情绪"报事贴"贴在额头上并向学生们进行询问。

教师还可以将所有描写情绪的单词或成语做成闪卡，玩"我变、我变、我变变变"的游戏：将学生分组，要求每组每次派一位代表出列。教师闪示情绪卡，让学生代表做表情，给同组组员猜。在限定的时间中，猜对最多的组即获胜。在玩第二轮或第三轮时，由于学生对于基本词汇已比较熟悉，建议教师把游戏的难度提高，要求学生们必须用完整的句子进行描述。再高一点的难度则是运用符合该情绪的语气进行描述。相信这会是一个很有趣的活动。如果教师可以利用录像机录下参演学生的表情，在活动结束后放给全班观赏的话，不仅可以再度复习所学内容，还可以把课堂的气氛带到最高点。

另一个分组合作活动则综合了语言、绘画、动作等多种因素。教师可将学生分组，每组分得一种情绪（羞愧、内疚、嫉妒、尴尬和骄傲中任一种），小组成员须用不同方式展示该情绪：善于用文字写作者，可在作文纸上描述；善于绘画的学生则用卡纸画出情绪中的重点情景；善于用肢体表达的学生，则可以用合作演默剧的形式呈现情景。最后全组学生上台表演"双簧"：负责写作的学生当旁白，画情景的学生展示画作，其余的学生用动作把故事情节演出来。台下的观众则边看边笑，猜测或印证台上学生表演的究竟是哪种感受。

上述分组活动结束时，教师可以结合活动中出现的情绪，继续训练学生的文化认知和语言表达能力。具体做法是：用"意思"进行贯连，使学生了解汉语中"意思"的不同意思和用法。如：当被称赞"够意思"时，可能会觉得很"骄傲"；当人家说你"很不够意思"时，说话的人可能对你很不满，想让你觉得"羞愧"或"内疚"；让人觉得"不好意思"的场合，通常会让人感到"尴尬"；人家跟你说"你好意思啊？"寓意是你该觉得"不好意思"或"羞愧"；同学生日时收到很多"意思"，你却什么都没收到，你可能会因为"羡慕"而有"嫉妒"的情绪。教师可让学生用不同的"意思"对话、画插画。然后让学生分组，选择部分对话，表演小品剧。在表演过程中，教师可用录像机进行拍摄，然后在课堂里播放。对这样的活动，一般学生们参与的热情都很大。此外，建议教师在平时的课堂对话中多多设计情景,利用机会反复练习诸多"意思"的多重意思,这样学生学习起来也比较有意思!

此外,在中国文化里,任何含有"自满""得意""骄傲"的姿态、行为或言语,都绝不适合出现在个人身上。美国学生虽然不见得了解中国人的"谦虚",但是身为教师的我们至少该教导学生:在被称赞时、被评价"很够意思"时,中国人会回答"哪里哪里""应该的""一般一般",而不是"谢谢"。我们应记得经常提醒学生:与中国人打交道时,要尽量注意语言谦虚、举止含蓄,如此才不会显得突兀,也比较容易获得中国人的喜爱和尊重。建议教师让学生再运用情景小品剧练习如何赞美别人和回应赞美。

教师在总结第二周的教学时,可以让每个学生以个人生活中的事件或经验为主题,撰写带有情绪性对话的短篇抒情文章或新诗,然后让学生练习以符合该作品内在情感的声音、表情进行朗诵。这是一种很好的训练活动,因为一般而言,学习外语的学生,在尚未将语言内化之前,很难在言语中正确运用与情绪吻合的语气、表情进行表达。通过这种稍显牵强的方式来教导学生,至少可以让学生了解语言表达中非语言成分的重要性。

在第三周,建议通过观赏电影《小孩不笨(2)》来探讨"冲动控制"(Impulse Control)的重要性,并整合第一、二周的教学内容。之所以挑选"冲动控制"当作主题,是因为笔者发现三、四年级的学生能够了解"冲动控制"的重要性,也有足够的持续专注力和认知能力来进行自我规范,但往往无法百分之百地压抑内在的冲动。将"冲动控制"当作主题还有一个好处:教师可以和学生们探讨不能成功进行冲动控制时,对个人、家人、朋友、班级学习可能造成的影响,譬如剥夺其他同学发言、学习的机会,耽误教师的教学进度,给人留下不好的印象等等。

在播放电影前,建议先让学生了解观赏电影的目的和在观赏电影的过程中应该完成的任务。观赏结束后,与学生讨论时,教师可以用下列几个问题来引导学生思考:"你认为电影情节中,哪些是没有很好地进行冲动控制的例子?""剧中人物没有控制好冲动的原因是什么?因控制不住情绪而引发的行为及语言有哪些?""剧中人物该怎么做,才不会让其他人受到不好的影响?""如果是你,你会怎么办?"

然后,将学生分组,发给每组数张3×5的索引卡。各组学生应分别进行头脑风暴,试着指出在自己的生活里哪些情况很容易叫人失控,例如:"弟弟常常把我的娃娃弄坏,我有想教训他的冲动。""我知道答案,而且我想让大家知道我很棒,所以我不想等老师叫我发言。"学生须在索引卡的一面画出易失控的情景,在另一面用一两个句子描述该情景以及可以用来控制冲动的策略。完成后,让学生挑出一两个情景,以小品剧的形式演示整个过程:从造成激动情绪的事件,到产生想让内在情绪完全爆发的冲动,再到成功地控制冲动。

小品剧表演结束时,教师可以归纳整理学生在小品剧中用到的冲动控制策略,带入"情绪控制不当或表达不合宜时,会有什么影响?"这个焦点问题,让学生继续在小组内讨论。这一过程可复习前两周已学过的词汇、句型,教师也可视情况再添加新的词语、句型。培养情绪管理能力的工作应从小做起,建议教师在教导学生控制冲动、调整情绪前,先取得校内或学区内心理咨询专家的协助,若可能,最好邀请这些专家到班级中介绍更多情绪调控的策略。

此外,手语是一种很有效的沟通工具,特别对有听力障碍的人士或尚在牙牙学语的幼儿而言。建议教师在此周将美式手语中有关情绪表达的几个简单手语教给学生。网络中有很多的视频资源可以运用。另外,*The Joy of Signing* 一书,对此也有很详细的文字、绘图说明。利用手语来辅助外语教学的手段很值得倡导,因为此举可以减少师生使用第一语言的机会;此外,教会学生用手语来表达个人情绪,除了可以为不善用口语表达或生性害羞的学生多提供一种表达的渠道外,在课堂里,用手语表达情绪,还可以缓和学生的冲动,减少教室中的嘈杂声。

本单元结束前,可以让学生创作一首综合所有情绪词汇的说唱作品,让学生们在一片欢乐声中,快快乐乐地结束这个单元。关于说唱节奏的选取,可参考印京华教授所著之《实用节奏汉语》。

单元主题:情绪与情感表达
(中文班三年级,三个星期)

引导问题

核心问题	焦点问题
1. 什么是情感? 2. 我们如何表达情感?	1. 你能用语言描述自己的情绪、感受吗? 2. 除了表情外,还有哪些线索可以帮助我们了解自己或别人的情感?

(续表)

核心问题	焦点问题
3. 造成情感及情绪表达多样性的原因是什么？ 4. 情感的表达方式会如何影响人际关系？	3. 你如何表达不同的情感？你的方式和别人的表达方式有什么不同？为什么？ 4. 情感表达不当时会有什么影响？

学习目标与技能

- 学生能够描述自己的情绪、感受，也能询问他人的情绪、感受
- 学生能够举例说明中国人表达个人情感的特点并可解释原因
- 学生能够举例说明在中国社会中哪些表现个人情感的方式是恰当的

学习评估

  a）过程评估：见各周教案详细内容
  b）总结评估：个人创作的说唱作品

每周教学计划

	第一周：情感表达的方式
教学目标	语言目标： • 学生能够描述表达情绪时掺杂的非语言行为 • 学生能运用有关情绪的词汇和句型来表达自己的感受，并询问他人的感受 文化目标： • 学生能简述影响中国儿童情绪表达的因素
课程内容	• 表示基本情绪的词语、句型 • 基本情绪的非语言表达方式 • 影响中国儿童情绪表达的因素
教学材料	• 基本情绪表情图片（维伯像卡） • 硬纸卡（制作不同形状的眉毛、眼睛、嘴巴、鼻子）、彩笔、剪刀 • 情绪词语卡

（续表）

	第一周：情感表达的方式
演练活动	• 教师在每次上课前，询问学生的心情，并让学生彼此询问。 • 复习低年级时学习过的词语和句型，然后加入其他表示基本情绪的词语。 • 分组活动：比手画脚→变换语气→语言、非语言方式总动员。 • 用硬纸卡制作不同形状的眉、眼、口，用以练习描述表情及情绪。 • 组织学生翻维伯像卡，学用符情绪的语气说话，或两三人一组玩"井"字游戏(Tic→Tac→Toe)，进行口语练习。 • 文化介绍及比较：展示中西儿童在公共场合，用不恰当的方式表达情绪的图片或影像。要求学生识别图片或影像中儿童的情绪状态，指出其中的非语言信息。
过程评估	• 比手画脚活动 • 描述不同眉、眼、口的组合所代表的情绪和情绪事件 • 维伯像卡情绪演示及说明
建议词语及句型	• 开心、高兴、快乐、愉快、生气、气愤、伤心、难过、害怕、紧张、担心、厌恶、感兴趣、惊讶、讶异、咬牙切齿、愁眉苦脸、眉开眼笑、心惊肉跳 • ……的时候，会……；看起来；听起来；一……就……
建议资源	• 《童言无忌》(李溎编译，北京外文出版社出版) • 维伯像卡

	第二周：自觉情绪
教学目标	语言目标： • 学生能运用有关自觉情绪的词汇和句型来表达自己的感受，并询问他人的感受 文化目标： • 被称赞时，学生能够用恰当的口语及非语言方式回应

(续表)

	第二周：自觉情绪
课程内容	• 有关自觉情绪的词语和句型 • 各种"意思"的用法 • 如何回应别人的赞美
教学材料	• 维伯像卡 • 报事贴 • 情绪词语闪卡 • 作文纸、图画纸、彩笔 • 电影四格纸 • 录像机
演练活动	• 复习八种基本情绪词语：教师询问学生的心情并让学生彼此询问。 • 介绍有关自觉情绪的词语。 • 报事贴：我感到……（认读词语） • "我变、我变、我变变变"（句型练习） • 多元智能分组创作：双簧 • "意思"的不同意思：请学生编写情景对话，表演小品剧（剧中应表现如何回应别人的赞美）。 • 写作＋朗诵
过程评估	• 报事贴：认读词语 • "我变、我变、我变变变"：句型使用 • 小品剧："意思"的使用及回应别人的赞美 • 学生创作、朗诵
建议词语及句型	• 羞愧、尴尬、内疚、嫉妒、骄傲、好意思、不好意思、没意思、有意思、够意思、不够意思、哪里哪里、真的吗 • 又……又……；既……又……
建议资源	• 电影《和你在一起》（陈凯歌导演，美国米高梅公司出品）

	第三周：冲动控制
教学目标	• 学生能够说明冲动控制的重要性并试着学习控制冲动 • 学生能够运用有关情绪的词语和句型来表达个人感受并询问别人的心情 • 学生能够使用美式手语表达情绪
课程内容	• 复习基本情绪和自觉情绪的相关词语与句型 • 冲动控制的重要性和方法 • 手语 • 说唱
教学材料	• 电影《小孩不笨（2）》 • 维伯像卡 • 3×5索引卡 • 投影仪、电脑（用以播放电影、网络资源）
演练活动	• 复习有关情绪的词语、句型。 • 观赏电影《小孩不笨（2）》，指出剧中人物情绪管理不当的情节，探讨比较理想的处理方式。 • 分组活动：发给学生索引卡，要求他们画出和描述生活中可能让自己情绪失去控制的情景，以头脑风暴的形式讨论对策。 • 小品剧演出：各组根据索引卡上所描绘的一、二个情景进行表演。 • 美式手语教学。 • 个人说唱活动：综合所有情绪词语、句型，设计一首嘻哈风格（Hip-Hop）的作品。（配乐可参考《实用节奏汉语》）
过程评估	• 索引卡描绘 • 小品剧演出
建议资源	• 《实用节奏汉语》（印京华、孙怡清著，北京：外语教学与研究出版社出版） • *Emotion Words*：*American Sign Language*（可自YouTube，expertvillage.com中搜索） • *The Joy of Signing*：*The Illustrated Guide for Mastering Sign Language and the Manual Alphabet*（Lottie Riekenol著，Gospel Publishing House出版）

郑莉玲　著

第五章 提升学习力：
五至六年级阶段的教学

引 言

依据学区制度的不同，在有些地区，五年级或六年级的学生可能尚处于小学学习的最后阶段，在有些地区，六年级学生可能已经进入了初中学习的过程。这个年纪（10 或 11 岁）的学生有的正处于青春期的发育过程中，有的正面临青春期的到来，他们在生理、认知、情感和人格方面都会有显著的变化。以下仅针对认知、社会心理和情绪发展三方面对语言学习的影响进行探讨。

在认知方面，五、六年级学生的注意力在集中性、稳定性、广度、分配和转移等方面都有不同程度的发展。在思维能力方面，虽然其抽象思维正逐渐萌芽，但仍以针对具体形象的操作（Concrete Operational）为主。此外，学生的逻辑思考能力也在逐渐发展，他们逐步学会了区分重点与非重点信息、主要成分与次要成分，符合客观现实的创造性思维也迅速地成长。根据上述五、六年级学生的认知发展特征，虽说其创造性思维正在逐渐萌芽，但教师在课程设计、主题选择上，仍不宜使教学内容过于偏离学生的日常生活。如果为了加速学生由"具体"到"抽象"的转变而使用与学生生活经验毫不相关的主题或教学方法、肤浅笼统的信息导入，反而容易造成学生的困惑。

教师在教授学生知识技能的同时,还有一项很重要的任务:培养学生的元认知(Meta-cognition)能力,提高他们对自身记忆、感知、计算、联想等认知能力的了解。因此在"传道"之外,教师还应该教学生如何利用自身认知发展的特色来提高学习效率。元认知能力的培养有助于学生发展高效的学习策略,学生在经历多次成功的学习体验后,"活到老学到老"的意识也会大大增强。

此阶段的学生正处于童年中期(6—10岁)或青春期(11—18岁)的早期。在社会心理发展方面,对处于童年中期(Middle Childhood)的学生而言,学校是其发展社会心理的关键场所,此阶段中成功的学习经验有助于加强他们对自身能力的肯定。随着学习经验的取得和成就感的养成,学生对学习的兴趣会随之提高,越发勤奋向上。此外,童年中期的学生仍会很大程度上服从教师的权威性。根据笔者的教学经验,学生常会因为迟交作业或考试成绩不尽如人意而对教师深感歉意。由此可知,某些学生会为了取悦教师而努力学习。教师如果懂得利用这个发展特性来督促、引导学生,在教学上往往能够达到事半功倍的效果。

至于正处青春期的学生,此阶段的中心任务是建立"自我",学生经常通过与同伴、师长的互动交流来不断确定自己的位置、角色。他们会有很强烈的团体归属感,同伴群体的重要性会逐渐取代学校或教师在他们心目中的地位。学生的自我意识、自我主张会逐渐增强,他们能够意识到他人的存在,关心他人对自己的观感。同时,其在社交情境中自我控制的能力也慢慢形成,逐渐开始渴望独立自主。因此,在设计课程时,教师必须特别了解学生的社会心理发展状态,多为其提供和创造独立自主的情境,使学生取得许多成功的经验。此外,还应信赖并尊重学生,引导学生参与课程内容的设计,给予学生主导课堂的机会,让学生选择自己喜爱的学习方式,或利用小组活动、群体目标等方式来引发其学习动机,激励学生不断努力。

除了生理结构的差异,男、女学生的语言表达能力也有不同:男学生利用语言表达情绪的能力比女学生差,再加上多数文化对男性都有"男儿有泪不轻弹"的要求,某些男学生往往会寻求一些"偏差行为"来表达情绪或情感,例如肢体的打打撞撞,或用愤怒来表示内心的挫败感。此外,男学生也比较倾向于隐藏自己的情绪,因为过多的情绪表达容易给他人留下"娘娘腔"的印象。相对而言,女学生比较善于利用语言进行自我表达,也有较多被社会认同的情绪输出渠道。教师必须了解两性发展的基本差异,从多角度观察学生在课堂上的语言或非语言的行为表现,以体谅、包容的态度来对待学生(尤其是男学生),并以灵活的教学设计来疏导男学生过多的精力,如此即可避免许多教室管理上的问题。

作为教师,我们除了希望学生能够发挥自身最大潜能获取更多知识外,同时也期待学生能够关注自身以外的世界。由于五、六年级的学生认知能力有所提高,知识获取量有所增加,社交层面有所扩展,教师这时可以逐渐地引导学生的思维发展,使之由"我的世界"转变为"世界和我",探讨个人、家庭、学校和社区等不同主题,加强其公民意识。此外,我们也应了解,这个年纪的学生可能已经或即将步入青春期,这是一个大脑前额叶皮质(Prefrontal Cortex)发展的重要阶段。大脑前额叶皮质与复杂的认知行动计划有关,其任务是统合个体的思考、行动以实现内在目标。我们期望教师在进行课程设计时,能够充分了解学生的身心、思维、感情等各方面发展特征,灵活调用各种教学手段,交替使用"以教师为主导"和"以学生为中心"的授课形式,多方启动学生大脑的"执行"功能,推动"认知"与"实践"的结合,实现提升语言技能、促进脑力发展的双重效果。

主 题 说 明

(一) 主题单元一:家庭

中国人特别重视家庭,见面时的话题八九不离家人或家庭。家庭是儿童社会化生活的基本单位,和儿童的生活、成长、教育紧密联系、息息相关。统观林林总总的外语教材,特别是针对儿童,甚至青春期学生设计的书籍,"家庭"或"家人"经常是学习的第一个主题,家庭的重要性由此可见。

在一到四年级的课程当中,学生对于以下主题已经有了初步的了解:家庭和家人在生活中的重要性、家庭成员的称谓及其与职责的关联、在传统中国家庭里男女地位的不同、孝道对中国家庭的意义。其中一再重复出现的行为文化主题包括父慈子孝、兄友弟恭、长幼有序等维系中国家庭伦常的行为准则。在语言学习方面,学生也具备了基本的听、说、读、写能力,能够完成简单的口头和书面任务。

进入五、六年级后,学生在情感、认知、身心发展、社会化方面皆有长足的进步，所以教师在设计课程时除了须延续前一阶段课程的中心，继续巩固学生的知识和语言应用能力外，还可以加入一些可以激发较高层次的认知思考，可以让学生进行分析、归纳、评价的主题，譬如：随着时代的不同，中国家庭出现了哪些变化？这些变化对家庭成员有何影响？为什么光耀门庭对中国人而言是很重要的家庭观念？各中国家庭之间有哪些相异、相同之处？

就学习目标而言，本单元以加强学生的沟通交际能力和对中国文化的体验理解为基础，进一步培养学生触类旁通的推理能力，提高其语言、文化比较能力以及在多元文化社区当中"学以致用"的能力。

由于这个阶段的学生的抽象思维尚处于起步阶段，其设身处地为他人着想的能力较为不足，因此，如果能够利用与学生切身经验密切相关的主题导入课程，比较容易得到学生的共鸣。花木兰代父从军是一个中美儿童都耳熟能详的历史故事，教师可以考虑利用这个故事来吸引学生的兴趣，讨论花木兰的家庭结构、男女角色的时代意义、传宗接代的重要性、家庭荣耀等文化议题。若想从目前转型中的中国社会入手来探讨类似议题，教师可以使用纪录片 *Mardi Gras Made in China*、电影《变脸》的某些片段或组织学生采访有中国背景的同伴。

教师必须明白，这个阶段的学生，绝大多数仍在学习如何用自身的经验来揣测他人的感受，所以，对于一些较严肃或艰深的主题，教师可以运用角色扮演的方式来激发学生的情绪反应。例如，教师可以在一两周内给予男学生诸多特权，给予女学生诸多限制，以酝酿女学生的反对情绪。学生可以藉此亲身体会到"重男轻女"带来的情绪震撼，进而体会到中国人由于性别差异而产生的角色、权责差异。当然，我们也希望可以试着培养学生简单评论、评判的能力。所以，在角色扮演结束后，可以让学生作个简短的分析报告或情绪发展总结（Closure）。教师还可以让学生分组，组成几个三代同堂的大家庭来学习其中的家人关系和称谓、角色和职责。这种类似于"过家家/扮家家酒"的游戏，可帮助学生学习复杂的中国家庭关系和不同角色承担的权利、职责，例如扮演孙子的学生必须为扮演祖父祖母的学生提书包、摆设午餐、陪他们玩等等。

在涉及家庭结构、成员等比较敏感的内容之前，教师最好对学生的家庭有初步的了解。虽说在美国多元的社会中，同性父母、单亲家庭、领养家庭都不足为奇，但是对某些学生或家庭而言，这属于个人隐私。为了避免学生在课堂上感到难堪，身为教师的我们必须多花一份心思，多为学生着想。笔者的某些学生是由同性双亲领养的,每当要学习"家庭"这个单元时,或观赏情节带有敏感成分的电影前,笔者都会事先和学生的家长联系,获得家长的支持后再开始教学。如果教师想让学生利用多代族谱来了解相关称谓,让全班学生分组去访问其他学科的教师是一个很可行的方式。学生可以把访问结果制作成族谱海报并贴上相片,然后手持海报在课堂里作报告。课后可组织学生将海报贴在教室外让其他学生参观。同时,教师也应该考虑让班级当中的少数族裔学生分享他们的家庭价值观、家庭成员职责等类似的信息,如此一来,学生对"家庭"这个主题的了解可以不只局限于中国家庭和当地主流家庭的比较。教师如果善于利用学生本身的背景作为教学资源,还可以让教室教学环境更加真切,对学生的学习而言也更有意义。

(二)主题单元二:食物与中药

"每天开门七件事:柴米油盐酱醋茶。"中国人"以食为天"的特性在这句话里呈现得淋漓尽致!谈到"食物与中药"这个主题,相信老师们和笔者一样,脑海里马上出现了种种新鲜、诱人的教学设想。当学生听到他们新的单元是"食物"时,也势必兴奋至极,迫不及待。是的,中国的美食文化举世闻名,我们不得不承认,许多学习中文的人可能就是慕中国美食之名而来。"食物"这个主题在教学操作方面经常取得事半功倍的效果,因为"吃"是一种很强的动力!

在一到四年级的课程当中,学生对中国人的餐饮方式已经有了初步的认识,包括饮食内容、基本中国菜名、饮茶文化、餐具使用等等。在课程当中一再重复出现的行为文化主题有餐具的使用、进餐的礼节、做客及待客之道等,学生也能够将自己家庭的饮食形态与中国人的饮食形态作初步的比较。在语言能力的培养方面,学生也已学会了陈述个人的喜好,可以说出常见的中国饮食名称。

到了五、六年级,我们都知道学生在情绪、认知、身心发展、社会化各方面皆有明显的发展,所以设计课程时可以在深度和广度两方面双管齐下。就深度而言,教师可以继续探讨中国饮食的多样性,以地理差异来说明各地饮食的不同,例如南方、北方的饮食差异。教师还可以再深入论及中国人使用饮食进行人情交往、祈福的传统。就广度而言,中国人利用食物来改善个人体质的"食疗"观念由来已久,可在此阶段作初步的介绍;此外,食物的属性(寒温冷热),以及中药、中医,都是很有意思的主题,都能给学生带来较大的认知震撼与失衡（Disequilibrium）。

"吃"是很具体的行为，如何利用具体行为来带动学生的抽象思维的发展是课程设计要解决的问题。笔者深信，利用学生切身经历过的情景或与之息息相关的主题，比较容易得到学生的共鸣并激发他们的学习兴趣。此外，通过对中国人健康饮食观念的了解，引导学生反思个人饮食习惯，在教学上也有很大的发挥空间。在进行饮食形态的对比时，教师可以让学生将他们常吃的早餐或点心带到教室里与同学分享，然后再切入中国人的饮食习惯。学生也可以利用网络研究中西方学生的在校午餐，从营养成分、进餐方式等方面出发对二者进行分析、比较，然后利用调查所得，根据他们对食物金字塔（Food Pyramid）的了解来设计学校的午餐菜单。如果可行，教师可号召全校学生参与此活动，最终向校方、学区提出菜单建议。这种教学方式，不但可以拓宽学生的视野，也能够激发学生的高层次认知思考能力（Higher Order Thinking Skills，HOTS，例如分析、归纳、评价、创造能力）。在教学中，教师可以斟酌、调整对学校、社区生活的参与度。

在讨论食疗和中药时，如有可能，教师可带领学生到校外参观中医诊所或邀请专家到校进行示范演说。笔者也曾将食疗的主要药材带到课堂上，让学生们先用眼看、用手摸、用鼻闻，再用心猜："这是什么？有什么用途？"之后，再将烹煮好的食疗品带到教室里让学生再一次看、闻，甚至品尝。这样的教学方式可以调动学生的情绪，刺激学生的多重感官，给他们留下深刻的印象，使他们比较容易形成与整个教学活动相关的"事件记忆"（Episodic Memory）。笔者认为通过这样的亲身体会，比较容易除去一些学生对中国文化的固执印象（Stereotypes）。

在某些特殊时机，例如庆祝毕业时，教师也可以带领学生到中餐馆一块儿吃圆桌饭。如果有学生过生日的话，教师可以根据自身成长的经验设计菜单，给寿星们来个"每月集体寿宴"，例如大伙儿一块儿煮个猪脚卤蛋面线。在这个过程当中，教师应该根据学生的语言基础来设计词汇和语法点，让学生在分组烹煮的过程中可以利用中文进行沟通。大伙儿一块儿洗洗切切、煎煮炒炸，身临其境地感受文化，此后学生对中文的热爱只会有增无减。在进行文化比较时，别忘了鼓励班上的"非主流"学生将他们自身的文化习俗用品带到教室里来与大家分享，切实做到"熟谙文化的教学"（Culturally Proficient Instruction）。

由以上的教学活动不难看出，本单元的教学目标除了加强学生的沟通交际能力和对中国文化的体验理解外,也注重培养触类旁通的推理能力、语言文化比较能力与在多元文化社区当中学以致用的能力。

各州对于教师是否可以给学生提供食品有不同的规定和限制,学生可能基于宗教原因而有不同的饮食禁忌,或由于体质关系而有食物过敏的可能,对于这些细节,教师都必须事先有所了解,以免危害学生的健康或涉及法律纠纷。总而言之,就"食物与中药"这个主题,可发挥的空间是无限的。光说不练,不动口吃、动手做,是很难说服学生的!

(三) 主题单元三:节庆活动

如果必须针对不同的民族或地区提出其最具代表性的文化产物,人们会很自然地联想到节庆。节日是每个民族或地区生活当中值得纪念或庆祝的日子,有的源于传统习俗,有的源于宗教信仰,有的则源于对某历史人物或事件的感怀、追思。节庆可说是每个民族或地区生活习俗、价值观念和信仰、理念的综合体现。由于节日拥有一定的规律性、重复性、可预期性,人们在庆祝时往往会遵循一定程序或规则,"传统"也就这样自然而然地形成了。

西北大学的杨景震先生在《中国传统节日风俗的形成及特征》一文中归纳出了节日风俗的八大特征:礼仪性、理想性、时代性、民族性、传承性、变异性、群众性以及地方性。教师们在就"节庆"这个主题设计课程时,如果能够以此八大特征为前提,必能使此主题的探讨面面俱到。在实际操作方面,教师必须考虑时令的合理度,如果不在过年期间庆祝春节,或是端午未到就赶在学期结束前包起粽子来,都是违背节庆时令合理性的。所以本主题的进行应该配合时令,以"年"为教学周期,而不是集中于一学年当中的一两个单元。

上文中提到了节日的传统性及传承性。在教学中,教师经常受限于地理空间,无法让学生亲身体验中国人庆祝节庆的热闹与隆重,不过教师还是可以遵循节庆内在的"大传统"来建立属于自己班级的"小传统"。譬如在迎接新年时可以组织全班打扫教室、书写春联、张贴窗花,一起除旧布新,年年如此。久而久之,大小传统可以齐头并进。此外,由于科技的进步,教师也可以组织学生利用卫星电话与中国的友谊学校进行视频沟通,让海外的学生也可以感受到节庆的欢腾气氛;如有可能,还可以组织学生到中国城或华人社区观赏花灯游行,这些都能为空间限制的遗憾做些弥补。

五、六年级的学生在经历过至少五年的节庆活动教学后，对中国传统节日或当代节日，都具备了相当具体的知识和实际操作经验。五、六年级学生的生理及认知发展又较三、四年级时有长足的进步，他们对同伴的兴趣提高了，自主学习的能力也有所提升。教师可以利用同伴互学的方式来进行较具知识性主题的教学，例如让学生收集、整理、分析、归纳资料并完成简报。当然，不是所有的教学内容都可以如此进行，举个例子：谈到中国传统节庆时，自然免不了介绍中国历法，特别是农历。如果授课的形式完全以口述为主，一般而言，五、六年级的学生仍然无法理解农历和公历的差别。在活动中，让学生在课堂里合作写出二至三年中全年（十二个月）的日期，然后从中找出中国四大传统节日对应的公历日期。这样学生会发现中国传统节日每年都会出现在不同的公历日期中，进而也可体会到公历与农历的不同。同时，教师也可以进一步组织讨论，探讨农历中"闰月"产生的原因以及二十四节气的由来、用处。这些都可加深学生对两种历法异同的了解。教师还可以进而介绍有关节气的词汇，让学生为节气制作插画，通过动手学习加深印象。

　　中国幅员辽阔，各地区或民族庆祝节日的方式虽然有普遍的共同性，但也带有民族或地区特色的差异：同样是春节，北方和南方人的节庆食品就不相同，庆祝的程序也有所不同。例如过春节时，在台湾地区，儿媳妇初二回娘家，北京的儿媳妇则初三回。五、六年级的学生在学习节庆这个主题时，可以开始试着了解这些地方性差异。此外，随着时间的推移，节日的内涵和庆祝方式也在发生变化，这就是所谓的变异性。当然，中国节日传到其他国家后发生的变化和对该国当地社区民众或华埠的影响也是一个很有趣的主题。例如，在美国俄勒冈州的波特兰市，每年六月玫瑰节时必举办划龙舟大赛。这时，教师可以趁机提问："中国人庆祝的外来节日有哪些？这些节日如何受到西方文化影响？某些节日中过节的意义和形式是否已有改变？如何改变？"

　　体验文化的同时，切勿忘记文化比较。教师偶尔会被家长质疑："我的孩子是学习中文的，为什么要像个中国人一样过年过节呢？"如果教师能够点出认识他国文化可以加深学生对自身文化的了解和体会，家长应该就能够明白文化教学的目的。所以教师在进行文化教学活动时，除了让学生就中华文化的产物、行为、观点进行分析讨论，还得让学生将自身文化与中华文化作比较。人们有时难以信任自己不熟悉的事物，所以教师应选择文化中的某些"优点"来激发学生的"正向思考"。

如何将中国人过年过节的程序有意义地带入学生的生活中,是对教师创造性思考能力的挑战。例如,在美国没有过年"回娘家"的习俗,不过对祖父母、外祖父母的思念情绪则中外皆然。教师可以在大年初二那天让学生写张问候卡寄给外祖父母,在卡上解释"回娘家"在中国社会中的传统意义,并在卡片中寄寓思念之情。

节庆的礼仪性是指礼尚往来,过新年时长辈给晚辈压岁钱,晚辈向长辈拜年祈福,就是一个例子。教师可以如法炮制:提醒学生向教师拜年,教师则给学生分发红包(里面最好是中国货币)。

节庆与饮食是中国人生活中的两大主题。和"吃"一样,节庆也是生活方式的展现,可是节庆涵盖的范畴又较"吃"这回事来得深、来得广。通过对这个主题的探讨,我们不只可以强调饮食文化对中国人的重要性,更可以深入探讨隐藏在节庆文化、庆祝活动和节庆产物背后的文化理念。另外,节庆饮食多有"祈福"的象征意义,教师可以让学生将不同国家、不同节日中的节庆食物进行比较,例如中国中秋节的月饼与美国感恩节的火鸡,中国七夕节的巧果与西方情人节的巧克力。

(四)主题单元四:地理与旅游

因为五、六年级的学生自我照顾的能力仍然局限于家庭和学校环境中,与师长、同学一起出国旅游时所需的独立自主、交流应变能力稍显不足,所以一般不是国际旅游教学的考虑对象。然而这个年纪的学生对异国旅游的憧憬并不会因此减弱。现代社会中科技发展突飞猛进,国与国之间的距离日益缩短,人类已经能够在较短的时间内"行万里路"。而想拥有"万卷书"般的知识,也非得靠"行万里路"来辅助不可。再说国际观的培养不应该受年龄的限制,培养国际公民当然得从小奠定基础。所以,在这个单元里,就让我们带领学生进行一段穿越时间与空间的虚拟中国之旅吧!

在三、四年级的课程中,学生已经掌握了基本的方位词,会使用与周遭生活相关的地图,对交通工具的种类、中国地理、世界地图都有了粗略的认识。在五、六年级的课程中,教师仍要继续增加学生的地理常识并强化与旅行有关的语言文化技能。

在"上路"前,最好有个知识技能的储备环节作为热身活动。提到旅行,绝对少不了花钱;提到花钱,当然得讨论汇率。学生经常会提出货币兑换的问题。笔者认为,与其让学生上网查汇率,不如拿出真钞实币,让学生看钱、摸钱、闻钱,再让学生比较中国货币与本地货币在钞票、硬币的面值、种类、尺寸大小、花样设计、购买力等方面的差别。在进行物价比较时,教师可以在教室中利用网络马上提供相关数据,例如:一个 iPad 价值多少美金?换算成人民币是多少?在购物网站(例如淘宝网)中被开价多少?为什么会有这样的差距?此外,让学生正确学习货币的量词和数目的位值也很有必要。笔者曾经将到中国内地、台湾地区旅游所收集的纪念品带到教室中,让学生玩类似美国猜价节目的游戏:学生练习出价,教师可以在呈现每一个纪念品的同时,在地图上标示购买该品的地点。游戏结束后,让学生"认养"一件纪念品,记住该纪念品的购买地点,为接下来的虚拟之旅作准备。

虚拟之旅可完全利用网络资讯配合图书馆资料进行。教师给每位学生一笔"旅费",学生必须利用这笔钱,在预算之内从其定居的城市出发,到自己挑选的中国某城市进行为期一周的旅行。学生必须先研究目的地的气候特征,再取得签证、整理行李。在旅途中,学生应记录每日的行程、食宿地点、使用的交通工具、参观景点、消费金额,还要试着与家人联络,解决旅行中不同的突发状况,譬如:到哪儿找洗手间?如何兑换货币?如何使用公用电话?生病时到哪儿就医?护照遗失了,到哪儿找大使馆?教师还可以设计某些包含文化冲突的情景,让学生试着体验、处理,例如:在景点碰到摊贩强力推销商品时应如何应对?如果当地人对自己品头论足,该如何反应?到当地人家中做客时该注意些什么?吃饭时如果不习惯主人家的饭菜怎么办?

在虚拟之旅结束后,别忘了要求学生作口头和书面报告,也可以组织学生制做简报、海报,呈现对旅游地的地理历史、人文经济、风俗习惯、饮食文化的了解。由于情景是虚拟的,学生可以勇敢地尝试不同的旅游计划并提出解决问题的方法。旅游计划可以完全依据学生个人兴趣量身订做,这是既有趣又有效的课程设计。当然,这个年纪的孩子基本上还无法独立处理上述诸多情况,若要求学生具备这些技能不免强人所难。不过,此阶段的学习重点之一在于为下一阶段的学习铺陈打底,所以可以先从扩大知识面的角度展开教学。更重要的是,这种课程设计提供给学生很大的自主性,容易激发学生的学习动机。教师可根据学生年龄、网络搜索能力、资源的数量来决定此项目是由一人独立完成还是由多人小组完成。此外,事先做好资料收集的工作可以确保本活动顺利进行。教师可事先收集一些提供可靠旅游资讯的网站(如谷歌地图),制定旅游所需的详细计划,好让学生在完成每一个步骤时打勾确认。

如果资源不足,上述教学活动不易进行,教师可以考虑利用个人的中国游记,配合旅游中保留的票根、收据,购买的风景明信片、纪念品,拍摄的相片或录像等来介绍中国地理、历史文物、风土人情。笔者建议,教师在下一个个人中国之旅中,不妨携带象征学校的吉祥物同行并在旅程中请当地人与吉祥物合影留念,或将吉祥物加进录像中、照片里。当教师在课堂中与学生分享这些影像时,学生较能体会到旅游地的真实性和到当地旅行的可行性。如果教师无法制作自导自演的旅游纪录片,可以考虑利用专门介绍旅游的录像带或网站来替代。

很多学生喜欢吃中国菜,但是有多少学生思考过中国菜是如何传入美国的呢?当学生向往着到中国旅游时,是不是对中国人何时开始移民美国也会感到好奇呢?除了大众媒体外,唐人街、中国城都可能是学生们首先接触到的有与中国相关知识的地方。想要了解中国人的移民史,笔者认为访问中国移民或是移民子弟是最理想的方式。教师可以邀请当地华人社区、华人教会或中文学校里的华人移民到校接受访问。上述诸地都可能有颇多可利用的资源,值得一探。如有可能,教师可考虑安排学生参观当地的中国城、中国移民博物馆,在中国城访问移民或吃饭。

旅游除了涉及空间的改变外,时区调整也在所难免。不同于中国的单一时区制,居住在美国的孩子一般都知道美国有六个时区。不同时区的概念其实不难理解,教师可以考虑和自然科学课教师进行课程内容的贯联,共同设计与太阳系有关的课程单元,帮助学生了解地球的公转、自转,太阳、月球的位置关系,四季、时差现象形成的原因。教师可藉此复习三、四年级曾探讨过的日晷、中国传统计时方式与现代记时方式的比较等课程内容。随着年龄的增长,学生的认知能力日渐提高,学习经验更加丰富,因此,即使类似的主题再度出现,依然会有学习的价值。为了激发学生认知的发展,拓展其认知思考范畴,教师可以再一次让学生思考:"时间不存在时,会出现什么现象?时间不存在是好还是坏呢?"

总之,"地理与旅游"经常是外语教学中触及的主题,在五、六年级的课程当中就旅游中可能出现的一些情景进行预设处理,普及地理常识,都是为下一个阶段奠定良好基础的重要步骤。让学生对未来的旅游充满憧憬,是激励他们继续学习中文的好手段;提升学生对他国文化的认识,则是帮助他们成为国际公民的好方法。

（五）主题单元五：历史、政治与宗教

中国有五千年的悠久历史，这不仅是中国人的骄傲，是凝聚民族的向心力，更是民族智慧的精华所在。这也说明了为什么有人认为中国人习惯在过去中寻求关于未来的答案。虽说"华夏五千年，文史不分家"，但是五、六年级学生的知识尚不足以让他们感受历史同语言之间的横向联贯。教师或许会担心五、六年级的学生可能认为这个主题稍显严肃、苦涩，或质疑"中国的历史、政治、宗教与我何干？"但有研究报告指出：中国学生对研习自身历史有较高的兴趣，美国学生则对学习他国历史兴致浓厚。其中原因不难理解：相较于中国，美国毕竟只有二百多年的历史，而学习历史就仿佛读故事书般有趣，能带来良好的学习体验。

中国历史源远流长，若以说书的方式来介绍，耗时一千零一夜可能也无法道尽。什么才是本单元教学的重点？如何联系语言和历史？笔者认为在回答这些问题之前，教师必须先了解学生的知识背景，并且与文史学科的教师沟通，了解本年级以及前后年级的语文课、历史课的课程重点，以实现学科与学科之间的横向或纵向贯联。接着，教师可以找寻学生的共同兴趣，依此选定单元教学重点、教学目标。

为了让学生对中国历史有整体性而非片断式的了解，教师可以将中国历史中有文明记载的时期切分成块，再讲述每一切块时期的著名历史人物或事件，并以此作为导火索来引燃学生学习的火花。以下的分期和历史人物可供教师参考：夏商周三代、春秋战国（孔子、屈原）、秦汉（秦始皇）、三国两晋南北朝（桃园三结义）、隋唐（玄奘、武则天）、宋元（苏轼、成吉思汗）、明清（郑和、慈禧太后）以及 20 世纪至今（孙中山、毛泽东、蒋介石）。学生可分成小组选定感兴趣的历史人物，利用图书馆或网络资源，依据教师所设定的研究重点来收集资料。研究重点可以包括朝代名称、起止年代、领域边疆、政治结构、科技宗教、最具历史意义的事件或人物等。学生可以利用录像、小品、简报、图表等方式呈现学习成果。在报告成果的时候，当听众的学生必须记笔记，以增强学习效果。最后，教师可汇集各组书面报告制作大板报，用时间轴的形式呈现各个历史时期的风貌。

在探讨历史时，中国早期移民到美国的历程是学生必须了解的一个主题。多数小学的社会学课对美国移民史都会有初步的研究，但是中国的移民史不一定是学生学习的项目之一。笔者认为，在帮助五、六年级的学生了解中国移民史时，可充分利用最靠近学校的华人社区进行课程设

计。教师可安排学生参观中国城,中国城内若有介绍华人移民历史的博物馆,也是一项非常好的资源。此外,为华裔专办的中文学校(特别是位于中国城内的学校)也是很好的资源。若学区内有华人聚集的社区,教师可以邀请华人长老到校,安排学生对其进行面对面访谈。加州的早期华人移民史是每位有意研究此主题者必须探究的,华人移民被拘禁在天使岛(Angel Island)等待入境或遭返的故事引人深思。教师可以利用这些华人被拘禁时在墙壁上书写的文章作为学生的阅读资料,甚至利用角色扮演或戏剧形式,重现当初华人移民美国时遭到移民官种种严格审查的过程。在了解华人移民史的课程当中,我们希望学生们能够发掘一下自己的祖先来到美国的经过,教师可以把这个主题作为课外拓展的项目之一。

丝绸之路是汉朝张骞出使西域时走过的路线,直到12世纪末,它仍然是中国与中亚、东欧各国经济文化交流的重要路径。三、四年级的学生对丝绸之路的概念已开始形成,到了五、六年级,教师可以让学生观赏电影,然后先对丝绸之路作个全面性的概述,再用张骞出使西域十三年的外交探险之旅来吸引学生的兴趣。最后可以让学生比较张骞和发现美洲大陆的哥伦布这两位探险家的事迹、成就。因为五、六年级的学生对哥伦布的故事都已经耳熟能详,因此利用哥伦布的冒险故事较易带动学生联系知识的能力。当然,教师也可以考虑让学生对比丝绸之路和网络之路,训练学生的分析、评价的能力。学生在五、六年级对丝绸之路具备了宏观的了解后,在七、八年级时就更容易在这个主题上进行微观的比较或较深入的研究。

中国的科举制度是政治结构中很重要的一个环节。在21世纪的今天,科举考试遗风尚存。五、六年级的学生可能知道亚裔学生非常注意在校的学业表现,但不明白在中国内地、香港、台湾地区,升学压力是学生生活中不可忽略的事实。教师在设计与此主题有关的课程时,可以考虑从之前学习过的"学校生活"这个主题来切入,讨论中美学校中课表的内容、每日课时、每学年总上课天数、寒暑假作业布置,以及课后学生活动等内容。在对比的过程中,学生须整理资料,综合并分析信息后形成自己的观点。此外,在中国接受过教育的教师也可以介绍个人求学经历,包括课后补习、面对高考的压力,来为学生观点的形成提供支持。《背起爸爸上学》这部电影对升学、"面子"与亲情都有很深切的描绘,可以当作辅助教学材料,或是本主题的"开场白"。培养学生的创造性思维,一直是教学的重点之一,教师可以把学业压力当作主题,让学生对中国学生面对的求学压力提出建议或解决之道,或为他们设计一份理想的课表来结束这个单元。

在美国,宗教是一个敏感的话题,这个主题绝对有很大的对比空间。在探讨这个主题时,教师可以先让学生从自身的经验出发,思考宗教信仰存在的意义和宗教信仰对自己生活的影响,然后可以利用绘画、写作或照片来呈现思考的结果。这个教学活动除了可以提高学生自我反思的能力之外,也可以通过分享的过程增进学生对非主流宗教的认识与尊重。接着,教师可以利用网络图片或视频来介绍存在于中国的宗教。道教是源自中国的宗教,和中国诸多传统节日有不可分离的密切关系,教师可以考虑将道教和中国传统节日相贯联,利用图像、影片来介绍在各个节日庆祝活动中受到特别推崇的神明和与之相关的历史故事或民间习俗。之后,教师可以让学生对自身的宗教再作进一步研究,找出受到高度推崇的宗教人物、著名典故等并在课堂中分享。

(六) 主题单元六:朋友、娱乐与时尚

人是群体动物,人际往来是无法避免的。儿童在与人交往的过程中尝试以不同的方式与他人进行沟通,建立和维系友谊。在这个过程里,儿童学会了与人协商、制定行为规范、解决问题,以及为达成群体目标而共同合作等社交技能。因此"交朋友"或"建立友谊"是儿童社会心理发展过程中必修的功课。

对五、六年级的学生来讲,由于其认知能力的增强,开始懂得如何设身处地为他人着想,对他人思维、情感的预测能力和从第三者的角度来探讨问题的技巧都大大提升,随着社会观点采择(Social Perspective Taking)能力的成熟以及生活空间的扩大,学生有了一定的交友技能,对寻求朋友、建立友谊的渴望也逐日提高,因此朋友、友谊的重要性也与日俱增。中国人对交友有"友直,友谅,友多闻"一说,对儿童或青少年而言,应无可厚非地再加上一"友":"友趣"。朋友间除了在心灵上彼此勉励、支持外,还有互动的乐趣。

提到娱乐,往往离不开大众文化的影响,这就包括了时装和时尚。时装(Fashion)指的是在某时期流行的服装及配饰,比如球鞋、眼镜、首饰或妆容。时尚(Fads)则是指某一时期中社会崇尚的流行文化。同于时装,时尚也受到潮流的影响,具有多变性,通常是年轻人表达个性、仿效和认同公众文化的方式。品牌追崇、人物崇拜、生活方式等都可以构成时尚。

由于本主题所涵盖的范畴很广泛,教师可以将"朋友和娱乐""时装和

时尚"视为两个小单元来进行教学。笔者认为教师还可以将"朋友和娱乐"的比例加重，因为这个年纪的孩子对时装、时尚的敏锐性还不及七、八年级学生和高中学生，而他们寻找朋友、建立友谊的欲望可能较追求时尚更胜一筹。

　　在探讨"朋友和娱乐"这个次单元时，教师可把友谊当作侧重点，先用电视剧（如《家有儿女》）片段、电影（如《长江七号》）情节或高班学生创作的小品剧来导入主题。接下来，教师可用语言贯联主题：让学生以"当我和我的好朋友在一起时……"为题作文，文中要介绍自己的好朋友、好朋友的个性以及和好朋友在一起时喜欢做的活动。为了提高学生的自学能力，教师可以让学生利用网络词典寻找切合个人学习需求的词汇，之后汇集所有新词汇，提供给全班学生。为了增加学习的乐趣，学生可以两人一组表演双簧：由甲生朗诵乙生的文章，乙生用肢体动作呈现文义，之后再互换角色。此外，利用简报方式、rap 歌唱或是连环画来诠释文章内容，都可以实现多元智能教学。为了避免有学生把某甲当好友，而某甲却不把他/她当好友，导致情感受伤害的情况，教师可以要求学生不在文中指名道姓。分享结束后，不难整理出学生和朋友在一起时常会涉及的娱乐或非娱乐活动。

　　教师还可以引导学生分组讨论以下焦点问题："什么是朋友？朋友间有什么该做或不该做的吗？"并要求在讨论之后作报告。在此，笔者必须特别提出的一点是，教师得让学生明白，中国社会有强烈的"敬老"意识和社会规范意识，年纪稍长者，即使是陌生人，也可以直接对年轻者的偏差举止提出纠正。因此，当朋友们一起在公共场合娱乐时，一定要尽量保证行为恰当。还有，同性好友之间的身体碰触，特别是女孩之间的碰触，在中国社会里是被完全接受、不会令人臆测的。

　　这个单元也是介绍中国传统玩具的一个好时机。抖空竹（扯铃）、踢毽子、打陀螺对五、六年级的学生来说都是很有趣的体验。此外，过生日是大多数美国学生向往的、充满欢乐的特殊日子，教师可以就中西儿童过生日的方式来探讨娱乐的方式和理念。当然，"过生日"也可以作为这个次单元的开场白："你要过生日了，你最想邀请的人是谁？为什么？""你被邀请参加生日会，你怎么挑选生日礼物呢？"在送礼这个话题上，教师可以和学生一起讨论收礼者希望送礼者如何为其挑选礼物。当然，对"好礼物"的界定难免会受到时尚潮流的影响。

　　进行文化认知和比较时，最有效的方式之一是与中国的友谊学校（姐妹校)进行视频或书信交流。如果双方可以制作录像,互相介绍本校学生在校内外的娱乐休闲活动,学生自然容易明白其他国家的同龄人和他们的朋友在一块儿时喜欢去哪儿和做什么,喜欢收到什么样的礼物。如果以上方式都不可行,利用优酷(YouKu)或是YouTube都不难找到具有教育及娱乐双重意义的影片。为了避免学生在上述网站看到少儿不宜的文字或图片,建议教师把录像嵌入PowerPoint中进行播放。

美国的教育方式多用架构思考方式:学生先体会、诠释,教师再进行引导。如果教师期待通过讲述有关友谊的中国历史故事达到教化的效果,对美国五、六年级的学生而言,这样做成效不会太大,因为学生举一反三的能力有限,再加上文化的隔阂,整个过程对学生来说仅是隔靴搔痒,况且教师难免有歌功颂德或以个人理念加诸他人之嫌。阐述友谊的历史故事可以用来进行文化观的比较。教师可以将美国有名的友情故事和中国的相提并论,在其中寻找异同,增进学生对双方文化的了解。

改革开放后,随着中国经济的发展,人民财富逐渐增加,购买力也逐渐提高,西方大众文化在中国社会逐渐找到立足之地。现代中国儿童的生活方式及其对科技潮流的追逐,已经和美国儿童有很多的相似之处。在介绍时装和时尚这个主题时,最容易上手的方式是利用网络中的音频、视频或图像,让学生了解到中国学生在很多方面和自己是颇为相似的。当然,教师不宜只给学生呈现中国社会的主流,少数民族、弱势团体的介绍可能会给学生带来更多的启示。

相较于中国学生,美国的学生一般而言都比较懂得穿着打扮,对流行事物较感兴趣,洞察度也较高。中国的校园规范强调"一致性",不鼓励个性表达,所以学生受制于较严格的服装仪容要求,在校园中染发或化妆仍未被普遍接受。突破规范的结果往往是人们会用异样的眼光,甚至带有强烈的偏见看待标新立异的学生。在探讨这个主题时,教师可以试着让学生制定一套服装仪容规范:每天只准穿同样的运动服来上学,不可以化妆、喷古龙水、抹发胶等。全班必须集体遵守该规范,若有违反须受到惩罚。在为期一两周的试验期结束后,学生们可以讨论这套规范有何优缺点。

根据维基百科的资料,美国92%的人口使用手机。这个数字说明手机等即时通信工具已逐渐成为人们维系社会关系的重要手段。对于青少年来说,"短信"则是他们的首选。教师可让学生知道使用汉语(普通话)写短信时也有类似于英文的缩略用法和完全利用阿拉伯数字谐音形成的趣味短语或"火星文"。这个主题不仅有趣，还可以提升学生的语言运用能力。由于时尚潮流具有强烈的时代感，为了能够在这个主题上拥有最新的知识，教师必须时时充实自我，确实跟上潮流发展，才不会有落伍老套、与现实脱节之嫌。

（七）主题单元七：艺术与科学创造

五千年的中华历史留下了丰硕的文化遗产，不论是绘画书法、音乐舞蹈、诗词戏曲、园林建筑或雕塑工艺，都显示了浓厚的艺术内涵和充满活力的历史痕迹。而中国祖先的高度智慧更体现在四大发明里，造纸术、指南针、火药、活字印刷术的出现不仅推动了中国古代政治、经济与文化的发展，更对世界文明的进步产生了不可磨灭的影响。

三、四年级的学生，对中国的四大发明、中国艺术以及语言文字已经有了基本的认识，到了五、六年级，可以继续就此主题进行深度和广度的推进。为实现这一目的，课程设计应实现"今古贯联，中外交叉"。此外，教师也可以引入其他外语教学常常探讨的主题，例如爱好、职业、国家和语言，让学生的语言知识和技能得以持续提升。

在外语教学的五大标准中，"贯连"（触类旁通）被列为其中之一。在此前提下，虽说中国四大发明对欧洲文明的发展有着深刻的影响，笔者并不认为在讲述四大发明时要将其与欧洲历史贯联，因为一般五、六年级的社会课教学都仍局限于各州历史或美国早期殖民历史，七、八年级则着重于古代文明或美国近代历史的学习，欧洲历史一般得等到高中才开始涉及。建议教师再度加深学生对四大发明的认知，特别可强调其对人类文明的重要贡献。为了避免枯燥乏味的讲解式教学，教师可采用富有变化的活动形式，如小组合作学习，运用网络信息来探究四大发明的相关内容；分派给各小组一项发明，让学生针对该发明的时代背景、产生缘由、人物、对当时与后来的影响等主题进行探讨。此外，也可以让学生探究美国早期发明对人类文明的贡献，例如电灯、飞机、汽车。这么一来，就轻易做到了"今古贯连，中外交叉"。

在笔者的成长过程中，书法、国画、国乐、传统舞蹈、民俗手工艺等文化内容即使不是正规课程，至少也是课外社团活动的一部分。为了帮助学生了解中国传统艺术不仅是历史产物，也融入了现代人的生活，教师可以利用录像或图片来阐释。如果能与友谊学校（姐妹校）进行视频交流，让中国学生表演其修习的艺术项目，说服力会更大。中国地大物博，各地民俗艺术精华荟萃，教师应该善加利用。在介绍民俗艺术时，很重要的是必须将地理风俗、人文知识也融入课程。教师可以利用投影仪，将中国地图投射在取代屏幕的白报纸上，让学生在报纸上用彩笔画出中国的主要山川、省份、城市的轮廓。然后让学生就感兴趣的民俗艺术主题，针对其特色、用途等方面进行资料搜寻并形成研究报告。学生可将研究报告张贴到中国地图上，将整份地图张贴于校内显眼之处，与全校学生分享，实现课堂与学校、社区的贯联，达到"学以致用"的学习目标。此外，可考虑邀请校外对中国民俗艺术学有专长的人士到教室里进行示范、教导，让学生亲身体验、实践操作，这么做不但可以加深学生对这个主题的认识，还可以增强学生学习汉语的动机。

音乐与人们的生活息息相关、密不可分。在美国的华人社区里，不难找到精通中国乐器、戏曲的人才。笔者认为，教师可以邀请这些人士到校，为全校举办一个小型演奏会，激发学生的兴趣和学习动机。

在教学中，教师可让学生进行头脑风暴并提出相关问题，再根据学生所提出的问题设计下一步的教学活动，避免主题过于松散或无法切合学生的学习兴趣。为了让教学活动更为生动活泼，教师可考虑在班上组织一场才艺表演。如果有学生表演了拉小提琴，教师可以在学生表演结束后，放一段演奏二胡的录像。同理，吉他可对琵琶，竖笛可对洞箫，西洋声乐可对中国地方戏曲。学生可以一边看/听一边画出该乐器，用教师事先给出的汉语词汇来描述听到的音乐，这些都有助于加深学生对中西音乐、戏曲的比较和了解。我们都知道五、六年级学生的抽象思考能力仍处于具体操作阶段，教师在进行课程设计时，不论教材还是教法，都要尽量先从学生的已有经验出发，再向外扩展、延深。利用与学生生活息息相关的，看得到、听得到、摸得到的教学材料或教学法绝对是实现高效教学的不二法门。

汉字是当今世上唯一仅存的高度发展的表意文字。虽然学生对学写汉字偶尔会有抱怨，但在授课时，汉字的演变经常是学生喜爱的主题。考虑到五、六年级学生的兴趣和认知能力，笔者认为老师们可以利用美术和游戏方式来进行此主题：教师先简短介绍汉字的演变过程并展示各种字体的范例，再让学生用各种字体来书写自己的中文名字，在每种字体下标明字体名称和该字体出现的朝代及对应公元纪年。教师也可以用行书或草书的字体呈现学生已熟悉的词汇，让学生猜字。现代科技的精进为汉字的学习也提供了不少的帮助，不少平板电脑或智能手机都有中文手写输入功能,这一点是很值得提醒学生关注的。

总之,本主题范围宽广、题材丰富,绝对足以引发学生的学习兴致,教师的发挥空间也无止境。若能针对学生的社会心理发展特征及兴趣进行设计,利用灵活的教学活动来带动课程,一定可为学生提供很好的学习体验。

(八) 主题单元八:情绪与情感表达

随着年龄的增长,学生情绪的种类和强度也变得较为多样。三、四年级的学生对情绪的类别、为何会产生情绪等都有了基本了解。他们明白多种情绪可以同时存在,知道个人的性格或成长背景都会影响情绪表达的方式。此外,由于他们已开始了解情绪表达的规则,所以也学会了隐藏自己的情绪。随着认知能力的提高,五、六年级学生的情绪表达方式会变得更加繁复和微妙,这个年纪的学生也开始学习利用认知策略来调整情绪。青春期的孩子因为控制情绪的大脑前额叶皮质正快速成长,情绪特征多为不稳定、易变、容易产生冲动、正确解码他人情绪的能力较低,他们常会通过音乐、电视、电脑游戏和其他媒介来疏解不愉快的情绪或压力。

五、六年级学生的社交仍然以处理和家庭/家人、学校/朋友的关系为主。他们对异性的兴趣一般还不明显,不及七、八年级学生来的浓厚,所以,会引发他们情绪反应的事件大多与家人、朋友、学业有关。基于此,在探讨本单元主题时,笔者认为除了可继续加强学生的语言能力外,教师可以考虑培养学生的后设情绪认知,例如引导学生审视自己的情绪特性,了解自己应如何觉察和处理情绪以及培养有效的情绪处理策略。以下是面对五、六年级学生时,教师可以提出的几个焦点问题:人有哪些情绪?为什么会产生正面情绪或负面情绪?你用什么方式来表达和调控情绪?你如何解读别人的情绪?对不同的人或在不同的场合里,你的情绪表达方式会有哪些不同?你认为男女生表达情绪的方式有哪些异同?情绪的表达方式有哪些文化差异?中国学生表达情绪和调控情绪的方式与其他国家的学生有什么不同?导致中国学生感受到负面和正面情绪的原因有哪些?

由于此年龄段儿童的认知能力仍倾向于具体操作,自我反思的能力较为不足,教师在引入新概念时,应尽量由浅而深,先具体再抽象,创设的情境必须关系到学生的切身生活。在进行跨文化比较时,教师应该由学生熟悉的自身文化切入目的语文化。为了在跨文化课程中切实对文化观念及行为体现进行面面俱到且深入的比较,教师必须对中美文化,特别是中美文化中的"情绪表达"这个主题,有一定程度的了解。例如:中国人委婉客气,美国人直接；中国人将人情与事理并重，美国人大多习惯于就事论事；中国人讲面子，看关系，重人情，美国人则较少有"丢脸"的想法，经常把成就当作个人努力的结果，与给家人面子无关。由于这些文化特征，两国人处理情绪的方式也存在一些差异。中国人比较依赖亲人、师长或朋友提供的指导，或读启发性名言警句来自我警醒；美国人则多注重隐私，寻求心理咨询。

在课程设计上，教师必须利用这个年纪的孩子感兴趣的或有意义的话题来调动学生学习的积极性。会造成高度情绪反应的例子有很多，如与家人的冲突、参加球赛或上台表演、学业的压力、遭遇欺凌、失去心爱的宠物、参加初中的第一个舞会或记忆中的第一个生日会等。我们都知道情绪是受到外界刺激后，综合感受、认知和行为交互作用后产生的一种心理和生理反应，而不同的人对同一刺激或事件所感受到的情绪会因为当事人的心情、个性、气质而有所不同。通过这些讨论，学生不只可以试着描述个人经验和产生诸如此类的情绪的原因，最重要的是可以了解自己内心的潜在意识以及情绪表现特点。例如，某学生会说："我考试的时候会很紧张，因为我担心考得不理想会叫父母失望。"很明显，这样的学生属于外控倾向型（External Locus of Control）。在分享的过程中，教师可同时对学生的性情作进一步的认识，还可以传授学生一些实用的情绪调控策略。此外，这个单元也是复习之前学习过的话题"爱好/兴趣"的好机会，因为在探讨情绪时，不免会提到这一话题；藉由对兴趣、爱好的追求，人们常常得以疏缓压力、改变情绪，使内心重新获得宁静。

在汉语语言能力的培养方面，教师除了可继续增加词汇量外，还可以考虑加入成语、古代诗词或现代散文作品。在选择时，应优先考虑富含感官信息、韵律清晰、实用性高、书写简易、易引发学生共鸣的成语、俗语、诗词。在教学上可利用故事、绘画、录像短片、肢体动作、歌谣吟唱等利用多重感官的教学方式来加深印象，然后，配以后续的口头表达或写作活动，提高学生灵活运用语言的能力。利用儿童喜欢听故事的特性来讲励志故事，可以让学生在欣赏文学的同时，了解文学、艺术是情感表达的有效媒介，也是将烦恼、忧愁等负面情绪转化成正面情绪的有效方式。学生更可以通过英文教师或图书馆员的协助，寻找以英文撰写的类似的文学著作，阅读后在课堂中用汉语作口头报告或写读后心得。教师可利用的其他教学辅助资源还包括音乐、视频、图片等等。教师如果懂得利用不同的资源教学，让教学动起来，学生的学习动机势必有大幅提高。

总之，情绪这个主题的探讨是非常实用、有趣的，因为人们每天都会面对它。接下来,笔者将就此主题提出一个为期四周的教学计划以供参考。笔者以人的四大基本情绪(快乐、愤怒、悲伤和恐惧)为架构,每周设置一个不同情境来探讨该情绪,同时采用美国外语教学的五大标准(5C)作为语言及文化教学的目标。虽然本书主要适用于沉浸式教学项目,在非沉浸式项目教课的教师仍可根据课程需求在课程内容、课时长短以及难易度上进行适度调整,加以利用。

单元主题:情绪与情感表达
(中文班五年级,四个星期)

课程简介:在这个为期四周的单元教学中,教师可组织学生先藉由观赏《背起爸爸上学》来探讨人类的四大基本情绪(喜怒哀惧),以及由这些基本情绪所衍生的更为复杂的情绪,然后利用个人经历过的事件当话题来继续学习。学生除了要对情绪有深入的认识外,还要反思自己的情绪表达特征、情绪调控方式。在教学目标上,应继续在词汇、句型等语言知识方面进行贯连及扩展,提高学生沟通、表达的能力,此外,还应帮助学生了解会影响情绪表达的文化因素。

引导问题

核心问题	焦点问题
1. 什么是情感?	1. 人为什么会有正面情绪或负面情绪?
2. 我们如何表达情绪和感受?	2. 你用什么方式来表达情绪或调控情绪?
	3. 你如何了解别人的心情?
3. 人们如何以不同的方式来表达情绪和感受?他们为什么会选择不同方式?	4. 对不同的人,或在不同的场合里,你的情绪表达方式会有哪些不同?
	5. 你认为男女表达情绪的方式有差别吗?有哪些差别?
4. 情感的表达方式如何影响人际关系?	6. 情绪的表达方式有哪些文化上的差异?
	7. 中国儿童表达情绪或调控情绪的方式与美国儿童有什么不同?
	8. 导致中国学生产生负面或正面情绪的原因有哪些?

学习目标与技能

- 学生能运用形容不同情绪的词汇和句型来进行口头交流、完成书面报告
- 学生能够口述或书面概括影片或文章所表达的大意
- 学生能举例说明中国儿童情绪表达方式的特征和背后原因
- 学生能比较中、英文在情绪表达方面的语言差异
- 学生能比较并总结中美情绪表达方式的异同

学习评估

a）过程评估：见各周教案详细内容
b）总结评估：小品剧创作演出及散文、短诗发表

每周教学计划

	第一周：快乐是什么？
课程简介	由谈论让学生感到快乐的事物开始，再探讨并呈现快乐的表现方式中的文化异同。最后，学生运用所选词语来创作与生日会有关的小品剧。
教学目标	• 学生能运用形容不同情绪的词汇和句型来进行口头交流、完成书面报告 • 学生能够口述或书面概括影片或文章所表达的大意 • 学生能举例说明中国儿童情绪表达方式的特征和背后原因 • 学生能比较中、英文在情绪表达方面的语言差异 • 学生能比较并总结中美情绪表达方式的异同
教学材料	• 《背起爸爸上学》 • 白色大字报 • 马克笔 • 胶条 • 表达欢乐情绪的传统及现代乐曲、美术作品 • 硬卡纸

(续表)

	第一周：快乐是什么？
演练活动	• 以观看《背起爸爸上学》作为本主题单元的序曲，在剧情的进行过程中，学生须记录剧中人物表现喜怒哀惧的形式。教师在播放电影前，应先介绍剧中的人物角色，让学生熟悉。 • 教师根据片中主人公的求学过程，将影片分成数段。同时将学生分组，再让各小组挑选某时间段，负责做该时间段内的主要观察记录的工作（如此可避免精神疲劳）。非主记小组也可以协助记录，在分享时提出补充。 • 观赏电影后，学生在分别标着"快乐""愤怒""忧伤"和"惊惧"的大字报上书写作答："剧中人物××有哪种情绪反应？他/她为什么会产生该种情绪？该种情绪是如何呈现的？"不善于书写的学生可以选择使用绘画进行阐述。 • 全体学生在"快乐"大字报上回答"快乐是什么？"这一问题。学生可以在大字报上张贴自己"快乐"时的相片来分享快乐的经历。 • 学生阅读全班在大字报上的图画或留言，共同思考快乐的特性。教师引导学生思考：电影中的人物与学生自己、家人表达快乐的方式有何不同？性别、年龄会影响表达快乐的方式吗？如何恰当地表达快乐才不会给别人造成困扰？ • 教师介绍有关"快乐"的词语，呈现表现欢乐情绪的的中国传统或现代音乐、美术作品，让学生练习用有关快乐的词语描述情感。 • 学生用不同的声调、肢体动作或情绪直线图来阐释不同程度的快乐情绪。 • 学生选择表现快乐或复杂情绪的词语，创作情绪符号图。 • 学生结合词语、句型，以"生日会"为主题进行小品剧创作。
学习评估	• 词语的正确书写与解释 • 情绪表达方式的初步比较 • 总结：小品剧创作

(续表)

	第一周:快乐是什么?
建议词语及句型	• 描写"快乐"的词语:开心、高兴、兴奋、惊喜、喜悦、满足、幸福、欢乐、快活、欣喜、痛快、眉开眼笑、笑逐颜开、满面春风、心花怒放、兴高采烈、乐不思蜀、欣喜若狂、喜上眉梢、喜笑颜开、满怀喜悦、怡然自得、喜形于色、乐不可支、喜出望外、沾沾自喜、手舞足蹈 • 掺有其他情绪的词语:惊喜交加、乐极生悲、喜极而泣、亦悲亦喜 • 描写快乐情绪的古诗词:骆宾王《咏鹅》 • 句型:既……又……;一……就……;……得很……;感到……;令……;让……
建议资源	• 《背起爸爸上学》(英文片名:*Going to School with Dad on My Back*,周友朝导演,北京紫禁城影业公司出品) • 传统乐曲试听:中国古曲网① • 现代乐曲试听:www.pandoroa.com • 情绪图标(可进行网络搜索)

	第二周:与家人争吵
课程简介	继续用《背起爸爸上学》一片展开教学,谈论让学生感到生气、愤怒的事物,然后比较父母和学生个人呈现愤怒的方式,再与剧中人物作初步的文化异同比较。
教学目标	• 学生能运用形容不同情绪的词汇和句型来进行口头交流、完成书面报告 • 学生能够口述或书面概括影片或文章所表达的大意 • 学生能举例说明中国儿童情绪表达方式的特征和背后原因 • 学生能比较中、英文在情绪表达方面的语言差异 • 学生能比较并总结中美情绪表达方式的异同
教学材料	• 电影《背起爸爸上学》 • 白色大字报 • 马克笔 • 硬卡纸

---

① http://www.guqu.net

(续表)

	第二周：与家人争吵
演练活动	• 教师重播电影中几个有愤怒情绪的片段，以勾回学生对剧情的记忆。学生阅读"愤怒"大字报上的内容后，在大字报上就"什么是愤怒？""家人做过的让我感到非常愤怒的一件事""对剧中人表达生气的方式的感想"进行书面表达。学生书写完毕后，教师选择性地带领全班关注学生书写的某些内容。 • 引导学生思考：你如何知道家人在生气？性别或年龄和气愤的表现形式有什么关系？别人对你做些什么会让你很生气？如何让别人知道你正在生气？生气时如何消气？ • 教师介绍有关愤怒的词语，让学生思考英文中表达愤怒的词语，再和中文作比较。 • 学生用不同的表情、声调、肢体动作或情绪直线图来阐释不同程度的愤怒情绪。 • 学生选择有关愤怒或复杂情绪的成语，画图表现其含义或创作情绪符号图。 • 学生结合新学到的词语、句型，为上周的"生日会"主题加入一个插曲："爸妈不让我参加好朋友的生日会"，继续进行小品剧创作。
学习评估	• 词语的正确书写与阐释 • 中美情绪表达方式的初步比较 • 总结：小品剧创作
建议词语及句型	• 描写"愤怒"的词语：讨厌、厌恶、憎恨、狂怒、恼火、责备、不满、反感、敌对、怒发冲冠、暴跳如雷、破口大骂、怒目而视、横眉怒视、怒火中烧、怒气冲冲、咬牙切齿、直眉怒目 • 掺有其他情绪的词语：爱恨交加、恼羞成怒、义愤填膺 • 描写"愤怒"的故事："怒发冲冠"与和氏璧的故事（秦王与蔺相如） • 含有愤怒情绪的古诗词：岳飞《满江红·怒发冲冠》 • 句型：因……而……；既然如此……
建议资源	• 《背起爸爸上学》（英语片名：Going to School with Dad on My Back，周友朝导演，北京紫禁城影业公司出品） • 情绪图标（可进行网络搜索）

	第三周：我为什么伤心？
课程简介	教师继续用《背起爸爸上学》一片当作主题，组织学生讨论哪些事物会让人有失落或悲伤的感觉。
教学目标	• 学生能够在交流中运用与"快乐""愤怒""悲伤"情绪有关的词汇/句型 • 学生能够用口述或书面表达方式说明影片或文章拟表达的大意 • 学生能举例说明中国儿童情绪表达方式的特色和背后原因 • 学生能贯连、比较用中英文表达情绪的语言差异 • 学生能比较中美情绪表达的异同
教学材料	• 电影《背起爸爸上学》 • 白色大字报 • 马克笔 • 硬卡纸
演练活动	• 教师重播电影中几个令人伤心的片段，以勾回学生对剧情的记忆。学生阅读"悲伤"大字报上的内容后，在大字报上就"什么是悲伤？""让我悲伤的一件事""对剧中人表达悲伤的方式的感想"进行书面表达。学生书写完毕后，教师选择性地带领全班关注学生书写的内容。 • 引导学生思考：你如何知道你的朋友正在难过？性别或年龄会影响表示痛苦的方式吗？别人对你做什么事或说什么话会让你很难过？心情不好时你会怎么办？ • 教师介绍有关"伤心""难过"的词语，之后让学生思考英文中表达悲伤的词语，再和中文作比较。 • 介绍马致远的《秋思》并让学生利用绘画来阐释其意境，然后讨论、分享自己思念家人的感受，讨论思念家人时会用哪些视觉形象来传达内心情感，再与《秋思》中的视觉形象做比较。 • 学生用不同的表情、声调、肢体动作或情绪直线图来阐释不同程度的悲伤情绪。 • 学生选择有关悲伤或复杂情绪的成语，画图表现其含义或创作情绪符号图。 • 学生分组运用所学词语写一篇关于"悲伤"的散文或短诗，再结合肢体语言、舞蹈动作，或以朗诵的方式在班级中展示该作品。

(续表)

	第三周：我为什么伤心？
学习评估	• 词语的正确书写与阐释 • 中美情绪表达形式的初步比较 • 总结：小组散文/短诗创作及发表
建议词语及句型	• 描写"悲伤"的词语/谚语：伤心；难过；哀愁；忧伤；痛苦；哀痛；唉声叹气；愁眉不展；忍气吞声；泪流满面；肝肠寸断；愁眉苦脸；呼天抢地；泪如雨下；声泪俱下；心如刀割；死去活来；少壮不努力，老大徒伤悲 • 掺有其他情绪的词语：悲喜交集、转悲为喜、乐极生悲 • 描写悲伤情绪的古诗词：马致远《天净沙·秋思》 • 带有悲伤情绪的歌曲：李叔同《送别》 • 句型：除了……以外；不但……而且……
建议资源	• 《背起爸爸上学》（英语片名：Going to School with Dad on My Back，周友朝导演，北京紫禁城影业公司出品） • 情绪图标（可进行网络搜索）

	第四周：心跳和呼吸加快的感觉
课程简介	教师继续用《背起爸爸上学》一片引入教学，组织学生谈论导致剧中人物害怕的事件以及学生自己的生活会让人紧张、害怕或恐惧的事物。
教学目标	• 学生能够在交流中运用与"喜""怒""哀""惧"有关的词汇、句型 • 学生能够比较中美呈现恐惧的语言及"恐惧"情绪表现形式的差异
教学材料	• 电影《背起爸爸上学》 • 电影 Ghost Buster 片段 • 白色大字报 • 马克笔 • 硬卡纸

(续表)

	第四周：心跳和呼吸加快的感觉
演练活动	• 教师重播电影中几个令人感到恐惧的片段，以勾起学生对剧情的记忆。学生阅读"恐惧"大字报上的内容后，在大字报上就"什么是恐惧？"和"让我害怕的一件事"（例如万圣节参观鬼屋或是在游乐园坐云霄飞车）进行书面表达。学生书写完毕后，教师选择性地带领全班关注学生书写的内容。 • 引导学生思考：你怎么知道你的朋友正感到紧张或害怕？性别或年龄会影响表示恐惧的方式吗？什么事会让你又高兴又害怕？什么事会让你又讨厌又害怕呢？ • 教师播放 *Ghost Buster* 与中国僵尸题材电影片段，让学生比较中美鬼故事的异同。 • 教师介绍有关恐惧的词语，然后让学生用不同的表情、声调、肢体动作或情绪直线图来阐释不同程度的恐惧情绪。 • 学生选择有关恐惧或复杂情绪的成语，画图表现其含义或创作情绪符号图。 • 学生分组运用所学词语写一篇会引发读者恐惧的故事，配合背景音乐、声光效果在班上进行展示。
学习评估	• 词语的正确书写与阐释 • 中美鬼故事文化比较 • 总结：故事创作及发表
建议词语及句型	• 描写"恐惧"的词语：刺激、紧张、害怕、畏惧、慌乱、惊恐、七上八下、毛骨悚然、心惊胆战、大惊失色、心惊肉跳、提心吊胆、坐立不安、一身冷汗、魂不附体、目瞪口呆 • 掺有其他情绪的表达：既担心又害怕、又敬重又害怕、又惊又喜 • 句型：复习前三周句型
建议资源	• 《背起爸爸上学》（英语片名：*Going to School with Dad on My Back*，周友朝导演，北京紫禁城影业公司出品） • *Ghost Buster*（美国哥伦比亚影业公司出品） • YouTube 搜索：僵尸电影片段 • 情绪图标（可进行网络搜索）

郑莉玲 著

第六章 建立成就感：
七至八年级阶段的教学

引 言

　　五、六年级学生在生理与心理两方面都较三、四年级学生成熟许多，认知理解力也相对增强，但是学生的创造性思维却仍未成熟，对于非具体形象的信息接收和转换仍然有着许多的困难。五、六年级是个适应和摸索的时期，同时也是青春期的萌芽阶段。到了七、八年级，学生已经慢慢地培养出一套自己的学习模式来应对学校的各项要求，学生的认知发展也逐渐成熟，自我意识也比较强烈，对于许多事物的看法开始反映出个人的喜好及主观评价。比方说，七、八年级的学生喜欢直接表达他们对于课堂中的教学内容、活动设计的好恶，评价老师教学法的优劣，甚至提出个人观点，否定他人的看法。多数学生对于同学的学习表现也敢于直接批评和评论（尤其在团队合作项目的分工过程中）。

　　中学生在七、八年级这个时期的生理成长速度很快，面貌和体态都已开始显出成人的形貌，在穿着打扮上也开始体现出自己的风格和特色；但其心理发展仍处于青少年的懵懂期，对人际关系的处理方式还很简单。比方说，当学生遇到学业上的压力或来自同伴的排挤时，他们常常无法直面问题，很容易陷入自我否定的情绪低潮之中。因此，本阶段课堂活动的设计要注意到青少年的好胜心,避免引发学生之间的能力或成绩比较,并且教师应注意针对学生的不同优点给予正面的鼓励。另外,男女学生因生理发展上的差异,语言和情绪的表达方式也不相同,男生比较偏向于通过肢体语言和动态形式进行表达。因此,团体项目的分工要尽量灵活,以长补短,让每个学生都有机会展现个人特色。

这个阶段社交技能培养的重点在于同情理解力的培养和团队精神的塑造,以及帮助学生学习如何建立良好的人际关系。此外,对意见沟通能力、矛盾与冲突化解能力的训练也相当重要。七、八年级中学生的汉语能力已由能完成基本对话沟通、意见交换进步到可进行团体讨论、表达个人观点。学生们对于生活中的事物已经有一定程度的理解以及逻辑思考,此阶段汉语教学的目标是训练学生多角度看待问题并且提出解决方案的能力,更进一步实现学生对多元文化的认知理解,加深对文化差异的比较。

此年龄段的学习中,课程内容可不仅限于学生自身,而是延伸到生活中的团体组织、自然环境甚至某些全球共同关心的话题。比如说,谈到情绪的表达方式,学生除了了解自己本身的喜怒哀乐之外,对他人的情感沟通和表达方式及其背后的文化因素也应该有基本的认识和尊重。由于资讯的发达,世界信息交流频繁,我们已经进入了无国界的交流时代。课程内容应该尽可能融入更多的文化、历史、地理、文学、艺术、宗教、民俗等多元化的题材,培养学生在跨文化交际中的思考、理解、诠释能力,提升学生对文化差异的认知。

在课程设计中,教师可安排听、说、读、写四方面的深度学习,但应注重坚持"以学生为中心"的教学形式来带动课堂教学。中学生的专注力虽然要比小学生持续的时间长,但是对于不感兴趣的学习内容,更容易产生排斥感,在上课时会表现出不合作或是不在乎的态度。将文化课程以趣味的方式融入教学可以充实语言学习。所以,教师应对课堂时间运用得当,绝对避免"一言堂"式的单向教学。课堂时间要尽可能平均地运用于听、说、读、写四方面的学习、演练活动,每一堂课都要设定短程学习目标。学习目标不要设置过多,通过一步一步地累积才能达到课程主题的最终学习目标。此外,在课堂中的分组讨论沟通、资料调查与搜集、团体创作、组织与阐述、多媒体运用等活动,最好设计为由学生带动学生进行的形式,提高其学习动机。

总而言之,我们现在所教育的学生在未来从事的许多职业是现在不存在的。在未来,学生们将面临一个科技发达的巅峰时代,对学生的创造力和想象力的培养是非常重要的。因此,各年级之间课程的内容在进行衔接与延伸、扩展时,除了应配合学生的认知能力及身心成长情况,符合学生的兴趣发展方向之外,一定要避免一成不变的教学模式和范围狭窄的学习题材。教师们必须跟上时代潮流的发展,随时充实、扩展个人知识领域,灵活运用教学法,不断更新教学内容和教学方式。"学以致用"是教师的目的,更是学生学习的最终目标。

主题说明

(一) 主题单元一:家庭

七、八年级的课程内容应该进阶到对家庭组合方式的多样性、家庭成员之间的相处、亲子之间的期望与冲突等问题的理解,并由此延伸到探讨中国家庭与美国家庭的不同,比如说鼓励与处罚方式的差异、对男女的不同要求、儿女对家庭的责任和义务等方面。学生应可从此处发现文化差异,并能思考其中的优劣,来理解中国家庭中的亲子关系。

在本单元中,不妨由学生的家庭规矩来切入,讨论家庭成员之间的关系以及来自家庭的压力。学生经过交流后,对于父母和兄弟姐妹之间的相对关系便有了一个基本的认知,教师可由此带入中国家庭的伦理观念来说明各家庭成员地位的差别以及个人在家庭中的权利和义务。教师可重点说明男孩在中国家庭中承担着"传宗接代"和赡养父母的责任,在家族中的重要地位,以及女孩对家务的负担和照顾老幼的义务。当学生学习到因为文化的差别,每个人在生活中必须面对不同的家庭压力时,许多观念的冲突会在讨论之中体现出来,尤其是父母对儿女的期望和要求。另外,中国传统的"重男轻女"的观念和"不孝有三"的说法对学生来说都是非常有趣的讨论话题。

教师可以先以一个"制定家规"的分组活动来引发学生对课程内容的兴趣:让学生以小组为单位制定"家规",然后各组轮流作报告。许多学生都会从自身的角度出发来订立规矩,而且大多以反对家庭对他们现有的束缚为标准。在各组的互相比较中,教师很容易总结出学生父母对他们的要求和期望。接下来可安排学生阅读一篇相关的故事或剪报,让他们针对文章中的人物遇到的不同问题提出个人的观点和解决方案。为了使学生对中国家庭的传统价值观念有更进一步的理解,可以组织学生欣赏某影片,请他们随时记录影片情节中与西方文化存在观念差别之处。观看影片的同时,教师应该进行段落性的简单提问,引导学生对某现象的关注和思考。《家有儿女》[①]是一套非常适合课堂教学使用的教学辅助材料。它是中国的一部少儿题材的情景喜剧,讲述了两个离异家庭重新组合后发生在父母和三个孩子间的各种趣事。这部电视剧不但体现了中国父母对儿女的教育观念,也同时呈现了手足之间的伦理亲情。

建议教师在本单元加入相关成语或谚语、诗歌的教学,例如:饮水思源(教育学生不忘父母养育之恩),家有一老如有一宝(尊重老人),母子连心(阐述亲子间的默契),唐诗《游子吟》等,培养学生对文化更深一层的认识。建议教师将本单元要学习的成语中的各字分别制作成字卡,以分组竞赛的方式,让学生用字卡把成语组合出来。这个活动由思考字的排列组合发展至理解成语表达的意境,对学生的思考很有挑战,也很有文字运用的趣味性。学生经过多次的错误后,对成语会有深刻的印象。

在中国心理咨询网亲子版[②]有一篇题为《三代同堂孩子如何管教》的转帖,其内容第一段可作为小品剧本。教师可以利用此剧本让学生表演,呈现三代同堂家庭之间的矛盾关系。文章对两代家长之间教育观念的差别也有详细的探讨,是个很不错的教学辅助材料。

进行此单元的学习评价时可以考虑让学生分析中、西家庭文化的优、缺点,配合教师的要求改写上述故事结局,并以幻灯片简报或表演的方式来呈现。另外也可让学生以图文配合,编写故事书的形式进行创作,表现相关故事情节。

课程内容在最后的阶段要延伸到现代中国家庭面临的新问题,让学生探讨目前中国的"计划生育"政策对家庭中男女地位的影响。学生可以上网搜寻资料,在整理的过程中进一步了解当代中国家庭和社会形态的变化,比方说,三代同堂的家庭已渐渐减少。如有可能,可组织学生举办一场小型辩论会,以辩论形式展现所学知识,锻炼语言表达能力。

---

① 参考网页:http://dianshiju.cntv.cn/city/jiayouernv/videopage/index.shtml
② http://bbs.xlzx.com/dispbbs.asp?boardid=10&Id=153256

(二) 主题单元二:食物与中药

在五、六年级的课程中,学生对中国南北方的代表食物、就餐的座位安排、基本的烹饪方法和食材都有了基本的了解。七、八年级的内容则衔接之前的内容,更多进入到有关文化层面的学习。中国菜的烹饪方式、食材、作料,餐桌上主客之间的礼貌用语和应对礼仪,中国人对于食物搭配的讲究和食疗观念,都可以在这个单元中引入。这个主题的教学时间可以稍微长一些,分成不同的阶段,循序渐进。

对于学生来说,上中国餐馆吃饭已经是很平常的事了。只要说到中国食物,学生们都能很快列出自己最爱吃的几道菜。那么,就从认识菜单来开始我们的主题吧!此时可用"猜猜看"的游戏来热身:教师先准备好五道菜的图片,发给学生一张生词记录单和一份菜名填写卷,学生们应一边辨认五道菜一边思考菜肴的名称,同时写出菜名、颜色和味道。在此活动中,教师可引导学生学习与味道相关的生词并在生词记录单上记下这些词语。在公布正确答案之前,请学生说出所写的答案,猜对最多的人获胜并可得到一个"幸运饼干"。教师应提醒学生,"幸运饼干"只有在西方的中国餐馆才有。(生词记录单可以让学生记下自己想知道的生词,经过学生的自主学习,学生对生词的意义和运用方式会有更深刻的理解。)

认识了菜单后,可指定学生各带一种中国菜常用的香料/作料到课堂中来。香料/作料必须装入小盒内,不可标示任何记号。在授课时,首先,教师展示香料/作料实物(另外准备的)并引入其名称,学生将所学名称记在生词表中。然后,教师将学生带来的香料/作料盒标上号码,摆放在不同的地方。学生应用三种感官(嗅、触、味)认出每一种香料/作料,并在纸上写出对应的名称。在活动中学生可以参考生词表,但活动必须限时。两三轮的辨认之后,学生对各种香料/佐料的名称和气味就有了很深刻的认识。这是一个学习物品名称的有趣的活动方式。

教师也可以将事前准备好的作业单分发给学生,布置一项课后作业,即让学生回家后查出作业单上列出的几种常用香料/作料的来源。学生经过这个小小的搜寻活动之后,对于香料/作料的历史会有基本的认识。接下来的活动是让学生设计一个在餐馆中因不满意饭菜口味而引发抱怨的情景对话,对话中必须详细描述菜品的味道和其中使用的香料/作料,再一次复习菜名和香料/作料名。

中国菜的基本烹饪方式有蒸、煮、炒、炸等,教师最好以影像展现这些过程,帮助学生更好地了解其中的差别。此外,还可以顺便介绍几道中国的名菜,包括其涉及的食材、作料和做法,让学生有机会认识烹饪方式和味道间的相互关系。笔者曾经给学生看过一个做家常豆腐的视频,其中把过程说得很详细。学生要一边听一边看,同时也要把这道菜所需要的食材和做法记下来,然后模拟电视烹饪节目,表演做菜的过程(学生必须边做边说明)。经过这样的演练,学生不但学会了写食谱,也学会了做菜的基本流程。若是学校有厨房设备,教师可以先教学生切菜的基本方式,比方怎样切"丝"、切"片"、切"碎末",再示范两三道菜的做法。在每一次教师示范的同时,学生必须听、看、写,也就是听着、看着教师一边做一边讲解,同时将食材及做法记下来。然后,学生可依照自己记录的食谱进行实际操作,看看谁做出来的味道与教师的最为接近。

　　经过三次的实际烹饪演练后,学生对于香料/作料的名称、某些菜肴的做法也都十分熟悉了。最后,可以举行一个美食竞赛活动:将学生分组,给每组发一份不同的食谱,让学生分组准备材料并在厨房中进行实际操作,看哪一组成品的颜色和味道最好。本活动的目的是让学生对中国菜的烹饪方式及食物的色、香、味有个比较完整的认识。若学校没有厨房设备,教师不妨要求学生录制视频:请学生选择一道菜的食谱,回家在自家厨房中进行实际操作并以录像机摄录整个过程。当然,学生必须完全用中文来解说食物材料和烹饪步骤。学生们都非常喜爱这项活动,并且常有令人惊喜的创意演出。

　　在进行关于到中国人家里做客时的应对礼节、食物的象征意义和中国人的饮食习惯等内容的教学时,建议教师采用短剧表演的方式:笔者通常喜欢自己编写短剧(短剧内容应该综合运用本单元的生词和句型),然后安排学生分组,每人选择自己的角色并进行表演。从表演中,学生可很快理解并学会相关礼仪。当然,表演的场景安排应尽量真实,人物的打扮也必须趣味化。同时,也可配合一份关于中国人饮食礼仪的简短资料阅读,让学生对就餐的座位安排、食物取用方式、喝酒的习惯以及主宾之间的应对礼仪有个比较完整的认识。

　　至于食疗的观念及中、西医的比较,则是扩展性的学习内容。在这部分的教学中,可要求学生读一些图文材料,做简单的阅读理解练习,从而引入基本的介绍。《新实用汉语课本》(北京语言大学出版社出版)的第四册第四十九课中有一篇有关"头痛医脚"的对话,教师可以放映与课本配套的光碟让学生观赏,介绍中医和西医的看诊方式及对人体认识的差别。

如有可能,也可邀请中医医生到课堂中实际展示中医的诊断原则(望、闻、问、切),介绍几种生活中常见的植物药材,然后简单地比较一下中、西方在医疗中常用植物药材的颜色、样子、味道和功能。教师若是能带些中国人在日常生活中常食用的保健品来,让学生看看、尝尝,也可大大增强学生对中国人所谓的"食疗"的理解。此单元的作业为完成一份依据课堂上所学内容设计的问卷。为回答问卷中的问题,学生须搜寻相关资料,有能力的学生可进行进一步的尝试——完成一份报告,简要介绍中、西医概况并比较二者的相同与相异之处。每个学生的能力不同,对于学习能力较强的学生,教师可多鼓励,引导学生思考更深层次的问题,形成自己的观点并举例说明,支持该论点。

本单元中可引入的与饮食相关的成语/谚语有:饥肠辘辘;众口难调;无米之炊;食之无味,弃之可惜;因噎废食;暴饮暴食;药补不如食补;心急吃不了热豆腐;肉包子打狗——一去不回;早吃饱,午吃好,晚吃少。教师可从中进行选择,配合教学。此外,"一瓢饮"(出自《论语·雍也》)从个人饮食的角度表现了对人生的态度,可以在七、八年级作为补充材料,培养学生对饮食人生观的理解。

(三) 主题单元三:节庆活动

谈到中国的传统节庆和当代节日,不论在哪一个年龄段的课程中都一定会涉及美工制作和庆祝活动。因此,在这个主题单元中,我们可以配合节庆的时间来设计教学内容。应注意课时不应该太长,因为节庆一过,活动的气氛就不再热络了。

在庆祝传统节日时,老师们都会设计相同的活动,比如每一年的中国春节会组织大家写春联、包饺子、剪窗花、说"年"的故事、进行新年歌舞表演等;在端午节、中秋节时,则组织学生包粽子或是打月饼,述说节日的由来和传说。但是七、八年级的学生并不会因此而生倦,他们还是很享受这些活动的乐趣,所以这些活动都应该持续下去。许多以往由教师一手包办的筹备工作,现在可以一项一项地交给学生,由学生自行负责,例如节目单的编辑、表演活动的设计和彩排、舞台布置、道具制作、广告传单张贴等。

中国的当代节日,如教师节、国庆节、儿童节、情人节、劳动节等,以及西方的万圣节、感恩节、圣诞节、国庆日,我们都应该适时带入课程,这些都是最好的生活文化学习机会。传统节日的由来及其庆祝活动对七、八年级的学生来说已经耳熟能详，因此，本单元的学习重点可以设定为对中国农历、黄历、节庆禁忌的认识，或介绍传统食物的代表意义及其与地理气候的关系，节庆对人类生活的影响以及传统节日在不同时代中的差别。

　　由节日传说故事来引入主题是一种很好的方式。比方在讲述农历七月七日（七夕）"牛郎与织女"的故事时，可引导学生由牛郎星和织女星的星象排列了解中国农历与公历的不同。同时也可教学生看"黄历"，学会辨别凶吉，了解中国人如何利用农历安排生活中的重要活动。此时甚至可以让学生模仿中国农历设计一份未来的新历法，理解中国人如何根据"黄历"为某些活动选择"吉日"。学生对于这样的活动会很有兴趣。

　　谈到中国节庆中的禁忌，教师可事先分派学生针对各国不同的节庆禁忌进行资料、图片搜集，在课堂上列出不同国家各节日的禁忌并讨论其背后的原因。之后，再整理收集到的资料并将其制作成壁报进行展示。学生可进行分组讨论，提出因为文化禁忌而引发的纷争事件并提出避免纷争的办法。如果能以学生在现实生活中知道的一些新闻事件为例进行讨论，则更能引起共鸣，帮助学生进一步了解节庆禁忌背后的文化因素，学习尊重不同民族、地区的礼仪和入乡随俗的态度。

　　传统节庆中少不了食物。在节庆活动中，教师每每会带着学生一起制作美味可口的传统佳肴。七、八年级的学生可以在更深的层面中学习传统食物的制作原料，了解当地的地理气候，进而理解食物的代表意义。教师可以先带几样出产于不同地区的粮食、蔬果到课堂上展示，请学生猜测其生长的时节、地区。之后，再展示一张大的气候地理图，让学生思考不同的地区会生产出不同农作物的原因并解说地理、气候对植物生长的影响。学生对此有了初步的理解后，教师可以分别选择中国、美国某节庆中的传统食物（课前预备图片），配合气候图，让学生谈谈这种传统食物的食材选择与当地气候的关联性，同时也可引入两个节庆的来源。比方说，美国人为什么会选择"火鸡""南瓜"作为感恩节的食物？为什么"饺子""腊肉"是中国春节中不可或缺的食品？学生可由这样的一个话题展开，探讨食物和当地气候及地理环境的相对关系，以及节庆食物制作的意义和其中蕴含的期望。最后，可让学生选择一个国家，制作一张该国的大地图，在不同地区加入文字说明和图片，展现各地的地理特点、气候特征、主要农作物、节庆活动食物及其象征的意义。

　　节庆对人类生活有哪些重要影响？谈论这一问题时，可以先以学生们最喜爱的节庆为主题来展开话题，请学生谈谈他们自己对节日寄予的期待，分享节日中最难忘的回忆。然后，让学生想象所有的节庆消失后的人类生活，分组制作一张海报来表现"节日消失后的未来"。学生可以用各种不同的形式和材料进行创作，完成后须上台说明海报表达的意义。这是一种让学生进行逆向思考的教学方式，由于学生无法想象圣诞节或是感恩节不存在了的情况，在讨论的过程中，他们会慢慢开始发现自己的心情和对节日的期盼受到了严重的影响，然后会意识到自己的失落感，同时意识到节庆的存在对个人生活的意义。这个活动除了可以刺激学生的创作、表现能力，同时还可以提高学生对话题讨论的兴趣和热情。

现代科技大大缩短了人与人之间的距离，不同地区的节庆活动因而开始互相影响。比方说，现在中国人也开始在圣诞节开派对，在情人节送巧克力；受到西方潮流的影响，一些之前中国并不存在的节日，也慢慢地演变成中国新的节庆日。为了让学生了解东、西方如何相互影响，教师可以先让学生列出现代社会中沟通的各种方式，讨论不同国家、地区在语言、生活习惯和时尚方面的共同点，进而讨论节日庆祝中的相同之处，思考其中的原因。教师可以布置一个"之前之后"资料收集竞赛，将学生分组并指派各组搜集、剪贴表现不同年代流行趋式的图片，比方说服装、发型、流行歌曲、明星、生活物品等。通过这项活动，学生会明白，随着资讯的日益丰富和各国间的开放交流，生活在不同地方的人正在经历某种程度上的同化。受到西方文化的影响，中国人对西方节日也逐渐认同，这就是"同化"的体现。

传统的节庆相传至今，有了什么样的改变？为什么？教师们不妨带领学生走出课堂，到自己生活的社区进行课外学习活动。学生可自行设计调查问卷，到当地的中国城（或中华会馆、华人服务中心、老人院）访问不同年龄的老人，了解他们在童年时期庆祝传统节日的方式，发现其中的改变之处并分析原因，写一篇简单的报告。这样一来，不仅可以给学生创造与当地华人沟通的机会，也能让他们体验另一种不同文化中的人文环境。

（四）主题单元四：地理与旅游

"旅游"是个很实用也很有趣的主题。在这个主题下，七、八年级的教学重点为：让学生学习使用地图，了解地理位置、方位与坐标；帮助学生了解不同时间、空间的区别；着重培养学生处理旅行中常见的状况的能力。

首先，在单元开始之前，教师可先请学生各带5件旅游中带回的纪念品到课堂上来，要求学生们说明物品的名称，描述物品样式，说一说这些物品分别是从哪儿带回来的，让自己回忆起哪些事情，也可以说说旅行的乐趣。然后，请学生看地图，找出自己去过的几个国家，写出其地理位置（包括四个方向上的邻国和海洋名称）。此外，还应请学生查看中国在地图上的地理方位。

之后可引导学生进入主题"到中国旅行"。旅行之前应该知道些什么呢？首先，让学生学看中文网页上中国某城市的气象预报，了解当地的天气状况，思考适当的穿着。此时可以先让学生分组讨论网页上呈现的资料内容，在学生掌握之后，再请各组分别选择一个中国的城市，上网了解其气象资料，然后请学生模仿气象员播报当地的一周天气概况并且提出出行建议。这个活动的目的是引导学生使用中文网页并且帮助他们看懂相关讯息（亦可以当地公交车、火车时刻表为范例）。了解天气后，可再发给学生一份分类调查表，请学生上网搜索旅行相关资料，比方说货币的汇率、是否要办理签证、签证手续时间、签证的费用、时差、行李重量及件数规定、当地食物、语言和应该注意的禁忌等。学生应该学习"入乡随俗"的观念，除了准备旅游必备物品外，旅行之前也要对当地的风土人情有基本的认识。最后，请学生就搜集到的资料，列出一份到中国旅行的物品明细单。

教师可以更进一步，让学生制作一个旅游广告板，训练学生的口语表达能力。教师先展示一个中文旅游介绍网页，让学生了解如何从不同的角度（如气候特色、历史文化、节庆活动、当地美食、人情风俗等）来介绍一个地区/城市。在教学中，可先以一个城市为例进行练习：将学生分组，每组负责说明一个方面。学生明白介绍的方法后，须选择中国的一个主要城市，查找以下内容：1)地理位置；2)气候/季节；3)当地五种特色；4)当地有名的餐馆及小吃；5)风俗节庆；6)相关图片。资料齐全之后，学生须在此基础上设计一份七天的旅行计划。这项活动的目标是训练学生的资料组织能力。完成旅游计划后，学生可利用搜集到的资料及图片制作一个广告板。学生可结合广告板中的内容，模拟旅行社的代表，介绍当地的特色、历史以及旅游价值。最后全班投票，选出最值得一游的地方。票选的标准是各组的旅游计划是否周全，有关当地的文化、历史、景点的信息是否丰富。票选结束后，教师可组织学生们就票选结果进行总结讨论，在白板上列出该处值得一游的主要原因。

在讨论中，教师可以引导学生进行延伸讨论："旅行将如何影响你对当地的认识?"当然,如有影片的辅助,本单元的教学会更有趣味。笔者曾经在课堂上播放过《中国月亮》这部影片,让学生一边观赏影片一边记录中美文化的不同之处。这部影片描写了一个美国人在中国的故事,影片里的人物很有趣,对中国的风俗、生活也有深度表现。其中有一些很有趣的文化冲突,非常适合作为参考材料。(影片前面有几段主角在美国生活的内容,不太适合用于课堂教学)结束观赏后,教师可以组织个简单的问题抢答游戏,了解学生对影片的理解程度,然后谈谈汉语在几大主要使用区中的异同。

因为笔者所在学校八年级学生的毕业旅行地是中国,因此在教学中可让学生练习填写入境表格,回答入关问题,认读航班信息表、列车时刻表。

本单元建议引入的成语有:跋山涉水、扶老携幼、呼朋引伴、风餐露宿、美不胜收、乐不思蜀、流连忘返。此外,还建议教师介绍描写游子旅途中心情的唐诗《枫桥夜泊》。

(五)主题单元五:历史、政治与宗教

谈到历史、政治、宗教这样的学习主题时,学生们都不太感兴趣,也非常缺乏学习动力。主要原因是这方面的中文材料的文字叙述常常十分冗长、生硬。笔者发现,很多历史方面的中文书籍都非常缺乏彩色图片,加上其中有很多因宗教、政治等各种错综复杂的原因引发的战争,很难引起学生的阅读兴趣。一般学生通常对与自身生活不直接相关的事物都不太有耐心和兴趣,除非这些内容涉及个人的兴趣、嗜好。因此,教师一定要摒弃传统的教学方式,尽量运用与学生现代生活密切相关的话题切入课程。还有,本主题的教学应该以开拓学生的国际视野以及培养对不同文化的理解为重。在此教师切忌输入个人主观印象,要忠实呈现历史中各方面的实际材料,引导学生理解、思考。

在本主题中,针对七、八年级的教学目标是帮助学生了解中国文明的起源、重要的历史朝代、传统社会阶层的划分对现代人的影响、政治管理方式的变化、宗教在人民生活中扮演的角色以及中国与其他国家的来往。这个主题中内容繁多,教师可以选择自己的教学重点,将课程再细分为几个不同的小单元。另外,本单元文化方面的内容多偏向于信息文化,从日常生活入手,利用学生感兴趣的事物来引入这样的内容是一项很有挑战性的工作,同时也是相当不容易实现的目标。不过,教师可以先用学生耳

熟能详的一些故事、影片或者是小说来引起他们的兴趣。例如,《花木兰》这部动画电影对古代中国和北方民族之间的战争、万里长城的重要性以及中国百姓对皇帝的顺服等都有很多呈现。教师可节选出影片的几个片段让学生观赏,再逐步引导他们进入学习主题。这是一部由西方人制作的影片,其中有许多对话和礼节是以西方人的方式来表现的,也正因为如此,这也是一个让学生理解文化误解的好机会。

欣赏影片后,教师可布置一项作业:让学生搜集资料,画出花木兰所处时代的中国地图,并注明当时的疆域分界线。然后展示少数民族分布图,让学生了解汉族和游牧民族居住地的差异。此时,教师可以回溯汉族文明的发源地:发给学生中国地图的拼图,限时请学生分组完成拼图并在地图中找出中国的两大河流,猜猜哪一条河的流域是中国文明的发源地。每组的学生都应有机会表达他们的意见。这个活动最主要的目的是让学生经过思考,表达自己的意见,至于所提出的意见是否正确,教师不应过多评论。只要曾经经历过这样的思考、表达过程,学生就能记住"中国文明的发源地是黄河流域",达到学习目的。

中国历史上朝代繁多,学生不可能完全理解并且记住每一个朝代。建议教师先让学生写出他们知道的中国朝代、各朝皇帝、历史战争和著名故事。教师可从中选出多数学生有兴趣的部分,然后将学生分组,为每一组指定一个朝代,要求各组以剪贴、歌剧、短剧、绘图等各种形式来呈现那个朝代的历史、文化。每组轮流上台报告时,其它组中的每个学生都必须在教师事先准备好的记录表上记下自己从每一组的报告中学到的重点。此活动的目的是让学生以自己喜爱的方式来表现对历史的理解并互相观摩、学习。在活动之前,教师应该留出至少两个小时的课堂时间供学生上网查询资料。因为在课堂上,教师可以随时掌握学生资料搜寻的方向并随时提供建议。教师也应该提供一些网页,以免学生在搜寻网页时浪费太多时间。另外,也可以带领学生到学校的图书馆查询所需资料。对教师而言,培养学生利用不同的资源进行学习的能力也是一项非常重要的教学任务。

为使学生了解中国传统的社会阶层、社会秩序及其对现代人的影响,教师可以设计一个类似于美国的"Revolution"的纸牌游戏:将原游戏中的国王、皇后、佃农和奴隶改换成士、农、工、商,让学生分组玩游戏,熟悉游戏中的角色。游戏之后,请学生根据自己的理解判断各角色的重要性,按照重要性排出先后顺序。此时也可以将中国的科举考试制度带入主题来讨论，请学生就其利弊进行辩论。接下来，教师可再提供一段表现中国学生在学校生活的视频给学生观看，让学生从中发现中国、美国学校在上课时间、学习科目、学校服装、课堂礼节、校规方面的不同之处；也可以提供一篇有关升学压力的故事，让学生讨论中国人看重学校教育的原因。新加坡有一部电影叫《小孩不笨》，对华人家庭中的孩子在学校承受的学习压力以及来自家庭、父母的压力都有很详细的描述。经由影片，学生能理解中国人对教育的看重源于对孩子将来发展的期许，这也是传统阶级观念对现代生活的影响。

学习中国政治管理方式的变化时，学生得先了解皇帝治理国家的方式，然后才能理解其与政府管理的差别。电影《末代皇帝》的片段欣赏是个很能吸引学生的热身活动，大家对中国宫廷中的种种事物都非常好奇，小皇帝在皇宫中生活的剧情尤其能够吸引学生。观看影片后，可以组织一个"扮皇帝"的游戏，用抽签方式来决定"皇帝"人选。当皇帝的人应提出三条治理国家的新政策，其他学生则为不同阶层的人民，须就皇帝的新政发表个人意见。在这项活动中，学生可以思考皇帝对百姓生活的影响，练习由"皇帝"和"百姓"的不同角度出发分析问题。

为了加深学生对皇帝制管理对百姓生活的影响的认识，此时也可引入"杨贵妃"和"武则天"的故事以及皇宫逸事。这些都颇能提高课堂学习的乐趣，尤其在配合图片来讲故事的时候。当然，教师在讲故事时一定要掌握好重点、方向，不时丢个问题给学生或请学生临场表演一段剧情，让学生在听故事的过程中与教师不断互动，如此才能保持学生的学习兴趣并加深他们对内容的印象。

之后，再请学生参考美国政府的管理方式，分别列出"一人管理"和"多党政府管理"的优缺点并根据所列内容选择自己支持的管理方式。至于多党政府和一党政府的区别，可以通过"模拟会议"的方式呈现：学生分别模拟多党政府和一党政府中会议的组织、表决方式，体会"多党"和"一党"之间的差别。在笔者供职的学校中，八年级的学生每年都到本州首府的议院观摩会议的过程，学生可由此对"多党执政"的管理方式有更深刻的理解。如有可能，建议教师安排学生体验类似的真实情境，一定能达到事半功倍的效果。

谈到宗教时，《西游记》里的故事很能引发学生们的兴趣。佛教的"好生之德"以及善恶观念都在《西游记》里的人物生活中表现了出来。教师可让学生从《西游记》的故事中了解佛教的基本教义，进而了解宗教信仰在人类生活中所具有的约束力和道德行为影响力。学生们来自不同的文化背景,成长的环境也不尽相同,所信仰的宗教当然也各有不同。教师可以让学生们按照不同信仰分组,轮流为大家说明本组宗教的教义,展示一些宗教图片、音乐或物品,说明在生活中必须遵从的礼仪和禁忌。这样的分享可以培养学生对不同宗教的尊重与理解,同时也可使其了解宗教对个人生活的意义和文化影响。

到二十世纪为止,中国和世界哪些国家曾经有过哪些交流关系?这对中国有什么影响?为回答这个问题,教师可组织学生进行信息搜寻竞赛:1)教师列出一张蔬果名单,列举从其他国家传入中国的各种蔬果,例如玉米、核桃、石榴、菠菜、胡萝卜、葡萄、香菜、西瓜、无花果、辣椒、茄子、绿豆等,让学生比赛搜寻这些蔬果传入中国的时间。2)请学生查出哪些中国技术传到了中亚、西亚和欧洲。3)请学生查出佛教、基督教、伊斯兰教传入中国的时间。经由这个游戏,学生可以了解中国与其他国家来往、交流的历史。另外,还可以再补充有关马可·波罗、玄奘、成吉思汗、郑和等历史人物的短篇阅读材料作为课后作业,要求学生阅读后在课堂上概述所读内容并发表读后感想(针对中国与外国之间交流的看法),同时由学生互相提问、质询。如此不但可以扩充学生的知识层面,也可以加深学生对材料的理解,提升思考能力。

建议教师到图书馆找一些有关汉朝"丝绸之路"及唐朝鼎盛时期对外交流的历史书作为教学参考。通常英语版的历史书中图片非常丰富,笔者曾经展示过一些表现唐朝长安城中交易场景的图片,让学生发现交易双方的服装、物品、发型的不同之处,引导学生们思考交流活动所产生的影响。此时教师还可以布置一项到图书馆借书的任务,请学生寻找与20世纪之前中国与世界的来往相关的图片和历史书籍,带到课堂上来展示并轮流报告所读内容。听报告的学生应记笔记,然后综合笔记内容画出一张时间表,针对有关中国和世界其他国家的交流情况写一篇题为"世界对中国的影响"的文章。我们希望学生从阅读、听报告的过程出发,总结所听内容,再根据个人的理解,形成并阐述自己的观点。

历史是活的,只要教师能不断创新,多运用各式各样的材料配合活动的进行,随时把握学生的兴趣方向,对学生周围的事物有一定的敏感度,历史课将不再枯燥无味。

本单元的成语、谚语和诗句应由教师选择并配合不同的重点内容带入教学,具体内容请参考主题总表。

（六）主题单元六：朋友、娱乐与时尚

"朋友、娱乐与时尚"这个主题单元的教学目标是让学生了解中国文化对"朋友"的定义及其对人生的影响，进而学习如何建立良好的人际关系，以及流行时尚如何影响社会价值观和社交关系。

随着年龄增长，七、八年级学生的自我意识也逐渐增强，对于任何事情，他们都有话要说。这时候学生的心理状态很微妙，也很敏感。笔者认为，七年级是个人风格的形成期，八年级是自我形象和格调展现的阶段。对于七、八年级的学生来说，对朋友的选择常会以学校社交关系为主要前提。换句话说，在校园里是否受到欢迎或是被崇拜意味着他们的社交成功与否。此时，朋友的选择标准常常取决于一个"酷"字，"酷友"远比所谓的"益友"更为重要。

如何进入教学主题而不引起学生（特别是一些没有太多朋友或是常被当作话题取笑的学生）的过度敏感？建议老师将学生分组，要求他们以"什么是朋友"为题创作四格漫画，用漫画的形式表现朋友间的相处之道。创作完成后，各组须面对其他小组进行展示、分享。本活动结束后，教师可以请学生在卡片上写出三个形容词描述"朋友"的意义，并将这些词都粘贴在一张事先准备好的壁报纸上，展示给全体学生。如果时间允许，教师还可以让学生听一首中国歌星周华健的《朋友》，要求他们一边听一边记下歌词，然后进行朗读（朗读过程中可以互相纠错）。朗读结束后，教师重播歌曲并要求学生尽量跟唱。最后，请学生写出三种自己最需要朋友在身旁的情况，并轮流念出自己所写的内容，教师则将这些内容都贴在壁报上。

经过这个活动，学生已经对"朋友"有了基本的概念。这时不妨玩个名为"谁是你的朋友"的游戏：抽一名学生甲到台前，向其提出几个关于个人嗜好的问题。甲回答问题之前，台下的学生须写下他们猜测的甲的答案。甲回答问题后，台下的学生相互展示所写内容，看谁写的和甲回答的一致。这个游戏可以增强学生之间的互动。然后，教师播放一段由韩国歌手安在旭演唱的《朋友》的音乐电视。这段视频中随歌曲穿插了几段小故事。学生观赏后，可参考其表现手法，以《朋友》为背景音乐，分组制作一段五分钟的视频。制作之前，老师可以提出一些问题，让学生思考如何以视频方式将其表现出来。例如：如何选择朋友？朋友可以为你做什么？有哪些方式可以表达你对朋友的关心？如何保持朋友之间的情谊？朋友

之间可用来联系情感的娱乐活动有哪些？学生可自由发挥，完成视频录制/制作，然后在全班范围中进行分享。除了分享视频之外，学生还要阐述他们对"朋友"的定义，并提出针对朋友之间交往方式的建议。学校若无可提供的摄像设备，可要求学生结合照片和文字完成上述任务。

教师可以分享自己的交友经历，引导学生进入"朋友之间如何互相影响"的话题，同时可带入中国人对子女交友选择的要求和对活动场所的限制，例如"近朱者赤，近墨者黑"的择友观念，和朋友出游的场合忌讳，男女之间的相处方式和行为，服装的穿着等等。教师可设计一份问卷，请学生以自己的父母或是学校的老师为采访对象，借由采访了解不同年代的人对"朋友"的定义、交友方式、情感表达方式以及社交场合选择的不同看法，然后形成一个报告并以 PPT 的形式呈现。课后还可安排学生阅读一篇有关"墨子对染丝的联想"的短文，要求他们读后写一篇有关"朋友如何影响你的生活"的文章。

对于流行时尚，不论是发型、服装、还是电影、小说、音乐、舞蹈、化妆，学生们都有说不完的话。笔者在教授地理历史课时，发现学生们对历史人物的肖像以及服装造型都非常好奇，甚至喜欢临摹不同朝代的服饰、发型，也会谈论当时社会的美丑标准。所以，建议教师给学生布置一个图片搜集任务，让他们用电脑搜寻中国 20 世纪 70、80、90 年代和现在的流行服装、发型、音乐、流行语，然后将所有图片、文字资料综合起来，剪贴制作成一份题为"过去与现在"的剪报（在图片之间穿插文字说明）。或者根据搜集到的图片，组织一个"时装表演"，活跃一下学习气氛。然后，请学生就搜集到的资料分组编排小品剧，表现"流行时尚及其对人际关系的影响"。最后，教师可组织学生讨论"时尚品牌如何反映社会价值观"，学生在讨论之前必须准备一些实际事件作为案例，支持自己的论点。

本单元建议引入的成语有：一诺千金；莫逆之交；志同道合；生死之交；手足之情；义无反顾；忘恩负义；见义勇为；近朱者赤，近墨者黑。教师也可讲述中国古代管仲与鲍叔牙的友情故事。

（七）主题单元七：艺术与科学创造

提到中国的艺术，一定少不了与传统文化、节日有关的民间剪纸、窗花、香囊、荷包、皮影、说书以及戏曲等民间艺术。在传统节庆主题中，学生们由幼儿园/一年级开始，每年都会有机会体会制作的乐趣，当然也会重温节庆的意义。因此，在七、八年级的"艺术与科学创造"主题中，笔者建议:七年级的教学内容侧重于中国的书法艺术、国画和乐曲。(此阶段中学生的领悟力和欣赏能力逐渐增强,适于培养学生的深度赏析能力。)八年级时则可引入中国的四大发明、文字演变、语言和科技等内容。

笔者以往喜欢直接以艺术画作的欣赏进入主题。具体方法为:先引导学生观赏几幅山水、花鸟画,说明"工笔"和"写意"两种画法的不同,同时让学生亲自用毛笔画几幅水墨画,深刻认识到两种画法的差别;之后,请学生就教师展示的几幅国画的内容说说自己的感受和看法。教师可鼓励学生将自己喜爱的中国画带到课堂上来,说说喜爱它的原因,或该作品对自己的心情有什么样的影响。再则,也可以展示几幅有名的西方画作,请学生讨论中、西方美术作品之间的相同点和差别。

在此主题中也可以介绍中国古代的孔子、孟子、老子、庄子等思想家及其主张,帮助学生理解中国士人的生活态度。这些主张与中国画的画风、意境常有关联。中国台湾漫画家蔡志忠有一套漫画,包括《老子说》、《孔子说》、《孟子说》等书(含光盘),以简短的篇幅说明了各家的思想、主张,通俗易懂。教师可以选择其中的某些片段辅助教学。

在由上述内容联系到中国画欣赏之前,教师应该先与学生讨论西方的写实画、抽象画,然后再请学生谈谈中国山水画与它们的差别。这个活动可以让学生理解:写实画是对实景、实物的真实表现,抽象画则是通过个人的想象力进行自由创作;中国山水画介于写实和抽象之间,表达的是一种意境。经过这个程序的学习,学生比较容易领会中国画中的思想表现。此外,也不妨请学生试着以中国画的方式,描绘大自然中的山水花鸟,呈现自己的风格、情感或者思想观点。通过这样的方式,学生也能在一定程度上体会中国画中的情感。最后,教师可以让学生观赏自己带来的国画,说说画中的意境。这个活动意在鼓励学生尝试表达自己对艺术的想法及体会,教师应尽量避免对学生的论述作对或错的评论。

对七、八年级的学生来说,揣摩画作的意境仍有相当大的难度,生活得无忧无虑的学生往往无法体会画家生活中的坎坷和他们的心理历程,对画的观赏多数仍停留在表面的色彩和线条的呈现这样粗浅的层面。所以,教师的教学目标不要太高,应着重培养学生对中、西方绘画的表达差异的理解,帮助他们形成基本认识即可。

如何欣赏中国乐曲,分辨其与西方音乐之不同?在进行此方面教学时,笔者会先准备好一份世界地图和六七首东、西方不同曲风的音乐,请学生在聆听音乐的同时记录个人对每首音乐的节奏和乐曲风格的感受,猜猜该乐曲来自于哪一个国家,并在地图上进行标记。欣赏音乐之后,学生轮流介绍个人的猜想和对音乐的描述,教师一一记录学生的答案。最后,教师再次播放各乐曲并公布答案,组织学生讨论、分析音乐中乐器的差异。教师可以展示各种各样的乐器(实物或图片),让学生认识东、西方的不同乐器,模仿其发出的声音。当然,对于不熟悉的乐器,学生可以通过想象进行模拟。此后可将学生分组,要求他们以西方乐器和东方乐器两种不同的组合来举行一场音乐会,每一个学生代表一种乐器,以模拟声响合奏一首曲子。这个活动非常有趣,可以很好地调动课堂气氛。

  为了加深学生对中国乐曲特色的印象,建议教师组织一次课外教学活动,带学生到当地华人乐社欣赏中国传统音乐,或以中国乐器和传统音乐为主题,访问当地的音乐家。笔者曾经布置过一项作业,请学生读一篇历史故事,然后自由选择他们喜爱的音乐或者歌曲,将这些音乐进行编排、串联、剪辑,表现故事情节的发展和自己在阅读中的感受。为了完成这个任务,学生们必须聆听许多不同的中国乐曲,熟悉各种乐器的特色,然后进行选择。(音乐总长度不可超过 5 分钟。)完成制作后,他们要将成品音乐置入光盘中,还可以为自己的光盘设计封面。在课堂上,学生要播放光盘并口头说明故事的段落、情节以及自己选择这些音乐的原因。对学生们来说,这个任务有些挑战性,需要的时间也比较长,但他们在制作光盘的过程中都特别投入,在最后的课堂播放环节中都会有极大的成就感。

  在学生对中国音乐有了基本了解之后,教师可分别播放一段欧洲歌剧和一段中国京剧,然后让学生分组比较这两者的表演方式和歌唱技巧,写出讨论的结果。此后,教师还可以展示京剧脸谱图片,讲解不同角色脸谱的区别。学生要搜集资料,了解京剧脸谱中常使用的红色、蓝色、白色和黑色等颜色代表的意义,然后根据颜色的不同含义进行搭配,绘制出全新的戏剧脸谱。如果条件允许,学生可以戴上面具,以西方歌剧或中国京剧的方式表演一段戏剧。这样的活动可以很好地引入有关京剧脸谱的知识,引发学生对中国京剧的兴趣。

  中学生都有自己喜爱的音乐,这些喜好代表着学生的个人品味、风格。教师可以让学生将他们最喜爱的音乐带到课堂上来进行分享。在播放音乐时,也不妨让喜欢跳舞的学生配合音乐展现舞姿。分享结束后,教师可播放几首中文流行歌曲,让学生听听中文流行音乐,看看它们与西方歌曲是否有相似之处。学生可以分别选择一首中文、英文流行歌曲,说明自己在其中发现的相同点。这是一个热身活动,意在由学生分享自己喜爱的音乐开始,提高其学习兴趣,然后进一步引入有关中国民族音乐的内容。

在这个单元的课程中,笔者会请学生上网听几首民歌,选出自己喜欢的一首,搜集相关资料形成报告(如该民歌起源于何处、有何含义、音乐的特色、与流行音乐的差别、自己喜爱它的原因等)。让学生自行选择歌曲进行资料搜集工作时,他们多半都会积极参与。这个活动同时也可培养学生对中国音乐的兴趣。

在"音乐"主题教学的最后,可以组织一个"音乐测验",进行有奖征答,让学生们比一比谁的音乐知识最多。在做这个活动之前,教师得花点时间,提前选出各式各样的音乐(比如传统音乐、民族音乐、古典音乐、经典流行音乐/歌曲)以及各种不同舞蹈的音视频文件。在课堂游戏的过程中,教师可先给学生每人发一个小白板,然后播放选出的音乐或舞蹈,在学生聆听、欣赏之后提出问题(问题必须配合单元的焦点问题来设计),要求学生在规定时间之内将答案写在小白板上,时间到后不得更改答案。每答对一题可得若干分,分数的高低取决于问题的难易度。测验完毕后,教师可为积分为前五名者分发不同的小物品作为奖励。此外,不要忘了给其余的学生发些巧克力糖,奖励他们的参与。虽然已经进入了七、八年级,但是学生们仍需要老师的"加油打气"。尤其是在游戏竞赛之后,小小的奖品将会给予他们大大的鼓励。

本单元还会涉及到部分有关汉字的内容。学生在五、六年级的课程中,已经对汉字的演变过程和各种字体有了一定的了解。教师可以先进行一个复习活动,以成语组合游戏进入教学:教师以几种不同的字体(行书、草书和隶书)写出成语卡片,一张卡片上写一个汉字。然后,将所有的成语都写在白板上,要求学生分组按照白板上所列的成语,找出每个成语包含的汉字并将其正确排列,率先完成的组胜出。然后,学生们要一起朗读每个成语,一一说明成语的含义。这一活动结束后,各组学生都将字卡集中放入一个纸盒,学生们依次从盒中抽出一张字卡,说出字卡上汉字的字体以及该字体出现的朝代。

为提高学生对汉字的学习热情,建议教师再组织一个活动:准备三张海报纸,让学生分成三组,分别在海报上写出自己学过的所有汉字。教师先介绍象形字、会意字和形声字的差别,再要求各小组相互交换手中的海报,让各组学生在拿到的海报上分别找出象形字、会意字和形声字,并在笔记本上进行记录。此外,还可以布置一项集体作业:请学生合作制作一个卷轴,在其中展示汉字的起源和演变。各组学生须先对内容进行讨论、设计,再分工进行资料搜集工作。这个任务除了可以加深学生对中国汉字的了解之外,同时可以培养学生的团队精神和合作能力。本主题中可以进行的活动有很多,带学生到当地的中国城进行拓碑活动,也是颇有乐趣的一种课外延展学习。有关汉字的动画片也能增加课堂学习的轻松气氛。教师可参考汉字相关动画①和《文字的故事》②。

在学生对文字的演变有了一定程度的认识和了解后,教师可以布置一项课后作业,请学生整合自己对中国汉字的认识,结合西方字母的演化过程形成口头报告,将汉字及其背后的中国文化与字母及自身文化进行比较。教师也可以展示来自不同地区的中文书籍、报纸和杂志,让学生自由选择阅读,自己去发现"繁体"和"简体"汉字的区别,以及"横版"和"竖版"两种不同形式。此时教师可说明形成这些差别的原因。学生们应该了解,在现在的几个主要的汉语使用区中,存在着使用不同文字形式的差异。此外,教师也可适时介绍、说明有关汉语记音方式的内容,讲解记音方式的演变及现行不同记音方式的差别。此时可以让学生以两种不同的方式为同一段文字注音,或者试着分别用纵式和横式的形式将其写出,学生由此可对汉语的不同记音方法、不同记音方法的排列形式有更深刻的印象。之后,可请学生针对中、西方的文字阅读方式以及语言的差异制作简易说明表,列出各项内容并配合图片和符号作为注解。

中国的四大发明也是本主题中的学习内容。经过三到六年级的铺垫,七、八年级的学习可以更进一步。指南针如何推动航海业的发展,火药在军事中的应用,印刷技术如何使知识得以传播,还有造纸术的发明对人类的贡献都是很好的话题。此外,老师们也可以把教学重点放在四大发明与现代生活的联系上。下面就以此为中心,从日常生活中的衣、食、住、行几方面展开论述。

首先,教师可准备四张大海报:在每张海报的中间都画上一个大圆并在圆形中分别写上一项发明(火药、印刷术、造纸术、指南针),然后在大圆的周围画上一些小圈。在活动中,教师先将海报分发给四组学生,请他们就大圆中的发明进行头脑风暴,讨论现代生活中的哪些事物与

---

① http://v.youku.com/v_show/id_XMTg1MTgxMDA=.html
② http://v.youku.com/v_show/id_XMTAwMTQ1OTk2.html

此发明有关系,然后把这些事物的名称逐一记录在大圆周围的小圈里。学生讨论时,教师可以就生活中的衣、食、住、行四方面举例,引导学生往更广的范畴思考。比方说,指南针除了推动航海业的发展,与我们日常生活中的"行"有什么直接关联?(搭机、开车、乘船、问路、登山……要辨别方向的场合以及活动中都可以用到指南针。)依此类推,学生按照这个思路进行讨论后,会发现四大发明与现实生活中很多事物存在间接或直接的关联。

从古代的四大发明进展到现代科技后,可选的教学内容更加包罗万象。笔者认为,老师们可以从学生最离不开的通讯、交流方式(比如电子邮件、电话留言、视频通讯和脸书等)入手,引入这一话题,例如,这些成果为我们的生活提供了哪些便利?为什么?学生对于这类话题都非常感兴趣。在每个人提出自己的看法后,教师还可以引入目前常发生的由网络沟通、交流引发的事件、案例,要求学生探讨事件的主要起因和网上交流的潜在危险并形成报告。这个年龄段的学生很容易接受新流行的事物,尤其热衷于新科技的应用。现在几乎每个学生都知道如何使用 iPhone、iPad 以及网络上的各种新式交流工具,但是他们普遍缺乏辨别力,难以判断资料、信息的真实性,对网络信息传播的伤害缺乏警惕。因此,教师在此应适时告诉学生如何判断网络信息的可信度,强调网络交流的安全规则。

科技在中国占据着什么样的地位?这个问题很大,也很复杂。我们可以把视野集中在中国如何因科技的进步而实现经济的快速发展以及随之而来的生活、文化方面的变化上。学生可以从衣、食、住、行四个生活层面来学习、了解科技在经济发展中的重要性。教师可以安排学生搜集20世纪90年代的中国和当下中国的图片并进行对比,制作比较展示板。然后在课堂上组织一个小型展示说明会,要求每个学生轮流展示自己的成果,说明图片中展现出来的变化及其影响。这是一个很好的活动,图片能很好地刺激学生思考,给他们留下深刻的印象。在制作展示板的过程中,学生们也很乐于分享自己所查阅到的有趣图片。

接下来可以让学生观看一个题为《2015人类未来可能的生活方式》的短片(教师可在网络中搜寻到本片),[①]记录生活中衣、食、住、行四个方面的改变并举出片中的例子进行说明。此外,短剧表演是多数学生最乐

---

① http://www.secretchina.com/news/12/07/19/459934.html

意参与的活动。如有可能,可以请学生以"我们未来的科技世界"为主题,分组设计、表演一段小品。在各小组互相观摩后,可以共同思考这样的科技对我们的文化有何影响,引发了哪些改变。

以上都是笔者个人的建议,老师们可根据自己学生的能力、需求以及兴趣随时修改、补充,并配合相关成语/谚语辅助教学,设计更丰富、有趣的课程。

(八) 主题单元八:情绪与情感表达

这个主题单元的教学目标应设定为对社交礼节的学习和对其后的文化背景的理解,个人情绪管理能力的提升,恰当的情感表达方式的培养。文化背景的差异会导致情感表达方式的不同,这是值得关注的问题。以七年级的课程设计为例,笔者由学生个人喜、怒、哀、乐的情绪表现开始,经由讨论对校规的看法引发学生的情绪,之后进一步谈到了家庭关系,帮助学生学习、理解中西方之间儿女同父母相处方式的差别,最后再把话题联系到男女之间的情感表达方式,从中国有名的"梁山伯与祝英台"入手,探讨中西文化在此方面的差别和情感表达方式的异同。到八年级时,教学重点则是"从家人间的相处及情感表达方式中发现文化差异"以及"中国人的社交观念和来往应对的礼节",内容较七年级时更为深入。

面对"情感"的问题,七、八年级是一个很尴尬的年龄阶段。此时的学生都喜欢以成人的态度处理事情,表现自己成熟的一面,但是谈到男女之间的情谊时就显得比较敏感、幼稚。这一阶段的学生们还有很强的好奇心,大多数的学生对初恋还比较懵懂。

在这个单元的教学中,为了避免学生的过度敏感,可以先从有关学校生活的话题进入教学,比方说请学生谈谈个人对校规有什么意见,在与同学相处时常有哪些情绪上的问题等。为了不让讨论范围偏离主题,教师可以先设计好一份有关情绪管理的情景问卷,让学生们互相采访,然后总结访问结果。在这个过程中,学生们也可以学习与此单元相关的新词汇和新句型。最后,请学生从情景问卷中选出一个情景问题,配合采访结果设计漫画,呈现并分享自己的看法。这个小的热身活动可以提高学生对下一个阶段内容的学习兴趣。

接下来,教师可以将话题转入父母和子女两代人之间的相处方式和两代人情感表达方式的不同。学生可以先在课堂上自由描述自己与父母相处的情况。他们的家庭作业是设计一份包含10到15个问题的问卷调查表，以此为基础采访自己的父母。学生在设计好问题之后，教师应该让学生先以老师为采访对象进行练习，在这个过程中教师可以对学生们设计的问题提出建议和修改意见。教师也可以提出以下问题，给学生作为参考：父母对你在学校的学习有哪些要求？你认为这些要求合理吗？父母是如何鼓励你学习的？你喜欢他们所用的方式吗？若是你达不到父母对你的要求，父母会有什么反应？你小时候做错事时，会受到什么样的责罚？父母责罚你后，会和你进行沟通吗？在日常生活中，面对父母时有什么礼节？你家有哪些规矩？为什么？……作业完成后，可将学生分组，要求各组综合比较各成员的访问结果，创作一段小品并在课堂上表演（观赏表演的学生必须记笔记）。此时也可以要求各组学生合作制作PPT，展示、说明父母和自己情绪表达方式的不同及其成因。大部分学生对父母都有一种"刻板印象"，这项活动可以帮助他们重新认识并理解自己与父母之间的关系。《家有儿女》这部电视剧也是一个很好的视听辅助材料，学生可以由此学习现代中国家庭的组合形式、父亲和母亲对儿女管教方式的差异以及现代家庭价值观。此外，笔者个人也建议老师们以朱自清的《背影》为阅读材料，帮助学生深刻体会"天下父母心"。

　　下一个要讨论的话题是男女之间情感表达方式的差异。教师可以用"谁是你的偶像"这一活动来引发学生对自己欣赏的异性的讨论。在这一活动中，学生首先应学习如何形容人的长相与特征，如何说明其魅力所在。然后大家一起票选出最受欢迎的人物，总结公认的"受欢迎"标准。然后，教师展示准备好的两组中、西方目前最受欢迎的偶像图片，请学生投票选出两位中、西最受欢迎的偶像。此后，再让学生玩"偶像配对"游戏，说说自己的配对标准。教师也可在此时引入话题，就男女适合约会的年龄组织一个简单的讨论。

　　男女之间互相表达爱慕的方式有哪些呢？相信学生们都能很快地说出各种方法，但其中大部分的方式都是非常直接的。笔者曾经尝试让学生避免使用"爱""喜欢"等直接的词语，以含蓄婉转的方式在卡片上向自己喜欢的人写一句表示情感的话。教师可将卡片收集在一个小盒里，然后把学生分成两组，要求各组派一名学生从盒中抽出一张卡片。两位学生要轮流大声念出卡片上所写的句子，所有学生举手选出更为含蓄委婉的句子。这个活动很有意思，在学生们读出这些有创意的表白时，课堂中总是一片欢声笑语，学生们都兴致勃勃。最后，可以将选出的"优秀表白"帖在公布栏上，作为对作者的表扬和鼓励。

在后面的教学中,教师可以让学生选择一首表达爱情的英文诗并将其翻译成中文。在翻译的过程中,学生们不但可以学习词语、句型,也有机会将其与自己的母语对照、比较,同时还可以更好地体会诗句中的感情。此后,可以让学生自己创作一首情诗。在创作时学生可以先写初稿,教师则应据此提出建议,帮助学生进行修正,直至完成创作。诗稿定稿后,学生须将其打印出来,并配以相应的图片。虽然这个教学活动需要的时间会稍微长一些,但是学生们在完成作业后,都会非常有成就感,所以很值得老师们采用。为加强学生的阅读能力,并且确认学习效果,此时教师也可节选一首现代情诗,要求学生口头或书面回答相关问题,进行理解程度测验。

影片可以很好地加深学生对中国文化的了解,进一步领会情感表达方式的重要意义。电影《中国月亮》很适合作为视听教材辅助教学。这部影片中有许多因为中美观点的不同而引发的误会,情节非常有趣。教师可以选择其中的几个片段让学生观赏并讨论,提升学生对中国人生活、文化的认识和尊重。不过,采用本片时建议省略前面一段男主角在美国生活的部分,选择适用的影片段落。

本主题中的最后一个活动是阅读"梁山伯与祝英台"的故事。阅读之后,学生们要分组在海报上画出故事中的重要情节,上台展示本组的图片并讲述故事梗概。此时建议老师们引入小提琴协奏曲《梁祝》,让学生在音乐中感受故事中人物感情和情绪的变化。比方说,可以播放不同段落的音乐,让学生猜想是故事中的哪一段情节,在表达什么样的情感,此时也可以请学生配合音乐,表演故事情节。

本主题的总体评估项目是一个团体创作任务,要求学生分组以"梁山伯与祝英台"的故事为纲,结合中美文化中不同的表达习惯,改编故事情节和结局并加以呈现。这样的创作给了学生很大的发挥空间,他们可以就自己对故事内容的理解,综合不同文化的情感表达方式,以戏剧的形式呈现自己的各种想法。这也是此教学主题中我们希望实现的最终目标。

单元主题：情绪与情感表达

（中文班七年级，四个星期）

引导问题

核心问题	焦点问题
1. 什么是情感？ 2. 我们如何表达个人情感？ 3. 人们如何以不同的方式来表达他们的情感？他们为什么会选择不同的方式？ 4. 情感表达如何影响人际关系？	1. 人的情绪是怎样产生的？ 2. 你认为用什么样的方式表达个人的"喜""怒""哀""乐"是合适的？ 3. 心情的表达方式有哪些？ 4. 行为表现与心情有什么样的关系？ 5. 什么样的因素会影响个人表达情绪的方式？ 6. 你认为中国人的情绪表达方式与西方人的有什么差别？为什么？ 7. 面对家人和朋友时，你的情绪表达方式有什么差异？为什么？ 8. 你认为男生和女生的情绪表达方式有什么不同？不恰当的方式会引起什么样的误会？ 9. 你和来自不同文化背景的朋友在一起时，是否曾经因为表达习惯的不同而引发有趣的事情或误会？请说明。 10. 你怎么解决朋友之间因文化差异而造成的误解？

学习目标与技能

- 学生能运用有关情绪的不同词汇和句型进行口头表达和书面创作
- 学生能举例说明中国儿童情绪表达的特色和背后原因
- 学生能比较并总结中美情绪表达方式的异同
- 学生能在课堂中及校外使用中文进行沟通

学习评估

a) 过程评估：

- 情绪管理情景问卷的采访结果汇报（口语；词语和句型运用/语法）
- 设计采访父母所用问卷（写作；词语和句型运用/语法）

- 短剧呈现两代人的差异（文化理解与比较）
- 阅读情书/情诗（内容理解）
- 情书写作（写作：词语和句型运用/语法）
- 回答关于"梁山伯与祝英台"的问题（内容理解）
- 讲述"梁山伯与祝英台"故事梗概（口语：词语和句型运用/语法）

b) 组别合作项目：
- 报告（PPT）：说明父母和自己两代人情绪表达方式的差异及成因
- 剧本编写：综合中美文化中的表达习惯和方式，重新设计情节和结局
- 戏剧表演：学生以戏剧表演方式展现上述剧本剧情

每周教学计划

第一周	
教学目标	学生能运用有关情绪的词汇和句型来表达个人的感受
课程内容	• 对"校规"的看法 • 对父辈的情感表达方式的了解
教学材料	• 问卷、空白表格纸、壁报纸 • 《家有儿女》（电视版、动画版）[①]
演练活动	• 学生以情景问卷互相采访。 • 学生轮流汇报访谈的结果，或用漫画形式将其呈现出来。 • 学生共同讨论对校规的意见和想法。 • 设计一份以父母为对象的采访问卷并采访父母。 • 学生分组，以短剧形式表演采访的结果并进行比较。 • 看《家有儿女》片断，加强对中国家庭的情感表达方式的理解，了解现代家庭的教育观。 • 阅读朱自清的《背影》。
过程评估	口头汇报采访结果、问卷设计、短剧表演

---

① 参考网页：http://dianshiju.cntv.cn/city/jiayouernv/videopage/index.shtml；http://www.tudou.com/programs/view/dgegzIgzGXA/

	第二周
教学目标	• 学生可理解男女之间情感表达方式的不同 • 学生能以适当的方式来表达个人情感
课程内容	• 对于"偶像"标准的设定和表达喜爱 • 同性和异性之间不同的情绪表达方式 • 异性之间表达好、恶感的方式 • 情绪表达中对误解的处理和对背景文化的认识
教学材料	• 中国明星和美国明星的照片、投票单、卡片 • 《中国月亮》(Nian A 导演,福建电影制片厂出品)
演练活动	• 投票选偶像,讨论偶像标准。教师准备两组中国和美国现在受欢迎的明星、歌手照片,由学生投票,选出两位"公共"偶像。 • 分组讨论,列出男学生和女学生对偶像标准的要求差别。 • 偶像配对游戏(一):通过这个活动,教师除了可以知道学生选择偶像的标准之外,也很容易进入有关男女约会年龄的讨论。 • "一句话":发给学生每人一张卡片,请学生避免使用"爱""喜欢"等直接的词语,以含蓄婉转的方式在卡片上写出一句向自己喜爱的人表示情感的话。然后收齐所有卡片放入一个盒子里,将学生分成两组,各组派一位学生抽卡片,朗读卡片上的句子。大家比较两个句子并投票选出其中比较含蓄婉转的句子。如此两人持续抽卡、朗读,一直到念完所有的卡片。最后,可将选出的卡片贴在白板或墙上供大家参考、欣赏。 • 观赏《中国月亮》中的情节,讨论影片中误解的成因,提出适宜的应对方式。
过程评估	口头报告:比较男女对情感表达及喜爱标准的差别

	第三周
教学目标	• 学生能理解并说明阅读材料——情书/情诗范例 • 学生能以文字来表达对异性的情感
课程内容	• 英文情诗分享 • 情诗阅读欣赏 • 情书写作

（续表）

	第三周
教学材料	• 情书范例材料① • 情诗:郑愁予——《错误》② • 手工材料、中文写作纸
演练活动	• 学生带来自己喜爱的英文情诗,将其译成中文并分享。 • 创作一首情诗,学习中英文写作中不同的表达方式。 • 分组阅读理解一篇中式情书,让学生以不同的呈现方式来说明对阅读材料内容的理解(例如图画、歌曲、立体剪贴、道具创作、短剧、音乐、动作等)。 • 情书创作:在写作过程中,教师应该从旁协助,检查情书中的词语和句型的运用是否得当。
过程评估	情诗的阅读理解,情书的写作

	第四周
教学目标	• 学生能理解中西文化背景对情感表达的影响 • 学生能比较文化差异,编写爱情剧本
课程内容	梁山伯与祝英台的故事
教学材料	• 动画片:《罗密欧与朱丽叶》 • 电影:《梁山伯与祝英台》(蔡明钦导演,上海美术电影制片厂出品) • 阅读材料:《梁山伯与祝英台》 (出自《读故事学汉语》,北京语言大学出版社出版) • 小提琴协奏曲:《梁山伯与祝英台》③ • 影片问卷、壁报纸、写作纸

---

① 参考网页:http://www.yiding8.com/qsdq/2007-3-9/QingShuFanLi-1-4-bmow0141.htm.
② 参考网页:http://blog.sina.com.cn/s/blog_4e0711140100bytm.html.
③ http://www.youtube.com/watch?v=5Egmjy8BbME

(续表)

	第四周
演练活动	• 安排学生阅读有关梁山伯与祝英台的故事,针对各段落进行提问,帮助学生理解故事内容。 • 请学生在阅读后写问题卷,测试其理解程度。 • 播放一段小提琴协奏曲《梁山伯与祝英台》,请学生配合音乐想象故事中的一段情节和对话,将其表演出来。 • 团体创作:分组讨论角色的分配、故事背景、情节发展,改编"梁山伯与祝英台"的故事。
过程评估	故事理解问卷、音乐短剧表演
总结评估	剧本、戏剧表演

教学建议

单元问题设置:针对单元主题设计的引导问题,应该以教学中使用的材料内容为基础。为了提高学生的学习兴趣,设计问题时应尽量以"什么""谁""为什么""如何"的形式来提问,连结整个教学过程中的内容。以下是针对本单元主题设计的一些问题:

1. 你心情好的时候喜欢做些什么事?喜欢和谁一起做?
2. 你心情不好的时候会做什么?为什么?
3. 学校的规定中,你认为哪一条不合理?为什么?
4. 在家里,父母对你有哪些要求?你认为这些要求合理吗?为什么?
5. 你会和谁谈心里的话?为什么?
6. 你如何选择朋友?
7. 你和朋友在一起时,喜欢做些什么事?为什么?
8. 如果你的朋友在大家面前说了让你不舒服的话,你会怎么样?为什么?
9. 如果你和朋友因意见不同而有了争执,你该怎么办?
10. 当你不同意父母说的话时,你怎么表达你的想法?
11. 你心情不好时,对家人和朋友的态度有什么差别?为什么?
12. 你怎么让你的家人知道你爱他们、你在乎他们?

13. 你如何对喜欢的男/女生表达你的感觉？请给出例子。
14. 你认为男生和女生的情绪表达方式有什么不同？为什么？
15. 为什么中国男女之间表达情感的方式同美国男女习惯的方式不同？
16. 你和来自不同文化背景的朋友在一起时，是否曾因表达方式不同而发生过有趣的事情或误会？请说明。
17. 你怎么解决朋友之间因文化差异而造成的误解？

　　词语与句型：词语及句型的设置应以教师在设计课程时准备的阅读材料及与主题相关的生词、语法为基础，依照学生的语言能力斟情处理。以下是与本单元相关的一些词汇和句型：

词语
紧张、担心、丢脸、烦恼、伤心、抱歉、惊讶、尴尬、害羞、内向、外向、活泼、谈恋爱、失恋、心情、压力、自由、约定、约会、暗示、直接、婉转、来往、表达、觉得、建议、应该、理会、了解、比较、合得来/合不来、含蓄、开放、冲突、理解、体谅、代沟、观点、角度、立场

句型
万一……该怎么办；对……有兴趣；为了……而……；如果……可以……；不但……反而……；由于……造成……；不仅……而且……

成语
七上八下；不知所措；男女授受不亲；一见如故；一刀两断；日有所思，夜有所梦

田凤英　著

第七章　更多探讨：关于教材选择、学生评估和教师培训

以上章节阐述了不同年级中的各种有创意的教学方法。需要再次强调的是，这些教学建议和文化主题仅供参考，每个教师必须因地制宜地自行设计课程。教师在设计过程中应该注意几个关键问题，这也是最后这一章主要讨论的问题：教学材料、学生评估和教师培训。

生动的教学材料

教师要不断努力，寻找、搜集有创意的、生动的教学材料。前面的章节中提供了很多资料来源（例如课文、歌曲、电影、游戏、网站等），都可以用来支持我们所提倡的"以学生为中心"的主题式教学。在传统外语教学方法中，课本及辅助材料决定了教学内容。我们的教学方法则要求课程设计者从一系列与主题相关的核心、焦点问题出发，围绕这些问题选择材料，激发学生的兴趣[1]。因为相关的话题和材料非常多，选择时应注意遵循以下几个原则。

一个最主要的原则是，选择与学生年龄相当、能引起其学习兴趣的材

---

[1] 我们在此借用的大致是威金斯（Wiggins）与麦克泰（McTighe）在《理解力培养与课程设计》(*Understanding by Design*, 2005)中提出的模式。

料。教师要记住的是，能使中国内地、香港或台湾地区的学生（及家长）感兴趣的话题，未必能够吸引来自各种不同的民族与语言背景的美国学生。① 教学经验不丰富的中文教师可以借鉴英语课程的教学内容和活动设计，这样既能估计学生期望达到的理解力标准，又能通过中英双语训练来加强教学效果。到设计三年级课程时，教职人员也应参考各州、各学区及各学校制定的社会学课程标准，②为中文课选择合适的地理、历史、政治及更广泛的全球性问题的内容和材料。教师须知，同一年级的学生在兴趣和能力上各有千秋，教师选择的主题与相关材料应当尽可能涵盖不同性别学生的多种多样的兴趣与生活经历，并照顾到不同学生的学习能力与学习方式。不是每个学生对每个主题或每堂课都有同样的兴趣，但教师应当有意识地选择不同种类的材料，设计不同的课堂活动，最终实现使所有学生都实际参与的目的。

除了考虑学生的兴趣与理解认知能力之外，教师在选择教学材料时，也应注意材料是否符合外语教学法的基本原则。下一主题的课程必须复习并反复练习前一堂课所学的词汇及语法结构，这样学生才能通过持续的学习、积累来掌握交流的技巧。语言与文化学习是个不断重复、积累的过程，因此，单一文化主题的课堂范例再怎么出色，也必须和其他系列课程结合在一起，共同服务于一组精心设计的语言与文化教学目标。③ 教师在选择语言和文化教材时必须时刻记住这一点。

关于具体的教学材料和资源的选择及使用，我们也想提供一些建议。语言教材与真实语料是所有可利用资源的两个极端，它们各有利弊。为低龄学生编写的优秀中文教材虽能系统地呈现词汇与语言结构，但通常缺乏系统性的中国文化教学内容（Li Yu, 2009），这些教材对中高年级学生也较无吸引力。教师在设计语言教学目标时可以参考教材，其中的某些课文也可能对学生有用，但总体来说我们不赞成用教材作为课堂教学

---

① 美国的中文课堂融合了华裔学生、亚裔混血学生和非亚裔学生。华裔学生在家庭中可能说粤语（或其他汉语方言）、普通话或英语，也有可能是由非华裔的父母领养，未接触或很少接触中文。

② 例如俄勒冈州的社会学课程标准（www.ode.state.or.us.）。

③ 例如，《外语学习的目标：为 21 世纪做准备》(*Standards for Foreign Language Learning: Preparing for the 21st Century*, 1996) 中的 "*Standards for Chinese Language Learning*" 部分提供了一些主题与教学方法都经过精心设计的示范课程。但如果只作为孤立的单元，没有再次复现与强化练习与之衔接，学习效果就会迅速下降。

的主要材料。与此相反,真实语料(指为某种文化内部的人们互相交流而设计的口头或书面材料,包括广告、报纸、目录、音乐、电视节目、地图、火车时刻表、诗歌、网站等)文化内涵丰富,具有鲜明的现实针对性,可引导学生把课堂中学到的知识与技能运用到真实的语境中,灵活地练习他们的第二语言。[1] 走访当地华人社区很显然能让学生亲身接触当地华人的语言、文化,在条件允许的情况下,应在课程中纳入这样的课外教学活动。不过,更普遍的与中国语言、文化接触的方式是上网,通过电脑网络了解信息。之前的章节中也经常使用网页中的内容辅助教学。一些语言学专家甚至认为外语教学材料应以这样的真实语料为主。不过这些材料也有局限,尤其对幼儿园至初中阶段的学生而言。中文网站中很少有专门针对儿童的内容,大部分都是针对成年人的兴趣和活动设计的。即使是为儿童设计的网站,也因为母语学生与第二语言学生的语言能力相差太悬殊,很难被美国学生有效利用。除了某些例外(比如图画故事书),语言类的真实语料最适合的对象是四至八年级(初三)的学生;[2]对更低年级的学生而言,真实的视觉与触觉材料可以丰富课堂教学,但教师须要使用其他教学材料来系统培养学生的语言能力,使学生可以理解更广泛的真实语料。在任何情况下,教师都必须考虑到真实语料是否适合学生的语言与认知能力。教师应注意避免学生接触青少年不宜的网络,必要时也应适当筛选材料内容。

除了互联网上的中国语言文化学习网站以外,我们还可以在美国和亚洲的主要城市的书店里找到越来越多的针对低龄学生编写的中文图书和杂志。网上书目和相关网站(例如 China Sprout 和 Cheng & Tsui)提供了一系列色彩缤纷的故事书、游戏、音乐、食品、地图和其它老师们认为有用的参考资料。我们有必要为学生们提供丰富的资源,以备在课堂中使用或作为补充阅读材料在课外使用。美国的小学生在学习阅读英文的时候,每天要在课外做至少 20 分钟的练习,因此也应对中文学习提出类似的要求。学校和老师们给学生们提供阅读材料时,应特别注意保证提供的阅读文本与学生的阅读水平和兴趣吻合。在笔者调查的学校中,很

---

[1] Jennifer Eddy 在她的"单元主题的设计与评估"研讨会(2010)上说:"熟练使用某一文化中的语言需要高度的适应性,能随时应付各种新情况和不完整的信息,不依赖任何提示也能解决问题。"真实语料有助于教师进行这方面的课堂训练。

[2] 即使是图画书,如果是为中国家长读给孩子听而设计的,其中的复杂词汇也常常是低年级的第二语言学生所无法掌握的。

多老师都在他们的教室里摆放了这样的书籍,这样他们不但可以了解学生的阅读内容,而且还能定期检测学生对阅读材料的理解情况。类似的方式很值得推荐,而且学校的经费应该可以用来资助这些课堂资源。学校的图书馆也最好可配备一系列适合学生年龄阶段和语言水平的资源,以此引导学生进一步用第二语言进行阅读和探索。中文儿童读物的难度各异,因此需要老师们给图书馆里或者教室里的图书按难易程度分级,这样有助于学生选择符合自己兴趣和能力的阅读材料。①

真实的评估

我们这一代人接受的学习评估经常以成绩单与期终等级评定的形式呈现。但评估方式可以是各种各样的,其目的不仅是考察学生对知识的掌握,并且为教师提供了重要的反馈信息,以便他们不断调整教学方式和步调,适应不同的学生。事实上,评估的目的是多重的,如用来检测学生的进步情况、明确学习目标、对学生提出鼓励、进一步教育学生、交流学习成果、记录学习成绩,以及评估教学内容等(Blaz,2001:6—8)。定期测试第二语言学生的听、说、读、写四种技能的做法由来已久,但近来的评估模式逐渐从传统的笔试转向较为动态的"以学生表现为基础"的评估方式,这种评估方式在 *Integrated Performance Assessment*(IPA)②一书中有所论述。这种模式所采用的评估方式渗透到了日常教学中,围绕阐释能力(使用各种书面、听觉与视觉材料的能力)、人际交往能力(学生在一对一或小组活动中互相交流信息与观点的能力)和表达能力(个人或小组进行口头或书面报告的能力)这几方面展开。本书中之前的各个章节中已经提供了许多这样的表现型的评估范例,其中隐含的一个共识是教师应随时观察学生的表现以评估学生的学习情况,从而调整之后的教学策略。

在每章结尾处,田凤英老师与郑莉玲老师列出了更为具体的学生评估方式,并对形成性评估(Formative Assessment)与总结性评估(Summative Assessment)分别进行了论述。总体而言,形成性评估渗透

---

① 例如,香港汉基国际学校有一本列出学校图书馆所有中文图书的难度级别的小册子。这个小册子被用来给各个不同年级的学生推荐适合他们的补充阅读材料。

② IPA 于 1997 年由 ACTFL 设计并得到美国教育部的赞助,旨在为学生的学习表现提供持续的反馈,"以此促进学习表现并改善教学方式"(Adair-Hauck 等,2006)。

在教学过程之中，就学习进度与目标接近程度向教师与学生提供持续的反馈。总结性评估针对的是学生在某一特定时间（通常在单元结束之时或学期、学年之终）的学习情况。Garrison & Ehringhaus 认为，"在一个均衡的评估系统中，总结性评估与形成性评估缺一不可，它们共同收集、提供完整的信息。过于偏重其中之一而忽视另一项，学生的学习情况就会模糊不明。"（2001）

评估学生表现的测量方式没有是非对错的明确答案（不像传统的多项选择题或填空题），所以教师必须制定出衡量学习水平的评估准则。Blaz（2001）与 Sandrock（2011）都为学生外语能力的评估与测量提供了各种范例。在针对文化行为与文化理解方面的评估中，我们应在设计评估任务/方式与评分标准时采取相似方式。Bartz 与 Vermett 在测试文化能力的章节中强调："语言与其文化是互相影响的。因此，文化能力的测试应当尽可能具体、清晰地测试交流互动中的文化成分。"（1996）他们列举并描述了针对十六种文化能力的评估方式，其中包括档案评估、测试学生对文化场景或跨文化冲突等情况的反应、要求学生对某些关键现象和事件进行评价等等。这些例子是为以法语作为第二语言的学生设计的，但对我们评估幼儿园至八年级的中文学生的短期与长期的文化知识的学习与理解有很大的启发作用。

最后要强调的是，学生应该积极参与评估，了解自己的学习情况，也向教师提供反馈（诸如关于课程中需要保持或者改进的地方）。这样的评估对学生与教师来说都要花一定的时间和精力，但为了进一步了解学生的个人需求以及课程有效性，这样的做法确有其存在的必要。

教师培训

虽然美国幼儿园至八年级教师的持续培训体制非常完善，不过就我们所提出的这种教学模式而言，其所需的教师培训稍有不同。目前为中文教师开设的各种研讨会、学术会议和教师培训课程并不区分学生的年龄段（且常以成年学生为默认对象），相关研讨也常以语言学问题为重点。如果采用我们推荐的教学模式，教师要适应新的教学方式，以新的方式理解并教授中国文化，教师应当组成教研组，合作设计适合各年级学生的逐级递进的课程框架。

美国学校中幼儿园至八年级的中文教师大多来自中国内地、台湾地区或香港,从小接受的课堂教育多以指定的教科书为主导,教学方式多"以教师为中心"。对这些教师的培训应更强调"以学生为中心",许多中文教师都要加强这个观念(Ning,2009)。参加诸如"星谈计划"这样的培训,可以使外语教师了解自主式学习策略,能更有效地帮助教师将教学重心从"教师"转移到"学生"身上。在研讨会上与其他教师交流,也能让大家分享成功的教学经验和优秀的教学资料。

如何将对中国文化的介绍纳入到语言课程中对教师及教学设计者而言是一个全新的挑战。大部分移民到美国的中文教师都曾将文化等同于以前在学校里学到的历史、文学与艺术类文化,经过引导才会想到日常风俗习惯这一类的文化。像其他许多外语教师一样,他们接受的教育使他们无法有意识地将文化习俗和文化产物联系起来(Schulz,2007)。因为行为文化已经成为移民教师自身行为的一部分,所以较难被移民教师有意识地认识并传授。我们研究小组的成员在合作设计行为文化的各种话题时,也学会了如何从新的视角看待这部分文化。教师可以阅读一些有关跨文化交流的书籍,如 *Doing Culture*(Davis,2001)和 *Writing and Culture*(Deng & Liu,1989),书中援引了许多因隐性的文化差异而引起跨文化冲突的事例。此外,老师们也可以参考关于具体情景中的语言使用问题的书籍,如 *When to Say What*(Feng & Liao,2008)和 *The Way We Communicate*(Kuo,2009),它们为中文教师提供了文化交流方面的有效教学策略。

中国文化多种多样,教师也应注意避免把中国文化过分刻板化。人们很容易把日常习俗与个人经历等同起来,一些移民教师对不同地区华人群体生活的差异性或不同社会阶层的情况所知甚少。我们应该鼓励教师通过阅读与研究,了解自己出生地以外的华人群体与习俗;或者将不同背景的中文教师召集起来,进行比较、交流。中文教师也应当了解一下中国以外的其他华人社会群体,比如东南亚、欧洲、北美等地的华人社会。越来越多的书籍与网站有相关的信息介绍。值得推荐的是2005年出版的一套介绍全球各地的唐人街的影碟(DVD),教师可自用或将其作为中学生的参考资料。

最后的一些感想

这项研究对我和我们小组的所有成员都是一个漫长的自我发现的过

程。我最初想将中国文化融入幼儿园至八年级的中文教学的动机既有理论的（人类学和语言学的基础）又有现实的考虑（如何维持小学高年级及中学生的中文学习热情）。对一系列幼儿园至八年级的双语教学项目的实地考察，证实了语言教学中的文化教学的重要性。而且，文化教学的方式多种多样，随学生的语言与文化背景、家庭背景、学校情况、学校机制的不同呈现出了多种面貌。但现阶段的教学中普遍缺乏与渐进的语言教学相配套的、连贯有序的文化主题系列———一言以蔽之，理想的教学方式是在文化中教语言，在语言中教文化。我们研究小组开发的以及本书所体现的正是这样一种教学模式。

我们相信我们所做的是幼儿园至八年级中文教学改革中重要的第一步。幼儿园至八年级的中文教学应结合并强调以下几个主要原则：

- 教学目标及方式与学生的认知和心理成熟程度相适应。
- 课堂话题及活动应结合学生们不同的爱好与经历设计。
- 文化主题在各个年级重复强化并逐步加深、扩展。
- 语言教学与文化教学相结合，使学生能灵活运用各种知识与技能，在不同社会背景下与不同的中国人自如地交流。

我们希望这个教学模式能在各个学校的幼儿园至八年级中文教学中得到运用，并进一步发展和完善。因此我们把自己的经验与探索过程总结出版，旨在与各界同仁交流切磋，共同致力于改进针对幼儿园至八年级学生的中文教学。

柯雪润　著

Chapter One   Mandarin and Chinese Culture Instruction in Diverse K—8 Programs

Introduction

In an increasingly globalized world, the ability to communicate effectively with people from diverse language and cultural backgrounds is an essential skill for students to develop as they prepare for satisfying and productive lives and careers. There are multiple paths to this goal, including lessons in intercultural communication that sensitize students to typical points of misunderstanding between people from different cultural backgrounds, even when speaking a common language. For those who wish to cultivate intercultural understanding in a deeper, more sustained way, learning another language is a crucial step. Historically, American students have waited until high school to begin foreign language classes, and two years of foreign language study remains a typical university graduation requirement for liberal arts majors. However, their foreign language skills have generally remained at a relatively basic level, with few opportunities for developing the more sophisticated language and culture skills necessary for truly effective cross cultural communication.

教汉语，教文化：美国幼儿园至八年级汉语及中国文化课程设计

More recently, acknowledging that languages are often learned more easily in younger years, foreign language programs have expanded to primary and middle school grades; in some schools classes meet several hours a week, while other schools have adopted immersion programs where a half day or more is dedicated to instruction in the foreign language. The relatively recent development of such programs in the United States has meant that effective curricular designs and resources are in many cases still in the earlier stages of development. Given that most foreign language and culture texts have been written for high school and college students whose cognitive abilities and interests diverge significantly from those of younger children, one of the crucial challenges is to identify and design language and culture materials and curriculum that address the needs of younger students. This volume aims to begin this process by presenting a framework for a Mandarin curriculum that intertwines language and culture instruction for K—8 students.

The project described here has grown out of both personal and professional involvement with one of the earlier US Mandarin immersion programs, which began in Portland, Oregon in 1998. Inspired by the success of Japanese and Spanish immersion classes in Portland Public Schools, Woodstock Elementary was chosen as the site of a Mandarin immersion magnet program, designed to attract additional students to an under enrolled neighborhood school. Final approval for the program did not emerge until the late spring of 1998, so initial decisions about staff, curriculum, materials and student recruitment were made quickly. When my daughter enrolled in the pioneer class in this program, I was one of the few Mandarin speaking parents with educational and cultural experiences in Chinese societies and quickly became involved in the planning. ① A native speaking Chinese teacher from the PRC was hired to teach the first mixed class of 26 kindergarten and first grade students, who came from a diverse set of family backgrounds: American Chinese who were mostly Cantonese speakers; adopted Chinese daughters; Caucasian children; and children of mixed Asian descent. The curriculum followed the format of other district immersion programs with a Mandarin half day that included instruction in language, math, and science and a half day devoted to English language arts and social studies. Mandarin language texts from Singapore were selected for two main reasons. Because Singapore Chinese texts had been developed for primary school students in a bilingual program where most courses were taught in English, the pace and level of language instruction seemed especially appropriate for our students. Over the next two years, a curriculum development committee drafted a set of Mandarin curriculum goals for K—5 students that included Chinese Language (listening, speaking, reading, writing), Cultural Themes, Science & Health, and Mathematics. ② Topics in Math, Science, and Health generally mirrored those in the regular English curriculum. As students advanced in grade level, Mandarin language goals in the four areas became increasingly complex and specific, while specified cultural themes remained quite general. ③

---

① My experience at this point included six years of university level Mandarin classes; a total of three years of language study (Mandarin and Hakka) in Taiwan from the early 1970s to the mid 1980s; three years research with Chinese communities in Malaysia and Singapore from the 1970s to 1990s; and a semester at Fudan University in Shanghai in 1985.

② The committee was composed of the Portland Public Schools Language Immersion Coordinator, three Chinese elementary school teachers, a Woodstock kindergarten teacher with some experience in China, and two Mandarin speaking parents.

③ For example, recommended cultural themes in Grades K—3 included children's songs, games, crafts, folklore, literature and Chinese holidays. K—1 students were also to learn about Chinese and American families and occupations and common greetings and forms of courtesy. Second and third graders were to develop "an awareness of life now and in the past in China." In grades four and five, cultural curriculum goals were simplified to a single statement: "Teachers will develop cultural units using a variety of perspectives that include contemporary, historical, environmental, and/or artistic information."

As with most new programs, the experiences of students in the first classes were both exhilarating and uneven. Parents, who had deliberately chosen to enroll their children in Mandarin classes, were generally very supportive and proud that their children were given the opportunity to learn a new and (for many) unusual language. Attentive parents volunteered in the classrooms, arranged for extra classes in Chinese dance and the abacus, designed Mandarin summer camps, and raised funds to support the purchase of supplementary educational materials for the Mandarin classroom. Nevertheless, by upper primary, the enthusiasm for Chinese expressed by students in their first years seemed to fade. Students struggled to learn math and science in Mandarin. Their Mandarin language skills lagged behind those of Singapore students, so that by fifth grade they were still reading stories and lessons in Singapore texts that had been designed for third graders with different cognitive skills and interests. Chinese culture lessons were generally limited to the repeated celebration of traditional Chinese holidays and selected art projects. The lack of cognitively challenging and culturally relevant ways for these students to use Mandarin seemed at least part of the problem. By the program's fifth year, with only one exception, all of the students who had originally entered as first graders selected non-Chinese options for middle school, leaving behind a small class of only nine fifth grade students. Some of this attrition was due to parental lack of confidence in district support for a robust Mandarin middle school program, but there was also a sense of disappointment in student Mandarin capabilities after five years of intensive language study.

As both a parent and initial advisor to this program, I began to wonder if there were not better curricular models for students like ours. What was the purpose of learning math, science, and health in Chinese when studying these subjects in English would have been much more effective? Why was so little attention paid to teaching our students about Chinese history, culture, and society which might more naturally enrich and stimulate Mandarin language instruction? As a university level Anthropology instructor of courses on Chinese society as well as culture theory, how might my own experiences and understandings be productively adapted to issues of Chinese language instruction for younger students?

Seeking to answer these questions, I first sought out what others had written: both on the general topic of teaching culture as part of foreign language instruction and on the more specific question of teaching Chinese culture in the context of Mandarin language programs. The scholarly literature revealed a lively and growing interest in this topic (Kramsch 1993; Heusinkveld 1997; Lange and Paige 2003). However, for the most part, discussions about the importance of cultural content in foreign language classes remained at the theoretical level, with few empirical and descriptive studies of how it was actually done (Paige et. al. 1999). I also quickly discovered that most writers focused on instruction for high school and university students, and it was not clear how their ideas and approaches could be productively adapted for younger students who were at very different developmental stages. ①

With little guidance from the scholarly literature, the next logical step was to investigate how current bilingual Mandarin programs incorporated the teaching of Chinese culture for K—8 students. Assuming that effective programs are always context specific, and aiming to better understand some of the important variables involved in developing and delivering K—8 language and culture curriculum, I decided to examine diverse schools in a range of different settings that included both China and North America. The result was an extensive investigation of curricular structures and teaching practices in seven different Mandarin bilingual programs in eleven schools in Beijing, Hong Kong, San Francisco, and Edmonton, Canada. The basic goals of my research were two fold. To begin with, I wanted to document the

---

① See, for example, discussions about teaching culture as part of Mandarin instruction by Bonin (1982), Myers (2000), Teng (2001) and Xing (2006).

multiple ways in which Chinese language and culture instruction were combined in actual classroom settings in different situations. However, my ultimate goal was to draw a set of lessons from these programs about how to most effectively combine Chinese language and culture instruction for younger students, and to use these lessons to develop a combined language and culture curricular framework for the growing number of K—8 students in American Mandarin programs.

The rest of this chapter describes the research findings from multiple school sites in some detail, highlighting both similarities and differences in approaches and outcomes for students in these diverse programs. Subsequent chapters draw on lessons learned from this research as well as additional research and collaborative work with four Portland based Chinese teachers to conceptualize and develop a framework for a more effective K—8 Mandarin language and culture curriculum.

K—8 Mandarin Bilingual Programs in Diverse Settings[①]

Initial research had revealed that the topic of cultural instruction in K—8 bilingual Mandarin programs was basically uncharted territory, so my research design was broadly exploratory, relying on classic ethnographic methods of participant observation, formal and informal interviews, and the examination of relevant documents such as curricular outlines, textbooks, and student projects. I hypothesized that children's acquisition of language and cultural understanding would be influenced by a number of factors that included family background; the cultural and linguistic environment outside of the classroom; the amount of time devoted to language and culture instruction; the types of instructional materials and practices employed; and other potential factors yet to be discovered. The schools and programs researched were

---

① The following account draws on research that has been discussed in more detail in Carstens 2008. Some sections borrow directly from this text.

deliberately selected to highlight the possible effects of such variables and included three differently structured international schools in Beijing, two international schools in Hong Kong, a private Mandarin immersion school in San Francisco, and the public Mandarin immersion program located in Edmonton, Canada. Beijing and Hong Kong represented Chinese cultural environments, although with significant linguistic and social differences. The San Francisco and Edmonton settings, by contrast, offered less opportunity for Chinese language and culture exposure outside of the classroom. However, since most of the students, especially in Edmonton, came from Chinese family backgrounds, it was possible that Chinese language and culture were reinforced in other ways.

Supported by a Fulbright Grant from the US Department of Education, I spent 11 months in China from August 2004 to June 2005, residing in Beijing but also traveling during school vacations to multiple historic and cultural sites throughout China. My daughter enrolled in Fangcaodi Primary School, a Chinese medium international school, which adapted the regular Chinese public school curriculum to teaching international students, who mostly came from Chinese and Asian family backgrounds. My daughter's experience at Fangcaodi provided interesting contrasts with the three bilingual Beijing schools that I researched: Yew Chung International School, the New School of Collaborative Learning (NSCL), and the Western Academy of Beijing (WAB). In April of 2005 I travelled to Hong Kong to research the Hong Kong branch of Yew Chung and the Hong Kong Chinese International School (HKCIS). Research in the San Francisco Chinese American International School took place in December of 2005, and the Mandarin program in the Edmonton public schools was investigated in June of 2006. In each school, initial interviews were scheduled with administrators and curriculum coordinators, who then made arrangements for me to observe a range of language and culture classes, followed, in turn, by interviews with the teachers of these classes.

These interviews followed a standard set of questions,① but also allowed for additional discussion of issues that arose from my classroom observations. In visits to eleven schools in seven different programs, I interviewed 17 administrators, observed 44 different classes and interviewed a total of 23 Chinese teachers in both English (19) and Mandarin (7).

The curriculum structures of these Mandarin bilingual programs were strongly influenced by their geographic settings and the family backgrounds of their students.② The Beijing schools ranged from completely bilingual with half day Mandarin, half day English instruction (NSCL); to 30% Mandarin, 70% English (Yew Chung); to a single daily required period of Mandarin (WAB). Because international schools in Beijing could not enroll local Chinese students, and the more mobile international students could enter these schools at any grade, Mandarin language classes had to offer multiple options for students at similar grade levels. The more intensive the language program, the more difficult this was to achieve. At NSCL, faced with student attrition from earlier grades, the Mandarin bilingual program turned to admitting a majority of Korean students, and eventually closely entirely. The less intensive language programs at Yew Chung and WAB, which had larger student populations, were able to be more flexible. At Yew Chung, with most students from ethnic Chinese families (60%) or of mixed Asian descent, Chinese language classes were divided into separate streams for native and second language students; each stream had three levels to which students were assigned based on ability and previous language experience. For WAB students, who were mostly from non-Asian families, the Mandarin curriculum was

---

① Questions were asked about the interviewee's educational and personal background, teaching and supervisory experience, their approaches to teaching Chinese culture as part of Mandarin language instruction, and the challenges they encountered in teaching Chinese culture to students at their grade level.

② See Table I for the comparative programmatic details discussed in the sections that follow.

divided into three streams, based on student language background and interest.

Chinese cultural lessons at NSCL were integrated into the Mandarin language arts and social studies classes; at Yew Chung, separate Chinese culture classes were taught twice weekly, mostly in Mandarin;① and at WAB, where grade level Mandarin language abilities were even more diverse, Chinese culture content was delivered in English, infused throughout the curriculum, with English stream teachers required to include some Chinese topic in whatever subject they taught.

Table I: Mandarin Bilingual Programs (2004—2006)

Beijing New School of Collaborative Learning

Students	Curricular Structure	Language Texts
All international. 80% Korean.	K—6 Fully bilingual: half day English, half day Mandarin.	PRC regular student texts.
Enter any grade.	7—9 Daily Mandarin class.	

Beijing Yew Chung International School

Students	Curricular Structure	Language Texts
All international. 60% Chinese, most from Chinese speaking families. Rest mostly Asian descent.	K—6 70% English; 30% Mandarin. Daily Mandarin language classes, leveled by ability. Weekly culture class.	Yew Chung developed and Singapore texts for native speakers; Yew Chung developed text for second language speakers.
Enter any grade.	7—9 Daily Mandarin class.	

---

① Because culture classes were taught at grade level to students with mixed Mandarin abilities, it was necessary for the teacher to adapt teaching strategies to incorporate some instruction in English.

Western Academy of Beijing

Students	Curricular Structure	Language Texts
All international. 40% European, 25% North American, 20% Asian. Enter any grade.	K—5 Daily Mandarin class (40 minutes); Chinese culture integrated throughout English curriculum. 6—8 Daily Mandarin class	3 streams for students of different ability/experience: PRC regular student texts; Singapore texts; PRC texts for second language learners.

Hong Kong Yew Chung International School

Students	Curricular Structure	Language Texts
Local Hong Kong. 85% Cantonese, 10% Mandarin speakers. Most enter K/1 or Grade 7	K—6 70% English, 30% Mandarin. 8 periods Mandarin language per week. Weekly Chinese culture class. 7—9 Daily Mandarin class.	Yew Chung developed texts for native speakers. Recognize 1500 characters by Grade 3, read Chinese newspapers by Grade 5.

Hong Kong Chinese International School

Students	Curricular Structure	Language Texts
International, but long term Hong Kong residents. 90% Chinese; 70% Chinese speaking families, mostly Cantonese. Most enter K/1 or Grade 7.	K—6 8 periods Mandarin language per week; 2 periods Chinese studies; 2 periods art in Mandarin. Each year one term Chinese music, one term Chinese library. 7—9 Daily Mandarin class, leveled.	K—6 Hong Kong regular student texts. 7—9 Level A: *Chinese for Today* (HK text); Level B: *Hanyu* (Australia).

San Francisco Chinese American International School

Students	Curricular Structure	Language Texts
Local. 50% Asian descent, 23% mixed race, 27% others.	K—5 Fully bilingual. Half day English, half day Mandarin.	K—5 Taiwan regular student texts, selected and revised.
20% Chinese speaking families, 10% Mandarin, 10% Cantonese.	6—8 Two periods daily in Mandarin; Chinese language arts and social studies.	6—8 CAIS developed Chinese materials.
Most enter K/1.		

Edmonton Mandarin Bilingual Program

Students	Curricular Structure	Language Texts
Local. 90% Chinese descent. 85% Chinese speaking families, mostly Cantonese.	K—6 Fully bilingual. Half day English, half day Mandarin.	K—6 Texts from Taiwan, mostly for overseas students, used selectively.
Most enter K/1.	7—9 Three periods Chinese language arts per week.	7—9 Teacher selected/developed materials.

In Hong Kong, although Yew Chung and the Hong Kong Chinese International School (HKCIS) were technically private international schools, students were mostly native Hong Kong residents who entered these programs in kindergarten or first grade. This allowed the Hong Kong programs to develop more unified and articulated language and culture curriculums and goals. Unlike Beijing schools, it was not necessary to provide multiple language streams for late entering students,① and the expectations for Chinese language fluency were

---

① HKCIS had recently decided to increase the number of late admitted students to its program and to offer them specially designed Mandarin language classes, but this had not yet been instituted at the time of my research.

significantly higher.① Like the branch school in Beijing, instruction at Yew Chung in Hong Kong was 30% Mandarin and 70% English, with a weekly Chinese culture class taught in Mandarin. HKCIS followed a similar pattern, with 8 periods of Mandarin language per week and an additional two periods of art and Chinese studies taught in Mandarin. The Chinese culture classes in both schools focused mainly on Chinese history, literature, arts and traditions with topics specified at each grade level.

As with schools in Hong Kong, the curricular structure for the San Francisco (CAIS) and Edmonton programs were based on expectations of continuous student enrollment from kindergarten through eighth grade. Although students in both programs had historically been drawn mainly from ethnic Chinese families, the students at CAIS were now more diverse and much less likely than those in Edmonton to speak any form of Chinese language at home. Also, while both programs featured half day classes in Mandarin and English, as a private school with smaller classes and more curricular flexibility, CAIS was able to offer instruction in math and social studies in both Mandarin and English, allowing for mutual reinforcement of language and content in the two subjects. Specific topics on Chinese culture were assigned to social studies classes at CAIS for students at every grade level. By contrast, the public school system in Edmonton required that subject contents follow provincial guidelines. Mandarin had been used for instruction in social studies, health, and art for some years through a translated curriculum, but the development of a new provincial social studies curriculum had convinced program administrators to gradually switch Mandarin instruction from social studies to math. Of all programs researched, Edmonton was the only program with no curricular guidelines for teaching Chinese culture; the inclusion of cultural topics in language arts classes was left to the discretion of individual teachers.

---

① For example, Yew Chung students were expected to master 1500 Chinese characters by Grade 3 and to read Chinese newspapers by Grade 5.

Beyond issues of curricular structure, what effect did geographic location have on the acquisition of language and culture skills for these students? Although I had expected that the Chinese environments of Beijing and Hong Kong would provide positive reinforcement and enrichment for Mandarin students in these locations, the reality was more complex. In Beijing, the Asian family backgrounds of most students at NSCL and Yew Chung facilitated their adjustment to Beijing Chinese society. However, the mostly non Asian WAB students often had a different experience. Living with their families in foreign compounds in the Beijing suburbs, many WAB students had limited daily encounters with local Chinese people, interacting mainly with the Chinese maids and drivers employed by their parents. WAB teachers and administrators commented repeatedly on the negative attitudes towards Chinese people and society developed by some students as a result of this living situation. [①] In retrospect, the range of responses to Chinese culture should not have been so surprising. Research on the linguistic and cultural adjustments of immigrants to new societies has shown that some individuals adapt more easily than others to unfamiliar cultural settings. (Klafehn, Banerjee, and Chiu 2008). Similarly, we cannot expect that immersion in Chinese society will necessarily generate a positive cultural response in all young students.

Issues with Chinese culture for Hong Kong students were both different and context specific. Hong Kong Chinese identity was based on Cantonese language, rather than Mandarin. Student attitudes were reflected in the remarks of an 8th grade Yew Chung teacher who claimed that most of her Hong Kong students did not like Chinese culture, but

---

[①] Asked about the special challenges she faced in teaching about Chinese culture, a middle school teacher at WAB replied: "I think from the students' side—most of the students don't appreciate Chinese culture because they don't have the chance to see the beauty of the culture. They see people spit, they see something very uncivilized around, so they get quite a negative, not respectful view towards this culture, this country, you understand?" Interview June 9, 2005.

preferred foreign things from Japan or the West.① These native Hong Kong students much preferred Hong Kong's version of a Cantonese based hybrid Chinese culture.

Cultural Instruction and Student Response

Although the curricular structures and student backgrounds in these K—8 programs varied in significant ways, the approaches to teaching culture followed several common patterns that were repeated in multiple settings. The three most common types of cultural instruction included: 1) the organization of dedicated culture classes and specified cultural curriculum; 2) teaching cultural ideas and practices through language arts texts; and 3) relying on the experiences of native Chinese teachers to bring cultural perspectives into the classroom.

Dedicated Culture Classes/Specified Culture Curriculum

The curricular guidelines in most programs identified topics for Chinese culture instruction for students at different grade levels. Of course, the extent to which these guidelines were followed varied, especially where cultural instruction was integrated with other subjects. Dedicated culture classes were offered at the Hong Kong Chinese International School and at Yew Chung branches in Hong Kong and Beijing. The culture classes, with specified topics for each grade, showed considerable sensitivity to students' cognitive abilities and interests. Early primary classes featured more hands on activities and projects along with Chinese stories, legends and the celebration of festivals, while topics for older students became increasingly more abstract and complex. The philosophy of this approach was clearly

---

① Yew Chung students traveled to Xian in 5th grade, to Australia in 6th grade, and to a mix of Asian and western countries in junior high and high school, giving them broad opportunities for comparison.

articulated in the Yew Chung guidelines, which espoused a pedagogical strategy based on the principles of proceeding "from emotion to reason, from concrete to abstract, from the outer characteristics to the essence."[①] The Yew Chung curriculum focused mostly on traditional Chinese culture while Hong Kong CIS topics paid more attention to contemporary Chinese society, but in both cases the approach reflected the sense of culture as *wenhua* (rather than *fengsu xiguan*), with considerable emphasis on history, literature, and arts. For Dr. Lui, the Yew Chung Hong Kong Chinese Curriculum coordinator, this represented in part the recuperation of a Chinese culture ignored by Hong Kong schools during British colonial times.

Chinese teachers, who were responsible for preparing culture lessons based on these curricular guidelines, drew on a variety of materials and resources that were shared with other teachers.[②] In most classes that I observed, teachers endeavored to make instruction appealing and culture come alive through a combination of text based lessons, multimedia materials, and student inquiry based projects. For example, a 3rd grade class studying the Beijing Summer Palace began with a field trip, continued with classroom instruction on its major geographic and artistic features, and ended with students exploring

---

[①] Introduction to Yew Chung Chinese Culture Curriculum Guidelines (my translation from Chinese): "Primary curriculum tends to emphasize student understanding of the concrete phenomenon of Chinese culture; what they grasp is the outer levels of the culture, emphasizing emotion as a way of molding education; the middle school curriculum tends to emphasize an understanding of abstract reasoning, an in depth investigation of the culture's essence, emphasizing logical knowledge."

[②] For example, Yew Chung Beijing had cabinets that stored a wide variety of material objects such as Chinese kites, masks, games, calligraphy materials, etc. A list of written resources for teaching Chinese culture divided by topics included: geography, history, Beijing sites, life styles (33); folk stories, geomancy, folk beliefs, religion (12); art: calligraphy, painting, paper cutting, handicrafts (30); ancient Chinese culture (26); food, tea (18); fairy tales, *chengyu* stories, dance (27); children's books—legends, including teacher recordings (51); language texts and books on other subjects that could be used directly by students in the classroom (58).

related materials on the Internet.① A 5th grade Beijing teacher lectured her class on the four great Chinese inventions (compass, printing, paper, gun powder) and then gave students the opportunity to make their own paper. Students in a 5th grade Hong Kong CIS class learned about traditional Beijing architecture, viewing and commenting in Mandarin about numerous shared photos before researching the topic further on the Internet. And a 6th grade Yew Chung Hong Kong class on Mao Zedong began with a period song that praised Mao and included a short video.

Schools provided no specific teacher training for teaching culture, and preparing these classes was viewed by many Chinese teachers as most the difficult and time consuming part of their job. Mei Lan May Tang, the Primary School Chinese principal of Yew Chung Hong Kong, described the development of materials as work that was continually ongoing:

> The original guidelines came from Dr. Lui and the teachers who did their best to find materials and to modify them with feedback from the students. Different teachers have different perspectives and students are different from year to year so that what worked last year may not suit this year's students, so (they) modify the materials every year. It's hard to keep the materials; Chinese culture is such a big pool and hard to make connections between very different materials.②

According to Dr. Lui, the difficulty in teaching these classes was due also to weaknesses in the colonial education system:

> So that's the problem we're facing. In Hong Kong in the local system they didn't offer Chinese culture lessons, so all our Chinese

---

① Although students clearly enjoyed using the computers, most Chinese Internet sites have been developed for adults, which limits what students, especially 3rd graders, can productively learn from them.

② Interview April 21, 2005.

teachers they themselves didn't have the training. They have no idea about Chinese culture, especially since we were a colony. And now suddenly they're asked to teach. They don't have the background, they don't have the training, they don't have the mentality. ①

In an effort to assist teachers and enrich culture lessons, a Yew Chung committee was in the process of preparing materials on Chinese culture which they planned to publish: both reference materials for teachers and supplementary reading materials that would include background information and suggestions for further exploration for motivated students. ②

Even where programs offered no specific classes in Chinese culture, most had curricular outlines that specified appropriate topics for students at different grade/language levels, either as part of Mandarin language arts (WAB) or social studies classes (NSCL, CAIS). Regardless of whether teachers actually followed these suggestions, the outlines conveyed informative statements about goals for student instruction. For example, the topics specified for second language students at WAB were minimal, focusing on festivals, a few stories, and some geography, while native Chinese speakers at WAB were expected to study Tang dynasty poetry, a range of traditional Chinese stories and idioms, famous Chinese scientists, and other subjects. At Beijing NSCL, topics in the social studies curriculum included folklore, handicrafts, and holidays for K—3 students, and the Confucian tradition, the Silk Road, Emperor and Peasants, and Chinese geography for students in grades 4—8. Because Chinese medium social science materials developed for native speakers were considered too difficult for second language students, the Chinese teachers at NSCL developed their

---

① Interview April 22, 2005.

② Yew Chung was also beginning to address issues of teacher training through annual Chinese teacher workshops held in Beijing (2006) and Huangshan (2007) with teachers from all of Yew Chung campuses in attendance.

own lessons on these topics using books from the school library and sharing their ideas with other teachers. A similar strategy was followed by teachers at CAIS San Francisco, who drew on a variety of materials in preparing lessons on cultural topics listed in the social studies curriculum.

Student responses to dedicated Chinese culture classes were generally positive, in part because these classes featured many hands on activities and were usually more relaxed than other classes. Student grades were based largely on effort and attitude rather than exams, something that students welcomed, but which also signaled that mastery of these lessons was of less importance than with other subjects. As materials and topics became increasingly abstract in upper grades, classroom observations and teacher comments revealed a waning interest among certain students. A Grade 6 Hong Kong Yew Chung Chinese teacher remarked on students' lack of interest in traditional Chinese culture, particularly with literature such as the 18th century *Dream of the Red Chamber* (*Hongloumeng*) which was too far removed from student lives and experiences. A Beijing Yew Chung teacher suggested that topics for culture classes had been organized too much around what adults considered important, and that a better strategy might be to focus on topics that appealed more specifically to children, creating in them a love and enthusiasm for Chinese culture that would fuel further exploration on their own when they were older.

Cultural Topics in Chinese Language Texts

Chinese language texts comprised a second important source of cultural instruction for students. However, there was considerable variation both in the cultural contents of these materials and in the extent to which teachers alerted students to the cultural perspectives that were often embedded in lesson contents. Language texts included both the "authentic texts" used by native students in mainland China,

Hong Kong, Taiwan, and Singapore① as well as texts developed specifically for second or foreign language students (See Table I). Some schools with multiple language streams used "authentic" texts for native speakers (and a few selected, more serious students) and various types of second language texts for other students. The selection of "authentic" texts suggested a desire to duplicate the education experience of native students, another type of potential cultural immersion. However, texts that were written to educate children in Taiwan, Hong Kong, or mainland China certainly functioned quite differently as instructional materials for second language students socialized in different linguistic and cultural settings. Teachers who used these texts reported doing so selectively, avoiding lessons with nationalistic references or other inappropriate contents and modifying vocabulary as necessary. Another problem with using such texts was that generally, by upper primary, students could not keep pace with native student levels and ended up studying lessons written for younger students with content that did not match their cognitive levels and interests.

The Chinese language texts for second and foreign language students ranged from those developed in Taiwan or the PRC to educate overseas Chinese students; to texts specially developed by Yew Chung teachers in Beijing and Shanghai; to more commercially developed texts aimed at younger students. Introductory lessons in second language texts typically focused on the acquisition of functional language, teaching students to use Mandarin to communicate what they might normally express in English. As a Yew Chung teacher who had helped develop such texts explained, teaching students through topics that were connected to their daily lives allowed them to use the language in

---

① The term "authentic text" is actually a misuse of the term which is usually "used in a reaction against the prefabricated artificial language of textbooks and instructional dialogues... (and) refers to the way language is used in non-pedagogic, natural communication" (Kramsch 1993:177). From this perspective, there is no such thing as an authentic textbook.

ways they found interesting.① More advanced levels of such texts usually included some Chinese stories that conveyed more distinctive cultural lessons. Overall, the amount of cultural content in second language texts varied considerably, with some continuing to focus on functional language even at the second and third levels,② while others, such as those developed by Jinan University for overseas Chinese students, featured lessons rich in cultural and historical information.

Upper primary teachers in Edmonton preferred what they described as "novel series" from Taiwan to regular texts, claiming that the longer, more developed stories were more interesting than short textbook lessons. However these teachers also commented that finding stories with subjects that appealed to their students could be difficult. In addition to the regular texts used in language classes, a variety of supplementary reading materials were available to students at every school, although the assignment of extra reading varied both between and within programs.

By middle school, Chinese language classes in programs where students had studied from an early age rarely used regular textbooks, but relied on a mix of teacher generated and selected materials, modified for student abilities and tailored to retain student interest. For example, students in an 8th grade class at CAIS in San Francisco selected a news article of their choice from a local Chinese newspaper (after reading a similar article in an English newspaper) and were asked to provide both written and verbal summaries in Chinese. Mandarin language instruction by this point in all programs was generally limited to a single period per day, and there was a sense among teachers and others that the language levels of many middle school students either leveled off or declined as Chinese classes became the least important in their overall

---

① Interview May 19, 2005.

② See, for example, texts developed for second language students by Yew Chung teachers in Shanghai, *Yukuai Xue Hanyu*, 2003.

academic program.

Culture Through Native Teacher Modeling

A third common means of cultural instruction in every program came through the employment of native Chinese teachers who not only taught culture through dedicated classes and language texts, but were also responsible for the more indirect modeling of culture in classroom practice. All of the teachers interviewed were of Chinese descent, and with one exception, born and raised in mainland China, Hong Kong, or Taiwan. Studies have demonstrated that implicit cultural instruction by native teachers can shape student language use and attitudes in language immersion classrooms (Falsgraf 1994), and this undoubtedly occurred regularly in these Mandarin programs. [1] Styles of teaching and classroom management often reflected stricter Chinese norms for respecting teachers and following proper classroom decorum, something that parents and administrators generally appreciated. However, some Chinese style teaching methods were viewed as less appropriate. Chinese curriculum coordinators at several schools commented on the tendency for their Chinese teachers to instruct students in the teacher-centered ways in which they themselves had been taught, noting that this was not a very effective approach for their students. Debates about the desirability of "rote learning" inevitably surfaced as students were required to constantly memorize new Chinese characters. In many cases, teachers' expectations for learning these characters were different for students from ethnic Chinese families and for non-Chinese students, who were generally deemed incapable of keeping up

---

[1] See, for example, the CAIS Fall 2005/2006 Newsletter that focused on cultural instruction at CAIS with an emphasis on the importance of indirect instruction by Chinese teachers (Anon. 2006).

with their Chinese peers. ① These sorts of "culturally shaped attitudes" suggest that implicit cultural instruction could be a two edged sword. Moreover, this aspect of culture comprised only a small portion of what Mandarin language students needed to know.

A considerable amount of "unscripted" instruction occurred in more direct ways. Asked about teaching culture in their classes, teachers often identified particular lessons that conveyed Chinese values, such as the lesson "Kong Rong and the Pear", where a younger brother chooses a smaller portion and gives his older brother a larger one in an acknowledgement of proper family order. One teacher spoke of the difficulty her young American students had in understanding this choice, and how the lesson exposed them to different attitudes towards family members. Another teacher taught her students to address envelopes in Chinese style with the country's name first and the individual's name last, pointing out that this conveyed different views of the relative importance of individual and country. Often examples of cultural instruction focused on proper forms of Chinese greeting which went beyond textbook lessons. For example, a teacher at WAB in Beijing described his great pleasure when a student greeted him with the old style Chinese question *chilema*? (Have you eaten?).

Certainly native Chinese teachers had the potential to bring rich cultural experiences to their classroom teaching, but the extent and ways in which they did so was shaped by a number of factors. Time was one issue, especially in bilingual programs such as Edmonton where provincial standards required coverage of specified content areas. Differences in teacher backgrounds could also make a big difference. From my observations, teachers with more limited personal and educational experiences outside of China tended to have narrower and

---

① I often felt uncomfortable with these types of comments, which seemed to verge on a kind of racism. But from another perspective, the teachers were responding to their own experiences with Chinese parents who were more likely to be able to help their children with Chinese homework and often pressured them to do well in school.

more conservative views of Chinese culture, seeing it largely in terms of classic knowledge of literature, art, and history. This was particularly true of a number of teachers in Beijing and Hong Kong who had lived their entire lives in these settings. For them, the anthropological sense of culture as everyday practices and perspectives was difficult to see because, as Jon Zatkin, the Beijing NSCL school head put it, it was too much a part of them, like mother's milk. ① Such teachers tended to have less appreciation for the more variable aspects of Chinese culture. For example, one Beijing teacher who had never left China observed that once Chinese went overseas, they became less Chinese. ② By contrast, teachers with wider experiences encouraged student discussions of diverse Chinese practices, often drawing on input from ethnic Chinese students in their classes whose families came from elsewhere. Some teachers even included units on overseas Chinese communities as part of their regular lessons. Other teachers questioned the relevance of teaching Chinese history and traditions to students living such different kinds of Chinese lives. A San Francisco CAIS teacher, who had grown up in a Chinese family in Thailand, expressed a personal view of the shifting cultural terrain when she remarked:

> I think it's important to teach the culture, but right now I think that the culture is shifting, you know like we develop our own culture here in San Francisco. We don't really have (an) exact culture like the one they have in China. Like celebrating New Year here, I think it's different from the one in China. I think we are developing our own also. ③

Ultimately, the quality and quantity of cultural instruction in whatever form it took varied more widely than language instruction as it relied on the native credentials of teachers for much of its delivery rather

---

① Interview November 16, 2004.
② Interview January 19, 2005.
③ Interview December 14, 2005.

than being systematically developed through curricular materials and teacher training. As a result, differences in teacher background and perspective significantly shaped and limited how Chinese culture was taught.

Lessons Learned

The research just described offered valuable insights into current practices in K—8 Mandarin language and culture instruction in diverse programs and settings and reinforced my belief in the unique opportunities and constraints of each situation. Decisions about curricular structure, teaching materials, staffing, and pedagogical approach clearly depended on key variables related to student family background, the local setting, and issues of resources and curricular flexibility in public and private institutions. The range of approaches and practices, however, also highlighted a series of strengths and weaknesses in teaching Mandarin to younger students that can offer lessons in how to improve curricular strategies for American students in the rapidly expanding programs emerging in our schools.

One of the strengths observed in all programs studied was the general dedication of the Chinese teachers in sharing their knowledge and love of Chinese language and culture with their students. This was clearly evident in both classroom observations and in subsequent conversations with teachers and administrators. More specifically, however, I would like to single out four areas of pedagogic practice that seemed especially effective in nurturing and advancing students' skills and enthusiasm for Mandarin language and culture. These include:

1. Differential instruction that took account of both student age and family background. Examples here would be the culture lessons that proceeded from more concrete to more abstract topics at Yew Chung; the use of different language texts and approaches for native and nonnative students in many programs; and the provision of dedicated Chinese culture classes rich in content knowledge for the mostly ethnic

Chinese students at Yew Chung and Hong Kong CIS.

2. Stimulating student interest through a variety of educational mediums, from visual aids, to encouraging student skits, to songs, riddles, use of the Internet and field trips. Such practices were especially evident in classes that targeted cultural learning.

3. The deliberate reinforcement of concepts and exercises shared with English classrooms. For example, the use of Venn diagrams for comparison and contrast; novel sets for more in depth literature studies; and math instruction in both languages. Teachers reported that building on such skills sets greatly enriched the cognitive development of their students.

4. The provision of supplementary reading materials beyond the classroom texts to students at all levels. This practice was emphasized more in some programs and some classrooms than others, but teachers who supplied and required extra reading for their students reported that such independent reading, even for their weaker students, not only reinforced what students were learning in regular lessons but gave them added confidence in their own individual abilities.

One of the major weaknesses in these programs was the absence of a truly integrated and articulated language and culture curriculum. Even where schools emphasized the teaching of Chinese culture through dedicated classes, culture was taught more as a series of facts rather than conceived as an integral part of language and communication. Programs without specific culture classes or a defined culture curriculum did not entirely ignore cultural instruction, but its delivery depended on individual teachers and lessons in selected language texts. The result was both uneven coverage and an inability to build on student knowledge and understanding from one year to the next. The relative unimportance of cultural instruction was further signaled in the absence of assessment goals in this area for students as well as a lack of teacher training.

Inattention to culture was most pronounced in public school immersion programs where required subjects were divided between

Mandarin and English instruction. Students were expected to master grade level subjects such as math, science, or social studies in Mandarin even though their second language skills increasingly diverged from their native English. Not only was classroom time at a premium in such programs, leaving little room for exploring cultural topics outside the standard curriculum, but the use of translated texts in math, science, and social studies suggested that knowledge and understanding were culture neutral: the same whether learned through Chinese or English. In texts such as these, language and culture connections were completely erased.

By far the greatest challenge faced by all programs was a declining student interest in Mandarin that began for many students in upper primary and became increasingly pronounced in middle school. The reasons behind the shift in student attitude were no doubt multiple. As with other subjects, and perhaps even more so with Mandarin, skill gaps between the best and worst students increased yearly, making it difficult for teachers to adjust lessons to appeal to a wide range of student abilities. Students also seemed frustrated with their limited abilities to express themselves in Mandarin, and often seemed to give up entirely, falling back on English (or Cantonese) for even simple expressions learned in early primary grades.

Both classroom observations and teachers' comments documented these trends across all schools and programs, suggesting that issues of motivation for my daughter's class were not an anomaly but part of a more general pattern. These results underscore the need to significantly rethink the K—8 Mandarin curriculum, so as to provide students with the types of skills and knowledge that remain cognitively engaging and personally stimulating at every grade level. We believe that one key way to do this is by systematically integrating language and culture instruction from the early grades, teaching ideas and understandings not available through the regular English language curriculum, and drawing on developmentally appropriate teaching methods to encourage sustained student engagement in Mandarin studies. The following chapter begins with a discussion of some productive ways to think about the relationship between language and culture in the context of foreign language instruction, followed by a description of some key pedagogical issues in teaching foreign language and culture to young children. The rest of the chapter describes the process followed by a team of four Portland based K—8 Chinese teachers and myself as we identified cultural themes and developed the integrated language and culture curricular framework that is featured in the remainder of this volume.

Carstens

Chapter Two   Conceptualizing and Teaching Culture to Young Students

Modeling Language and Culture Connections

The first step in developing an integrated language and culture curriculum must begin with an understanding of the multiple relationships between language and culture in language instruction. Asked about the importance of cultural understanding to language learning, most teachers and administrators in the schools that I researched tended to view language and culture as naturally intertwined—part of an unproblematic whole. For example, a middle school teacher at the Western Academy of Beijing put it this way,

> Culture is as crucial as the language. If you just know the language and don't know the culture, you really don't know it. You can't separate these two. The more language you learn, the more culture you need to go with, otherwise... it's like a robot speaking the language; it doesn't mean that he understands everything. And language is just a tool. And when you come into the country you don't just use a tool, you go as a person and use emotions and deal with people and that's

why you can't separate language and culture. ①

However, there were also teachers (included the San Francisco teacher quoted in the previous chapter) who recognized the potential tension between a more general view of Chinese culture and the complex linguistic and cultural worlds of their students. A second grade Chinese teacher in Edmonton put it this way,

> Culture is an important component of this program but sometimes I think that I have some dilemma about teaching the cultural elements of the program. I don't know if you mean a very traditional culture or the global culture. Because of communication and transportation nowadays culture is becoming more global; it's not really the Chinese culture per se. So when we talk about teaching culture, we teach language, we teach art, we have the connection with our habits, out traditions, but nowadays it seems more global—everybody is doing more or less the same thing. If I'm talking about teaching very traditional culture, like what we used to do with *Rujia* (Confucianism), *Kongzi* (Confucius), *Daojia* (Taoism), when we teach all these very old traditions, it seems to be very remote to the students. Sometimes these young children don't quite connect with it. When we talk about the Chinese New Year—they do practice Chinese New Year at home. So do we teach the very traditional culture or do we teach the culture that they practice nowadays in Chinese families? Even Chinese families in Hong Kong and China are quite different from what we used to do before. ②

Teachers such as this recognized a more complex connection between language and culture, echoed in the words of linguists such as Karen Risager, who argues that in an increasingly globalized world, "languages spread across cultures and cultures spread across languages

---

① Excerpt from interview June 9, 2005.
② Excerpt from interview May 31, 2006.

(2006:2)." Her point is most obvious when considering the global expansion of colonial languages, most notably English, but it is equally relevant to the flows of Chinese languages and cultures both within and outside of China. There is no natural connection between Mandarin Chinese and any single set of cultural beliefs, ideals, practices, and understandings. In fact, Mandarin has a somewhat different status in mainland China, Hong Kong, Taiwan, and Singapore, as well as among different segments of the population within these countries.

Given that students may be using Mandarin in diverse cultural contexts, it is important to carefully consider what types of cultural knowledge will be most useful to them. I believe that students need three basic types of cultural skills and understanding, which might be broadly divided into behavioral, interpretive, and content types of knowledge.

From a behavioral perspective, students need to know how to use Mandarin appropriately in different social contexts. This requires a basic understanding of the rules of etiquette and how they apply to people in different social positions and settings. Students not only need to understand how to use the words and phrases that are most suitable for interaction with adults and peers, but also what types of information are appropriately shared with people in different settings and what sort of behaviors are expected. For example, when is it proper to ask people's age? How do you politely refuse food or drink when it is offered in different settings? How and why do you express your appreciation and thanks in different ways to close friends and strangers? While this type of knowledge for the youngest students usually consists of memorizing appropriate words and phrases, as students mature, they should be able to adjust their language styles to fit a range of different social contexts.

From an interpretive perspective, students need to be able to decipher the social and cultural implications of messages that they read or hear. How do different styles of communication convey the diverse intentions of writers and speakers? How does language use signal social status and social relationships? Why would someone from a rural area speak or write differently from someone raised and educated in a large city? If Chinese parents do not praise their children to their face, does this mean they are not proud of them? These types of cultural understandings, which encourage student recognition of the implicit meanings conveyed through different styles of communication, could be integrated into instructional materials beginning in early grades and receive more explicit attention as students matured.

In terms of culture content, students need some basic knowledge of the historic, geographical, and cultural backgrounds of the Chinese people with whom they communicate. While the study of Chinese history, geography, and culture could easily be a life time endeavor, some types of basic shared knowledge are essential for mutual understanding to occur. Here students should not only be exposed to the key components of traditional and contemporary Chinese history and culture, but also, as they mature, they should understand some of the basic political and social divisions in the core Chinese areas of mainland China, Taiwan, Hong Kong, and Singapore, as well as other Overseas Chinese communities.

The question then, is how to integrate instruction of these types of cultural understandings into language curriculum. To answer this, we need to begin with a basic review of the most commonly used models of culture in language instruction. One way that culture is often conceptualized is by distinguishing between "big C" culture: the high culture of arts, literature, history, etc. and "little c" culture: the beliefs and practices of daily life. A similar distinction occurs with the usual Chinese translation for culture, *wenhua* (文化), which carries the connotation of high culture (civilization, arts, history, literature) as opposed to the term *fengsu xiguan* (风俗习惯), or customary beliefs and practices. Although these were the terms that I used during my initial research and interviews with Chinese teachers and administrators in the different Mandarin bilingual programs, I eventually realized that other models that relate more specifically to culture and language instruction are more useful for curricular development, in particular those of Hammerly (1982) and those outlined in the *Standards for Foreign Language Learning in the 21ˢᵗ Century* (1999). ①

In his *Synthesis in Second Language Teaching* (1982), Hammerly divides culture into three types: achievement, informational, and behavioral culture. *Achievement culture* refers to venerated accomplishments in areas such as art, literature, music or even technology. *Informational culture* consists of the common knowledge held by the average person about the geography, history, resources, politics, or other important features of his/her country. *Behavioral culture* is defined as accepted patterns of linguistic and physical behavior and the values placed on these types of behavior by people within the culture. While the domains of both achievement and informational culture emphasize the more typical sorts of factual cultural knowledge taught in the Chinese culture classes that I observed, instruction in behavioral cultural is equally essential, not only for proper communicative performance but also in interpreting cultural practices in both real time interactions as well as in other areas of culture such as literature, music, and art.

A model more familiar to American foreign language teachers was developed in the late 1990s as part of the National Standards in Foreign Language (NSFL) project (Phillips 2003), and subsequently adopted by the K—12 Chinese Standards Projects (K—12 Chinese Standards Project 1998). Here culture was designated as one of the "Five C's" of second language learning, along with communication, connections, comparisons, and communities. Goals for cultural instruction were organized around the "Three P's": students should understand the relationship between *cultural perspectives* (meaning, attitudes, values, ideas), *cultural practices* (patterns of social interaction) and *cultural products* (books, tools, food, laws, etc.).

---

① The key points of these two models are nicely summarized and critiqued in a recent article by Li Yu (2009) entitled "*Where is Culture: Culture Instruction and the Foreign Language Textbook.*"

Table II: Models of Language and Culture Connections

Hammerly		National Standards for Foreign Language	
Achievement Culture	Arts, music, literature, technology, etc.	Cultural Products	Books, tools, food, laws, etc.
Informational Culture	Geography, history, resources, politics, social organization, etc.		
Behavioral Culture	Accepted patterns of linguistic and physical behavior	Cultural Practices	Patterns of social interaction
	Values placed on patterns of linguistic and physical behavior	Cultural Perspectives	Meaning, attitudes, values, ideas

In comparing the two models, cultural products in the NSFL model would encompass both the achievement and informational culture of Hammerly's categories, although it is less clear where geography or politics would fit in the NSFL category of cultural products. Cultural practices, while similar to Hammerly's category of behavioral culture, do not include the cultural values that shape these practices, but fall in the separate category of cultural perspectives, which are said to interact with and shape both cultural products and practices (Yu 2009:82). In addition to somewhat different categories of culture, these two models differ in their emphasis on what aspects of culture deserve the most attention for foreign language learners. The "Three P's" model does not privilege one area of cultural understanding over another. Hammerly, however, advocates special attention to behavioral culture over achievement and informational culture, emphasizing the importance of a more performative understanding of language and culture. ① Each of these models has strengths and weaknesses, and practitioners often find themselves more comfortable with one approach or the other. Nevertheless, the deliberate and systematic incorporation of these different components of culture into language instruction is an important first step in curricular development. The following chapters provide one example of how we have endeavored to do this.

Language/Culture Pedagogy for Young Children

A second crucial step in developing effective curriculum for K—8 Mandarin students is to understand some of the ways that cognitive and emotional development in younger students affects foreign language learning. Research on cognitive development has shown that thinking in younger children generally progresses from more concrete understandings for younger children, to the ability to think beyond their personal experiences and comprehend more abstract ideas as students mature. Younger children learn concepts through "hypothesis evaluation" where they repeatedly (and somewhat haphazardly) compare new information to their current understandings. This suggests that active styles of learning which enable children to generate hypothesis and repeated exposure to a variety of experiences, along with teacher guidance, work best for younger children. However, discovery learning, which allows students to internalize and personalize their understandings, also needs to be balanced with teacher instruction that systematically guides student explorations of problems (Langford 1989).

---

① The performative approach to language and culture instruction has been further developed by subsequent practitioners such as Walker and Noda (2000) and Christensen and Warnick (2006) who have argued for a more contextual and experiential approach to language learning, even within the confines of the classroom. For a critique of this approach see Tang (2006), who argues that over emphasis on correct performance often ignores the cultural perspectives that shape this behavior.

Studies of foreign language learners frequently contrast the different learning capabilities and outcomes of child and adult learners (Griffiths 2008). Some theories of brain development have suggested that there is a critical period of language development during childhood after which learning new languages becomes more difficult. These theories would support the advantages of beginning foreign language study with younger, primary school students. However, the results of studies seeking to test these theories do not always agree. In general, research shows that younger children in classroom settings acquire new languages at a slower rate than older students and adults, who are able to apply their more advanced cognitive skills to a more conscious understanding and mastery of new language structures. Younger students, however, often acquire more native like pronunciation skills than those who begin foreign language instruction later in life. In some situations children also have an advantage because they can be less self-conscious about experimenting with languages than adults, although such attitudes usually shift as students approach adolescence. Beyond this, studies show that differences in younger and older language learners depend on a variety of factors, most particularly the settings in which second languages are learned and utilized, the intensity of instruction, and the motivations for language learning (Munoz 2006). For example, children who learn a second language in an environment where the language is commonly spoken have both experiential and motivational advantages over students who rarely have access to their second language outside of the classroom.

English speaking students who learn Chinese as a foreign language in K—8 classroom settings in North America cannot be expected to acquire spoken, written, and reading comprehension skills in the same way or at the same rate as they would their native language, even where Chinese and English are given equal periods of instruction time during the day. This would be true of any second language, but is particularly true for Chinese. Unlike other common immersion languages such as Spanish or French, which share an alphabet and some similar grammar and vocabulary, Mandarin is completely different from English, and usually requires four or five times longer than easier languages for an English speaker to master.① There is also usually little reinforcement for students' nascent Chinese language skills outside the classroom. Even in North American cities with large Chinese speaking populations, the most commonly spoken form of Chinese has historically been Cantonese, not Mandarin. This means that as K—8 students progress, the gap between their English language abilities and Mandarin abilities grows almost geometrically. In English, students in primary grades are expected to gradually progress from learning to read, to reading to learn; thereby using their English literacy skills to access knowledge about the world in increasingly complex and cognitively challenging ways. However, their comparatively weak Chinese skills generally do not allow them to use Mandarin to engage with similarly complex materials, and thus to feel that the language is ultimately very useful to them.

This growing competency gap between the two languages not only explains much of the waning enthusiasm for Chinese classes exhibited by upper primary and middle school students, but is also a common trend observed among students in K—8 foreign language programs in general (Tragant 2006:239). One of the key factors here is the issue of the perceived relevance of the second language to student goals. Studies of second language learning motivation in relation to student age suggest that enthusiasm in foreign language learning for younger students is tied most directly to their satisfaction with classroom practices, while older students are more focused on the current and future utility of the language (Tragant 2006:240). Such findings challenge Chinese teachers to develop curricular models and materials that not only teach foreign language in imaginative ways that connect with current student interests, but also systematically develop student skills that enable them

---

① See *Language Learning Difficulty*, http://www.foreignlanguagesweb.com/essentials/difficulty-1.htm.

to work with materials that are cognitively satisfying and clearly applicable to real world interests and problems, particularly in upper primary and middle school grades.

From Theory to Practice: A Team Centered Approach to Curricular Development

The urge to translate these research findings into more tangible schemas and curricular plans suitable for classroom use set the stage for this project's most significant contribution. My previous observations and conversations with teachers and administrators in multiple schools had underscored not only the wealth of knowledge, understanding and empathy of individual teachers, but also the synergy and stimulation that resulted from sharing ideas and insights in team settings. As a next step then, I decided that I needed to work with a team of experienced Chinese teachers who understood younger students. The Confucius Institute at Portland State University generously provided financial support for my proposed project, and offered logistical assistance in identifying a list of potential teacher candidates with appropriate experience and interests. In late summer of 2009, I made arrangements with four Portland based K—8 Mandarin teachers to work on what I estimated as a year long project to develop a combined language and culture curricular framework for K—8 Mandarin students in American schools.

The rest of this chapter describes the processes that our team has gone through to identify and develop the suggested cultural themes, topics, and teaching strategies presented here. My rationale for sharing this process is to encourage teachers and curriculum design teams to follow similar (although not necessarily identical) procedures in developing curricular goals and plans that will best serve the students and situations in each of their own unique programs. Given variations in student and family backgrounds, the different curricular and budgetary constraints of public and private schools, and variations in local cultural settings, it is vital that curricular models be tailored to local needs. In addition, involving teachers in the type of planning process described below (and perhaps students and parents also) greatly enriches their understandings of not only what should be taught, but why it needs to be taught and learned in these particular ways.

In my initial individual meetings with teachers, I briefly described my research in bilingual Mandarin programs and my goals for a new type of integrated language and culture curriculum, but also confessed that I was not certain what this would look like or how we could get there. Our project was breaking new ground in its focus on combined language and culture instruction for younger K—8 students, and my previous experience in curriculum development was with university level anthropology courses. With full time teaching schedules, we initially arranged to meet for a few hours on a monthly basis to share and comment on ideas and materials gathered individually around topics determined at monthly meetings. During our first group session in September, I shared with the team some of the key lessons about teaching language and culture garnered through my research, and we then brainstormed about how to organize the project, what we hoped to achieve, and where to begin. We agreed that one potentially productive way to start was with a backwards design: to specify what 8th grade students who had been enrolled since kindergarten in a Mandarin immersion program should know about Chinese language and culture and then begin to figure out how to teach students grade by grade to attain this level. This was the team's first homework assignment.

At our October meeting, we discussed the results of our first attempts at setting model goals for language and culture proficiency by the end of middle school. Our lists of goals followed different formats and ranged from very specific and dissimilar suggestions for Chinese character recognition (from 600 to 2500!); to more general statements about expected student proficiency in speaking, writing, and listening; to cultural topics generally linked to themes such as history, geography, food, holiday celebrations, Chinese medicine, traditional arts and crafts, and Chinese folktales and idioms. As we discussed the disparity in our language proficiency goals, we observed that students might have more passive understanding of a larger vocabulary in written and spoken Chinese than they could actively use in their own written and oral communication, so we might want to propose two sets of goals for vocabulary acquisition. One team member suggested using goals linked to the five stages of cultural topics and learning objectives from the *International Curriculum for Chinese Language Education* (OCLCI 2009), but we noted that the list here seemed more appropriate for older students or adult learners.

In terms of specific culture topics, we returned repeatedly to the question of why American kids would be interested in these subjects, especially those of a more abstract nature. And what materials were available for teaching these subjects to younger children? Two ideas raised in this meeting that we returned to repeatedly in our subsequent sessions included the proposal to integrate instruction in Chinese idioms (*chengyu*)[①] with broader cultural themes that could be repeated on a yearly basis (rather than treat them as a separate topic), and the suggestion that cultural themes be linked to the social studies benchmarks in the English curriculum.

Our assignment for our November meeting was to identify potential K—8 teaching materials for the culture topics on our lists and to bring examples where possible. The (often unsuccessful) search for appropriate culture and language learning materials for K—8 students (in bookstores, libraries, on the Internet, etc.) was something I had actively pursued throughout my research, and I was hoping that the teachers in our group would be able to suggest new resources. Not surprisingly, however, although a range of different resources were proposed, the materials identified by team members mirrored what I had

---

① Knowledge of and the correct usage of idioms (*chengyu*) are important ways that Chinese signal education and cultural fluency, and thus play a much more important role in Chinese social interactions than similar idioms would with English speakers. Because of this different cultural perspective, teaching American students how to use these idioms is usually a challenge.

found in my own investigations. Most materials were either more suitable for very young students (for whom there exists a wide range of colorful picture books) or for older students with more advanced cognitive and linguistic capabilities, with a large gap in between. One of the more promising collections of easier readings on Chinese culture (a book on Chinese Traditions and Festivals) was already out of print, another common problem. We found ourselves questioning the appeal of certain culturally rich texts for American students with little background in Chinese history and culture. Two potentially useful websites were recommended, one from Taiwan[①] and one from Beijing[②]. Both sites have language and culture lessons and include short videos of contemporary Chinese society. Some textbooks developed for Overseas Chinese students included culture related lessons, but the textbook style language and lack of thematic organization limited their usefulness. Although we had not expected to find perfect sets of materials for our purposes, it was clear from this research that relying on available materials to determine culture topics was not a useful way to proceed. As a next step, we divided the group into four grade levels, and individual teachers were asked to focus on language and culture topics appropriate for students in grades K—2, 3—4, 5—6, and 7—8.

Our January meeting featured presentations of plans for appropriate grade level Chinese language and culture topics for American students. Team members had invested considerable thought and energy into their recommendations, which ranged from suggestions for typical topics such as geography, food, festivals, history and customs; to ideas for thematic units organized around subjects like the Silk Road, the great Chinese inventions, and the Monkey King; to topics linked to student learning outcomes, which often asked students to compare American and Chinese cultural practices. Much of our discussion again revolved around how to make these topics relevant to American students.

---

① http://edu.ocac.gov.tw/home_htm
② http://www.myechinese.org

We also noticed that most suggestions focused on the categories of informational and achievement culture from the Hammerly model, with almost no attention to behavioral culture. However, if we hoped to teach our students how to communicate in culturally appropriate ways, a focus on behavioral culture was essential. As we discussed this concept in more detail, we realized that most language teachers have not been trained to think of culture in this way, in part because it is a "taken for granted" part of most daily interactions. The rest of this meeting was spent brainstorming ideas for behavioral culture topics suitable for students at different levels. Our first attempts produced the following lists:

1st—2nd grade:
- greetings: answering personal questions
- riddles; tongue twister; games
- how to take compliments
- daily routines

3rd—4th grade
- surnames
- buy candy/shopping
- chores
- meeting new friends
- visiting friend's house
- family trips: Chinese style transportation/destination

5th—6th grade:
- eating etiquette: at restaurant, at home, with friends, use of chopsticks
- food serving/sharing, symbolic food, different foods
- writing messages/emails, leaving messages
- telephone etiquette
- praises/insults: being humble vs. being confident
- classical stories on relationship between siblings
- addressing friend's family members

7th—8th grade:

- dating: asking for a date, make-up and dressing up
- behaviors in public, things considered cultural taboos
- brand names/fashion vs. creativity
- places to hangout, things to do
- slang

We decided to continue to focus more specifically on developing topics and lesson ideas around behavioral culture at the different grade levels as our next step, with an emphasis on lessons that would appeal to American students. I also asked the teachers to think again about how to teach Chinese idioms (*chengyu*). Knowing the story behind an idiom might be a start, but how are these idioms used in contemporary speech and writing? How would Chinese kids activate this sort of knowledge? Are there practical, behavioral applications? We also considered the time frame for Mandarin lessons and decided that a daily two hour period for combined Chinese language arts and social studies seemed the most logical, because even with half day Mandarin instruction in Chinese immersion programs, other subjects such as math, science, health, etc., would also need to be taught.

Our February meeting began with team member presentations of lesson topics and lesson plans focused on behavioral culture, and we exchanged suggestions for improving teaching strategies at all levels. Once again, however, there seemed to be quite a diversity of approaches and potential topics, and we wondered how we might begin to identify and organize a series of cultural topics that could begin at lower grade levels and lead in a natural/systematic way to the next higher grade levels. The consensus was that it would be useful to construct lists of potential cultural topics organized around a series of themes. Returning to our brainstorming mode we selected as our initial categories: Family, Food, Festivals, Friends & Fun, Fashion, Feelings, Famous People, Famous Places. We decided to begin to list possible topics for each of these themes at different grade levels, separating these topics into the

Hammerly categories of Behavioral Culture, Informational Culture, and Achievement Culture.

Team members brought draft charts of cultural topics for our eight designated themes to our March meeting, with specific suggestions for behavioral, informational, and achievement culture. However, rather than discussing these charts in detail, we decided to focus on developing a single common theme for our upcoming conference presentation at the Chinese Education Conference, hosted by the Chinese American International School in San Francisco in April. Our goal was to develop combined language/culture unit plans built around a theme that would be interesting, developmentally appropriate, and build in a spiral manner with reinforcing and expanding lessons at subsequent grade levels. Rather than gravitating to a theme that is usually well covered by Chinese teachers, such as food or festivals, we choose to develop our unit plans around the theme of feelings. Part of our discussion focused on the different ways that Chinese are taught to express feelings, and how this might be integrated into classroom lessons. One team member questioned whether the focus on feelings was the best topic, given that Chinese students are encouraged to hide their feelings inside. However, we noted that teaching culturally appropriate vocabulary associated with feelings beginning in early grades made sense, in part because this topic was one that American students could connect with their own experiences. Then, as students matured, lessons could begin to focus on cultural differences in the way that people are expected to expression emotions. After brainstorming and listing possible language and culture contents for this theme at different grade levels, we decided to follow the backward design of the "5C" standards for developing model unit plans. Each teacher would first identify learning goals, objectives, and assessment tools before deciding on teaching contents and suggested student activities.

The next few weeks were very busy as each team member worked on their own Power Point sections which were previewed, critiqued, and revised multiple times before our final group presentation in the second week of April. Attending and participating in this conference not only exposed us to additional valuable ideas and perspectives, but gave an added boost to team spirit. Our presentation, titled *"Developing an Integrated Language/Culture Curriculum for K—8 Mandarin Students"* was well received, although in retrospect, in terms of our project, the major benefit was the push it gave us to organize our ideas even more carefully. I also attended a valuable day long workshop titled *"Developing and Assessing Thematic Units"* led by Dr. Jennifer Eddy which, among other things, reinforced my conviction that culturally relevant topics belong at the core of language instruction. According to Dr. Eddy, the ultimate goal of language learning is the flexible transfer of knowledge and skills learned in one context to new, unfamiliar situations. Students should be given experience with transfer tasks early and often, preferably with culturally authentic materials drawn from the target culture. This workshop also introduced me to useful ways of organizing units around nested questions that served as the framework for an array of interpersonal, interpretive, and presentational activities (Eddy 2010).

In the meetings that followed the Chinese Education Conference, we focused increasingly on identifying our ultimate goals for this project and decided to return to the thematic charts initially drafted in March around our seven categories: Family, Food, Festivals, Friends & Fun, Fashion, Feelings, Famous People, Famous Places. Beginning with the theme of Family, we talked at length about what should be taught at different grade levels, again paying attention to behavioral, informational, and achievement culture, but now collapsing this into the two categories of behavioral and informational/achievement culture. The issue of age appropriate topics was repeatedly raised: we should not expect American students to comprehend ideas that are either too abstract for them or that could not be connected in some way to their own experiences, especially for younger children. Thus, there might be little in the achievement culture column for lower primary students because these are not suitable topics for this age. A focus on behavioral culture, with active learning strategies, makes more sense for younger students, and informational culture can be carefully included to help students begin to understand cultural differences and different cultural perspectives. As we looked at our original thematic categories, we decided that information for some themes would be more usefully integrated into other topics/themes, so we eliminated Famous People and combined Famous Places with Geography into a single theme. This process of revision and refinement of key themes continued throughout our subsequent meetings as we slowly worked our way through our evolving thematic chart. By this point, we also realized that we were most productive when working together and began to schedule longer group meetings to accomplish our goals.

In late May, as we turned our attention to the Food and Festivals themes, we decided to organize food lessons for different grade levels around two key questions, with the first focusing more on informational culture and the second including behavioral understandings:

1. What do Chinese people like to eat and why? (Informational)
   - daily family meals (breakfast, lunch, dinner, snacks)
   - special occasions (birthdays, restaurants, dim sum, etc.)
   - festivals (save this for when festivals celebrated?)
   - regional foods (north, south, etc.) beliefs about food and health

2. How is food served/ shared in different settings? (Informational & Behavioral)
   - formal and informal occasions (etiquette)
   - round tables and shared food
   - chopsticks
   - going out for snacks (*xiaoye*...)

These questions would help direct student attention to variation in foods and eating practices in different contexts. The same topics would not necessarily be covered at every grade level, but lessons would address these questions in ways that appealed to students of different ages and levels of cognitive development. Students could learn about

Chinese food beliefs and practices through stories, poems, art, music and a range of hands on activities, including cooking and eating. Rather than organizing a unit around Festivals, as we had earlier envisioned, we decided that annual festivals should be celebrated as they occurred throughout the school year, at the same time including lessons about the Chinese lunar calendar and the Chinese almanac with lucky and unlucky days as appropriate. We identified three key questions for this theme (How do Chinese people organize activities throughout the year? How do Chinese people celebrate festivals and holidays? Why are these celebrations meaningful?), and we drafted a chart with lists of topics for different grade levels.

Table III: Annual Festival/Holiday Cycle

Kindergarten—Grade 2	Grades 3—4	Grades 5—6	Grades 7—8
* Teacher's Day: Sept 10	* Teacher's Day: Sept 10	* Teacher's Day: Sept 10	* Teacher's Day: Sept 10
* Autumn: Seasonal poems, music, art	* Autumn: Seasonal poems, music, art	* Autumn: Seasonal poems, music, art	* Autumn: Seasonal poems, music, art
		* Lunar calendar	* Lunar calendar and Chinese almanac
* Moon Festival: Moon cakes, moon gazing	* Moon Festival: Moon cakes, legends, poems	* Moon Festival: Moon cakes, legends, poems	* Moon Festival: Moon cakes, legends, poems, strolling couples in parks (Taiwan)
* National Days: October 1	* National Days: October 1	* National Days: October 1	* National Days: October 1
		* Halloween and Ghost Festival	* Halloween and Ghost Festival
* Winter: Seasonal poems, music, art	* Winter: Seasonal poems, music, art	* Winter: Seasonal poems, music, art	* Winter: Seasonal poems, music, art

(Continued)

Kindergarten—Grade 2	Grades 3—4	Grades 5—6	Grades 7—8
* Chinese New Year: Common practices, zodiac animals, paper cuts and decorations, music▲	* Chinese New Year: Common practices, legends, lion dance, good luck symbols, music	* Chinese New Year: Common practices, good luck symbols, taboos, regional practices within China, travel during Chinese New Year, CCTV extravaganza	* Chinese New Year: Common practices, stove god and door gods, travel during Chinese New Year, celebrations in overseas Chinese Chinatowns
* Yuan Xiao: Rice balls, lantern parade	* Yuan Xiao: Lanterns and lantern riddles	* Yuan Xiao: Legends, lantern riddles, temple festivals	* Yuan Xiao: Lantern displays, lantern riddles
		* Valentines and Qixi festival legends	* Valentines and temple festivals
* Spring: Seasonal poems, music, art	* Spring: Seasonal poems, music, art	* Spring: Seasonal poems, music, art	Spring: Seasonal poems, music, art
		* Labor Day: May 1	* Labor Day: May 1
* Children's Day: June 1	* Children's Day: June 1	* Children's Day: June 1	* Youth Day: May 4 (May 4th Movement)
* Duanwu Jie: zongzi, hats with 5 poisonous animals	* Duanwu Jie: zongzi, Dragon Boat legends	* Duanwu Jie: different types of zongzi, dragon boat legends	* Duanwu Jie: Qu Yuan poetry and history

▲ Every Chinese New Year season, students would expect a series of activities organized around a core set of practices: cleaning the classroom, writing spring couplets（对联）, family reunion dinner with special foods（饺子）, midnight firecrackers, hong bao（红包）, auspicious sayings（吉祥话）, visiting family and friends.

In the meetings that followed throughout the summer and into the fall, team members not only continued to work on identifying appropriate topics for thematic units at each grade level, but also constructed sets of essential questions for each theme that were matched to different grade levels. For example, the question "How and why are families important?" was considered appropriate for all K—8 students, while the question "Why is family honor important?" targeted only students in grades 5—8. Individual teachers then developed more specific focus questions for their grade levels that connected to essential questions (see Master Thematic Chart). We also continued to discuss our project's ultimate goal, a publication that shared our endeavor with a wider audience. Our objective was neither a textbook nor a conclusive recipe for an integrated K—8 language and culture curriculum, but rather a set of guidelines to help people think about the why, how, what, and wherefore of integrated culture and language instruction. Ultimately, each program's curriculum would need to be designed by the people involved in student instruction within that program at all levels. We decided that individual teachers would write grade level chapters that described their approach to teaching integrated language and culture lessons, drawing on the themes and topics in the continually evolving thematic master chart and ending with the more developed unit plan on Feelings initially prepared for the Chinese Education Conference.

I proposed that each teacher begin their chapter with a short introduction that described students' social, emotional, and cognitive development at that age level and the effect of this on language arts skills and teaching strategies. I had naively assumed that this information could be easily drawn from other sources, but we quickly discovered that writings on social, psychological, and cognitive developmental stages tend to be highly theoretical and abstract. After we had shared and discussed the first chapter of Peter Langford's *Children's Thinking and Learning in Elementary School* and previewed some textbook charts on child development, I encouraged teachers to draw on their own rich experiences to write about the developmental challenges and promises of students of different ages. Ideally, this should also be a model for other programs to follow in encouraging teachers to consciously and actively consider issues of social, emotional, and cognitive development as they plan lessons for their students.

The next four chapters, written by two of the four teachers in our group,① describe approaches to integrated culture and language instruction for students at four different grade levels, offering specific suggestions for each of the eight thematic topics, and ending with an example of a more developed unit plan for the topic: Emotions. Having teachers personally write their own chapters underscores the distinct flavors and somewhat different perspectives that instruction will always carry when delivered by individuals with their own unique experiences and personalities. These chapters were originally written in Chinese, and I have taken responsibility for their English translation as well as the English translation in the bilingual Master Thematic Table (Appendix I), which provides an overview of topical development for our eight themes at the four different levels.

Carstens

---

① Two team members, Wen-Chyou Guo and Lily Tsang, who were initially responsible for the K—2 and 3—4 levels and contributed much to our group discussions, were unable to find sufficient time to write the narratives for these chapters. Fortunately, Tien Whyte and Li-Ling Cheng were able to draw on their past experiences with K—4 students as well as ideas proposed in group meetings to write these chapters.

Chapter Three Guiding Curiosity: Kindergarten to Grade 2

Introduction

Children's mental and physical capabilities increase with age, and each stage of development has its own definite patterns and special characteristics. For example, four year old children are extremely capable of expressing themselves both linguistically and physically; not only do they love to talk, but they love to ask why and love to put things together for themselves. In circumstances where family involvement is not necessary, they can play quietly by themselves and very easily play happily together with other children. They are also able to interact with playmates in group games and learn simple rules of the game. Five year old children have increased abilities to grasp ideas, a growing curiosity, and a desire to have answers for everything. This is a period of exceptional love of learning and questioning; they are particularly fond of using their own ways to explore new things. As they begin to have conscious awareness of their own self-expression, they do not like others telling them how to do things. Six year old children sleep for shorter periods and are more active and mobile; they are increasingly interested in learning; beginning to care about their status in a group; able to express their individual views, and starting to learn how to debate with others. Therefore, teachers who guide children of this age group need to have a definite understanding of the changes in these children and the teaching methods most appropriate for this stage.

Cognitively, children aged five to seven are extremely sensitive to sight and sound and are able to understand numbers. This is a period of rich oral vocabulary development and an important stage in the shaping of moral character. In curricular design, teachers should utilize colorful visual images in their demonstrations, and should use music to stimulate all kinds of physical activity. Classroom rules and proper ways for students to treat each other should also be taught, and students should be encouraged to talk to nurture their expressive language abilities.

In kindergarten through second grade, children progress from the mostly play based learning of kindergarten to the more regular style of school classes. In this transformation of environment and roles, as children psychologically adjust to the situation, they can feel impatient and have difficulty controlling their behavior. The teacher must create a sense of security in the learning environment so as to stabilize the student's mood for learning. For example, every morning when the students enter the classroom, the teacher must first take the initiative to say hello; by making sure to maintain a cheerful mood, and getting the day off to a good start, students can quickly forget the difficult parting from mom. Especially with kindergarten students, a gentle hug can often calm a student's nervous feelings. Sometimes you can negotiate timing with students, allowing them to talk awhile with their mother before entering the classroom. By encouraging students to behave in a more grown up manner, children will enjoy having the opportunity to show off their more mature sides.

Younger students are still grappling with social skills, still learning how to make friends and how to get along with friends. Children of this age are most afraid of being rejected and isolated by others, and are also afraid that others will not listen to them; therefore, it is extremely important for students to cultivate compassion and learn good communication skills. Students need to change from their usual forms of self-centered behavior to caring for and sharing with others. This is truly not an easy task. The teacher needs to guide them step by step, constantly setting an example in both large and small daily matters, helping student establish habits of speaking well about things to encourage other people to have a positive attitude toward life.

The culture study contents for K—2 students should emphasize behavioral culture, including polite behavior between teachers and students, required rules for school and classroom; cherish the young, respect the elderly, obey one's parents; using bowl and chopsticks to eat Chinese food; Chinese festival activities; ways of expressing positions and directions, etc. These are all part of the behaviors of daily life. The teaching goal is for students to demonstrate appropriate manners in their daily life. I especially recommend that teachers with students in the lower grades use stories from Chinese fables and idioms to raise students' cultural awareness.

In learning about the culture of daily life, you need to establish a foundation of vocabulary and sentence patterns. Thus language proficiency training is a primary learning focus for lower grades. The main themes in language study should revolve around things and relationships in student lives such as family, friends, and school. The curricular goal is to train students to communicate orally and understand short phrases connected to individuals and daily life; to be able to simply introduce their own and others' basic situations; and to able to communicate with others about familiar subjects of daily life such as numbers, time, and place. In terms of teaching idioms or verse, I think that using imitative performances or images to explain are the easiest ways to help students understand. The teacher just needs to prepare some supplementary visual props before class, and students will quickly understand the idioms and the contexts in which they are used.

I propose that language teaching activities for K—2 students use

Chinese character/word cards that students read and compare, using a variety of visual and auditory stimulation and body movements to deepen the impression of these words. Reading short stories will enhance student comprehension skills, but in reading these stories, teachers should divide them into smaller sections and use different voices to represent different characters so as to create an atmosphere for the story and to transform the story's abstractions into concrete descriptions. Each time a character appears, especially in the dialogue section of the story, assign one student to imagine how to mimic this character. After the teacher has demonstrated this, have the student pick a partner, to practice with. When the whole story has been presented, the students will be very interested in performing the story, and during the performance the teacher will just need to guide them a bit in using proper dialogue. After several practices and mutual observations, the students will be able to explain the plot of the story in simple terms.

In addition, teach through the singing and chanting of nursery rhymes; this trains student pronunciation and oral tempo while transforming the lesson into a pleasurable activity. Of course, don't forget games, whether the more static activity of matching playing cards and bingo games, or the active games of kicking the shuttlecock, losing the handkerchief, or the wooden headed man losing at cards. So long as the teacher first establishes a few simple rules, such as when playing there must be certain oral exchanges, these games can certainly benefit language study.

Kindergarten students just need to have novel and interesting things and they are willing to follow along. Because the students are still rather young, their muscular coordination and organizational skills are just developing and they need many opportunities for guidance and practice, so teachers need to spend more time doing preparatory work before class. These younger students, who like to ask questions, to study and have a strong sense of curiosity, seem to soak up knowledge like a sponge. No matter what the teacher teaches, the students are impatient to absorb it; but they still have a short attention span, so the teacher must have at least five different types of learning activities for each class period to maintain student motivation for learning. I recommend a book published by Beijing Culture and Language University Press *Games for Learning Chinese* ("游戏学中文") compiled by Zhou Yanzhuo and Shu Yibing, which teachers can consult as a reference in planning games and activities.

In addition, the culture learning objective for lower level students at this stage is to nurture a foundation of understanding, so when choosing stories about Chinese traditional cultural perspectives, try to avoid books with stereotypical old fashioned writing styles and those with complex historical backgrounds and select instead illustrated books with more modern forms of expression.

Finally, I want to say that teachers of younger students must always maintain a youthful sense of humor in order to appreciate the unrestrained creative imagination of children. They need to be able at any time to squat down to see things from a child's perspective, to feel their frustrations, and understand their challenges in learning. In this way you can be like a "fish in water" and the students can take pleasure in their Chinese class.

Unit Topics

Unit Topic One: Family

The lives of younger students are still focused around family, friends, and school, so it is easy with the family unit to inspire warm student discussion on this topic. The learning objectives for this unit are for students to understand Chinese ideas of filial piety; the different relationships and forms of address for Chinese family members, and the ethical views of sibling relationships.

Forms of address in Chinese families are much more complicated than American families. I think it is sufficient for kindergarten students to learn terms for father, mother, older brother, younger brother, older sister, and younger sister. First and second grade students can add paternal and maternal grandparents, aunts and uncles. In order for students to quickly remember family titles, the classroom can exhibit a chart of family members. Students can refer to this every day and this can help to create a visual impression and memory.

Practical manual work is very important for students of this age because the sense of touch can help to concretize visual and mental memories. Small motor skills are still developing in kindergarten students, so I suggest that students cut and paste shapes to assemble the family member display chart (cutting and pasting is a very beneficial exercise for developing small motor skills). For first and second grade students you can use a diversity of materials such as fabric, yarn, clay, and recycled bottles to make cloth or bottle dolls, with each class completing two sets of family members, while at the same time learning corresponding nursery rhymes about the relationships of family members. For example, today you are studying paternal grandfather and grandmother; take the nursery rhyme "Father's father is *yeye*, father's mother is *nainai*" and while reciting this, write it on the whiteboard; by the time the dolls are completed the students will have learned the nursery rhymes, while at the same time understanding the relationships between family members. Afterwards, every day select two students to take turns to display the constructed family, and one by one introduce each doll; for example, this is *yeye*, father's father, this is *nainai*, father's mother. Don't forget to ask students to bring their favorite photo of their whole family to class, so that they all become acquainted with each other's families.

To provide impetus for learning from repeated phrases, ask students to disguise themselves as different family members, and each time their position is read aloud, they have to act in an appropriate way. For example, when they hear *yeye* (paternal grandfather), the student has to imitate how a grandfather walks or dances. Another way is to not directly say a form of address, but say father's older brother and then *bobo* would have to come out and dance. This activity not only reviews words, but at the same time reviews family relationships. It also fits with the "Go Fish" game where students match picture cards.

Recommended children's songs:"家族歌""世上只有妈妈好""宝贝女儿好妈妈""咱们从小讲礼貌"。Idioms:母子连心、虎父无犬子、孟母三迁、知子莫若父/知女莫若母。Poem:"静夜思"(Grades 1—2).

In terms of reading materials, it is fine to read stories about family relations to kindergarten students as long as the text is not complicated and pictures illustrate the story. In selecting reading materials for younger students, there are stories of modern families as well as the 24 stories of filial piety.① In narrating the stories, the teacher should emphasize Chinese filial piety concepts of obedience and deference (听话和顺从) and the concept of love and respect between brothers (兄友弟恭). The focal point of studying these stories is to allow students to obtain basic understandings of different cultural forms of polite daily expressions. The teacher can assign homework for students to borrow one book from the library about showing filial piety to parents and one story about sibling affection (in either English or Chinese) to bring to the classroom, and students take turns relating the stories. This assignment allows students, as they select their stories, to think about the concepts of filial piety and friendship. The reason why books do not have to be in Chinese is because students can more easily read and select an English book. Although this phase of study is focused on training Chinese language skills, selecting reading materials that can initiate a student's desire to speak can help them become more engaged in this topic.

Finally, give students nine large cards and have them draw three representing filial piety, three expressing fraternal affection, and three expressing courtesy/manners. After completion, the students have to guess the meaning of each other's pictures, then exhibit them on the classroom walls. I recommend an animated film that students enjoy

---

① http://www.icpcc.cn/edu/student/leyuan/200612/972.html

titled *"Big Ear Tutu"*[①], a family movie very suitable for lower level students.

Younger students are at a stage where it is easy to spur them to learn; as long as the teacher repeatedly changes learning activities and gives students more opportunities to speak and perform, the children will never tire.

Unit Topic Two: Food and Chinese Medicine

Food is a topic of endless interest for younger students. The learning objectives of this unit are to understand the names and flavors of common Chinese foods, learn how to use chopsticks, and practice common table manners.

As a start, students can learn common foods for breakfast, lunch and dinner. The teacher can clip supermarket ads from newspapers and have students cut and paste, dividing them into three trays of food (for their three different meals). Students practice explaining the contents of the three meals they eat each day. The teacher then shows pictures of the common foods that Chinese people eat for breakfast (steamed buns, soy milk, sesame coated baked biscuits, deep fried breadsticks, rice porridge) and for lunch and dinner (white rice, noodles, dumplings, and stir fried vegetables). Of course, if the teacher is able to buy some foods from Asian markets and bring them to the classroom for students to see and taste, it will stimulate more active sensations and allow them to learn tastes such as sour, sweet, bitter, and spicy.

Making onion cakes or dumplings are always very popular activities, and if there is a school kitchen, the teacher should give the students the opportunity to practice this to enhance student knowledge and love of Chinese food. If there are no kitchen facilities, the students can make dough models of their favorite Chinese foods. The teacher can design a bingo game using pictures of different kinds of Chinese foods as an exercise to strengthen

---

① http://www.tom61.com/ertongyingyuan/ertongdonghuapian/2010-09-19/2538.html

student mastery of vocabulary. See also *Games for Learning Chinese* ("游戏学中文"), "The smelling game" (page 81).

Next, assign students to bring snacks of different shapes and sizes to the classroom. The teacher prepares chopsticks for a snack competition game where the snacks are placed in different bowls. Students divide into two groups; each group selects one student at a time to compete to see who can place the most snacks in a bowl in one minute. In the end the winning group gets to share the snacks. There are many different games to play with chopsticks and the teacher can vary them for student practice, such as picking up noodles or meatballs. The purpose of this activity is to train students in using chopsticks to eat and to understand the Chinese practice of eating food with chopsticks. At the same time, the teacher should display images or movies of Chinese and western styles of utensils and meals so that students can compare and contrast the differences.

Arrange classroom tables and chairs to make a large table, and have students practice setting out bowls and chopsticks. Students can take turns playing the roles of different family members: grandfather, grandmother, father, or mother. Have students practice the order of seating positions and ways of holding bowls and chopsticks when eating. As students perform spontaneously, the teacher will remind them of mistakes and students can correct themselves so that after doing this a few times students will know how to set out bowls and chopsticks, how to take their seats in the proper order, and how to hold bowls and chopsticks when they eat a meal. Because this is a very spontaneous exercise for students, it is a very effective way for them to learn.

What are inappropriate eating behaviors? Have students make a diagram with symbols for prohibited behaviors. Hand out a round card to each student and ask them to design a chart that can be used in a restaurant with symbols of prohibited behaviors. After this is completed, have them give a simple explanation of the meaning and then post this on the classroom wall.

Finally, put students into groups and ask them to perform short skits about eating at a Chinese friend's house. The teacher first explains the requirements that students must follow in their performance; their dialogues should include and demonstrate all of the table manners that they have previously learned. Before being scored, each group has the opportunity to first discuss their story line and style of performance. Although this is very challenging for younger students, don't underestimate the students' abilities. As long as the teacher explains clearly the contents required for the performances, students can definitely express these ideas.

Chinese songs about food are very limited. I suggest that the teacher revise Chinese or English songs or rhymes that the children are already familiar with. First and second grade students especially love these types of creative activities and the teacher might as well utilize this. In the process of classroom learning you can also insert Mavis Fan's *Health Song* as a warm up singing exercise and a way of enhancing the classroom learning atmosphere. Recommended songs:"饭前要洗手""吃饭歌""大米饭". Tang poem *Compassion for the Farmer* ("悯农"). By reciting this poem every day before beginning lunch, students will soon unconsciously remember the verse and quickly understand the profound meaning of the value of food.

Unit Topic Three: Chinese Festivals

Days devoted to festivals and celebratory activities are greeted by younger students with great excitement and anticipation. Festivals inevitably include food, drink, games, and music. Chinese annual festivals: Teacher's Day, Mid-autumn Festival, New Year, Lunar New Year, and Dragon Boat Festival all have their own types of celebrations and special foods. Although these festivals are celebrated every year, as the students get older, their comprehension and learning abilities increase, so even if the activities used by the teacher are constant from year to year, the level of student knowledge deepens and the teacher should preserve traditional ways of teaching. Students who have passed through kindergarten and first grade should have a basic knowledge of the meaning and activities of Chinese traditional holidays.

The culture learning objectives for this unit are that students have basic knowledge and understanding of the origins and celebration of traditional Chinese festivals and festival foods (dumplings, moon cakes, sticky rice cakes). The teacher needs to understand students' cognitive levels and functional maturity, and particularly with manual activities needs to design projects according to students' practical skills. In gaining new knowledge, younger students need to go through the process of touching, seeing, reflecting on, and then remembering in order to learn. Each child may have a different way of remembering. After students have finished listening to stories of festival fables and legends, use cartoon style sketches to show their level of comprehension of the story. After going through this type of reflective drawing process, students can once more digest the story and retain a lasting impression.

Kindergarten students still need training in many types of physical activities, so materials for handicrafts should be prepared before class begins. In the production process, you must slowly explain and demonstrate step by step. Muscles are better developed in first and second grade students, who also have better organizational skills. For manual activities at this level, where appropriate, the teacher can assign preparation of materials to students, giving them the opportunity to participate and perform. The teacher, however, still must explain the sequence and procedure.

The teaching content for this unit should include knowledge of the names of festivals, short illustrated mythical stories of festivals, festival music/ songs, the making of handicrafts, and other corresponding festival activities, for example: cutting and pasting window flowers; making small lanterns; decorative firecrackers; tracing spring couplets on paper; wrapping dumplings; making moon cakes; eating pomelos; drawing the image of Confucius; performing the lion dance/dragon dance; wrapping clay dumplings; making dragon boat origami; or making stage props for festival performances; watching festival animation and performances. See also *Games for Learning Chinese* ("游戏学中文"), "Lantern riddles" (page 33) and "My favorite holiday" (page 37).

I believe that teachers already have a wealth of ideas about teaching contents for Chinese festivals, so I don't need to say much more about this. I would just like to remind teachers that festivals have a set time period, so the course plan needs to correspond with this timing. For example, the spring festival period is relatively long, and the abundant materials can be spread over two weeks. Other festivals, at the most, do not extend for more than three days; by comparison this allows students to experience the festive atmosphere of the moment and not find it tedious and lose interest. Just as after receiving Christmas gifts, children quickly look forward to the arrival of the New Year, and then again look forward to the next holiday, my wish is that students have these same types of expectant feelings as they look forward to Chinese festivals throughout the year.

Don't forget to have "Show and Tell" to give students the opportunity to talk about their favorite American and Chinese holidays and to show the things that they have collected. See also *Games for Learning Chinese* ("游戏学中文"), "My favorite holiday" (page 37).

Unit Topic Four: Geography and Travel

Key topics for the geography and travel unit should train students in the concepts of time, direction, and position as well as training them to explain locations and understand modes of transportation and travel.

To begin with, students should understand how to explain positions, that is the basic concepts and expressions for front, back, inside, outside, above, below, and in between. "Hiding Things" is a good warm up game; students learn through this game how to say the position of things and at the same time achieve the goal of understanding positions. In order to better understand and use sentence patterns, the teacher shows a large scale picture prepared in advance and asks students in turn to describe something's position. Each student is given a small white board, listens to the teacher say a sentence, and then draws this position on their white board. After practicing several times, students will grasp how to explain positions.

The teacher can also draw things like houses, trees, cars, parks, dogs or cats on the large white board, and have students take turns drawing themselves in the positions they like. Their human figures must show movement; for example, they will draw themselves eating something. After each person is finished drawing, they will guess who is doing what and where. This game as much as possible allows students to create as they wish. The more comical and exaggerated the drawings, for example drawing yourself sleeping inside the dog's stomach, the more intense the student interest. After the drawing game have another "I say, you do" activity to once again review. This lesson is highly entertaining and guaranteed to generate endless laughter.

Next, have students draw tables and chairs in a classroom with things arranged in position on the diagram. The amount of detail required in the picture will depend on student capabilities. Then, collect all of the drawings together. Kindergarten students can select a drawing and talk about the drawing for their activity; first and second grade students, in addition to talking about the drawing, can be asked to write a sentence about the drawing. Then have students draw maps of areas outside of the classroom. Before drawing the map, lead students in a walk around the schoolyard (the teacher determines the size range), to give the students the opportunity to understand their own schoolyard. The teacher can explain the location of things throughout this tour, or use questions to have students practice explanations. In this way help students to have a basic conception of directions and locations before drawing their maps. For younger students, this is a big project, but also a fun challenge. Teachers should keep in mind not to judge whether student maps are realistic or not; as long as they are able to show the positions of things, this is sufficient. Students at this stage are afraid of being laughed at, so teachers should display their own imaginative abilities in understanding student artistic creations. An accompanying homework assignment asks students to draw the position of their house with the surrounding landscape on all four sides, and bring this to the classroom to explain and display. An accompanying song game can be played in class. "Where is my friend" is a children's song where the students are asked to change the usual answer "over here" to above, or inside, or in the back, etc. making this a practice review.

If students can draw a map, then they also have basic skills to read a map. So the teacher can display a community map with captions, and have students practice how to get from A to B. At this time words for means of transportation can be brought in. In learning new words it is best to use picture cards for main characters to assist students in recognition and reading. Then play a travel game to learn how to give directions (left turn/right turn/straight ahead/stop). Two students are going on a trip and select two different points (A to B) and the mode of travel, a third student gives directions, and the students going on the trip must imitate riding in the kind of transportation they have selected. If they can go outside and practice this in the actual schoolyard setting, the learning process for the students will be even more realistic. For games about directions and traffic, teachers can also refer to *Games for Learning Chinese* ("游戏学中文"): "A good driver" (page 19); "Flag carrier" (page 27); "On the right train" (page 42); "Walking with eyes closed" (page 136). Recommended children's songs: "红绿灯""交通秩序歌""造飞机""火车快飞". Nursery rhyme: "碰碰车，车碰碰".

Once students have a basic understanding of geographic location, the teacher can show a map of the world and teach students the location of China and the United States. Younger students should learn to recognize on a map the names of the seven continents and four oceans. Having students use different colors of clay to make a three dimensional world map is a very effective learning activity.

In terms of time, kindergarten students must first have number concepts and learn to count before reading a clock. Teachers can have students practice counting while doing exercises and can use nursery rhymes for this practice. First and second grade students ought to learn how to say dates and to read a digital clock, including minutes and seconds. The teacher can coordinate with prior travel activities and add time, so each time students travel they must clearly state the date (drawing a date card) and time (according to the time indicated on a clock).

Finally, have kindergarten students bring a souvenir from a family trip to the classroom and talk about where they went, who they went with, what they brought with them, how they got there, how long they went, and what they did. First and second grade students can make a simple schedule: the teacher must prepare in advance a form for them to use that includes dates, location, transportation, time/activities. Based on their own preferences, students design a holiday travel schedule and give an oral report.

Recommended idioms:景色如画,走马看花,人山人海,一路顺风,一路平安. Recommended poem:"山村咏怀"(一去二三里,烟村四五家.亭台六七座,八九十枝花.) This poem allows students to express their own understanding and imagination through drawing with a Chinese brush. I usually ask students to use four images to express the contents of the poem. Students in the course of creation have their own ideas, so each work of art is a child-like free form ink painting.

Unit Topic Five: History, Politics and Religion

Younger students have no specific conceptions of history, government, or religion and are not yet capable of even understanding these words. I think that telling stories is the best mode of instruction. Kindergarten students still lack a concept of time and only understand "long ago" and "the present". First and second grade students understand the meaning of the words for years, months, days, and weeks but although they can also talk about today, tomorrow, yesterday, last week, or last year they are easily confused. Therefore, the focus of instruction for younger students in this unit is school education, and students learn to understand the main functions of school, and the courtesy and attitudes that show basic respect for teachers. The story of Confucius, school regulations, and relationships between teachers and students are types of culture learning goals.

In approaching these topics, how do you attract student interest? Ask students to come to the front and act as teacher for one minute; allow students to freely select a subject to teach to everyone: reading, math, drawing, or singing. From this activity students can experience and talk about the fun and difficulty of teaching and learning. After letting them lead discussion, draw on students topics to introduce the main points of the lesson. For example, give students five "why" questions (Why go to school? Why learn to write? Why learn to read? Why have tests? Why have homework?) and write these on the white board, then paste on a display board. Students chose a partner to discuss. When they have a solution I ask the students to come forward one by one and explain. The student answers are written down and attached next to the questions on the display board. The teacher can also use "why not" questions and achieve similar good results. The teacher should not forget to reward students, because they have solved a question that the teacher does not understand. This exercise is a means by which students can use discussion to understand the functions of school and the importance of education. The concluding summary discussion must be connected to things related to their lives. Recommended songs and nursery rhymes: "上学歌""小二郎""拍手歌""做早操".

After the discussion activity, have students watch Cai Zhizhong's animated series *"Confucius Says"* to see how Confucius taught students and how teachers and students treated each other. [1] This cartoon is still too difficult for kindergarten students and you can use a different illustrated story book to introduce Confucius. But for first and second grade students, as long as the teacher explains as the cartoon is being shown, students can basically understand. Also, because the timing for each segment is very short, students will not feel discouraged if they

---

[1] Refer to the website: http://www.tudou.com/playlist/id/10435985/

don't understand. There is also a documentary called *"Please Vote for Me"* recorded in Wuhan, China in 2007 of a class election for student monitor in third grade. The teacher can select clips showing the actual situation of students in Chinese schools: for example, the class seating arrangement, the playground, etiquette for entering and leaving classes, student uniforms, relationships between fellow classmates, etc. You can also refer to a book published by Beijing University Press titled *"A Comparative Guide to Chinese and American Culture"*. The author, Mr. Shu Yibing, talks about the many cultural differences between China and the United States, illustrating his points with many contrasting images. Teachers can use selections from this book as supplementary teaching materials, modifying and simplifying them according to student levels.

The classroom rules required by teachers and the interactive relations between students both provide education through daily life. For example, students should greet their teachers when they see them; should report when entering or leaving the classroom; should get the teacher's permission to talk in class or leave their seats; and should not eat in class or lie on the desks. In this unit there is no harm in emphasizing respect for the rules. Have a competition for keeping the rules: each day give students a card with 100 points; each time a student breaks the rules they lose two points; within a given time period, tally the points on student cards. The teacher needs to set standards ahead of time for the number of points to win a prize. By giving students control during the time of competition, students will usually work very hard for these prizes. This activity allows students to unconsciously adapt to the rules and to develop good manners.

In this unit I also like to introduce occupational vocabulary (doctors, teachers, firefighters, librarians, businessmen, cooks, police) and play the "Fly Swatter" racing game to become familiar with words. The teacher posts all of the images on the white board or the wall and selects two students at a time to compete with each other. The teacher says the word and whichever student hits the correct picture first with the flyswatter receives a point. Once they are familiar with the words have students play the game "What do I want to do when I grow up" where students guess their classmates' ambitions. Have students take turns coming forward to state their strong points in five sentences or less: for example, I can read and write, I am polite, I love friends, I can sing and dance, I am a good student. The other students select cards with drawings of occupations prepared by the teacher that are suitable and say for example "You want to be a teacher" and see if this matches the student's own aspirations. The reason for putting this activity at the end of the unit is to help students understand the important relationship between their studies at school and their future occupation.

Recommended ancient story: "铁杵磨成针", a supplementary cultural material for younger students that encourages studious attitudes in students. ① Suggested verse excerpts: 一日为师,终身为父;少壮不努力,老大徒伤悲;一寸光阴一寸金,寸金难买寸光阴。Idioms: 光阴似箭,有教无类,努力不懈,勤学苦练。

Unit Topic Six: Friends, Fun, Fashions and Fads

"Friends" at this stage represent the first step in the development of interpersonal relationships for children. Kindergarteners especially need to have playmates; as long as they play together or sing together they are friends. From the viewpoint of younger children, in addition to serving as a companion in joint activities, friends also need to share some common interests: for example, they need to like the same colors, eat the same candy, like to play soccer, or enjoy dancing. The learning objectives for this unit are to guide students to cultivate empathy, to learn to understand that their treatment of others will shape how others treat them, and through activities to study and practice the basic

---

① Refer to the webpage *Epoch Times Chinese culture class lesson plan* (6): http://www.epochtimes.com/b5/3/10/27/n401012.htm.

methods and skills of making friends. The culture goals are for students to understand Chinese children's games and toys.

"Myself in the Mirror" is a game that stimulates enthusiastic student participation. With two person groups, student A is the person outside of the mirror who makes movements and student B is the person in the mirror who imitates these movements. At the end of the activity ask student A to discuss that they saw and then ask student B to share what they were feeling as they tried to imitate student A. Through this active process students experience the relationship between the different internal and external mirrors, similar to the principles for getting along with friends. In another "How much do you know me?" activity, students are given white boards. One student is chosen to play "Me" and the teacher suggests several personal hobbies, habits, or situations and the other students must write down the answer that they think the person on stage would select. After comparing the answers they see who understands "Me" the best. This is a game that my younger students never tire of playing. The important point is that the teacher must design topics that the students find interesting; the kinds of perplexing situations encountered in life are always student favorites. For example, if there is no toilet paper when you go to the restroom, what do you do? 1) call out; 2) don't use toilet paper or; 3) sit on the toilet and wait for someone to come. These types of active games not only narrow the distance between students but also give students the chance to see the humorous side of each person and to establish mutually good impressions.

In presenting illustrated stories, the teacher can select one or two stories about friends, such as "*Lion makes friends*"[①]; for different types of Chinese fables (almost 3000)[②]. Focusing on the contents of the story, guide the students to ask questions and let the students quiz each other about the moral of the story, in order to nuture students'

---

① Refer to the website: http://www.wretch.cc/blog/misseshome/5789975
② Refer to the website: http://www.vastman.com/fable/traditional/index.htm

basic skills in social interaction and making friends. You can have the students read the story together in small groups. After students first try to understand the general meaning, have students personally select a partner to perform the story. Encourage the younger students to exchange and play different roles; dramatic imitations are a most effective way to create deep student memories. After the story, divide the students into two groups: one group asks a question and the other group must answer. From this the teacher understands the level of student comprehension of the story.

After the story relax and play a musical game "Looking for Friends." One student starts first to sing and look for a friend; when the student finds a friend they put their hands on the new friend's shoulders; with one in front and one in back they connect like driving a train; the new friend then looks for another new friend until the whole class of students has found friends and they form a large circle. Recommended song: "*Looking for a Friend*". See also *Games for Learning Chinese* ("游戏学中文"), "Looking for friends" (page 9).

Next, the teacher can write questions on cards of various scenarios (or allow students to write): for example, how do you make friends with a new student who comes to your class? If your friend is hurt, what do you do? If you want to share toys or candy with a friend, how do you do it? If you are refused or rejected, what can you do? These are good ways to stimulate further student reflection. Ask a student to come to the front, choose a card, and read it out loud; let this student select the student who raises their hand the quickest answer the question; then the student who read the card can decide how many points to give to this answer. The teacher should prepare point cards ahead of time; one with a small smile awards three points and one with a large smile awards four points; the point differences should not be large because students who participate in the discussion should have the opportunity to receive points. The teacher can also distribute a variety of items; after students have divided into groups, ask them to divide the items evenly and distribute them to fellow members of their group. This activity gives students practice in sharing with others and helps cultivate a caring attitude towards friends.

For the next interview activity "What do you like to do with your friends?", the teacher designs a simple questionnaire and has students interview each other and record their results; kindergarten students can record with drawings. After the survey is finished, the teacher writes the numerical results on the white board. For example: play games—6 people, do homework—4 people, play soccer—5 people.

Afterwards, as a concluding activity, choose one of the games that students like. Use this opportunity to bring Chinese toys into the unit. Teaching the students to make Chinese shuttlecocks, sandbags, and kites will increase the culture learning atmosphere and also give students the opportunity to compare Chinese games and American games. Of course, don't omit the birthday parties that children love so much, and help students in the class set up a collective birthday party. That day each student has to do three good things for their friends; encourage students to practice what they preach and remind them that they cannot spend money on gifts.

Recommended idioms:将心比心,和睦相处,情同手足,一言为定,相亲相爱,不分彼此. Through learning activities, students actually practice the meaning of idioms; teachers must seize the immediate circumstances to use the idiom to describe and explain so that students reach understanding in a natural learning environment.

Unit Topic Seven: Creative Arts and Sciences

In addressing Chinese creative arts and sciences, younger children should first start with characters, calligraphy, and music to guide their study and understanding; the teacher, moreover, must construct a learning environment and opportunities for practical physical experience. The culture learning objectives for this unit are to recognize common traditional musical instruments; to appreciate Chinese music; to understand basic concepts of Chinese ideographs; and to study the recitation of Tang poetry.

Refer to the webpage for *"The Story of Characters"*,① the teacher can use the same style as the video to teach students the development of Chinese characters from the shape of simple drawings. I am especially partial to this teaching method, which produces excellent results, because using the written forms of Chinese calligraphy to introduce Chinese writing conveys a more artistic flavor. Students not only study the changes in Chinese characters but at the same time learn about the four treasures of the Chinese studio and the use of the brush. Allow students to take their own written characters and mount them simply like a Chinese style painting and hang them on the classroom wall. Have students take turns talking about their work and their understanding of the changes in Chinese characters. Painting scenery, birds and flowers, or writing spring couplets or copying a short poem are good practice writing and drawing activities. Alternatively, you can display a few simple ideographic characters such as 日,月,山,水,木 and use calligraphic style to change them into a picture as a way of introducing the common features between pictographs and natural landscapes. Following this show animal pictographs and let the students from their own imaginations transform the pictographs into what they believe are the correct animal pictures. In this way you can emphasize the basic variations in Chinese characters to students and increase interest in the classroom teaching of Chinese characters.

With a basic understanding of pictographs, the teacher can take common characters that the students have already studied, make cards with complicated and simplified characters, and have students compete to match the complicated and simplified characters. Then use an illustrated story book with complex characters to play a recognition game; see who can read the most complex characters in the story and find the matching cards with simplified characters. Often after reading a short story, my students are surprised at their ability to read

---

① http://v.youku.com/v_show/id_XMTAwMTQ1OTk2.html

complicated characters. By comparing the differences in complex and simplified characters, students become more interested in characters and more proficient in learning to write them. For teachers, I recommend the book *The Beauty of Chinese Calligraphy* ("汉字书法之美") written by the famous painter, poet and writer Chiang Hsun. The book is divided into four topics: the development of characters, the aesthetics of calligraphy, education on perception, and modern Chinese characters. I personally love this book, especially the lively explanation of the elements of characters in the section on perception. This book not only improved my own aesthetic appreciation of Chinese characters, but also enriched my knowledge of the historical and cultural aspects of characters and has improved the quality of my teaching.

Before introducing Chinese music, have the students play a warm up singing game, allowing them to review Chinese children's songs they have already studied and guiding them to understand the rhythm of the songs. Next, have each student select a different item that can produce sounds and use this to keep beat with the songs. The combined activity of body movement and sound encourages student interest in participating. I often have students find partners to form a small band and perform to the beat of a favorite song. Afterwards, I take turns playing American and Chinese music, allowing students to hear the sounds of different musical instruments. In the discussion that follows, I ask students to imagine the appearance of the musical instrument producing the sounds they hear, try to imitate a similar sound, then draw on the classroom white board the type of instrument. From hearing to image, the students can construct the concept of linking sounds and instruments. They also can learn from the pictures of musical instruments to distinguish the differences and similarities between western and Chinese instruments.

At the same time, coordinate an activity for the manual creation of Chinese musical instruments to help students recognize the specific forms of the zither, flute, erhu, pipa, and gongs. When the hand made instruments are complete and each student has their own Chinese musical instrument, the teacher can select some songs played by the "Twelve Girl's Band". The students are organized into an orchestra and when they hear the sound of an instrument, the student holding the instrument must perform. After several repetitions, the students can quickly identify the sounds of Chinese instruments. When selecting the music, the teacher should not start with fast-paced pieces, because students will not have enough time to distinguish the music and perform the actions. So I propose that the teacher starts with a slow pace and gradually speeds up, with the last song being very fast-paced, so though the students will be all in a flurry, they will have a great time. Finally, the teacher can arrange for a small performance, with some students dancing, some students singing, and some playing musical instruments (imitating the sound) as an end to this lively learning unit. You can also use the game of "Musical Chairs" as a review activity. Play a variety of Chinese music and songs with different rhythms. The students with no seat must say the name of the music and one musical instrument or be eliminated.

For this unit, I propose that teachers use Chinese idiom stories related to music and sound: 滥竽充数, 五音不全, 对牛弹琴, 不声不响, 不闻不问.

Unit Topic Eight: Expressing Emotions and Feelings

Emotional expression is a unique language; it is how people exchange feelings and a way to achieve mutual understanding. You must learn to recognize others' facial expressions in order to accurately understand how messages are passed and expressed. Therefore, teachers should use every opportunity and activity to guide younger students to understand all kinds of facial expressions in their environment; to be aware of the emotions and facial expressions connected to joy, anger, sadness and happiness, etc.; and to know ways of expressing positive attitudes and feelings towards people and things. Younger students naturally understand emotions in terms of "I" as the center of performance and as the basic form of expression. The focus of learning for this stage is to train students to recognize facial expressions.

For the first week, our starting activity can be to observe different expressions. For example, we can use a facial expression chart and have students observe and say what they see. Do you think they are happy or sad? Then guide students to look at different facial expressions, to compare the five different facial features such as types of eyebrows and eyes. Allow students to look in the mirror and make all kinds of expressions. Have them observe both more general impressions and individual delicate details and from this to experience how different people's facial expressions reflect different moods.

Then have students explore how likes and dislikes are expressed in different ways. Have students recall, what was your facial expression when others praised your drawings? (beaming with joy) What was your expression when others refused to let you join their game? (sad and dejected) What emotions showed on your face when your friends had finished eating lunch and wanted to go play, but you had not yet finished eating? (anxiety) What was your facial expression when your teacher criticized you? (embarrassment and pain)

Use a variety of situations to display different facial expressions. For example, you can ask students to draw emotional expressions by drawing different facial features, or ask students to draw a facial expression chart on their small white boards and explain each emotional expression. In the musical performance game "If you're happy clap your hands" allow students to practice self expression, showing their feelings in facial expressions and physical movements. Also, the performance of lively stories, nursery rhymes and songs not only allow students to experience the feelings of the images, but also influence and educate students in fully expressing their own emotions. (I recommend the Chinese children's resource network website, with children's animation, audio stories, movies, books and other rich content, that provides a database to support teaching that teachers should utilize.)

Finally, give each student eight cards and ask students to use stories about personal things that have happened in their own life to draw an individual mood booklet.

In the second week, start by reviewing the words and sentence patterns from the first week, using the fly swatter game to match cards with characters and pictures. Next, play music and ask students to use physical ways to express the mood and emotions of the music. By studying musical influences students will understand how people can have very different emotional responses to the same things. Have the students listen to the reading of a story and talk about the dialogue of the characters and their emotional expressions; ask students to imitate in performance their favorite and least favorite characters in the story; then discuss the reasons for this to help them understand how the emotions between the characters in the story affect each other.

Give each student a mood record card previously prepared by the teacher. Have the students watch the cartoon movie "大头儿子小头爸爸" and mark the grids of the card to show the different expressions next to the characters' names. When the movie is finished, use questions and answers to make sure that students understand the story and to practice sentence patterns. Afterwards, have students take turns showing their mood record cards; using different colored pens mark the difference between good feelings and bad feelings and explain their categories.

I hope that students can develop the habit of having good things to say, so I like to do scenario simulation exercises. First, have students take turns coming to the front to draw a practice scenario card that lays out a problem or dispute. Have students practice how to avoid reacting directly in a bad frame of mind and how to express a good mood in communicating with their classmates, that is how to speak in different ways to express their emotions. This activity trains students to learn to control their negative emotions and to express a positive attitude.

The goals of the third week are to teach students to understand how their emotions affect their relations with friends; to learn to use more appropriate ways to express their feelings; and to learn how to establish good relationships with friends.

After reviewing the vocabulary and sentence structures connected to feelings and emotions, the teacher will put cards with event descriptions written on them into a cardboard box. Each student will draw a card and display the emotional response triggered by this event. Have student A perform some type of emotional response to student B and student B must explain his/her feelings and ideas. Each student will have an opportunity to take a turn to display emotions and express personal feelings. The students learn from this activity how events affect an individual's moods and how emotional responses can affect relations with other people.

The teacher then posts four large sheets of poster paper indicating delight, sadness, anger, and happiness on four different classroom walls. Students draw cards indicating delight, sadness, anger, or happiness from a small bag prepared by the teacher and students with the same emotion cards are organized into groups. Each group discusses and shares their own stories, then writes on the emotion posters pasted to the wall the things/situations that affect emotions, drawing icons that represent moods. Each group takes turns explaining their results on the mood posters and classifies their displays in terms of good and bad moods. For bad moods, ask students to share the methods they use to relieve these types of moods. At the same time, the teacher can display a chart of how to relieve emotions as a way of giving students suggestions for this exercise. Playing fitting music will help students to relax and experience changes in their moods.

Returning to the first exercises, ask students to do a performance of emotional reactions. B must describe with a positive attitude the negative feelings created by A toward B, and let A understand their impact on B. A must then select a suitable way to express the emotions triggered by this event. For example, A has been deprived of his favorite toys by his mother because he did not do his homework and his teacher will not let him go out to play. A vents his unhappy mood toward B, who needs to understand this emotional reaction and to learn to use a gentle way of expressing his feelings towards A, who in turn must learn how to breathe deeply and change his feelings. This exercise sounds a bit challenging, but it is not terribly difficult in practice. As long as the teacher guides them step by step, having different combinations of students repeatedly acting out the situation, the students will quickly understand the main focus of this learning activity, especially first and second grade students. For kindergarten students you must design the most basic situational problems to practice. The teaching objectives are focused on recognizing emotions and choosing ways of communicating using words rather than hitting or touching.

Before the end of the unit, have the students listen to a story about moods; rearrange the dialogue of the characters in the story and change the end of the story. Play music to accompany student discussion and performance of the story. Finally, have students once again sing the song "If you're happy and you know it..."

Unit Plan Example: Expressing Emotions and Feelings (Kindergarten, 3 weeks)

Guiding Questions

Essential Questions	Focus Questions
1. What is emotion? 2. How do we express our feelings? 3. How do expressions of emotions affect social relationships?	1. Do you know the differences between happy, angry, sad and scared? 2. What kind of things would make you happy, angry, sad or scared? Why? 3. What do you do when you are happy, angry, sad and scared? 4. How do you make people understand you are angry? 5. What causes you to argue or fight with your friends? How do you get along with friends?

Functional Outcome/Skills

- Students engage in conversation, provide and obtain information, express feelings and emotions, and exchange opinions in Chinese
- Students present information, concepts, and ideas to an audience of listeners or readers on a variety of topics in Chinese
- Students understand and interpret written and spoken language in a variety of topics in Chinese
- Students reinforce and further their knowledge of other disciplines through the study of Chinese

Assessment

a) Formative Assessment
- Can draw emotion cards that distinguish between good and bad moods
- Can use physical and facial expressions to show different emotional reactions
- Can identify pictures and explain the reasons for different emotional expressions
- Can answer situational questions

b) Group Project
- Draw a picture that tells a story: Students draw a story about their own emotional expressions and share this with the class
- Performance of a short skit: imitate a narrative situation the displays different kinds of emotions

Weekly Lesson Plans

Week One	
Teaching objectives	• Students can recognize and read basic words about emotions • Students can use words and sentences related to emotions to express their personal feelings

(Continued)

	Week One
Lesson contents	• Emotion words and sentence patterns • Recognizing moods and facial expressions • Emotional and physical reactions • Reasons for moods/emotions • Nursery rhyme (If you're happy and you know it clap your hands...), songs
Materials	• Chinese words and pinyin cards • Emotions wall chart • Emotion icon game cards①(prepared in advance by teachers, each face icon has two cards) • All kinds of daily life photos, pictures, cartoons, comics • Small mirrors • Nursery rhyme/Emotion song② • Small white boards and markers • Cardboard cards and colored pens
Learning exercises	• Using a wall chart showing emotional expressions, learn how to use related vocabulary and sentence patterns. • Students divide into groups and play the "Go fish" matching game with emotion cards. • Looking at photos, pictures, cartoons, comics, describe their contents and the emotional reactions of the characters. • Students analyze the differences in changing emotion icons and facial features, use mirrors to practice a variety of facial expressions. Use nursery rhymes to encourage physical expressions of emotions. • Looking at the face icon, draw on a white board a scenario that could have caused that emotional expression. • Students create their own mood booklet.
Formative assessment	Match cards, describe pictures, draw a scenario

---

① Refer to the website: http://www.icosky.com/iconset/emotions-2s-icons/
② Refer to the website: http://www.ergel00.com/erge/cn/1539.html

	Week Two
Teaching objectives	• Students can distinguish between different positive and negative emotions • Students will understand how others express their personal feelings • Students can express their feelings toward other students in appropriate ways
Lesson contents	• Emotion words and sentence patterns • The difference between positive emotions and negative emotions • How others are affected by the expression of personal feelings • Appropriate emotional expression • Family animation：“大头儿子小头爸爸”
Materials	• Mood chart • Fly swatter • Mood icon cards • Music tape • Mood stories：*Mr. Happy* + *Mr. Grumpy* • Animation DVD：“大头儿子小头爸爸” • Cardboard cards (teacher designed grids) and colored pens • Description of scenario game cards (prepared by teacher)
Learning exercises	• Use the card/fly swatter game to review vocabulary and sentence patterns. • Looking at Chinese words, practice drawing the mood chart/looking at the mood chart, write out the proper words. • Play a musical tape and have students use physical means to express emotions; students understand that there are different emotional reactions to the music.

(Continued)

	Week Two
	• Listen to the reading of a story, talk about the emotional expressions in the dialogues of characters in the story. Ask students to imitate in performance their favorite and least favorite characters in the story, discuss the reasons for this, and understand how characters in the story influence each other. • Watch the animated DVD "大头儿子小头爸爸" and ask the students as they are watching to mark the grids on the cards for each type of emotional expression. After the movie is finished, use a question and answer format to check student comprehension and practice orally their words and sentence patterns. Then have students take turns showing the records on their mood pictures cards and using different colored pens divide them into good and bad moods. • Scenario card exercise; have students draw a card and practice their responses to problems and disputes: how to express their feelings towards their classmates in good ways.
Formative assessment	Story simulation with emotional dialogue, making records on mood cards while watching a video, dialogue and communication scenarios

	Week Three
Teaching objectives	• Understand how displaying negative emotions can affect friends • Understand how to control your negative feelings • Learning to speak in positive ways
Lesson contents	• Emotion words and sentence patterns • The relationship between events and moods • Approaches and activities to relieve negative emotions • Styles of expression and communication

(Continued)

	Week Three
Materials	• Negative emotions generated by causes "cards" (written by teacher) • Emotions picture cards • Four large poster boards, markers, tape • Relieving emotions wall chart • Relieving emotions music CDs • A story about moods
Learning exercises	• Each student draws a card on which is displayed an event that triggers an emotional response. Ask student A to display an emotional response to student B, and student B explains how this makes him/her feel. Each student has an opportunity to take a turn to display emotions and to express how they feel about emotions. • Tape four large poster boards on four different walls of the classroom. Students divide into four groups based on drawing the same emotion cards for joy, sadness, anger, happiness. Each group discusses and shares their own small stories, then writes on their corresponding emotion poster the things and situations that affect their moods, using the representative icons to draw moods. • Each group takes turns explaining their resulting poster, classifying the feelings into good and bad moods. • Students share their methods of relieving a bad mood. • Display ways of relieving emotions on a wall chart according to the student recommendations to encourage students in this exercise. • Play music, allow students to relax with the tunes and experience mood changes. • Return to the first learning exercise; ask student to once again make a chart of emotional responses. B must use a positive attitude to explain to A the effect of his/her negative feelings on B. • Students listen to a story about emotions, rearrange the negative dialogue of the characters in the story and change the ending. Play matching music and allow students to discuss.

	Week Three
	• For the concluding activity lead the song "If you're happy and you know it...".
Final assessment	Explain the causes and effects of moods, create a good and bad mood poster, how to express negative emotions in a positive way, adaptation of emotion story dialogue

Teaching Suggestions

Designing unit questions: Guiding questions for the themes of this unit should be based on the contents of the teaching materials. In order to improve student interest in learning, when designing questions use basic what, who, why, and how questions as much as possible to connect teaching contents and processes. For reference, here is a sample list of questions for themes in this unit:

1. What makes you happy/hurt/angry/sad/scared?
2. When you are happy/hurt/angry/sad/scared how do you feel and how do you react?
3. How do you express your emotions?
4. What do you like to do when you are in a happy mood? With who?
5. When you are in a bad mood, what do you do? Why?
6. How do you understand your own feelings?
7. What are "good" moods?
8. What are "bad" moods?
9. How do "good" moods affect your friends? Why?
10. How do "bad" moods affect your friends? Why?
11. How can you change your bad moods into good moods?
12. How can you express your bad moods in a way that does not hurt other people's good moods?

Vocabulary and sentence patterns: These should draw from the educational reading materials prepared by the teacher according to the course design and related themes and can increase or decrease in relation to the language levels of the students. The following are some examples of vocabulary and sentence patterns related to this unit:

◆ **Vocabulary**
喜、怒、哀、乐、高兴、快乐、幸福、生气、伤心、难过、害怕、紧张、看见、听见、想到、摸到、微笑、大笑、哭、流眼泪、尖叫、发抖、拍手、跺脚、如果、可以/不可以、会/不会、喜欢/不喜欢、客气、不礼貌

◆ **Sentence Patterns**
一……就……；……的时候，会……；因为……所以……；虽然……可是……；有的时候……

◆ **Idioms**
唉声叹气、泪流满面、大惊小怪、兴奋不已、欢天喜地、得意洋洋

Whyte

Chapter Four
Inspiring Creativity: Grades 3 to 4

Introduction

Third and fourth grade students, ages eight and nine, continue with the steady physical, psychosocial, cognitive and emotional growth of middle childhood. Compared to first and second grade students, they have longer attention spans, improved self-control, a more mature ability to care for themselves, and they adapt more easily to school activities. As a result, academic requirements for these students will gradually increase in difficulty, and greater attention will be paid to school work that enhances academic performance.

In terms of physical growth for children at this stage, aside from a few more rapidly developing girls, most students will not be experiencing the type of fast growth associated with adolescence. However, certain physical skills, especially fine and large motor development will show particular progress. With improving speed and smoothness in fine motor skills, students are more nimble and competent than their younger peers in holding their pencils, cutting paper with scissors, painting and pasting. Therefore, children can begin to develop their Chinese writing abilities, use arts and crafts in the classroom, and accomplish their tasks in a more independent manner.

Progress in large motor development, including the muscles of arms and legs, will be even more striking, especially in terms of balance and the coordination of large body movements. Interestingly, once children become aware of their progress in physical development and motor abilities, they begin to enjoy challenging themselves and testing each other with things like somersaults, handstands, racing, throwing balls or other team sports. Children of this age can also tend to overestimate their own physical abilities and lack the higher level thinking skills to preview and predict consequences and design coping strategies. In some of my earlier teaching experiences, children would insist on playing games in their own way and would make an effort to ensure they did not fall down or injure each other. In order to gain the trust of the students, I allowed them to continue, but the result, of course, backfired! The conclusion is that when leading children in this age group, teachers need to trust their own instincts. Once students reach 7th or 8th grade, the teacher can let go and give students more autonomy. Finally, to emphasize once again, when using games and competition to stimulate learning for 3rd and 4th grade students, teachers need to consider the environment, teaching aids and flows of activity, and handle everything with safety as a clear prerequisite.

Physically speaking, children of this age have a lot energy but may not know how to adjust their pace, often playing to the point of total exhaustion. Thus, in designing classroom activities, as much as possible intersperse dynamic and static activities, so students learn how to settle their mind and body through alternating rest and exertion. I often use music sites (such as Pandora.com) and the slow rhythm of classical music to relax student moods and raise their levels of concentration.

Children at this stage also begin to show significant individual differences in physical size and physical performance, and these differences can further affect a child's perception of self, degree of self-confidence, and physical modes of communication with others. In organizing activities and dividing students into groups, teachers should pay attention to this and provide positive opportunities for the somewhat physically disadvantaged students to cultivate their self-esteem and self-confidence; at the same time they should guide the physically dominant students to use their special talents to lend a helping hand with their peers and work together on teams to enhance the peaceful atmosphere of the classroom and reduce the possibility of bullying.

It is well known that school is the foundation for social and psychological development for students of this age. Because school is the intermediary point between a child's family and society, children learn to follow norms within the smaller school community, learn to respond to elders outside of their family, and learn teamwork, compassion, empathy and social negotiation skills in dealing with peers in daily life. Although 3rd and 4th grade students desire friendship with other children and peer group acceptance, they still seek the approval and permission of adults. In other words, teachers still play very appealing and influential roles for eight year old children, and teachers can take advantage of this feature to promote teaching and learning. Third and fourth grade students understand teamwork and like competition, so there is a lot of space for competitive team games. However, you need to remember that some of these students will not like to be put on a team with members of the opposite sex, so teachers must take into account the preferences of the students in arranging group activities to promote favorable group dynamics.

How to enhance male student motivation and achievement is a much discussed subject among experts. From my experience, using competitive small group physical activities can often produce a positive response among male students. The attention span for eight or nine year old children is usually about ten to fifteen minutes, so as much as possible try to cut down on passive lecture styles, because once passive activities go beyond an acceptable limit, students become fidgety and classroom management issues arise. In speaking, avoid making comparisons between male and female students as a kind of motivation. If necessary, try to use non-verbal gestures to communicate and reduce situations of "power struggle" between teachers and students.

Third and fourth grade students show increased creativity and stronger independence. Their cognitive development remains in the Piaget period of concrete operations: their style of thinking depends on concrete images, and they often learn through trial and error or use their direct experience of actual materials in order to understand things and obtain knowledge and skills. Therefore, avoid abstractions in teaching because these children think in highly concrete ways, and the borders between fantasy and reality are not always clear. I recommend providing a variety of concrete and personally related activities to give children the opportunity to explore and find answers. Children at this stage have greatly enhanced written language skills and are able to use written records to convey their own ways of thinking. So, in addition to gradually increasing the difficulty in language and culture instruction, teachers can begin to use brainstorming in the classroom as a way to explore issues and to cultivate children's reflective thinking and meta-cognitive capacities, building for the future of higher level thinking that is needed to pave the way of learning. These children also particularly like to read adventure stories and fantasy novels, so teachers should as much as possible provide opportunities for learning language and culture through story books and dramas, etc.

In short, based on their physical, psychological, emotional, and cognitive development, third and fourth grade students should focus on enhancing their ability to learn and their desire for accomplishment, so they can become excellent students. In Chinese language teaching, in addition to continuing the culture training from previous years, the goal of strengthening language skills is self-evident.

Unit Topics

Unit Topic One: Family

When imparting knowledge to students, it is most effective to begin with materials from their own experiences. Using this as a catalyst, you can introduce new concepts and knowledge and finally engage in cross-cultural and cross-language comparisons. That's why during the family theme, you cannot avoid talking about personal, sensitive family situations. No one can select their own kinfolk, and certainly third and fourth graders cannot change their living environments. Moreover, in today's pluralistic society, there is a gradual trend towards more diverse family forms and the definition of family gives rise to multiple answers. Therefore I recommend that before this lesson begins, teachers need to understand something about student family backgrounds, including ethnic background, family composition, their housing situation, etc. There are many benefits in doing things this way, but the most important is that when teachers use students background experiences, they should carefully select themes that take account of student feelings, respect their privacy, and arouse a sympathetic response.

Learning objectives for this unit continue to focus and expand upon the same core issues as first and second grade: investigations of Chinese filial piety, family education, and gender roles and responsibilities. With the increased creativity of third and fourth grade students, the class can brainstorm an adventure story about a three generation family living under one roof, inspiring student interest and motivation through story production. There are many reasons why we select "three generations under one roof". For one, we can review the names for family members studied in first and second grades. Second, because most students live in two generation families, the concept of three generations living together is a novelty. In addition, as family members increase, their duties and responsibilities become more specified, which can raise potential problems.

Third and fourth grade students still think in concrete ways, so teachers must provide clear instructions and standards for students. When writing this story, the teacher can provide the necessary family rules and the responsibilities and conflicts of the main characters in the plot. To enhance language learning knowledge and skills, in addition to reviewing the terms for family members learned in previous years, words for relationships between family members can be added, for example: son, daughter, grandson, granddaughter, nephew and so on. When describing the family, the house structure can be also introduced, such as the names of rooms, furniture, etc., so this unit will have a more coherent feel.

In order to develop children's ability to work in small groups, this project should include group activities, where students study in collaboration with their peers and have the opportunity to negotiate. First, the children can brainstorm to decide on their family members; the roles and responsibilities of these members, and the residential distribution of family members: who lives where and why? Using their imaginations, students write the plot of their story: the adventures of family members and their significant contributions in solving a crisis or conflict. Students can choose their own methods to convey their ideas such as making a comic book, or a story book with hand painted or cut and pasted pictures. When the project is completed, students share their results with the class. Teachers use the plot of the story and characters to ask questions and stimulate learning, for example: What is the importance of the family to the characters in the story? How is this importance of family similar and different for you? Why? What are the tasks and responsibilities for different family members? How does this work in your family? In the course of questioning, due to the limited attention span of children at this stage, the questions should be answered in terms of the main point without unnecessary lengthy detail. Because more than one story will be shared, at the time of sharing, the same concept can be repeated for a different time and place, adding depth and breadth to the effectiveness of this lesson.

When the students have finished presenting their story books, the teacher can have students cast votes to select the most popular works and change them into a stage performance. Before the vote, have the candidates, who are selected issue a "political publication" or promotional posters as a prototype of democratic practice.

Converting a story book into a stage play involves writing a script. Transforming a written story into spoken language can help students develop their speaking abilities. Stage plays require the creation of different props, sound and lighting effects, and even dancing and singing, conducive to the teaching/nurturing of multiple intelligences. As students rehearse their dramatic performances, the concepts of family relations, responsibilities, and roles are immediately clarified. In the process of stage rehearsals, teachers can introduce aspects of Chinese behavioral culture in popular idioms such as "Respect the wise and honor the worthy"（尊老敬贤）, "Fathers and sons are close"（父子有亲）, "Order of younger and elder"（长幼有序）, "Male and females are different"（男女有别）to give students practical experiences with the relationships expressed in these idioms through drama. I personally think that the responsibility of Chinese teachers is not to make students into Chinese people, but to teach students to understand how to adapt their language to properly fit specific times and places (code-switching). In order to shift cultural behaviors, students must respond to frequent influences and intentionally understand how to code switch at different times, so it is enough to have students try out different cultural roles through dramatic performances.

When informed that most Chinese people do not consider pets as family members, students will often voice their amazement and protests. This is due to differences in both culture and language. Teachers can use the topic "Do pets count as family members?" to discuss "What is home/family（家）?" "Who is family（家人）?" "Who can be part of the family?" "What are the different forms of family?" Students can use drawings or writings to give examples of different types of families and family members from television, film plays, or story books and then summarize. When exploring these issues, you do not necessarily need to give answers to students; students only need to realize that the form of family will vary with the culture. This is a very important connection in developing views of global citizenship.

In the United States, Chinese language teachers are likely to have contact with children from single sex parents or adoptive families. As mentioned earlier, children cannot select their family or household, and there are no good or bad family structures, just good or bad family functions. If, as teachers, we understand this point and show tolerance, respect, and love for children from different family backgrounds and do not let prejudice or bias influence our teaching, we will provide a good example of mutual encouragement to our students.

Unit Topic Two: Food and Chinese Medicine

Talking about the subject of eating is guaranteed to lift the spirits of the vast majority of people. From eating just to survive, this topic ascends to complex behavior with manifold social and cultural meanings, and these changes in eating behavior also involve many complex social norms. So when the subject turns to food, there is a lot of scope for expansion.

First and second grade students already have basic knowledge of the names and flavors of commonly eaten Chinese foods; the placement and use of utensils; and inappropriate dining behavior. In the third and fourth grade curricular design, in addition to consolidating existing student knowledge and skills, you can explore similar themes in increasing depth and breadth. In addition, as a result of the physical and emotional development of students and their more mature ability to care for themselves, teachers can consider taking the students out into the community for practical experience to reinforce their previous knowledge and skills.

When investigating the topic of Chinese people's three daily meals,

I like to begin by presenting comparisons of breakfast foods. First have students share their favorite breakfast foods. In order to add to the fun, invite parents to participate by making photographs or videotapes of students eating breakfast, then bringing to the class to share. In the process of sharing their videos, students can make a simple oral report that includes the names of breakfast foods, their quantities (review the use of quantifiers), and their flavors. If there are ethnic minorities in the class who continue to maintain their traditional diet, the teacher should make special introductions that encourage the goal of multicultural education.

Teachers can take this opportunity to record a *"Teacher's Breakfast Video"* and revise the *"Monkey Wears New Clothes"* nursery rhyme: On Monday the teacher eats fried dumplings and egg cakes with rice broth; on Tuesday the teacher eats *shaobing youtiao* with a rice ball snack; Wednesday the teacher eats steamed bread and a stuffed bun with soy milk; on Thursday the teacher drinks cow's milk with a sandwich; on Friday the teacher eats rice porridge and fermented bean curd; on Saturday the teacher eats left over fried pork; on Sunday the teacher goes to a teahouse for tea and refreshments. If the video is made by the teacher him/hersrelf or a restaurant, it will create more interest for students. Teachers can use this video to show China's cultural diversity and the traditional importance of breakfast, which is why Chinese people have so many breakfast choices. I have in the past uploaded videos made for students on YouTube as personal use teaching materials to share with networks of other Chinese teachers.

After the students have watched the video made by the teacher, they will be interested in personally making and tasting things. In my personal experience it is not difficult to buy soy milk, *mantou*, *baozi*, and even *shaobing youtiao* at the local Chinese grocery store. Teachers can use a rice cooker (to steam) or small oven (to bake) some immediate treats for the students. If you want to personally make things, I suggest wrapping rice balls: the teacher will need to prepare the ingredients in advance and let students do the hand work. In addition to the cooking activities, this is a good opportunity to learn certain expressions and students can explain their hands on activities step by step. Before doing the cooking lesson with students, teachers need to be aware of government regulations about food handling (food handling license) and need to know whether students have food intolerances, a history of allergies, or other personal or religious dietary restrictions.

Community based lessons are very suitable for eight and nine year old students. When investigating the differences between Chinese restaurants and other restaurants with students, the best way to teach them is to first take them to a meal in a Chinese restaurant: have students become silent detectives, observing with their ears, eyes, and hearts. Teachers should communicate with restaurant staff in advance and explain the purpose of community education and the corresponding expectations of the people involved. Students should have basic abilities to order food and know proper dining manners, so that they have the opportunity to apply their knowledge in a community setting. After the community lesson, they should return to the classroom and immediately begin their discussion and use charts, such as a Venn diagram, to draw their conclusions. One focal point of this trip to the Chinese restaurant is to consolidate what students have learned in lower grades about the arrangement of food and utensils at the table and proper eating manners.

Third and fourth grade students will have better hand-eye coordination for using chopsticks than students in lower grades, so I propose at this stage using physical demonstrations and a hands-on approach to re-emphasize the proper use of dining utensils. An ideal approach is to have students eat their lunch in the Chinese classroom. First have students eat using western cutlery, plates, cups, napkins and table settings. In this process teachers can invite students to demonstrate (becoming teachers to the teacher) correct and incorrect table manners and make a record. The teacher can then select another opportunity to have students eat lunch in the classroom, changing to Chinese style utensils to eat, with a rule that they cannot use their hands. Students will inevitably face some challenges, such as how to use chopsticks to eat a sandwich? Gradually guide students to understand from this experience that Chinese people do not use a knife and fork, so almost all the food on the table will be pre-cut. Teachers can record the doubts and understandings expressed by students, and have students use this experience to compare Western and Chinese eating utensils. Encourage students to extend their understanding of the proper ways to use forks and knives to the proper use of Chinese utensils, and consider improper ways of using bowls and chopsticks. The teacher can sum up the main points and include additional items that the students have not thought of, so that the lesson achieves multiple effects.

Finally, teachers can involve students in a guessing game that compares Chinese chopsticks with chopsticks used in other Asian countries such as Japan and Korea, offering differences and explanations. Teachers can collect chopsticks from different countries and regions and different kinds of chopsticks; by investigating the etiquette of using chopsticks they can give students different examples of the correct and incorrect ways of using chopsticks. Teaching through personal experience is not only interesting, but helps students better remember the proper way to use chopsticks. Usually, if students perform well in the classroom, the teacher can organize speed games with chopsticks and award small prizes.

In terms of celebratory foods and activities, birthday celebrations are a good way to approach this topic: have students design their own birthday menu including food and drinks. Teachers can first seek out a Chinese elder at a nursing home or community center and have students become familiar with the elder and identify this person as the grandfather or grandmother of the Chinese class. While the students are designing their own birthday party menus, the teacher will design a birthday menu for a long life birthday feast for the elder. When students have finished designing their menus, the whole class can first share in pairs (Think—Pair—Share); students must report on what they will prepare and why. After the students have finished sharing, the teacher can present her menu design. Teachers can have students brainstorm, and guess the reasons why certain foods have been chosen, such as birthday noodles, eggs, and long season vegetables. In concluding this lesson, the teacher should give a brief description of the long Chinese tradition of using the colors, special characteristics, and names of foods to seek out luck and good fortune, such as New Year cakes that symbolize a promotion; presenting pomegranate fruits (whose many seeds symbolize multiple offspring) to newly married couples; and foods that symbolize longevity when designing a birthday feast.

The teacher might also consider arranging another community education activity. Pick a less busy time for business to go to a Chinese grocery store and shop for food for the elder's birthday feast. The teacher can arrange in advance for students to select appropriate birthday foods according to the basic principles of food symbolism previously introduced. Students can use cameras or simple video recorders (eg. Flip Video) to capture images to bring back to the classroom, so they can shop but avoid unnecessary costs, and the images can be later used as teaching materials. When teachers purchase the necessary fruits and vegetables for the birthday party, they should select things that are suitable for students to help in a classroom project, such as cooking soup, to give them a sense of participation.

On the day of the birthday, the teacher should invite the elder to a classroom party, and use this opportunity to demonstrate showing respect for elders while at the same time giving students opportunities to try to copy this behavior. This birthday party can provide a variety of learning opportunities: from decorating and setting the table, to the meanings of foods, to the traditional culture of respect for elders, to the utilization of Chinese community resources.

Numerous themes can be explored in this unit and a variety of teaching strategies can be used, and these are just a few brief proposals. Chinese food culture is wide-ranging, allowing us to make good use of its essence to promote the success of Chinese education overseas.

Unit Topic Three: Chinese Festivals

Everyone loves the festive atmosphere of holidays, especially children, who are not part of the labor force and do not face financial pressures. For children, holidays mean eating, drinking and playing—no wonder they always look forward to the arrival of holidays! However, for Chinese living overseas, whether children or adults, there is less festive atmosphere in celebrating festivals abroad; because Chinese festivals are not public holidays outside of China, festive activities and their meanings are diminished. As a result, the most difficult part of teaching about holiday celebrations is creating a festive atmosphere that gets students excited. A comparatively useful strategy to overcome this difficulty is to strengthen the depth and breadth of celebratory activities: to enhance the depth of understanding of traditional festivals through classic holiday legends, traditional foods, and an understanding of regional differences; and to broaden these celebrations to extend out of the classroom into the school and community.

As a way to enhance student participation, the teacher can have students make collective decisions about how to celebrate festivals, while following a policy of not deviating too far from traditional meanings. Also, to advance student abilities in making cultural comparisons, when celebrating mainstream American holidays, have students try to compare how Chinese people today celebrate them as modern Chinese holidays. Many contemporary Chinese holidays have been derived from or influenced by Western culture, so students can contrast the modes of celebration and their meanings. When celebrating traditional Chinese festivals, it is natural to let students brainstorm to look for matching mainstream heritage festivals: for example the Jewish festival of lights (Hanukkah) and a Chinese festival related to lights (Lantern festival).

The teaching objectives for this unit are to enhance student understanding of the origins of traditional Chinese festivals, their celebration, and traditional festival foods. I personally believe that teachers have many ideas for teaching about traditional festivals; in what follows I would like to share an example for teaching about the Mid-Autumn Festival.

Mid-Autumn Festival is one of the three major traditional Chinese festivals and also the first traditional festival to arrive after school has started. At the beginning of the school year, the teacher can post the daily lunar calendar and the western calendar dates in a prominent place in the classroom. Students who are comparatively weak in understanding abstract notions of time can concretely watch the date of the festival gradually arrive. For a nightly homework assignment, students can be asked to observe and draw the shape of the moon; the next day they take the moon shape drawn the previous evening and transfer this drawing to a place near the date on the lunar calendar. In this way students can use visual images of the shape of the moon to gradually establish an initial understanding of the relationship between the moon and the lunar calendar. The time used to celebrate the Mid-Autumn festival may be longer or shorter; I have used baking moon cakes as a three week lesson plan, from helping students understand the different types of moon cakes in different areas of China, to the materials and processes used to make moon cakes, to having students make moon cakes themselves. Third and fourth grade students enjoy stories, and may also have sufficient language abilities to put on a performance of the three traditional Mid-Autumn legends for students and teachers of the whole school (Chang'e Flies to the Moon, Wu Gang Cuts Down the Laurel, Jade Rabbit Pounds Medicine). This performance can bring the festive atmosphere to the whole school, and the moon cakes can be baked the day before the festival to share with other teachers and students. On Mid-Autumn evening, teachers can have students recite poems about the moon to their families (for example: Su Shi "水调歌头", Li Bai "关山月") or sing a song about the moon (for example: Wang Fei "明月几时有") thus taking the study from the classroom out to the family and community.

In investigating the topic of comparative differences between

American and Chinese holiday celebrations, teachers can have students at the beginning of the school year arrange a list of the major annual American holidays: from New Years at the beginning to Christmas at the end; students can use drawings and representative festive colors such as red for Valentine's Day, orange and black for Halloween, and red and green for Christmas. After the chart has been arranged, students can brainstorm as a group and share how and why they celebrate these holidays. Then have students play an educational guessing game: do the Chinese people also celebrate Christmas? Do Chinese have a Lover's Day? The teacher can ask questions and write answers on the board, developing a comparison table and transfer the results onto the classroom calendar. Throughout the school year the calendar can be used to introduce modern Chinese holidays and the ways that Chinese people celebrate these holidays. If there are ethnic minority students in the class, I suggest choosing a special time to allow them to share the ways in which they celebrate their unique traditional festivals. This can expand student views and their respect and understanding of different cultures.

In making cultural comparisons with the Mid-Autumn Festival, although no mainstream American holidays have a relationship to the moon, according to Wikipedia, in American myth and folklore each full moon has a specific name, and students can find their full moon name according to the month of their birth. In addition, India, the Philippines, Vietnam, Singapore and other countries have their unique ways to celebrate the Moon Festival, and the teacher can introduce this through stories, having students draw filmstrip type depictions as they listen. Students can use their drawings to repeat the story in small groups, giving them practice in speaking. In addition, you cannot neglect food when celebrating a traditional festival. So in making cultural comparisons of festivals, teachers can highlight the types and meanings of traditional foods, linking this to the food themes in the previous unit.

In addition, if you wish to emphasize the study of vocabulary related to festivals, students can divide into groups and use charades to present different festivals. In this process, because students have to find the movements that best represent festivals to achieve group consensus, they must think carefully about the full significance of festivals, and this sets in motion students taking initiative for their own self-study. Moreover, as mentioned earlier, if the celebration of traditional Chinese festivals in the US often lacks a festive atmosphere, when talking about unique contemporary Chinese holidays such as Teachers' Day or Children's Day, although students feel a sense of novelty, it is more difficult to use their own experience as a springboard, because they may have zero experience. At this point I suggest that teachers introduce network resources, videos, or photos and if there is a sister school relationship, they can use Internet phones (Skype) for video access. Or they might pose the following questions: do you think the United States should have a Teachers' Day or a Children's Day? This trains students' speculative and higher thinking skills.

Since festival activities have their own timing, when designing courses, teachers should plan these activities as close to the festival day as possible. If this timing doesn't work, they should be celebrated in advance, so that students might on that day celebrate the holiday with their family or participate in community celebrations. In addition, knowledge of multi-ethnic cultures for third and fourth grade students is still in the beginning stages, so teachers should start from students' own experiences, then draw in other different ethnic cultures to train students to view things as international citizens. Finally, use community resources as much as possible, bringing the classroom into the community and community into the classroom, bringing life and fire to the festival celebration.

Unit Topic Four: Geography and Travel

The teaching objectives for this unit include understanding the meaning of time; using directions and maps to understand the relationship between time and space; understanding the benefits of travel to gain knowledge of culture, history, and customs; becoming familiar with modes of transport; and learning about Chinese communities in the United States. Students in first and second grade will have acquired basic knowledge and skills dealing with time and space, including descriptions of directions and locations. In third and fourth grade, in addition to continuing to consolidate previous knowledge and skills, consider increasing the diversity of skills, to develop students' adaptive capabilities. For example, first and second grade students can read a digital clock, but at this stage students should have the mathematical skills to read a traditional clock. Most school districts set social studies standards for the third grade curriculum in humanities and history, and I suggest that Chinese teachers consider linking their curriculum with other teachers while at the same time adding topics in Chinese culture and history.

  Students in first and second grades will already have drawn maps of their school yard and neighborhood, and will have used these maps to describe the relationships between buildings or give directions. In the third grade you can add the directions north, south, east, and west. Given that the four cardinal directions (north, south, east, west) are defined by the earth's relationship to the sun, but relative directions such as front, back, right, left, up, and down change according to what directions the communicator is facing, it is easy for people to get confused. Although relationships between north, south, east, and west do not change, because the reference points used are not the students themselves and because students are not accustomed to commonly using these terms, it might require more time. You can start by studying the earth (a social studies theme for third grade) and use balloons and paper mache to make a globe. Then color the globe, marking north and south with the equator as the first dividing line, and east and west with the prime meridian, then the northern hemisphere, southern hemisphere, eastern hemisphere, western hemisphere, the Antarctic, the arctic and so on. Students can then indicate and review the seven continents and four oceans and the positions of the United States, China, or any other countries of student interest. This type of lesson helps students understand that in describing positions they can use a flat plane (like first and second grade) or three dimensional forms. The equator is based on the axis of rotation of the earth and serves as the dividing line for the northern and southern hemisphere. The idea of eastern and western direction is easy to understand, but the location of the Prime Meridian has no special physical meaning and is something set by humans. If students ask, you just have to say this is the way it is. Following the earth's rotation, morning is in the east and west is opposite, and you can use the paper mache globe to explain. The sun rising in the east and setting in the west is a very important concept, because students' determinations of the basic directions of north, south, east, west are based on this knowledge. Teachers can take advantage of the sun's early morning progression in the east and take the students to the school yard or playground. Have students stretch out their arms with right arms pointing to the sun rising from the east; their left arms are naturally the west, their face is north and their back is south; this is easy for students to remember. (Note: ancient Chinese used to refer to the east as the left, but because the usual map directions show east on the right, in order to prevent confusion, it is better to use the right arms to stand for east.) If you can't go out in the morning, you can use the afternoon when the sun is setting in the west. The main point is to have students use body movements as much as possible, giving them a multi-sensory experience to aid learning and memory.

In addition, on the playground or in another suitable space, teachers can give students an experience familiar to students at schools in China: the team line up experience to reinforce their memories of directions. Teach students to count off and form rows in a group according to height, then practice standing at attention, face forward, look left, look right, turn to the back, march, at ease, and other military commands. Students who are still not very clear on directions and sometimes make mistakes are bound to stimulate laughter.

The next focus of study is to have students use the basic directions and relative orientations that they have learned. Students can use their basic directions for a treasure hunt in the school yard. Before embarking on the treasure hunt, the teacher can have students make a simple compass, which students use during the treasure hunt with instructions given by the teacher. In addition, practicing relative directions in the classroom building by searching for hidden candy is also a very interesting game. When playing the candy finding game, students read slips of paper and the teacher gives oral directions. Or you can blindfold the student who is responsible for looking and have other students practice giving oral directions. You can have a group competition with the victorious team being the one finding the candy safely in the shortest period of time. When playing this game, you must be certain to set safety rules to avoid students stumbling or bumping into things and having fun turn into sorrow.

Once students are very familiar with giving directions, they can design a small skit about asking directions on the school campus (a prerequisite is that students must be very familiar with the names and locations of school buildings). Allow students to use very simple photographic or video equipment and act out short skits with scenes of asking for directions; students will have very high motivation for completing this project. In addition, students can try to record a short video introducing the school campus, using shots from different orientations and different positions to introduce the school. Chinese teachers can join with other foreign language teachers at their school and have students use different languages to co-produce a short video about the school that can be used as a public relations gift in the future, given to visiting foreign dignitaries, used in the establishment of a sister school, or simply used as a tool to promote foreign language education.

In reference to "time", given that third and fourth grade students have good hand/eye coordination, they can make a sundial, marking time on the sundial in the ancient Chinese way, with each day divided into twelve two hours periods, using the names of the 12 earthly branches for these periods. Because of the difficulty in calibrating the sundial, the purpose of this project is to introduce the multiple ways of telling time, and to compare and contrast ancient Chinese and modern ways of measuring time. In extending this theme, the teacher can have students compare different timing methods and explore the meaning of time. Ask them "If instruments of time were to disappear, would this be good or bad? What could be done if there were no sun and no tools to measure time?"

If basic skills in geography and travel are being nurtured in third grade, teachers in fourth grade can consider how to integrate these skills and design a simulated trip to Beijing. The teacher can compose travel notes along with students, with each student in the class selecting a role to play during this travel. If the school has a mascot, you can consider taking it to China and have students care for the mascot during their journey. The focus of this lesson should include preparation for departure induding the type of transport used to go from home to the airport; making individual passports, preparing travel money and air tickets; reading the time table during airport check-in, getting a boarding pass, checking luggage, going through the security check, finding the location of the boarding gate, finding the flight, etc. In addition, design some interesting incidents that will occur aboard the plane such as turbulence, becoming airsick, and ordering food to increase the fun of travel. Some students can play the roles of parents, ground crew, and passengers and some can play the roles of captain, flight attendant, and doctor. The teacher and students can rearrange the positions of tables and chairs to make the classroom look like the cabin of an airplane. While students are on the plane, the teacher can broadcast a satellite map of China to introduce important Chinese landforms such as mountains, rivers and bordering countries, inserting geographical knowledge into travel as a focus of study. When the students have arrived in Beijing, the teacher can play travel videos that introduce different historic features, famous scenic spots, the modern landscape of Beijing (including the remnants of the *hutong*), creating realistic effects as much as possible. The teacher can also emphasize the special ways that Beijing people talk with the variety of "r" sounds and consonants produced on the back of the tongue, and can have students study a few Beijing verses, and watch Beijing opera as an exciting conclusion to their trip to China.

These are some suggestions for teaching geography and travel. Although third and fourth grade students have less opportunities to travel abroad with their school, through flexible teaching design teachers can still give students many interesting and practical learning experiences. The trick is that even when we cannot take students around the world, we can bring the world into our classrooms.

Unit Topic Five: History, Politics and Religion

In talking about topics of history, government, and religion with third and fourth grade students, it is hard to avoid worrying about lack of student interest because the subject might be too boring. However, if you use the fact that students love to listen to stories, and your mode of entry is based on students' personal experiences, it is relatively easy to overcome these difficulties. The contents of this unit do not need to focus on expanding the breadth of knowledge because after all one or two months is certainly not sufficient to understand five thousand years of history. Moreover, most American students still have little knowledge of their own country's history, so expecting students to understand the ins and outs of Chinese history is rather futile. So I propose using *The Journey to the West* to introduce Chinese history and religion, or the Qin Emperor and the Great Wall to narrate early Chinese political patterns and history.

Before investigating religion, I recommend that you first contact parents in advance so that they understand the purpose of this lesson and can discuss with students at home their religious beliefs and the form and purpose of their participation in religious activities. If the students' parents do not have any special religious beliefs, you can change the discussion to how they maintain spiritual/mental health. By allowing parents to participate in preparation, you can reduce the degree of parental rejection of the subject and obtain their cooperation and assistance in teaching. Also, when students and their families have discussed topics of religion and psychological health in advance, students can more easily and quickly enter into the following learning activities.

After talking with their families, have students share with others in the classroom what they have learned from these discussions. Students can use drawings to demonstrate: Who are the important people on religious occasions? What types of activities are held in these places? What are the special features in architectural design and how are religious ceremonies conducted? Then students can be divided into groups according to religious faith, with students of the same religion in the same group. Students can share their drawings with the group and integrate their personal religious knowledge. They should add new information to their drawings based on their discussions. Afterwards, the teacher can reorganize the students and have each faith group appoint a member to the "Religious United Nations". where they introduce a summary of their group's religious knowledge. Students with no particular religious beliefs must also share in the "Religious United Nations". This activity is an example of using students as a resource and using students to teach students. In addition, during the sharing process of the "Religious United Nations", teachers should help students understand that even though people may have different religious beliefs, these religious faiths may serve the same functions. Also, even where there is no special religious belief, people can still used philosophical beliefs to pursue spiritual/mental health.

If teachers themselves have different spiritual beliefs from their students, they should be encouraged to share this with the students. In the process of sharing, it is best to allow students to see how religious beliefs are implemented in that religion, such as styles of prayer or the special items and clothing required for ceremonies. If parents have non-mainstream religious beliefs, the teacher may consider inviting the parents to class to share with the students. As this activity comes to an end, have students use two ring or three ring Venn diagrams to draw comparisons. Students can select one or two other religious faiths that they find interesting and compare them with their own.

Finally, teachers can arrange to take students to visit a Buddhist temple, if one is available in their community. Have students bring a hard board, drawing paper, and colored pencils and sit quietly in a corner of the temple, becoming silent detectives using eyes to see, ears to hear, noses to smell, hands to draw, and hearts to make conjectures. In order to allow students to completely gather information, the teacher can in advance assign students to focus on different important themes, for example: people and activities, the external temple construction, the interior furnishings, etc. After returning to school, teachers can sum up the information, collect the results, and display outside of the classroom the work completed by the "Religious United Nations". Including the student drawings from the field trip. In this way students and teachers from the entire school can benefit.

After visiting the temple, you can proceed to the Monkey King story. Many American students know that China has a Monkey King, but they don't necessarily know the historical facts about Xuan Zang going to India to fetch the scriptures. Third and fourth grade students especially enjoy reading adventure stories and fantasy novels, so *Journey to the West* is very suitable for children of this age group. Teachers can use story books or download a video from the Internet (for example the Youku website: www.youku.com) and select sections to focus on within this classic tale. In teaching behavioral culture, you might highlight the relationship between Xuan Zang and the Monkey King as master and disciple but also like father and son, thus emphasizing traditional Chinese ethical relationships. At their level of knowledge, students can learn through the story of *Journey to the West* the geographical relationship between India and China; the early contacts between China and Western countries; that Buddhism travelled from India into China, etc. In order to enhance their interest, teachers can have students make a Monkey King headband and then go to a building supply place such as Home Depot to buy a rod to make the Monkey King golden cudgel. They can invite outside experts from the Chinese community who know how to teach dance or martial arts to come to the school to teach the students golden cudgel Monkey King dance. Have students imitate the Monkey King's shape, and accompany the performance with traditional Chinese percussion music and it will be very lively!

Most third and fourth grade students have heard of the Chinese emperor, but they don't necessarily know that this is a historical fact. American student understanding of the Great Wall is like their recognition of the panda: they are both features of China. So in talking about history and politics, you can use the topic of the Great Wall to introduce China's first emperor and the early Chinese political situation.

To penetrate this subject, use an entire week to advance a fictitious/virtual story: two empires are fighting against each other and urgently need a Great Wall to prevent foreign invasion. The Great Wall must be built in the high mountains of a remote border region. Due to the inaccessible terrain, the border can only be reached on foot. The style of government of the two emperors is totally opposite: one is a controlling tyrant and the other is a good king who shows universal kindness. The teacher can divide the class into two empires (you can use two country names from the warring states period). Because this was not a democratic era, the roles of emperor in this activity can be assigned by the teacher. The two emperors must follow the governance characteristics assigned by the teacher, and they must gather people to build the Great Wall in the shortest period of time. Teachers in this project must at all times provide assistance to students so that political forms can be maintained. Before the start of this project, students work together to determine how tyrants and benevolent monarchs control people. Students who are serving as ordinary people, after promising their emperor to help build the Great Wall, must bring empty milk cartons or bottles to school to "construct the Great Wall". Teachers must stipulate how many milk cartons are needed to complete the Great Wall. In this simulated political environment, students can experience different political styles, they can understand political patterns, and become vaguely aware of the governing style of the first Chinese emperor. Students acting as emperor must also learn negotiating strategies, or they will be totally useless. After whichever country first finishes construction of the Great Wall, the teacher can have students sum up the knowledge they've gained. The teacher can finally take the opportunity to present the story of the first emperor and his positive and negative influences on Chinese history. At the end of the unit, the teacher can use a DVD to introduce spectacular images of the Great Wall.

In short, when investigating Chinese history, government, or religion with third and fourth grade students, as it involves a lot of information about culture and cultural achievements, the teaching objective should not necessarily focus on greatly increasing student knowledge, but should first select several topics of interest to students and by using fun and energetic small group activities raise student interest in learning. If students are willing to continue learning Chinese, the teacher need not worry about not being able to finish the long history of five thousand years!

Unit Topic Six: Friends, Fun, Fashions and Fads

Third and fourth grade students attach much greater importance to friends than students in earlier years, and the influence of peers is also growing. In first and second grades, this topic has emphasized training students in empathy and skills in making friends, and in learning about Chinese children's games. At this stage, besides continuing to investigate the meaning of friendship, styles of expressing friendship, and how to balance fun activities, we can also include understanding fashion, and the impact of popularity on students' friendships and lives, because interest in and sensitivity towards fashion is gradually increasing.

In the school where I serve, each spring term features a "pet day". On that day students can bring their pets to school for other students to observe, to tease, or to engage in a variety of competitions. This activity not only gives students access to different pets, but can also challenge everyone's definition of pets because some students will bring pets like snakes, lizards or turtles to school.

Personally, I think that pets fit well with the topic of friendship, because most children are enthusiastic about animals, and this gives them great incentive to participate. The teacher first has students bring a photo of their own or a close friend's pet to the classroom and give an oral introduction. Depending on school regulations, as well as conditions such as size, temperament, and safety of the pets, you can decide whether or not to allow students to bring the pets themselves to the classroom. If this is possible, it is bound to create an exciting class atmosphere. Students from families that do not have pets can use Internet resources to search for images, and have teachers help them construct a PowerPoint that enables them to make a short class presentation.

Students can then conduct a mini-debate on the questions "Can pets be friends? Why?". Third and fourth grade students may not have previous experience in debate, so teachers can use a jury system and have members of the jury listen to the positive and negative sides of the arguments and make a joint decision on whether pets can or cannot count as friends. Before the debate begins, the main arguments can be determined through the process of brainstorming in small groups about the positive and negative sides, collecting ideas by pooling student wisdom. Teachers must help students arrange their lines of argument so they can be more eloquent during the debate. Using this event, students are trained in their presentational capabilities and students on the jury will be trained in their interpretive capabilities. Winning the debate is not the main point. For students, understanding the true meaning of friendship is the main objective of this activity, because during the preparation of positive and negative sides of the debate and the subsequent competition, they will be able to investigate and understand friendship in a deeper way.

In order to increase the effect of this debating activity, students can make drawings of what their ideal animal friends would look like. What are the special characteristics of a good friend? Also, how should you care for your animal friends so they will not despise you? Students can use their creative imaginations, and it doesn't matter if their ideal friends are like nothing else on earth. One reason for having students pick their ideal animal friends is to avoid having students publically declaring that they want certain named individuals to be their good friend. Also the teaching strategies for this activity draw on the cognitive orientations of students of this age, which fall between fantasy and reality. Using a harmless theme to study the meaning of friends and how to maintain friendships is the most important element. If students wish to explore this topic further, they can use the preceding questions to interview students in the rest of the school.

Next, teachers can use the fact that third and fourth grade students love to listen to stories to narrate stories of friendship from Chinese history, such as Sima Guang's rescue of a friend; Guan Ning's diplomatic break with the Hua Xin; or the influence of social environment on Mencius. [1] In sharing these stories, teachers should not preach to students, attempt to reach conclusions for students, or impose their own views, which would deprive them of an opportunity to think independently. The ideal approach is to use guided questions, such as: If you were Guan Ning, what would you do? When friends are in difficulty, why do you want to help them?

When friends are together, an inevitable question is what to do to have fun. This unit presents a good opportunity for introducing abundant vocabulary and sentence patterns related to entertainment and hobbies. Teachers can use graphic organizers such as KWL to collect

---

[1] The teacher can locate these stories through a keyword search on Internet sources for primary students such as www. vastman. com, www. baidu. com or others.

and arrange the vocabulary that students want to learn. I've discovered that students really like to use physically oriented guessing games such as charades. Third and fourth grade students are still learning about small group organization and collaboration, so teachers must be patient and willing to provide assistance step by step. Because self-control is still an issue, some students can be temperamental or make trouble for no reason. Teachers can use group pressure to provide appropriate mediation, or change the roles and duties of the student in the group. In addition, you can use incidents of conflict themselves to interpret the meaning of friendship, providing the opportunity for a "teachable moment". Of course, not every conflict should be handled in this way.

Most American children spend a considerable amount of time watching television, similar to students in China. Students can be asked to vote on their favorite television programs and explain why they like them. Then, the teacher can collect contemporary popular programs from mainland, Hong Kong, and Taiwan of China and find out reasons for their popularity. They can show students some excerpts of episodes in the classroom, both as a means for teaching language and as a tool for cultural comparison. Teachers can ask questions such as: What is interesting about the program? Why? Because cultural definitions of what is interesting will vary, there may be large differences that make it difficult to understand how to appreciate each other's programs. So, if students cannot understand what is interesting about a television program, the teacher can use this opportunity to guide students to consider why Chinese children might enjoy a program which they do not like. Hopefully, through this process of sharing and discussion, students will understand that there can be different cultural definitions of what is interesting for Americans and Chinese and that this is influenced by different systems of cultural values. Teachers do not need further explanation or analysis of the reasons for cultural differences because this will not be very meaningful for students. As long as students understand that there might be different views of the same thing (perspectives), planting the seed is sufficient.

Unit Topic Seven: Creative Arts and Sciences

For the topic of creative arts and science, younger students will have gained a beginning understanding of characters, calligraphy, and music. In the third and fourth grade curriculum, we can add in China's four great inventions to pave the way for the fifth and sixth grade classes, as well as continuing to explore and expand on the themes of Chinese folk arts, music, and written language, so that students both consolidate and add to their knowledge.

In American courses on the history of world civilizations, the first mention of China usually leads to discussion of the four great inventions. The compass arose out of the great navigational advances of the Southern Song maritime industry. The invention of paper making and printing with moveable type allowed for the preservation of the lasting contribution of Chinese classic literary works. The invention of gunpowder brought about the emergence of firearms in the late Tang period. The four great Chinese inventions also contributed to the rapid development of Western civilization. When third and fourth grade students talk about the four great inventions, at their level of knowledge it is enough to let them know about the four inventions, have students speculate about how they influenced China, and then have hands on learning projects.

In setting the stage, teachers can first show students pictures of the four great inventions, and have students guess what they were and what they were used for. In terms of pictures, teachers can use the SOSO website (www.wenwen.soso.com) and find information with the keyword search of "four great inventions of China." Wikipedia has a diagram of the five step process for making paper that you can print out and have students try to arrange the proper sequence for making paper. If there is a paper mill near the school, you might try to arrange a field trip. Also YouTube has a Chinese version of the four great inventions of ancient China that can be downloaded.

By using hands on methods to study the four great inventions students can become a "modern Cai Lun" or "modern Bi Sheng" as they make paper and moveable type printing in the classroom. If teachers have questions about paper making methods, they can search for self-study videos from YouTube or ask for guidance in the classroom from an art teacher. When having students study simple printing with moveable types, you might need to alter the methods and materials.

Teachers and students can brainstorm together to design a flyer or an invitation, such as an invitation to parents to visit an exhibition of Chinese year-end projects at the school. After determining the content of flyers or invitations, teachers can distribute tasks in making the moveable type: so and so is responsible for carving this character, etc. Use a safety block and a simple carving knife for student engraving. Before the activity begins, be sure to emphasize safety rules for the handling of tools. When students have all completed the characters that they are personally responsible for, the teacher can collect them together and then have students begin typesetting. In the process, the study should involve the review of reading characters. The teacher can even use typesetting to have small groups compete with each other to see who can accomplish the typesetting the quickest. When the typesetting is finished, the students can help the teacher brush ink on the characters arranged in a row and use paper made by students to print the flyers or invitations. Of course, it is difficult to guarantee quality in the printing process, but for students, the experience of learning through making things with their own hands is far more important. As for the compass, the teachers can have students engage in hands on production as part of the unit that investigates geography and travel. And because gunpowder would involve laws and regulations, it is of course not suitable for hands on classroom production!

As students investigate the influence of folk arts and music in people's daily lives, I recommend connecting this with topics in other units. For example, when celebrating traditional festivals or special days, selecting very traditional and colorful classical music and folk arts to add to the festive atmosphere is a good way to introduce traditional folk arts and music. New Year celebrations feature traditions of paper cutting and pasting spring flowers, and teachers can make special arrangements to include these in the course curriculum: presenting paper cutting materials, tools, techniques and special colors from each region, as well as the uses of paper cuts. At the end of the lecture, the students make their own paper cuts and decorate the classroom. In this way, it is easier for students to understand the different uses of these folk arts on appropriate occasions.

As for music, younger students will have gained some understanding of traditional Chinese musical instruments and might even identify their sounds. The focus at this earlier stage was on learning the names of instruments and their special characteristics. For third and fourth grade, I recommend that as the teacher introduces folk arts, they make use of educational opportunities to have students make multiple connections. For example, what types of musical instruments are more often used in the traditional happy music celebrating Chinese New Year and other holidays? Do these instruments have counterparts with Western musical instruments, such as the *huqin* and the violin, the dulcimer and the zither, the *bangdi* and the clarinet? Then, students who are studying Western musical instruments can try playing traditional Chinese melodies and compare this with traditional melodies played on traditional Chinese instruments. This type of activity not only increases students' curiosity and interest in learning, it also allows students to have a deeper impression of Chinese music and to experience the special characteristics of music from one's own culture.

The final theme focuses on China's written language. The emphasis for teaching in lower grades was the study of pictographs and the comparative recognition of simplified and complex characters. In third and fourth grades, because the vocabulary and characters that students encounter are no longer limited to pictographic characters, teachers can gradually shift their focus to combined ideograms and characters that are mostly based on phonetic compounds. Teachers can systematically organize the common radicals （eg. 提手旁,秃宝盖,单人旁） and introduce them as a topic. Encourage students to make connections, linking radicals and pictographs in their writing (eg. "手" vs. "提手旁", "心" vs. "竖心旁"). Learning radicals is very helpful in advancing student reading abilities.

Teaching comparative Chinese and Western language and literature, as occurs with university classes, is generally not appropriate and ill-suited to the cognitive levels of students of this age. For a systematic introduction, I think that you must wait until at least eighth grade. For example, with syntax, third and fourth grade students may not even know the English terms for basic sentence structures. If you want third and fourth grade students to experience or detect differences in Chinese and English, you do not need to rush this, because when they are sufficiently mature they will automatically raise questions or bring up new discoveries. Besides written characters, the most significant characteristic of Chinese language is the tone. In teaching the language, you can as much as possible lay a solid foundation for the control of tone with third and fourth grade students. According to research from language experts, children who are learning a second language have diminished ability to discriminate tones as they reach adolescence. In the process of language instruction, teachers can use more physical movements and gestures to especially emphasize tones. When teaching singing, you can begin with nursery rhymes: read the song lyrics aloud very expressively several times or use the lyrics to create a short skit; then finally learn to sing, because when singing, all of the tones are first tones, unless you are singing Hip-Hop.

Unit Topic Eight: Expressing Emotions and Feelings

In investigating emotional expressions, it is very important to understand the emotional development of children, including the special characteristics of different stages of development, as well as the identification and ability to control emotions, in order to design teaching goals and activities in compatible and practical ways. In addition, teachers must not play the role of psychological counselors and attempt to solve students' emotional problems, because this is not the domain or focus area of Chinese language teachers, and Chinese teachers do not have this ability or training. So, if a teacher discovers that a certain student seems to have emotional difficulties, they need to make the necessary referral for counseling. I insist that when Chinese teachers investigate this topic the emphasis should be placed on language functions and cultural comparisons. The following is a brief outline of a three week teaching plan for fourth grade students.

The vocabulary and sentence structures in the first and second grade curriculum focus on basic emotions such as happy, angry, sad, and scared. At this stage you can add other basic emotion vocabulary including the so called conscious emotions of disgust, interest, and surprise. Another teaching priority for lower grades is to train students in their ability to recognize facial expressions. Facial expressions are external and can be visually observed, and for younger elementary students the study of facial expressions is an appropriate and interesting topic. By third and fourth grades, children know that a variety of emotions can exist simultaneously; they are learning to judge or speculate on the reasons for emotional reactions; and they are trying to comply with the social standards for expressing emotions. Once students understand some of the basic norms for emotional expressions, they also can try to hide their personal emotions.

Given the above characteristics of emotional development, I believe that the emphasis for the first week should be to connect with what students have learned in lower grades. Since third and fourth grade students already know how to hide their emotions, students can further investigate the many styles of emotional expression, especially non-verbal communication. In addition to facial expressions, are there any clues that can help us understand our own or other people's emotions? Teachers can use questions and let students brainstorm: "In addition to facial expressions, what other methods do people use to let people understand their emotions or feelings in their heart?" Afterwards, teachers can bring non-verbal ways of expressing emotions such as through eyes, gestures, body movements, tone of speaking, etc. into the curriculum. So, the focus in the first week is to concentrate on language and study the vocabulary and sentence patterns related to basic emotions, and in addition to language and facial expressions, the use of other non-verbal ways of expressing emotion.

The teacher can mix together male and female students in groups and have students discuss how to use body movements and hand gestures, but not facial expressions, to convey emotions. Students must come up with the most effective means of expression. By mixing male and female students the hope is that this discussion will lead them to explore whether there are male and female differences in body movements and hand gestures. The next game is similar to charades: group A assigns a representative to wear a mask that shows only the eyes. Following flash cards shown by the teacher, the student makes body movements or gestures to represent this emotion, which must be guessed by group B. The way to determine the winner is to announce at the end of the game which group received the most points. If group B receives the most points, then group A is the winner because members of this group will have most effectively communicated emotions through body movements and gestures. During this phase, the teacher can have students provide feedback on whether only using gestures and body movements provided ideal results.

Teachers can then give the class a simple, short sentence with no emotional color, such as "I want to buy an apple", so that the students practice using different moods to speak this sentence. Then pick a volunteer to come to the front. With their back to the class, have the student use different tones of voice to produce the same sentence in different emotional colors, and have the class guess whether the speaker is happy, sad, angry or disgusted. Finally, with the same short phrase, allow performers to demonstrate using facial expressions, gestures, eye contact, and body movements. Through these several activities, teachers can easily help students learn that to understand someone's mood, in addition to facial expressions there are other methods, and communication works best when these are used simultaneously.

Then, using the different emotion vocabulary, students can draw different possible shapes for eyebrows, eyes, and mouth on cardboard paper. When students have finished drawing they can color, cut them out and put them together to describe different emotional expressions. For example: when eyebrows are down, mouth is down, the eyes are not shining, this person might be sad. Then the teacher distributes four character idioms that describe emotions to the students and has them use their picture cards to show the facial expressions of emotion that match the contents of the idiom.

A recommended activity for training students in oral skills is to consider using the Webber Photo Cards published by Super Duper Publications. Webber has a set of 264 image cards that contain images of emotional expressions. Teachers can first extract the emotion cards that they desire students to be familiar with, and put all of the cards face down in the middle of the table. Have students take turns drawing cards, and if the card shows a happy emotion the student must use that emotional tone to explain something that has made her/him happy. Because of the non-competitive nature of this event, students can make full use of their time to reflect on how to express this content verbally. Teachers can also put students in groups of two or three and give students in each group nine Webber cards and they can do oral drills from words, to phrases, to complete sentences.

In teaching culture, the teacher can have students look at pictures or videos that display school age children making an unreasonable fuss in a public place and ask students how they would feel if they were this child's father or mother. What they would do, and why? Students can discuss in pairs and then share with the class, while the teacher sums up the main points. Then show several pictures of Chinese children making a big fuss and again ask the students, if this were the father or mother of a Chinese child, do you think they would have a different reaction? Let students speculate and discuss. At this point I recommend that the teacher present a summary of Chinese people's concept of "face" and explain that Chinese children pay particular attention to behavior in public places so as not to make parents lose face. If students cannot understand, it does not matter, because if the seeds are planted at this age, the harvest will probably increase at the next stage. In short, at the third and fourth grade level, the cultural emphasis is to have students start to realize that there is a concept of "face" in Chinese society. When they reach fifth and sixth grades, you can again emphasize the importance of "face" and point to cultural differences in expressing emotions.

Before the age of eight, in addition to basic emotions, children can also experience self-conscious emotions such as shame, embarrassment, guilt, jealousy and pride. In the second week, you can add further descriptive emotional vocabulary and sentence patterns, so that students' oral abilities in describing their inner feelings can continue to take root. The teacher can connect with patterns of emotional expression from the previous week and investigate how these patterns of emotional expression are different. For examples, can you see emotions by merely relying on facial expressions? What emotions can be hidden? When you have these inner feelings, can other emotions also be present?

In presenting and practicing vocabulary, teachers should make greater use of the concept of multiple intelligences in their instruction by integrating movement, visuals, texts, and small group situations into their design. The teacher can first have students take the emotion booklets made in the previous grade and add new vocabulary for emotional expressions, using drawings to explain. As for reading the terms, the teacher can write the words describing emotion on post-it notes, one on each, and attach them to students' foreheads. The students cannot see the words pasted on their heads in advance, and must walk around the classroom and ask other students questions such as "Do I feel awkward?" "Do I feel jealous?" Students must be able to read the word on the forehead of the student who inquires in order to give a helpful answer. After students have received the correct answer three times, they can remove the note. To help students understand this activity, the teacher should serve as a model, sticking a mood word on their head and asking the students.

Teachers can also take the words or idioms describing emotion and make flash cards to play the game "I change, I change, I change change change". Students divide into groups and send a representative forward. This student makes a facial expression corresponding with the emotion word on the teacher's flashcard and members of their group must guess. Within a limited time, the group that guesses correctly the most times wins. In the second or third round of play, because students are already familiar with the basic vocabulary, I suggest that teachers increase the difficulty of the game and require that students give descriptions in complete sentences. Another way to increase the difficulty is to use an emotional tone of voice in the description, which makes this a very interesting activity. If the teacher can record student facial expressions on video, after the activity has ended, they can have the whole class watch and not only review the vocabulary once again but also bring the classroom atmosphere to a high level.

Another group collaboration integrates language, drawing, and movement. Students use words to describe five circumstances where people feel shame, guilt, jealousy, embarrassment and pride. Those who are good at writing can write the description on cards; those who are good at drawing can draw scenarios on the other side of the cards; those who are good at physical expressions can cooperatively present the situation in the form of mime. Finally, the whole group of students put on a performance; those responsible for writing become the narrators on stage, the students drawing scenes display their drawing, and the rest of the students act out the plot of the story. The audience watches, laughs, and makes guesses about the actual feelings of the students performing on stage.

At the end of the small group activities, teachers can use the situations designed by the students to train students further in cultural awareness and language skills, using use the Chinese term "意思" to help students understand the different uses and meanings of "意思" in

Mandarin. For example, when praised with "够意思", you may feel very proud, but when people say that you "很不够意思" they are expressing dissatisfaction and want you to feel shame or guilt. The occasions that cause people to feel "不好意思" often make people embarrassed. When people say that you "好意思啊？", the implication is that you should feel embarrassed or ashamed. When classmates have birthdays and receive a lot of "意思" while you have received nothing, you might feel envy and jealousy. Teachers can use four frame movie paper and have students use different meanings of "意思" to make illustrated dialogues. Then have students divide into groups and select some of the dialogue for a dramatic comedy, make a video recording, and show this to the rest of the class. The general student motivation for participating in such activities is very high. During ordinary classroom dialogue, teachers should manufacture many situations to use opportunities to repeatedly practice the many meanings of "意思", making student learning very interesting and fun（很有意思）!

In Chinese culture, it is not appropriate for individuals to display self-satisfied pride or arrogance in their attitudes, behavior or speech. While American students might not understand the Chinese concept of modesty（谦虚）, as teachers we should at least guide our students to reply when being praised with phrases such as "哪里哪里""应该的""不好不好", and not thank you（谢谢）. Remember to constantly remind students that when dealing with Chinese people, you should pay attention to modest language and subtle manners, because in this way you will not seem abrupt and will have easier access to Chinese people's respect and love. Teachers can have students once again perform a small situation comedy to practice giving praise and responding to praise from others.

At the end of the second week, have each student select a subject from personal life events or experiences and use emotional dialogue to write lyrics or a new poem. Then have students read this aloud with facial expressions and voice corresponding to the emotions of the piece. This is very good training because foreign language students, before they have internalized the language, generally find it difficult to properly express themselves using the correct facial expressions and emotional tone. Through this somewhat implausible way to teach students, you can at least help them understand the importance of non-verbal components in linguistic expressions.

In the third week watch the movie "*I Not Stupid* (2)", using this to discuss the importance of "impulse control" and to integrate with the first two weeks of teaching content. I select "impulse control" as a theme because I have discovered that third and fourth grade students understand the importance of this concept and have enough powers of concentration and cognitive abilities for self-regulation, but they are often not able to suppress their inner impulses one hundred percent of the time. "Impulse control" as a theme has another advantage: the teacher and students can take the initiative to investigate the effects of poor impulse control on family, on friends, and on classroom learning, such as not allowing other students opportunities to speak and learn, delaying the progress of their teachers, or giving others a bad impression.

Before showing the movie, you should first help students understand the purpose of watching the movie and the tasks they should accomplish as they watch it. When discussing with students at the end of the movie, use questions to guide their reflections, such as: What are some examples of poor emotional control? Why did the characters in the movie not control their impulses? How did they show this in their behavior and words? What could the characters do to not give other people a bad impression? If it were you, what would you do?

Then have students divide into groups, give each group some 3×5 index cards, and have them brain storm and try to point out which situations in students' personal lives most easily cause a loss of control. For example: my younger brother often breaks my doll and I have the urge to teach him a lesson; I know the answer and I want everyone to know that I'm very smart, so I don't want to wait for the teacher to call on me to speak. Students draw a picture of the situation on one side of an index card and on the other side write one or two sentences describing the situation and strategies that can be used to control impulsive behavior. After drawing and writing, have students select one or two situations and use a small skit to act out the circumstances: from creating an exciting emotional event, to producing the complete internal emotional outbreak, to the process of successfully controlling the impulse.

When the short skits are finished, the teacher can summarize and sort out the strategies used by students in the skits to control their impulses. The teacher then asks a focus question "What is the impact of controlling emotions or expressing inappropriate emotions?" and has students continue discussions in their groups, using a variety of vocabulary and sentence patterns for expressing emotions. Training students to manage emotions should start small, and I suggest that before teachers instruct students in controlling their impulses and adjusting their emotions that they first obtain help from psychological counseling experts at the school or school district, and if possible, invite these experts to the classroom to teach students more strategies to regulate their emotions.

In addition, sign language is a very effective communication tool, especially for the hearing impaired person or for young children who are still babbling. During this week, teachers can use American Sign Language and instruct students in how to use simple sign language for some emotional expressions. YouTube has many useful video resources. Also a book, *The Joy of Signing* (Riekehof 1987), has many carefully written descriptions plus drawings. Using sign language to supplement foreign language teaching is worth promoting, as it can reduce the opportunities for students to use the first language. Teaching students to use sign language to express personal feelings, in addition to offering an additional form of emotional expression in the classroom for students who are shy or not fond of oral expressions, can also buffer student impulsiveness and reduce noise in the classroom. Clearly, there are many benefits to sign language.

Before the end of the unit, have the students compile a type of hip-hop creation using the combined vocabulary for emotions, and let the students come to a happy end of this unit with fun sounds. For the selection of hip-hop rhythms, consult *Practical Rhythmic Chinese* (Yin

& Sun 2008).

Unit Plan Example: Expressing Emotions and Feelings
(Grades 3, 3 weeks)

Guiding Questions

Essential Questions	Focus Questions
1. What is emotion? 2. How do we express our feelings? 3. How and why do people express emotions in different ways? 4. How do emotional expressions affect social relationships?	1. Can you describe your emotions and feelings? 2. In addition to facial expressions, what other clues can help us understand our own or other people's feelings? 3. How do you express different types of emotions? How is this similar and different from the ways that others express these emotions? 4. What are the effects of inappropriate emotional expressions?

Functional Outcomes/Skills

- Students are able to describe their own and inquire about other people's emotions.
- Students can explain and give examples of the special characteristics and causes for individual emotional expression among Chinese people.
- Students can explain and give examples of appropriate forms of individual emotional expression in Chinese society, in both language and behavior.

Learning Assessments

a) Formative assessments: See details of weekly lesson plans
b) Summative assessment: Individual creative rhythm rap

Weekly Lesson Plans

Week One: Patterns of Emotional Expression	
Teaching Objectives	• Students can describe a mix of non-verbal behaviors when expressing emotions • Students can use the vocabulary and sentence patterns related to emotions to describe their own emotions and ask about the feelings of others • Students can outline the factors that effect emotional expressions for Chinese children
Lesson Contents	• Basic vocabulary and sentence patterns relating to emotions • Basic non-verbal patterns of emotional expression • Factors that influence emotional expression for Chinese children
Materials	• Basic facial expression images (Webber cards) • Cardboard cards (to make different shaped eyebrows, eyes, noses, mouths), crayons, scissors • Emotion vocabulary flashcards
Learning Activities	• Each class, ask students about their feelings and have them also ask each other. • Review vocabulary and sentence structures from previous grades, then add other basic emotional terms. • Group activity: Use gestures to interpret the emotions shown on the flash cards, let teammates guess. Vary the tone of voice while speaking the same phrase or sentence for teammates to guess what emotion the presenter tries to express. Combine different facial expressions, gestures, and tones of voice while saying a phrase or sentence for teammates to guess.

(Continued)

	Week One: Patterns of Emotional Expression
	• Use cardboard cards to make different forms of eyebrows, eyes, and mouths in order to practice describing emotions and feelings. • Turning over Webber cards, learn to match emotion with tone of voice, or divide into two and three person groups to play Tic—Tac—Toe for speaking practice. • Introduce cultural comparison: Show PowerPoint pictures of Chinese and Western children in public places using inappropriate ways to express their emotions. Students identify the children's emotional state, pointing out information from non-verbal behavior.
Formative Assessment	• Gesturing activities • Describe the emotions and emotional events represented by different expressive combinations of eyebrows, eyes, and mouths • Present and explain different emotional expressions on Webber cards
Recommended Vocabulary and Sentence Patterns	• 开心、高兴、快乐、愉快、生气、气愤、伤心、难过、害怕、紧张、担心、厌恶、感兴趣、惊讶、讶异、咬牙切齿、愁眉苦脸、眉开眼笑、心惊肉跳 • ……的时候,会……;看起来;听起来;一……就……
Resources	• Li Yuan, 2006. *Childlike Innocence* ("童言无忌") • Webber Cards: Emotions

Chapter Four Inspiring Creativity: Grades 3 to 4   277

Week Two: Being Aware of Emotions	
Teaching Objectives	• Students can use vocabulary and sentence patterns related to self-conscious emotions to express themselves and ask about other people's emotions • When being praised, students can use appropriate oral and non-verbal responses
Lesson Contents	• Vocabulary and sentence patterns dealing with self-conscious emotions • All kinds of uses of "意思" • Cultural knowledge and behavior: how to respond to compliments
Materials	• Webber cards • Post-it notes • Emotion vocabulary flash cards • Essay paper, drawing paper, colored pencils • Film strips • Video recorder such as Flip Video
Learning Activities	• Review eight basic emotional expressions: ask about student feelings and have students ask each other. • New knowledge: vocabulary for self-conscious emotions. • Post-it notes: I feel that...? (recognize and read words) • "I change, I change, I change change change" (practice sentence patterns) • Multiple intelligence group creation: Double reed • The different meanings of "意思". Using four frame movie paper write a situation dialogue, then act out a short skit that includes how to respond to compliments from others. • Writing and recitation

(Continued)

Week Two: Being Aware of Emotions	
Formative Assessments	• Post-it notes: recognize and read words • Change change change: using sentence patterns • Short skit: How to use "意思" and respond to other people's compliments • Student writing and oral recitation
Recommended Vocabulary and Sentence Patterns	• 羞愧、尴尬、内疚、嫉妒、骄傲、好意思、不好意思、没意思、有意思、够意思、不够意思、哪里哪里、真的吗 • 又……又……；既……又……
Resources	• Movie: *Together* ("和你在一起") Chen Kaige, Director, 2003. United States: MGM.

Week Three: Impulse Control	
Teaching Objectives	• Students can explain the importance of impulse control and try to learn to control impulses • Students can use vocabulary and sentence patterns to express their own personal feelings and ask about other people's feelings • Students can use American Sign Language to express their emotions
Lesson Contents	• Review vocabulary and sentence patterns for basic emotions and self-conscious emotions • The importance and methods of impulse control • Sign language • Rap
Materials	• Movie: "*I Not Stupid* (2)" • Webber Emotion Cards • 3×5 index cards • Projector, computer: Play movies, Internet resources

(Continued)

	Week Three: Impulse Control
Learning Activities	• Review emotion vocabulary and sentence patterns. • Watch the movie "*I Not Supid* (2)", point out places in the plot where characters do not appropriately manage their emotions and explore more ideal ways to do this. • Group activity: Distribute index cards to students; have them draw and describe daily situations that cause them to lose self-control and brainstorm about what to do. • Perform a short skit: based on one or two situations described on index cards selected from each small group. • Instruction in American Sign Language. • Individual rap activity: integrate emotion words and sentence patterns to design a type of hip-hop work. Use *Practical Rhythmic Chinese* as a reference.
Formative Assessments	• Describe index cards • Short skits
Resources	• Yin & Sun, 2008. *Practical Rhythmic Chinese* • Expertvillage or YouTube: *Emotion Words*: *American Sign Language* • Riekehof, 1987: *The Joy of Signing: The Illustrated Guide for Mastering Sign Language and the Manual Alphabet*

Cheng

Chapter Five Promoting Learning Ability: Grades 5 to 6

Introduction

Depending on school district systems, fifth and sixth grade students might be in the final stage of primary school, or sixth grade students might have just entered middle school. Students who are 10 or 11 years old are just on the verge of or have already entered adolescence, and they are undergoing significant changes in personality, as well as in their physical, cognitive, and emotional development. My comments below explore the particular effects of the students' cognitive, psychosocial, and emotional development on language learning.

In terms of cognitive development, fifth and sixth grade students are at quite diverse levels in their ability to concentrate on topics (focus, stability, breadth, distribution, transfer, etc.). In thinking abilities, although abstract thinking has begun to emerge, more concrete types of approaches still dominate. As for logical evaluation, students are gradually learning to assess the relative importance of things, as well as primary and secondary elements. At this stage, their creative thinking about objective reality is also rapidly maturing. Yet even with the emergence of this creative thinking, given the overall cognitive characteristics of fifth and sixth grade students, teachers should not diverge too far from the concrete phenomenon of students' daily lives in selecting topics and themes for course development. In training students to go from more concrete to more abstract reflections, if the themes and teaching methods do not connect strongly with student experiences, or if a broad range of information is presented in superficial ways, students will be easily confused.

As teachers impart knowledge and skills to students, it is very important to nurture students' metacognitive abilities: to enhance their understanding and reflection on their own processes of memory, perception, calculation, association and other cognitive skills. Thus, in addition to lecturing, the teacher should instruct students in how to utilize their own special cognitive talents to improve their learning efficiency. Students who use their metacognitive abilities to develop an efficient learning strategy, will, after several successful learning experiences, increase their motivation for life long learning.

In terms of social behavior, students are between the stages of Middle Childhood (6—10 years) and Early Adolescence (11—18 years). For students in Middle Childhood, school is the key place of psychosocial development. Successful learning experiences at this stage promote confidence in personal abilities. The acquisition of positive learning experiences and a sense of achievement increase student interest in learning and willingness to work hard. In addition, students in Middle Childhood still have a high level of confidence in the teacher's authority. From my experience, students will still apologize to teachers when they turn in late assignments or do poorly on tests. Given this, some students will study hard to please their teachers, and if the teacher knows how to use this feature to guide their development, classroom teaching can become even more effective.

For students just reaching puberty, the central task for this stage is the establishment of a personal identity; students often develop their personal roles through interactions with peers and teachers. They have a very strong sense of belonging to groups, and the importance of peer groups will gradually replace the importance of school or teachers in their minds. Students' self-awareness and self advocacy are gradually strengthening; they can sense the presence of others and care about their perceptions; their abilities for self control in social situations are progressively forming and they are gradually becoming eager for more control over their own affairs. Therefore, in designing the curriculum, teachers must be particularly aware of the stages of their students' psychosocial development; by providing and creating opportunities for students to act independently, they can achieve many positive successful experiences. In addition, teachers should show trust and respect for the students by guiding students to participate in the design of the curriculum: give students the opportunity to lead, let students choose their favorite learning styles, or use group activities and target groups to lead and motivate students.

In addition to physical differences, variation in language skills and hormonal development affects levels of performance for male and female students. Male students find it more difficult than female students to express their emotions through language, in part due to cultural expectations that "real men do not cry". Some male students will use deviant behavior to express their feelings: for example, using body language to strike out, or angry outbursts to express their inner frustrations. Male students tend to hide their emotions because expressing emotions too easily can get them branded as a sissy. In contrast, female students are generally better at using language to express themselves and also have more social support for their displays of moodiness. Teachers must pay attention to basic differences in gender development and must understand the verbal and non-verbal behaviors of students in the classroom from different perspectives. Through a perceptive and tolerant attitude towards students, particularly male students, and flexible curriculum designed to ease excessive male energy, many classroom management problems can be avoided.

As teachers, in addition to our hope that students gain knowledge and skills to reach their full potential, we also expect students to care about the outside world. Fifth and sixth grade students have increased cognitive ability, greater knowledge acquisition, and expanded social contacts, so teachers can lead students gradually away from thinking only in terms of "my world" to an awareness of "the world and I" by exploring the individual, family, school and community with different themes to enhance civic awareness. Also, for older students entering or about to enter puberty, this is an important stage in the development of the brain function of the prefrontal cortex, where complex cognitive functions are connected to plans of action; its role is to unify and internalize individual thinking and action. As teachers design their curriculum they need to fully understand the special characteristics of their students' emotional, physical, and mental development, and to transfer this in flexible ways to different types of learning activities. Trading off between teacher led and student centered types of activities stimulates the brain function that unites cognition and manipulation, resulting in a positive learning situation that trains students' cognitive abilities and brain development.

Unit Topics

Unit Topic One: Family

Chinese people pay special attention to the concept of the family. When meeting each other, they will inevitably talk about family members or their household. The family is the basic unit of socialization for children and is closely and intimately related to children's lives, growth, and education. In consulting the wide range of foreign language materials, especially books designed for students from childhood through adolescence, the first topic for student learning often focuses on family or family members, which clearly reinforces the importance of family as a topic.

In the first through fourth grade curriculum, students will have reached a basic understanding of the following topics: the importance of home and family to their lives; titles for family members and their associated responsibilities and roles; the different status of males and females in traditional Chinese families; and the meaning of filial piety in the Chinese family. Among the topics of behavioral culture to reappear are sayings that support Chinese family ethics and codes of conduct: affectionate father and dutiful son （父慈子孝）; love and respect between brothers （兄友弟恭）; family order in age and generation （长幼有序）. In language learning, students have the basic listening, speaking, reading and writing skills to engage in simple oral and written tasks.

At the fifth and sixth grade levels, students will have made great progress in physical, mental, social, emotional, and cognitive development. So, in curricular design, in addition to continuing the central themes of previous stages and continuing to strengthen student levels of knowledge and understanding, beyond language proficiency, you can add some higher levels of cognitive thinking to stimulate students. Allow students to practice analyzing, synthesizing and evaluating topics. For example: How have Chinese families changed in different time periods? How and why have these changes affected family members? Why is the idiom "Splendor shines on the family door" （光耀门楣） an important Chinese family concept? What are some common similarities and differences in Chinese families?

In terms of learning objectives, this unit seeks to enhance student communication skills as a basis for experiencing and understanding Chinese culture; to further train students in analogical comprehension; to improve student abilities in comparing languages and cultures; and to enable students to apply their knowledge in a multicultural community.

Working with abstract concepts and putting themselves in someone else's shoes are still comparatively weak abilities for students of this age, so drawing on personal experiences and themes to guide the curriculum will resonate more clearly. The historical story of Mulan substituting for her father in military service is familiar to American children, and teachers can consider attracting student interest with this story, while also bringing up cultural issues related to the structure of Mulan's family; male and female gender roles in this era; the importance of continuing the family line; and the issue of family honor, etc. To explore transformations in similar topics in contemporary Chinese society, teachers can use clips from a documentary such as *Mardi Gras Made in China* or the film *Face Changing*（变脸）or interviews with peers from a Chinese background.

Teachers must understand that most students at this stage are still learning to use their own experiences to speculate on the feelings of others, so for some more serious or hard to understand topics, teachers can use role-playing scenarios to stimulate emotional reactions in students. For example, the teacher may, for the period of a week or two, grant many privileges to male students and impose many restrictions on female students in order to provoke an emotional reaction among female students. Students of both genders can in this way experience the emotional shock caused by the preference for males over females（重男轻女）and further experience the different powers and responsibilities associated with gender for Chinese people. Of course, we also hope that students can try to develop a simple ability to evaluate and judge, so after playing these situational roles, have students make a brief analytical report and a final summary of their emotions（closure）. The teacher can also divide students into several three generation family groups to study family relationships and titles, roles and responsibilities. When playing the childhood game of playing house（过家家/扮家家酒）students can learn about complicated Chinese family relationships and the responsibilities conferred by different roles: for example, students playing the role of grandchild must carry the bags of students playing the roles of grandparents, must serve them lunch, and must accompany them when they go out.

In relation to family structure, family membership, and other somewhat sensitive topics, it is best for the teacher to have a preliminary understanding of the families of their students. In the pluralistic society of the United States, while it is not surprising to have same sex parents, single parents, and adoptive families, for some students and families these are private matters. In order to avoid embarrassing students in the classroom, we as teachers must have multiple approaches for our students. Some of my students are adopted by same sex parents. Whenever we are studying the family unit or watching movies with plots about sensitive social statuses, I will contact the parents of the students in advance and obtain the support of parents before going ahead with the course of study. If teachers want students to use multi-generational genealogies to understand forms of address, dividing students into groups to interview teachers from another class is a practical method. Students can use their interview results to make a family tree poster, adding the teachers' photographs, and making reports in the classroom. Afterwards they can display these posters outside of the classroom for other students to examine. At the same time, teachers might also consider having minority students share their family values, the duties of family members, or similar themes with the class. In this way students can understand that the theme of family is not just confined to the comparison of Chinese families with American main stream families. If teachers make good use of the background of students themselves as a teaching resource, it can also allow for a more realistic classroom teaching and learning environment, and one that is more meaningful for students.

Unit Topic Two: Food and Chinese Medicine

每天开门七件事：柴米油盐酱醋茶. (The seven necessities of daily life: firewood, rice, oil, salt, soy sauce, vinegar, tea.) The centrality of food for Chinese people （以食为天） as the number one basic instinct and central requirement is obvious in this saying. In talking about the topics of food and Chinese medicine, I believe that we teachers find our heads full of fresh and attractive teaching ideas. When students hear their new unit is about food, everyone is excited and cannot wait. Yes! Chinese food culture is world famous, and we must acknowledge that many people studying Chinese language were first attracted because of their admiration for Chinese food. The use of the food theme in language teaching often has a magnificent result, because eating is a very powerful force!

In the first through fourth grade curriculum, students will already have gained a preliminary understanding of Chinese styles of food and drink, including dietary content, the names of basic Chinese dishes, tea culture, eating utensils, etc. They will have repeatedly reviewed such behavioral culture themes as the use of utensils, dining etiquette, hospitality towards hosts and guests, etc. The students can also make basic comparisons between the forms of food and drink in their families and the patterns of food and drink of Chinese people. As for language ability, students will have learned how to state their personal preferences and the basic names of Chinese foods.

At the fifth and sixth grade level, students are developing in obvious physical, mental, social, emotional, and cognitive respects, so the curricular design should become both deeper and broader. As for depth, teachers can continue to explore the diversity of Chinese cuisine and how geography explains certain differences in food and drink, such as typical diets in the north and south. Teachers can also discuss in more depth how Chinese people use food to represent social relationships and traditional blessings. In terms of breadth, the therapeutic use of foods for personal health is an old concept that can be introduced in simple forms at this stage. This may include ideas about "hot" and "cold" foods, along with traditional Chinese medicine and healing, all very interesting topics that can shake up and unbalance student understandings.

Eating is a very specific behavior; the focus of course design is how to use this specific behavior to guide students towards higher abstract thinking abilities. I firmly believe that if you use the circumstances of students' personal experiences or closely connected topics, it is relatively easy to gain their sympathy and stimulate interest in learning. In addition, through understanding Chinese principles of healthy eating, you can guide students to review their eating habits, another important educational development. In making comparisons of eating patterns, students can be asked to bring their common breakfast or snack foods to the classroom to share, and use this to also talk about Chinese customs. Students can also use the Internet to research the contents of school lunches for students in mainland China or Taiwan, analyzing and comparing them in nutritional value and style of meals. Students can use these findings and the Food Pyramid to understand how to design a school lunch menu. If feasible, have all students in the school participate and as a final result make menu recommendations to the school district. This approach will not only broaden their knowledge horizons, but also inspire students to higher order thinking skills (HOTS) such as analysis, synthesis, evaluation, and creativity. The teacher can, as appropriate, adjust this activity in terms of degrees of participation within the school and community.

In discussing diet and medicine, if possible, take students to visit the school clinic, or invite experts to the school for demonstrations and lectures. I have personally also brought key therapeutic ingredients to class for students to see, touch, smell, and guess: What is this? What is it used for? Afterwards, bring therapeutic foods that have been cooked to the classroom and once again have students look, smell, and even taste. By emotional arousal and multi-sensory teaching methods, students not only gain deep knowledge, but also can more easily remember the teaching activities associated with "episodic memory". In addition, I think that the first-hand experience of such activities helps students get rid of their fixed impressions and stereotypes about Chinese culture.

If there is a special occasion, such as a graduation celebration, teachers can take students to a restaurant to eat together in a round-table dinner. When students have a birthday, teachers can design a special menu from their own childhood experience, a monthly collective birthday feast. For example, everyone can cook a noodle dish with stewed pig's feet and eggs. Based on student language skills, teachers should design vocabulary and grammatical points that allow students to communicate using the target language throughout the cooking process. Working together, washing, chopping, boiling, and stir frying, will make the students feel like they are immersed in a family culture, and will increase their love of Chinese language. In making cultural comparisons, do not forget to encourage non-mainstream students in the class to share their own cultural practices, another type of culturally proficient instruction.

From the above teaching activities, it is easy to see the teaching objectives of this unit. In addition to strengthening student communication and interpersonal skills and nurturing student understanding of the Chinese cultural experience, the focus is also on training students to make analogical connections as they compare languages and cultures and apply their knowledge to multicultural communities.

Because each state has different requirements and restrictions about teachers providing food to students, and students may have religious or other types of dietary restrictions related to food allergies, the teacher must know these things in advance, so as not to endanger student health or provoke legal disputes. All in all, the food/medicine topic presents unlimited opportunities. When teaching about cooking or eating, it's hard to convince students with all talk and no action!

Unit Topic Three: Chinese Festivals

When thinking about the most representative products of different ethnic groups or regions, it is natural to think of festivals. Ethnic and regional festivals are memorial or celebratory occasions in the midst of daily life; some are derived from traditional practices, some are based on religious beliefs, while others memorialize historical figures or events. Festivals connect to ethnic and regional customs, bringing together and reflecting upon a system of values and beliefs. Because festivals have assigned patterns, repetition, and predictability, people celebrating festivals often follow certain procedures or processes, making "traditions" their natural form.

In *The Characteristics and Forms of China's Traditional Festivals and Customs*, Yang Jingzhen (1998) summarizes eight characteristic forms: a focus on ceremony, ideals, time period, ethnicity, inherited tradition, transformation, the masses, or local regions. In designing curriculum around the theme of festivals, teachers who draw on these eight features will be able to cover everything in their discussion of this topic. In practice, teachers must take the seasons into account: for example, celebrating the New Year during Spring Festival period or finding time to wrap *zongzi* (粽子) for the Dragon Boat Festival before the end of the semester. So festival topics should correspond with the seasons and the annual cycle rather than being concentrated into one compact unit during the school year.

Speaking about the traditional characteristics of these festivals, it is worth noting that teachers often face the limitations of geographical location, which makes it difficult for students to experience the excitement and grandeur of these festivals. However, teachers can still follow the great traditions of the festival by creating little traditions within their classrooms, such as with New Year, having the whole class participate in cleaning the classroom, writing spring couplets to paste on the sides of the windows, and getting rid of the old to bring in the new. By doing this year after year, over time large and small traditions become a force of habit. With the advancement of technology, the teacher can also use satellite phones to make video connections with sister schools in mainland China or Taiwan, so that students can feel the festive and celebratory atmosphere. If feasible, students can also watch a lantern parade in Chinatown or the Chinese community, thus making up for the limitations of the local setting.

Having participated in festival activities over the past five years, fifth and sixth grade students all have very specific knowledge and practical experience with Chinese traditional festivals and contemporary holidays. Compared to fourth graders, fifth and sixth grade students have advanced tremendously in physical and cognitive development; they have heightened interest in their peers and their self-directed learning ability has also improved. Teachers can use a peer learning approach to investigate a subject and have students collect, analyze and summarize data for classroom presentations in PowerPoint format. Of course not all teaching content can be handled in this way. For example, when talking about Chinese traditional festivals, the Chinese lunar calendar is inevitably introduced. If taught about entirely in an oral-based format, fifth and sixth grade students generally have difficulty understanding the difference between the lunar and Gregorian calendars. The teacher can use two light colored ribbons or lengths of cloth, providing symbols for the lunar calendar on one strip and the Gregorian calendar on the other. Have students work cooperatively in the classroom to mark the dates for twelve months over two or three years on both strips. Then have students find the Gregorian dates for the four major Chinese festivals. Students will find that Chinese festivals occur every year on different dates of the Gregorian calendar and become aware of the two different ways of recording dates in the lunar and Gregorian calendars. The students can also further explore the reasons for the Chinese lunar leap month and the origins and use of the sexagenary cycle. This project can deepen students' understanding of the similarities and differences between the two calendars. Teachers can also introduce the Solar Terms Glossary, and have students make illustrations for the solar terms, using hands-on learning to create a deeper impression.

With China's vast territory, although there are many similarities in approach to regional or ethnic holiday celebrations, there are also some different characteristics. For example, during the Spring Festival there are different festival foods in the north and south and also different visiting schedules. Beijing wives will return to their natal homes on the third day of the New Year, while wives in Taiwan make this visit on the second day. When learning about festivals, fifth and sixth grade students can begin to understand such local differences. Also, with the passage of time, the meaning of festivals and the ways they are celebrated continue to change. Of course, changes that come from foreign places or influences from the local community or Chinatown are very interesting topics; for example, the dragon boat competition that is part of the Portland, Oregon Rose Festival in June every year. The teacher can take advantage of the situation to raise the question of outside modern influences on Chinese festivals. How have these festivals been influenced by western culture? How has this changed the forms and meanings of these holidays? In what ways have they been transformed?

As the students are experiencing culture, you must not forget to do cultural comparisons. Teachers sometimes encounter parents who question why children who are studying Mandarin should celebrate the Lunar New Year in the Chinese way. If the teacher can point out how the understanding of other cultures can enhance student understanding of their own culture and experience, parents should be able to appreciate one purpose for teaching Chinese culture. Whenever teachers are involved in teaching culture, they are bound to have students analyze and discuss cultural products, practices, and perceptions, comparing their own culture with Chinese culture. Of course, teachers should choose a certain affirmative cultural trait to motivate student behavior and positive thinking, for it is only human nature to distrust what is strange.

How to bring the celebration of Chinese New Year and festivals into student lives challenges the creative thinking of teachers. For example, in the United States although it is not customary for wives to visit their natal families at New Year, the emotion of missing paternal and maternal grandparents is the same both within and outside of China. The teacher can have the students on the second day of the New Year write a greeting card to send to their grandparents, explaining the traditional meaning of wives returning to parental homes in Chinese society, and also include their thoughts of love.

Festival etiquette calls for reciprocal politeness. For example, at

New Year the older generation gives money（压岁钱）to the younger generation and they in turn ask for blessings for the older generation. Teachers can do the same: students wish the teacher Happy New Year and the teacher gives the students red envelopes with Chinese coins inside.

Festivals and food are the two main themes of Chinese life; like food, festivals emerge as a way of life, but the categories covered by festivals are much deeper and broader than that of food. In investigating the topic of festivals, we not only emphasize the importance of food culture for Chinese people, but we also explore the hidden depths in festival culture, festival activities, and the cultural perspectives behind these products. Moreover, Chinese festival foods are rich in symbolic meanings, so the teacher can have students make comparisons, for example contrasting Mid-Autumn Festival's mooncakes with Thanksgiving turkey, or the special foods of the Double-Seven Festival with the chocolates of Valentine's Day.

Unit Topic Four: Geography and Travel

Fifth and sixth grade students are still limited in their ability to care about things beyond their families and school environment, and if traveling abroad with teachers and fellow students, they are not capable of taking care of themselves independently and adapting to different social situations. So in general, teaching about international travel is not a serious objective. However, longing for foreign travel is not lacking among students of this age. Rapid technological development has reduced the distance between countries, and people are capable of traveling thousands of miles in the shortest period of time. With the ability to read, even without the possibility of traveling thousands of miles, teaching an international outlook should not have age restrictions. In shaping global citizens, the foundation needs to be laid while people are young. Therefore, in this unit, let us lead students on a fictitious journey to China through time and space.

Before hitting the road, you must have a reserve of knowledge and skills, and it is good to begin with warm up exercises. In the third and fourth grade curriculum, students will have studied the vocabulary for basic directions that they can use with maps and related activities, and they will have gained a rough understanding of Chinese geography and world maps. In the fifth and sixth grade curriculum, teachers should continue to strengthen student geographical knowledge and travel-related language and culture skills.

In raising the subject of travel, spending money is absolutely unavoidable, and with money comes a discussion of exchange rates. Students themselves will often raise the subject of changing money. I think that rather than allowing students to check the Internet exchange rates, it is better to take out real money so that students can see, feel, and smell the money. Compare paper money and coins from China with similar types of American money: size, pattern design, and the basic value differences. In making price comparisons, the teacher can use data that is immediately available on the Internet in the classroom, such as the US price of an iPod. If converted to Chinese money, how much would it cost? What would be the opening bid on an online auction site (eg. 淘宝)? Why might there be a disparity in price? In addition, having students study the proper measure words for money and numerical values is a very practical exercise. You can also bring the souvenirs collected in travels to China to the classroom and have students play a game similar to the American program of guessing the price. Have students practice bidding and as each souvenir is displayed, the teacher points to a map showing where it was purchased. After this game, have students "adopt" a souvenir and the place where it was purchased in order to prepare for a make-believe journey.

The virtual tour uses information from the Internet in conjunction with library materials. The teacher gives each student travel expenses and the student must use that sum of money to budget a one week trip from their US city to the place selected by the student in mainland China, Hong Kong, or Taiwan. Prior to their trip, students must first study the weather patterns at their travel destinations, then make arrangements for luggage, visa applications, daily itinerary, accommodation sites, modes of transport, places to visit, and daily expenses. Students also need to arrange for contact with their families and think of how to resolve situations that arise during travel, such as how to find the bathroom, where to change money, how to use the public phone, where to find a doctor if they fall sick, or where to find the embassy if they lose their passport. The teacher can also design some culture shock situations and have the students try to resolve them: for example, how to respond to stall keepers who pressure you to buy their goods at scenic spots? If local people find fault over minor details, how do you respond? What should you pay attention to when you are a guest at local people's homes? What do you do if you are not accustomed to the food served by your host?

At the end of the virtual tour, students can give oral classroom or written reports, using newsletters or posters to present their understanding of the geography, history, culture, economy, customs, food, and art in their place of travel. Because the situation is simulated, students can bravely try different travel plans and different problem solving strategies. Also, because travel plans can be completely customized to the personal interests of students, it produces a very appealing and effective curriculum design. We are, of course, very clear that children of this age are largely unable to independently handle many of these described situations, and if you demand that students have these skills, you will inevitably be placing undue pressure on them. However, the focus of this phase of study is to lay the foundation for the next phase of study, so students enhance their knowledge to carry them to the next level. More importantly, this curricular approach provides students with great autonomy, making it easy to stimulate student motivation to learn. The project can have students working independently or in small groups based on their age, their Internet search capabilities, and the available resources. In order to ensure the smooth progress of this lesson, teachers need to collect reliable information on travel sites well in advance of student data collection, using, for example, Google maps. In order to help students complete their plans, have them use a check list to mark their progress step by step.

If computer hardware resources are insufficient, it will not be easy to implement the teaching activities described above. Teachers can consider using things from their personal travels in mainland, Hong Kong, or Taiwan of China such as ticket stubs, receipts, scenic postcards, souvenirs, and photos or videos that were taken to introduce Chinese geography, history, heritage, and customs. I suggest that when teachers plan a personal trip to one of these places, they bring a symbol of their school mascot with them and on their journey have local people take souvenir photos with the mascot, or include the mascot in street scenes and videos. When they return, teachers can share these images with students in the classroom, so that students can feel both the authenticity and the feasibility of travel to these places. If teachers are unable to obtain a self-guided, self-directed travel documentary, they can consider using a supplemental video or website devoted to travel.

Many students like to eat Chinese food, but how many students have thought about how Chinese food came to America? As students are yearning to travel to China, might they also not feel curious about the immigration of Chinese people to the United States? In addition to mass media, Chinatown may be where the students first come into contact with local China related knowledge. If you want to understand the history of Chinese immigrants, I think that interviewing Chinese immigrants or their children is the ideal approach. Teachers can invite people from the local Chinese community, Chinese churches, or Chinese schools, all of which have abundant resources. If possible, teachers can arrange for students to visit the local Chinatown or Museum of Chinese Immigration in Chinatown to interview Chinese people and have a meal.

In addition to changing geography, rapid travel to far away countries involves adjustments in time zones. Unlike China's system of a single time zone, children living in the United States are generally aware that the US has six time zones. The concept behind time zones is not difficult to understand. The teacher can consider linking up with their school's natural science teacher and curriculum to design a unit on the solar system. Students can learn about the earth's revolution and rotation; the relationship between the positions of the sun and the moon; and the reasons behind the time differences of the four seasons. Teachers can take advantage of this topic to review the exploration of the sundial from third and fourth grade, and compare Chinese traditional ways of telling time with modern ways of telling time. As students have advanced in age, their cognitive abilities and learning experiences will have increased, so even when returning to similar themes, there is still great value in this study. In order to stimulate and expand the scope of cognitive thinking, teachers can once again allow students to brainstorm "If time did not exist, what would happen? Would the non-existence of time be good or bad?"

In short, geography and travel are topics that ought to be included in foreign language teaching. In the fifth and sixth grade curriculum, even if travel lessons involve some advance set up and preparations, they aim at strengthening geographic knowledge and preparing students for the next stage. Laying a good foundation is a significant step. Giving students a future vision of travel is a good way to motivate them to continue learning Chinese. Increasing student knowledge of the cultures of other countries is a good way to help them become global citizens.

Unit Topic Five: History, Politics and Religion

China's five thousand years of history are not only the pride of the Chinese people, but a centripetal force of national cohesion and a compilation of national wisdom. This also explains why some people think that Chinese people use the past in search of answers about the future. Although China has five thousand years of literature and history, fifth and sixth grade students do not have sufficient language skills to understand the mutual coherence of history and literature.

Teachers may worry that fifth and sixth grade students may find this topic rather serious and inevitably agonizing, or students may ask why they should care about the political and religious history of China. However, studies have shown that similar to the relatively high interest among Chinese students who study their own history, American students also have a strong interest in the history of their own country. The main reason is not hard to understand: compared to China, the US after all has only two hundred years of history, and students have a good experience of learning history from interesting story style books.

With China's glorious and extensive history, if you used storytelling to introduce Chinese history, it would be like trying to read to the end of *The Book of One Thousand and One Nights*. Therefore, what are the important points of focus for this unit? How can you consistently link language and history? In answering these questions, teachers must first understand the background of students, and need to understand what important points have been covered in previous years to accomplish the horizontal and longitudinal connections between history and language. Then teachers can seek out the common interests of students and from this select the unit's main points and learning objectives.

To give students a more holistic understanding rather than a piece of Chinese history, teachers can divide the recorded history of Chinese civilization into periods, then talk about the famous persons or events from each period of time as an introduction to spark student interest. The following is a reference for teachers on periods and historical figures: Spring and Autumn and Warring States Period (Confucius, Qu Yuan); Qin Dynasty (Qin Shi Huang, Mulan); Wei, Jin(Peach Garden Oath), Sui, Tang Dynasties (Xuan Zang, Empress Wu); Song, Yuan Dynasties (Su Shi, Genghis Khan); Ming, Qing Dynasties (Zheng He, the Empress Dowager Cixi), and the twentieth century to the present (Sun Yat-sen, Mao Zedong and Chiang Kai-shek). Students are divided into groups and select an historical figure of interest to them, then use the library or Internet resources based on research priorities set by the teacher to collect data. Research emphasis may include dynastic names, dates based on the Gregorian calendar, the boundaries of the state, political structure, religion, science and technology, and the most significant historical events or people. Students can use video, drama sketches, presentations, charts, etc. to show learning outcomes. When reports are being made, students in the audience must take notes in order to increase the effectiveness of their learning. Finally, the teacher compiles the written reports from each group and constructs a large wall poster, using a time line to display the results.

In exploring history, students should understand something about the early immigration of Chinese to the United States. Most primary school social studies texts include a preliminary study of the history of immigration to the US, but the history of Chinese immigration is not necessarily one of these topics. To help fifth and sixth grade students understand the history of Chinese immigrants you might draw on the following teaching plans: use the Chinese community that is geographically the closest to your school to design this lesson. Students can visit Chinatown or a museum that introduces Chinese immigrant history as a resource. In addition, schools that teach Chinese language to ethnic Chinese, especially those in Chinatown, are an excellent resource. If the school district includes communities with many Chinese, the teacher can invite Chinese elders to the school and have students interview them. The history of early Chinese immigrants in California is an interesting topic to explore, including thought provoking stories of Chinese immigrants detained at Angel Island awaiting entry or repatriation. The teacher can use the writings on the walls etched by Chinese held in custody as reading materials for students, or can use role play or skits to reenact the kinds of rigorous examination suffered by Chinese immigrants to the US. As part of the curriculum aimed at understanding Chinese immigration to the US, we hope that students can also discover how their own ancestors came to the United States; teachers can use this topic to further expand on this theme.

The Silk Road was the path of the envoy Zhang Qian during the

Western Han Dynasty; until the end of the 12th century the Silk Road was an important route for economic and cultural exchanges between China, Central Asia, and Eastern Europe. The concept of the Silk Road has begun to take shape for students in third and fourth grades, so by grades five and six the teacher can have students watch movies about the Silk Road that give them a comprehensive overview, then use the envoy Zhang Qian's thirteen years of diplomatic travels and exploration to the western regions to stimulate student interest. Finally students can compare the accomplishments of the two explorers, Zhang Qian in China and Columbus in America. Because fifty and sixth grade students are already familiar with the story of Columbus, it is easy to use the adventure stories of Columbus as a means of connected learning. Of course, the teacher can also consider having the students contrast the Silk Road with the "road" of the Internet to deepen students' skills in critical analysis. Once fifty and sixth grade students have gained knowledge of the Silk Road at a macro level, it is easier for seventh and eighth grade students to advance to a deeper microscopic and comparative understanding.

China's imperial examination system was very important to the structure of China's political economy, and the influence of these examinations continues today in the 21st century. Fifth and sixth grade students may know that Asian students pay great attention to academic performance in school, but don't realize that the academic pressure on students in mainland China, Hong Kong, and Taiwan is something that cannot be avoided. In designing curriculum related to this topic, the teacher should consider using topics learned previously in "School life/ discipline" including curriculum content, daily lessons, the number of total school days in the school year, summer vacation homework arrangements, and after-school student activities. Have students compare, contrast and organize information and research results to make inferences. In addition, teachers who were educated in China can share their personal experiences of schooling, including after-school tutoring and facing the pressure of college entrance exams, to provide additional evidence for students' research results. The movie *Going to School with Dad on My Back*（背起爸爸上学）depicts connections between going to school, "face" and family affection in great depth and can be used as a teaching aid or opening theme. Training students in creative thinking is always a major focus of education. The teacher can take "school pressure" as a topic and ask students to propose suggestions or solutions to the pressures that Chinese students face in attending school, or have them design an ideal schedule for Chinese students as a concluding exercise.

Religion can be a sensitive topic in the United States. The topic of religion has a lot of space for comparison and contrast. In exploring this theme, teachers can let students brainstorm, starting from their own experience; reflect on the meaning of religious belief and the influence of religious beliefs on their lives; students can present their results through drawing, writing, or photographs. This type of activity, in addition to increasing the self-reflective abilities of students can also, through the process of sharing, enhance students understanding of and respect for non-mainstream religions. The teacher can use the Internet or videos to introduce religions in China. Taoism, which is the only faith that originated in China, has close and inseparable connections to many traditional Chinese festivals. The teacher might consider drawing on this relationship between Taoism and Chinese traditional festivals and use video images to introduce the celebratory activities during Chinese festivals that include reverence for deities and interrelated famous historical stories and superstitious customs. The teacher can allow students to further their own religious research and search out highly respected religious figures or parables to share in the classroom.

Unit Topic Six: Friends, Fun, Fashions and Fads

People are social animals, and interpersonal exchanges are inevitable. In the process of human interaction, children try out different ways to communicate with others and to establish and maintain friendships. In this process, they develop codes of conduct to address issues and work together to achieve group goals and social skills. So "friends" or "establishing friendships" are required subjects in the social and psychological development of children.

The enhanced cognitive abilities of fifth and sixth grade students promote greater empathy, an increased ability to predict other people's feelings, and improved skills in exploring things from a third party perspective. Adopting a more mature social perspective and an expanded space of daily life gives students more flexibility in finding and making friends. With this desire to make friends, it is obvious that the importance of friends or companions continues to grow. Chinese people have a saying about good friends "friends are forthright, friends understand, friends listen". In terms of children or adolescents, it might be understandable to add "friends are fun". Friendship, in addition to mutual emotional support and encouragement, includes friends doing fun things together.

Entertainment is inevitably linked to the influence of popular culture and this includes fashion and lifestyle. Fashion refers to popular clothing and accessories, such as shoes, glasses, jewelry or makeup of a certain period. Fads refer to things that society worships from pop culture at a certain time. Like fashion, fads are also influenced by trends but still have variability; usually young people express their individuality by copying and endorsing styles of mass culture. Worshipping and chasing after brand names, worshipping film characters or their lifestyles can all constitute fads.

Because the area covered by these topics is extensive, the teacher can divide this into two smaller units comprised of friends/fun and fashion/fads. I think that fifth and sixth grade teachers can weigh more seriously the topic of friends/fun because the keen attention to fashion is more typical of middle or high school students than those of this age, and their desire to seek out friends and establish friendships is stronger than their pursuit of fads.

For the part of the unit that investigates friends and entertainment, in focusing on friendship, the teacher can first introduce the subject through a segment of a television show, such as *Families with Children*; a film plot, such as *The Yangtze River VII*; or student creative drama sketches. Next, teachers can use language connected with this theme and have the students describe in writing "When I'm together with my friends, we..." In this paper they need to introduce a good friend, the good friend's personality, and the activities that they enjoy doing together. In order to improve student self-learning skills, teachers can allow students to use the Internet dictionary to find words that meet individual needs, and afterwards make the collection of new words available to the entire class. One way of adding pleasure to the class is to have students divide into groups to play "double reed"(双簧) where student A reads their paper to student B, who gives a physical demonstration of the meaning of the writing, and then the two students swap roles. In addition, you can use different presentation methods, such as rap songs or comic illustrations to interpret the papers, thus achieving multiple-intelligence education. In order to avoid potential emotional hurt, such as where student A is disappointed not to be named someone's best friend, teachers can ask students to not name names in the text. After sharing, it is not hard to sort out the activities that students like or don't like to do with their friends.

    Teachers can also guide students to discuss and report on the following focus questions: What is a friend? What things should friends do or not do in relation to each other? Here, I must highlight the point that teachers have to help students understand that Chinese society has a strong sense of respect for elders and conscious awareness of social norms. People who are somewhat older, even if they are strangers, can directly correct the behavior of younger people. Therefore, when friends get together to have fun in public places, they must be sure to understand appropriate behavior. Also, body contact between same sex friends in Chinese society, especially girls, is completely acceptable and does not cause people to wonder about them.

    In terms of entertainment, this unit presents a good opportunity to introduce Chinese folk toys. Playing with Chinese yoyos, shuttlecocks, and tops are very interesting experiences for fifth and sixth graders. In addition, celebrating birthdays is something that most American students look forward to, a special day full of joy. Teachers can investigate different approaches and ideals in the ways that birthdays are celebrated by American and Chinese children. Of course, celebrating birthdays can be used in the beginning stages of this unit by asking students questions such as who they would invite to their birthday and why, or how they choose birthday presents when invited to birthday parties. On the topic of gifts, teachers and students can brainstorm and discuss ways of choosing gifts that others like. Of course, definitions of good gifts will inevitably be affected by fashion trends.

To advance the understanding and comparison of culture, one of the most effective ways is through sharing letters or videos with a Chinese sister school. If both sides can create video productions that introduce entertainment and leisure activities outside of their schools, students find it naturally easier to understand where Chinese children like to go with their friends and what they like to do. What kinds of gifts do they like to receive? If the above strategies are not feasible, it is not difficult to use videos with combined entertainment and educational value from YouKu (优酷) or YouTube. In order to prevent students from having access to text or pictures that are not suitable for children on these sites, I advise teachers to embed the videos into a PowerPoint for viewing.

American educational methods use a reflective approach, where students comment and explain from their experience following the teacher's guidance. If teachers are looking forward to telling stories about Chinese historical friendships (Three Kingdoms, Immortals) to achieve their teaching goal, they will have limited success with American fifth and sixth grade students, who are not accustomed to learning by analogy or example. In addition to cultural barriers, not only will students completely miss the point, but teachers will inevitably be imposing on others their own personal philosophy. Using historical stories of friendship does have a possibility if used for cultural comparison. Students can suggest famous American stories of friendship to discuss along with Chinese stories, and the search for similarities and differences will enhance student understanding of both cultures.

Under the open door policy, in tandem with China's economic development, western mass culture has gradually found a foothold in Chinese society. With increases in personal wealth and purchasing power, children's lifestyles in contemporary China and their pursuit of popular science and technology already bear a close resemblance to children in the United States. In introducing the theme of fashion and style, the teacher can easily start by using audio visual images from the Internet to help students understand that Chinese students on many levels are very similar to them. Of course, teachers should not only show students the side of China's wealthy developments, but should also enlighten students by introducing ethnic minorities and disadvantaged groups.

Compared with Chinese students, American students in general are more knowledgeable about styles of dress, and they have more insight and interest in things that are popular. Chinese norms that emphasize uniformity are less encouraging of individual expression; students there are still subject to more stringent dress codes, with hair dye and make up still not generally accepted. The consequence of breaking these norms is that people regard you as peculiar, and there are clear biases against brave students with strong self-expression. In exploring this theme, teachers can try to have students set a class dress code: each day only allow the same type of athletic clothes to be worn to class with no make-up, no cologne, and no hair gels, etc. The class must collectively comply, with violations punished by class rules. When the one or two week trial period is over, students can discuss the pros and cons of this type of class rules.

According to Wikipedia, 92% of Americans use cell phones. This data shows that the use of cell phones and instant messaging has gradually become the most important method for maintaining social relationships among adults and young people, for whom text messaging is especially important. Teachers can let students know that using Mandarin to send text messages is similar to using English abbreviations; styles of completely using Arabic numerals as homonyms for short phrases or Internet slang is not only a fun theme, but can enhance student language proficiency. Because fashion trends are closely connected to the times, in order to have the latest knowledge about the topic, teachers must constantly work at self-enrichment to keep up with the development of trends, otherwise we will be left behind as old fashioned and suspected of being out of touch with reality.

Unit Topic Seven: Creative Arts and Sciences

Five thousand years of Chinese history has left a rich cultural heritage; painting, calligraphy, music, dance, drama, landscape architecture, sculpture, and crafts, all show strong artistic content and the dynamic traces of history. The wisdom of Chinese ancestors is also revealed in the four great inventions; the emergence of paper making, the compass, gunpowder, and printing with moveable type not only promoted political, economic, and cultural development in ancient China but also had an indelible impact on the development of world civilization.

Third and fourth grade students already have a basic understanding of the four great inventions, Chinese art, and the Chinese writing system, so in fifth and sixth grade you can continue to increase the depth and breadth of this subject. I think that the ideal way to do this is to "unite the modern with ancient, and intersect Chinese with foreign." In designing this curriculum, if the teacher connects this with other frequently discussed foreign language themes such as hobbies, occupations, the nation, or language, student language skills and knowledge will continue to grow.

In the five foreign language teaching standards, and consistent with other disciplines, analogy is often listed as one of the goals of teaching.

In this context, although China's four great inventions had a profound impact on European civilization, I don't think it is necessary to connect the four great inventions with European history. Generally social studies teaching in fifth and sixth grades is limited to the history of individual states and early American colonial history, while seventh and eighth grade students focus on ancient civilizations and modern American history. European history is not taught until high school. I suggest that teachers can further enhance student understanding of the four great inventions, especially their important contributions to human civilization. In order to avoid tedious and boring modes of explanation, teachers should employ a variety of different activities such as cooperative learning groups, using the Internet to explore the relevant contents of the four great inventions. Assign a different invention to each group, and have students investigate topics such as that invention's background, causes, and the people involved, as well as modern and ancient impacts. In addition, having students explore the contributions of early American inventions to human civilization is a very interesting topic, such as electric lights, airplanes, and automobiles. In this way it is easy to accomplish the intersection of old/new, Chinese/foreign.

When I was growing up, calligraphy, painting, traditional music, traditional dance, folk arts and crafts, if not part of the formal curriculum, were at least a part of extracurricular activities. In order to help students understand that traditional Chinese art is not just a product of history but is also integrated with modern life, teachers can explain by using videos or images. If you are able to show a video from a Chinese sister school with Chinese student performances of artistic activities, it will be even more convincing and powerful. China is a place of abundant resources, with each region featuring its own collection of outstanding folk arts which teachers should put to good use. In introducing folk art, it is important to integrate knowledge of geography and local customs into the curriculum. The teacher can project a large map of China on a screen of white newsprint, and have students use colored pencils to draw outlines of China's important geographic features: mountains, rivers, provinces, and large cities. Then have students, based on their interests in Chinese folk arts, their special characteristics and uses, do a simple search for information on this topic. Students can paste their research report on the Chinese map and then post the map in a conspicuous place on campus. By sharing with the entire school, students truly connect with the school community and achieve the learning goal of the application of their knowledge. You can also invite people from off campus who have special knowledge of Chinese folk arts to personally demonstrate and instruct students and give them first hand practice and experience, which will not only enhance student understanding of this topic, but provide added motivation for language learning.

Music is inseparable from people's daily lives. In American Chinese communities it is not difficult to find people who are skilled in playing Chinese musical instruments and singing Chinese opera. I think that teachers can invite these people to present a small concert for the entire school to stimulate student interest and motivation.

Have students brainstorm to propose relevant questions, and teachers can design the next teaching activities based on these questions. This way you can avoid problems with topics that are too unfocused or incapable of meeting student interests. To make things livelier, teachers can consider holding a classroom talent show. If a student plays the violin, following the student performance the teacher can play a music video of the *erhu*; for the guitar they can match with the *pipa*; for the clarinet match with the *xiao*; and for Western vocal music match with Chinese opera, etc. Students can draw musical instruments while listening, and use the Chinese vocabulary given by the teacher in advance to describe the music they are hearing; this will help students understand and compare Chinese and Western music. We all know that fifth and sixth grade students' abstract thinking skills are still in the concrete operational stage. In designing curriculum, whether considering materials or teaching methods, teachers should try to proceed from the students' personal experiences and then expand outward, to use the things that are intimately related with what students see, hear, and touch in their lives. This teaching method can be at once magical and very effective.

Chinese characters are the only remaining highly developed ideographic system in the world. Although students occasionally complain about learning to write characters, the evolution of Chinese characters is often a topic of interest to them. Considering fifth and sixth grade student interests and cognitive abilities, I think we can use art and games to advance this topic. The teacher first briefly introduces the evolution of Chinese characters and presents examples of various calligraphic styles, then has students write their names in each of the different styles and underneath each style indicate the name of the style, the dynasty in which it appeared, and the corresponding western date. Teachers can also use familiar vocabulary and present these words to students in semi-cursive or grass scripts and have students play at guessing the characters. Sophisticated modern technology for learning Chinese characters also provides a lot of help; it is worth reminding students that many tablet computers (iPad, android devices, etc.) and smart phones have functions for Chinese handwriting input.

In short, the broad scope of this topic and its rich subject matter are guaranteed to attract student interest, providing teachers with endless space for further elaboration. If you are able to take account of the social and psychological development of students and their interests in shaping flexible teaching and learning activities, the students will definitely have a very positive learning experience.

Unit Topic Eight: *Expressing Emotions and Feelings*

As children increase in age, the types and intensity of emotions become more diverse. Third and fourth grade students have a basic concept of the categories of emotions and what causes them. They understand that a variety of emotions can co-exist and that personal temperament and background both affect emotional responses. As they have begun to understand the rules of emotional expression, they have also learned to hide their feelings. With the improvement of cognitive ability, fifth and sixth grade students have become more complex and subtle in their emotional expressions, and by this age children have started to learn to use cognitive strategies to adjust their mood. Because the prefrontal cortex of the brain that controls emotions is experiencing rapid growth in adolescent children, their moods are characteristically unstable, volatile, and prone to emotional impulses, and they are less able to correctly decode the emotions of others. Adolescents often relieve unpleasant or stressful feelings through music, television, computer games and other media.

Social relationships and contacts for fifth and sixth grade students focus mainly on home, family, school, and friends. Their general interest in the opposite sex is much less obvious than the strong interests of seventh and eighth grade students. So incidents that trigger emotional responses mostly relate to family, friends, and school work. Based on this, in this unit, in addition to continuing to enhance the language proficiency of students, teachers can consider training students in meta-emotional understanding: for example, teaching students to examine the characteristics of their emotions, how to understand their own emotions, how to deal with emotional awareness, and how to develop effective strategies for dealing with their emotions. Teachers might consider several focus questions directed toward fifth and sixth grade students: What are emotions? Why do positive and negative emotions occur? What methods are useful for expressing and controlling emotions? How do you interpret other people's emotions? How do you express your emotions differently with different people and in different situations? How do you think that males and female express emotions differently? What are the cultural differences in ways that emotions are expressed? Do Chinese school children express and regulate their emotions in different ways? What are the causes of positive and negative emotions for Chinese school children?

Because cognitive abilities for children this age still tend toward more concrete abstractions, with less ability for self-reflection, when teachers introduce new concepts they should as much as possible proceed from shallow to deep and from concrete to abstract, with situations related to the personal lives of the students. In conducting cross cultural comparisons, the teacher should approach this topic through the cultures with which students are personally familiar. In order to accomplish a deep and extensive cross cultural comparison of cultural and behavioral perspectives, teachers must have a certain degree of understanding of Chinese and American culture, especially of emotional expressions. For example, Chinese can be more tactful and polite, while Americans are often more straightforward; Chinese pay equal attention to human emotions and logic, while Americans discuss things on their own merits; Chinese people talk about "face", pay attention to connections, and exchange favors, while Americans are generally less concerned about loss of face, and often see success as a result of individual effort that has nothing to do with family reputation. The cultural characteristics of how people handle emotions also show some differences. Chinese are more dependent on relatives, teachers, or friends to provide guidance or are influenced by inspiring phrases; Americans put more emphasis on privacy and also can seek assistance through psychological counseling.

In designing this curriculum, teachers must use subjects that are interesting or meaningful to children of this age to mobilize their enthusiasm for learning. There are frequent examples from daily life that create a high degree of emotional response, such as conflicts with families, participating in sports competitions or performances on stage, pressures from school work, bullying, loss of beloved pets, participating in the first middle school dance, or memories of a birthday party. We all know that emotions provoked by the outside world are integrated with and mutually affect impressions, cognition, and behavior, producing both psychological and physiological responses. Also different people can have a different emotional response to the same stimulus or event due to differences in individual personality and temperament. As teachers discuss these topics, students will not only try to describe their individual experiences and the reasons for their emotional responses, but most importantly they should understand their inner feelings and the special ways they express their emotions. For example, some students say "I get very nervous when I take exams because I worry that if I don't perform well I will disappoint my parents." Obviously this type of student is oriented toward an external locus of control. In sharing this process, teachers can advance student understanding of personal temperament and can also teach students some practical strategies for controlling their feelings. Also, this unit is a good opportunity for students to review the hobbies and interests studied previously, because when investigating emotions, the topic of hobbies will inevitably arise since people often relieve emotional pressures and regain inner peace through the pursuit of their hobbies.

In respect to training in Chinese language and literature, in addition to continuing to increase vocabulary, teachers should consider adding idioms, ancient poetry, or modern prose works. In making selections, priority should be given to idioms, sayings and poems that are rich in sensory information, have clear rhythm, high practicality, simple language, and allusions that resonate easily with the students. Using multi-sensory teaching methods such as story telling, painting, video clips, body movements, and songs will deepen student impressions. Accompanied by oral or written follow up activities you can increase students' abilities to flexibly use these literary sources. Making use of children's fondness for listening to stories, the teacher can tell inspirational stories that not only give students an appreciation of literature but also help them understand literature and art as an effective medium of emotional expression, where people can sublimate the negative emotions of sadness and worry and transform them into positive emotions. With the assistance of their English language teacher or the librarian, students can find similar writing in American literature and after reading this can give an oral report in Chinese to the class and afterwards write about this experience in Chinese. Other supplementary teaching mediums can include music, movies, or fine arts. Through the flexible use of different resources and teaching methods, education can move forward and student motivation is bound to increase.

In short, the theme of emotions is practical and fascinating, because emotions are something that people deal with on a daily basis. In what follows, I recommend a four week teaching plan that can be used for reference. I use as its structure the four basic emotions: happiness, anger, sadness, and fear, using a different theme each week to explore that emotion. I'm also using the American teachers of foreign language model of the Five C's as my language and culture teaching objective. Although this book is mainly targeted at immersion education, teachers in non-immersion programs can adjust the plan and curricular contents to the requirements of their class with appropriate revisions according to degrees of difficulty and longer or shorter class periods.

Unit Plan Example: Expressing Emotions and Feelings (Grade 5, 4 weeks)

Course Outline: In this four-week unit, fifth grade students will first watch the movie *Going to School with Dad on My Back* (背起爸爸上学) to explore the four basic human emotions: happiness, anger, sorrow, and fear, as well as the secondary, complex emotions derived from them. Then we will use the individual experiences of events as continuing topics in the class. In addition to gaining deeper understanding of emotions, students should reflect on and assess their own characteristic emotional expressions and methods of control. The course objectives, in addition to increasing knowledge of vocabulary and sentence patterns and improving communication and presentation skills, are to help students understand how cultural factors affect emotional expressions.

Essential Questions	Focus Questions
1. What is emotion? 2. How do we express our feelings? 3. How and why do people express emotions in different ways? 4. How do expressions of emotion affect social relationships?	1. How do positive and negative emotions arise? 2. How do you express and control emotions? 3. How do you understand other people's emotions? 4. How do you express emotions differently with different people or in different situations? 5. Do you think that boys and girls express emotions in different ways? What are the differences? 6. What are cultural differences in emotional expressions? 7. What are the differences in the ways that Chinese children express and control their emotions? 8. What are the causes of positive and negative emotions for Chinese students?

Learning Objectives/Skills

- Students are able to use correct words and phrases to communicate information, ideas and opinions about emotion in ways that are comprehensible to a native speaker
- Students are able to explain orally or in written form the main ideas expressed in films or literary works
- Students can give examples that illustrate the special characteristics, backgrounds, and reasons behind emotional expressions among Chinese children
- Students can consistently compare the language differences in emotional expressions between English and Chinese
- Students can compare and contrast similarities and differences in Chinese and American emotional expressions

Learning Assessment

a) Formative Assessment: See details of each week's lesson plans

b) Summative Assessment: Creation and performance of short skits and short poems and essays

Weekly Lesson Plans

Week One: What is Happiness?	
Lesson Overview	Start by talking about something that makes students feel happy, then investigate cultural differences in the ways that happiness is demonstrated. Finally have students use the vocabulary they have selected to create a short skit about a birthday party.
Learning Objectives	• Students can use different vocabulary and sentence structures to describe emotions in oral communication and written reports • Students can explain orally or in writing the main ideas expressed in a movie or an essay • Students can use examples to explain the special characteristics and reasons behind the ways that Chinese children express emotions • Students can connect and compare differences in emotional expressions in English and Chinese language • Students can compare and contrast American and Chinese ways of expressing emotions
Materials	• Movie: (DVD) *Going to School with Dad on My Back* • Large white poster • Markers • Tape • "Happy" traditional and contemporary music and art • Cardboard

(Continued)

	Week One: What is Happiness?
Learning Activities	• Watch *Going to School with Dad on My Back* as a prelude to this unit topic; as the story line advances, students must record the ways that the characters in the drama demonstrate happiness, anger, sorrow, and fear. Before showing the movie, the teacher introduces the main characters and their names, allowing the students to gain familiarity with them. • The teacher can first divide how the main character seeks schooling into several stages. Divide students into groups and have each group select a certain stage as their responsibility for principle observation, so as to avoid mental fatigue. Small groups that are not the main recorders can still provide assistance in recording, bringing up additional information during class sharing. • After watching the movie, students paste large characters for happiness, anger, sorrow, and fear on a wall poster and answer the questions: Which character in the drama had which kind of emotional response? What generated this kind of emotion? How was that kind of emotion displayed? Students who are not good at writing can elect to use drawings to elaborate on the topic. • All of the students must answer "What is happiness" on a large character poster. Students can post their photos on a poster to share their experience of happiness. • Students view and read the words and drawings of the whole class on the large character poster and brainstorm about the characteristics of happiness, as the teacher continues to encourage the students to reflect: What are the differences in how happiness is expressed by characters in

(Continued)

	Week One: What is Happiness?
	the film and the students' own families? How is this affected by age and gender? What are appropriate ways to express happiness that will not cause distress to others? • The teacher introduces vocabulary related to happiness, then plays joyful Chinese traditional or modern music or shows students joyful art and has students use their happy words to describe their emotions. • Students use different tones of voice, body movements or emotional line graphs to illustrate the varying degrees of the emotion of happiness. • Students create an emotion symbol chart using vocabulary words selected in relationship to happiness or other complex emotions. • Students combine vocabulary and sentence patterns to create a short skit about a birthday party.
Assessment	• Use proper words to write and explain • Preliminary comparison of forms of emotional expression • Summative: creation of short drama
Language Reference and Examples	• Vocabulary describing happiness：开心、高兴、兴奋、惊喜、喜悦、满足、幸福、欢乐、快活、欣喜、痛快、眉开眼笑、笑逐颜开、满面春风、心花怒放、兴高采烈、乐不思蜀、欣喜若狂、喜上眉梢、喜笑颜开、满怀喜悦、怡然自得、喜形于色、乐不可支、喜出望外、沾沾自喜、手舞足蹈 • Other mixed emotion vocabulary：惊喜交加、乐极生悲、喜极而泣、横眉吐气、喜出望外、亦悲亦喜 • Ancient poetry describing happiness：骆宾王《咏鹅》 • Sentence patterns：既……又……；一……就……；……得很……；感到……；令……；让……

(Continued)

	Week One: What is Happiness?
Recommended Resources	• DVD: *Going to School with Dad on My Back* • Traditional music: "China's Ancient Classical Network" ① • Contemporary music: www.pandoroa.com • Emotion symbols: Wikipedia (keyword "emoticon")

	Week Two: Family Feud
Lesson Overview	The teacher continues to use the film *Going to School with Dad on My Back* as a theme. Discuss how students feel about things that make them angry. Then compare the way their parents or individual students express anger, and make a preliminary comparison of cultural differences with characters in the film.
Learning Objectives	• Students can use different vocabulary and sentence structures to describe emotions in oral communication and written reports • Students can explain orally or in writing the main ideas expressed in a movie or an essay • Students can use examples to explain the special characteristics and reasons behind the ways that Chinese children express emotions • Students can connect and compare differences in emotional expressions in English and Chinese language • Students can compare and contrast American and Chinese ways of expressing emotions

---

① http://www.guqu.net/

(Continued)

	Week Two: Family Feud
Materials	- Movie: (DVD) *Going to School with Dad on My Back*
- Large white poster
- Markers
- Cardboard
Learning Activities	- The teacher replays several sections from the movie displaying anger to jog student memories of the plot. After students read and view words and drawings about anger on the large character poster, they answer the questions on the big character poster: What is anger? What does my family do to make me especially angry? What are your impressions of how characters in the film express anger? After students have finished writing, the teacher selectively gives the whole class some of the written contents for students to read.
- Stimulate student reflection: How do you know when your family members are angry? How does gender or age affect the way that anger is expressed? What do other people do that makes you angry? How do you let others know when you are angry? How do you cool down when you're angry?
- The teacher introduces vocabulary related to anger. Allow students to brainstorm words that express anger in English and compare this with Chinese.
- Students use different facial expressions, tones of voice, physical movements, or emotional line graphs to illustrate different levels of anger.
- Students select an idiom that illustrates anger or complex emotions, or create an emotion symbol chart.

	Week Two: Family Feud
	• Students combine the vocabulary and sentence patterns used to write about the birthday party last week with an additional episode: "My parents do not let me attend my good friend's birthday party…" and continue to create a small skit.
Assessment	• Individual accurate interpretation and writing of words • Basic cultural comparisons • Summative: Create a short skit
Language Reference and Examples	• Vocabulary describing anger: 讨厌、厌恶、憎恨、狂怒、恼火、责备、不满、反感、敌对、怒发冲冠、暴跳如雷、破口大骂、怒目而视、横眉怒视、怒火中烧、怒气冲冲、怒目切齿、直眉怒目 • Other mixed emotion vocabulary: 爱恨交加、恼羞成怒、义愤填膺 • Story describing anger: "怒发冲冠""和氏璧"(秦王,蔺相如) • Song describing anger: 岳飞《满江红·怒发冲冠》 • Sentence patterns: 因……而……;既然如此……
Recommended Resources	• DVD: *Going to School with Dad on My Back* • Emotion symbols: Wikipedia (keyword "emoticon")

	Week Three: Why Am I So Sad?
Lesson Overview	The teacher continues to use the film *Going to School with Dad on My Back* as a topic to talk about things that make people feel lost or sad.

(Continued)

	Week Three: Why Am I So Sad?
Learning Objectives	• In communicative exchanges students can use the vocabulary and sentence patterns relating to happiness, anger and sadness • Students can explain orally or in writing the main ideas expressed in a movie or an essay • Students can use examples to explain the special characteristics and reasons behind the ways that Chinese children express emotions • Students can connect and compare differences in emotional expressions in English and Chinese language • Students can compare and contrast American and Chinese ways of expressing emotions
Materials	• Movie: (DVD) *Going to School with Dad on My Back* • Large white poster • Markers • Cardboard
Learning Activities	• The teacher replays several sections from the movie displaying sadness to jog student memories of the plot. After students read and view words and drawings about sadness on the large character poster, they answer the questions on the big character poster: What is sadness? What things make me sad? What are your impressions of how characters in the film express sadness? After the students have finished writing, the teacher selectively gives the whole class some of the written contents for students to read.

(Continued)

	Week Three: Why Am I So Sad?
	• Stimulate student reflection: How do you know when your friends are sad? How does gender or age affect the ways that sadness is expressed? What sorts of things done by others or said by others make you sad? What do you do when you are in a bad mood? • The teacher introduces vocabulary related to sadness. Allow students to brainstorm words that express sadness in English and compare this with Chinese. • Introduce Ma Zhiyuan's *"Autumn Thoughts"*. Students use drawings to interpret the artistic mood and share their experiences about missing their family. Then discuss the visual images used to depict one's inner feelings when missing one's family and compare this with the visual images produced through *"Autumn Thoughts"*. • Students use different facial expressions, tone of voice, physical movements, or emotional line graphs to illustrate the different levels of sadness. • Students select an idiom that illustrates sadness or complex emotions, or create an emotion symbol chart. • Students divide into groups and use the vocabulary they have studied to write an essay or short poem about loss and combined with dance moves and body language read aloud their works to the class.
Assessment	• Individual accurate interpretation and writing of words • Basic cultural and linguistic comparisons • Summative: small group essay or short poem

(Continued)

	Week Three: Why Am I So Sad?
Language Reference and Examples	• Vocabulary describing sadness：伤心；难过；哀愁；忧伤、痛苦、哀痛、唉声叹气、愁眉不展、忍气吞声、泪流满面、肝肠寸断、愁眉苦脸、呼天抢地、泪如雨下、声泪俱下、心如刀割、死去活来、少壮不努力，老大徒伤悲 • Other mixed emotion vocabulary：悲喜交集、转悲为喜、乐极生悲 • Sorrowful Yuan poem：马致远《天净沙·秋思》 • Song describing sadness：李叔同《送别》 • Sentence patterns：除了……以外；不但……而且……
Recommended Resources	• DVD：*Going to School with Dad on My Back* • Emotion symbols：Wikipedia (keyword "emoticon")

	Week Four: Feelings that Accelerate Breath and Heartbeat
Lesson Overview	The teacher continues to use the film *Going to School with Dad on My Back* as a topic to talk about things that have frightened characters in the drama, and also what things in their own lives make people nervous, scared, or afraid.
Learning Objectives	• In communicative exchanges students can use the vocabulary and sentence patterns relating to happiness, anger, sadness, and fear • Students can compare and contrast different patterns of showing fear in Chinese and American language and popular culture
Materials	• Movie：(DVD) *Going to School with Dad on My Back* • Ghost Buster movie clips • Large white poster • Markers • Cardboard

	Week Four: Feelings that Accelerate Breath and Heartbeat
Learning Activities	• The teacher replays several frightening sections from the movie to jog student memories of the plot. After students read and view words and drawings about fear on the large character poster, they answer the questions on the big character poster: What is fear? What is one thing that I fear? (For example a haunted house at Halloween, or the experience of a roller coaster at an amusement park.) After the students have finished writing, the teacher selectively gives the whole class some of the written contents for students to read. • Stimulate student reflection: How do you know when your friends are feeling nervous or afraid? How does gender or age affect the way that fear is expressed? What things do you like that also make you afraid? What things do you hate that also make you afraid? • The teacher plays clips from *Ghost Buster* and zombie movies and has students make comparisons between Chinese and American ghost stories. • The teacher introduces vocabulary related to fear. • Students use different facial expressions, tones of voice, physical movements, or emotional line graphs to illustrate the different levels of fear. Students can also select an idiom that illustrates fear or complex emotions, or create an emotion symbol chart. • Students divide into groups and use the vocabulary they have studied to write a story that will frighten their readers; they should coordinate this with background music, sounds, and lights and perform this for the whole class.

(Continued)

	Week Four: Feelings that Accelerate Breath and Heartbeat
Assessment	• Individual accurate interpretation and writing of words • Cultural comparison of Chinese and American ghost stories • Summative: creative story
Language Reference and Examples	• Vocabulary describing fear：刺激、紧张、害怕、畏惧、慌乱、惊恐、七上八下、毛骨悚然、心惊胆战、大惊失色、心惊肉跳、提心吊胆、坐立不安、一身冷汗、魂不附体、目瞪口呆 • Other mixed emotion vocabulary：既担心又害怕、又敬重又害怕、又惊又喜 • Sentence patterns：review sentence patterns from week three
Recommended Resources	• DVD：*Going to School with Dad on My Back* • Emotion symbols：Wikipedia (keyword "emoticon") • Ghost Buster • YouTube：Zombie movie clips • Emotion symbols：wikipedia (keyword "emotion")

Chapter Six Establishing a Sense of Achievement: Grades 7 to 8

Introduction

While 5th and 6th grade students have advanced considerably in terms of physiological, psychological, and cognitive development, their creative thinking skills remain relatively immature, and they face considerable difficulty in dealing with abstract concepts. This is a period of adaptation and exploration as well as the budding of adolescence. By 7th and 8th grades, students have gradually developed their own learning style, have adjusted to the demands of school and from my perspective, have advanced considerably in cognitive maturity, so that their view of many things is beginning to reflect their individual preferences and subjective evaluations. For example, students are fond of directly expressing what they like and dislike about lesson contents and activities. They will critique the teacher's instructional methods as good or bad and use personal subjective arguments to assess or negate other people's views. They will also dare to directly critique and judge their fellow classmates' academic performances, particularly when having to divide up work in group projects.

Middle school students in 7th and 8th grades are experiencing rapid physical growth. However, although their appearance and deportment are beginning to take on adult characteristics, with clothing styles and cosmetics beginning to give expression to unique styles, their emotional development is still in a stage of teenage confusion and their methods of handling interpersonal relationships are still rather naive. For example, when students face pressures from schoolwork or find themselves being ignored by their classmates, they are often unable to deal with this directly and easily sink into a self-critical mood. Thus, it is very important when planning language curricular activities to pay attention to the teenage desire to excel, to avoid student comparisons of ability or achievement, and to point out individual strong points and give positive encouragement. Also, because of differences in physical development in male and female students, their ways of expressing ideas and emotions can also vary, with male students favoring more dynamic types of body language. Therefore, flexibility in organizing group projects is important, so that all students have an opportunity to display their special characteristics.

At this stage it is very important to help students develop sympathetic understanding in dealing with others so as to establish good social relationships and team spirit. Learning how to deal with contradictions and conflict in expressing personal opinions is also extremely important. In terms of Mandarin abilities, 7th and 8th grade students are able to converse at a basic level, to share opinions, and in group discussion are beginning to be able to express personal views about events. Students have a basic level of understanding about things and their own points of view, so that an important goal in Mandarin training at this stage is to teach students to understand different perspectives on things, and to be able to put forward decisive plans so as to move toward a multicultural understanding of comparative differences.

The scope of studies at this stage is not just focused on the individual but should expand to include topics that deal with concerns about local groups, the environment, and the wider world. For example, in talking about ways in which people express their moods, students should not only focus on their own moods, but the ways that other people communicate emotions, to understand and respect factors related to cultural backgrounds and to begin to show concern for the local community environment. With the rapid development of Internet information, we are exposed to frequent world news, and our lives have entered an era of global communication. I believe that curricular contents at this stage should include diverse lessons and assignments on cultural history, geography, literature, arts, and religious customs so as to nurture student reflections on intercultural communication and their interpretation skills, and to increase their level of comprehension of cultural difference.

In addition to working in depth with students on the four skills of listening, speaking, reading, and writing, it is important to emphasize a student centered approach to instruction. Although middle school students have longer attention spans than primary students, when contents do not interest them they can quickly exhibit negative attitudes during class, becoming uncooperative or acting like they do not care. Thus, integrating interesting cultural lessons in a timely manner can enrich language learning. Teachers need to remember to utilize appropriate classroom methods and especially to avoid a "single voice" unidirectional teaching style. Classroom time should be used as much as possible in active exercises focused on the four skills of listening, speaking, reading and writing. In terms of approaches to small group discussion, active discourse, researching and collecting materials, team projects, organization and analysis, or multimedia activities, it is best to involve students in planning and implementation so as to attract and stimulate the interests of students of this age.

For this generation of educators, there are many future occupations that do not now exist. In the future, students will face an intensely technological age, so students' creative abilities and imaginative skills will be extremely important. Because of this, each year's curricular content needs to build and extend, not only matching students' cognitive and psychological development, but also understanding the directions of students' developing interests, avoiding as much as possible unchanging and narrow materials and topics. Teachers also must keep up with the trends of the times, expand their individual areas of expertise, retain flexibility in teaching, and create innovative classroom activities. "Applied knowledge" is the teacher's objective, and even more the ultimate goal of mature student learning.

Unit Topics

Unit Topic One: Family

The curriculum topics for the family unit for 7th and 8th grade students should advance understanding of the complexity of family structures, including the relationships between adult family members, expectations between parents and children, and conflicting views. This should extend to contrasting Chinese families with American families: for example, forms of encouragement and discipline, male and female standards, and the responsibilities of children toward their families. Allow students to discover cultural differences and their strengths and weaknesses and to understand how Chinese parents and children cope with family relationships.

For the family unit, I propose using family rules in students' families as an entry into discussion about family relationships and family pressures. After the students have exchanged views about relationships with their own parents and siblings and have a basic understanding of the concepts, it is appropriate to introduce Chinese family ideals and to clarify the differences in family structures, as well as individual rights and responsibilities in the Chinese family. Of special importance is the central position of males in Chinese families with their responsibilities to carry on the family line and support their elders, and female domestic responsibilities for the care of young and old. Once students have learned that due to cultural differences individuals face different family pressures, many diverse ideas can enter into discussion, especially the aspirations and demands of parents towards their children's future. In addition, the Chinese phrases "to value males over females" and "the three types of unfilial behavior" should provide interesting topics of discussion.

The teacher can begin with a small group activity organized around "setting family rules" to stimulate student curiosity about the topic. Allow students to list family rules, with each group reporting to the class in turn. Many students will draw on their own experience to set rules, and will set standards in opposition to the current restrictions they face from their families. After the groups have compared their lists, the teacher can easily list the demands and expectations that parents have for their children. Following this, students can read a related story or newspaper clipping, allowing them to connect the different positions of the characters, put forward personal views, and propose solutions.

In order to further advance student understanding of the traditional values of Chinese families, students can watch a video, taking notes on the plot development and the differences from a western cultural viewpoint. As they watch the movie, the teacher should provide simple questions for students to take note of and reflect upon. In terms of videos, I think that *Families with Children*[①] is a very appropriate supplementary teaching material. This is a Chinese situation comedy with interesting stories about three children in a blended (divorced) family. This television program not only reflects how Chinese parents discipline their children, but also demonstrates family ethics and affection between siblings.

I recommend teaching the following idioms and proverbs relevant to this unit to help student gain a deeper cultural understanding: 饮水思源; 家有一老, 如有一宝; 母子连心 and the Tang Poem "游子吟". In terms of suggestions for teaching idioms, the teacher can take the idioms studied in this unit and separate them out into printed word cards, and use small group competition where students use a jig saw puzzle method

---

① Refer to the website: http://dianshiju.cntv.cn/city/jiayouernv/videopage/index.shtml

to assemble the idioms in the proper order. By thinking about the combination of the meanings of individual words, this activity helps students understand the creative concept expressed in the idiom. This is a very challenging mental exercise and a very interesting way to learn to use characters. As students go through many mistaken understandings, they will retain a much deeper impression of this idiom.

The first section of China's Counseling Network site[①] features short plays on disciplining children in three generation families. The teacher can use these short plays to allow students to demonstrate contradictory relationships in the three generation family. The essay also has detailed discussions of the differences in educational viewpoints between the two generations and thus is a useful supplementary teaching material. In terms of evaluative projects for this unit, you might consider having students synthesize the strengths and weaknesses of Chinese and western family culture, combined with writing a revised version of the conclusion of the television story, using PowerPoint or a puppet drama as a form of presentation.

You could also have students write an illustrated story to advance their language creativity. The curricular content in the last section of this unit can extend to new challenges facing the modern family in China, such as having students investigate the effects on family gender values of China's current one child policy. Students can go on the Internet, and through the process of searching for and arranging information can begin to understand changing patterns of Chinese family and society, such as the gradual disappearance of the three generation family and the increase in the elderly population. Students can organize mini debates, using this format to demonstrate both knowledge and language skills.

Unit Topic Two: Food and Chinese Medicine

In the 5th and 6th grade curriculum, students will have learned about

---

① http://bbs.xlzx.com/dispbbs.asp? boardid=10&Id=153256

typical foods in northern and southern China, proper seating when dining, and basic cooking methods and ingredients. The contents for 7th and 8th grade will connect to ideas in the previous lessons and go into more detailed cultural aspects of study such as understanding Chinese cooking methods; ingredients and seasonings; polite forms of social manners and speech between host and guest; and ideas about harmonizing food and health. I think that the time period spent on this unit might be a little longer, divided into different sections taught in sequence.

For students, eating at a Chinese restaurant will already be a common event, and just the mention of Chinese food will quickly elicit from students the names of a few of their favorite dishes. So we might use understanding a menu as a way to begin this topic. Use a guessing game as a warm up. The teacher prepares a Power Point with five dishes and distributes to the students a list of new words and a fill in form for the names of Chinese dishes. As students identify the five different dishes, have them speculate on their matching names; at the same time have students write down food names, colors and flavors. In the course of this activity, guide the students to learn new Chinese words related to flavor and write them down on their new word list. Before announcing the correct answers, ask students to report on what they have written down, see who made the most correct guesses, and award the winning students with a fortune cookie prize. Remind the students that fortune cookies are only found in Chinese restaurants in the west. (The list of new words allows students to remember new words they think they want to know; by going through the process of self-determination, students will have a deeper understanding of the meaning and usage of the new words.)

After the menu activities, have students bring to class one type of spice/seasoning (a type commonly used in Chinese food). The seasoning must be in a small box with no notations. First, the teacher will show real spices (another preparation), and teach the students their names, with the students writing this down on their new words list. The teacher will take the boxes of spices brought in by the students and give them numbers, place them in different places, and have the students use three senses (smell, touch, taste) to recognize each spice and write the name on an answer sheet. The exercise should have a time limit and students can refer to their list of new words. After two or three rounds of identification exercises, students will have a deep understanding of the names and aromas of these seasonings. This is an interesting activity for studying the names of things.

The teacher can also distribute prepared work sheets for students and arrange a homework assignment for them to compile a list of the sources of some commonly used spices; after students have done this small research, they will have a basic understanding of the historical background of the spices. In the following activity, have the students prepare a dialogue where they complain about the taste of food while eating in a restaurant; when ordering they must give a detailed description of the flavors and ingredients to be used, thus reviewing again the names of dishes and names of seasonings.

Basic cooking methods for Chinese food: steaming, boiling, frying, and deep-frying, are best learned through demonstration, so students are better able to understand the different methods. By introducing a few famous Chinese dishes, their ingredients and cooking methods, students have the opportunity to compare the mutual relationship between cooking practices and tastes. I have had students watch a video about preparing "Home-style Doufu", where the process is explained in detail. Students watch and listen, taking notes on ingredients and cooking methods. I then let students simulate television cooking shows, demonstrating the sequence and process while giving explanations. With this exercise, students not only learn to write recipes, but also learn the basic process of cooking. It is even better if the school has kitchen facilities. I first teach students the basic ways to chop meats and vegetables: for example cutting thin threads, thin slices, or smashing; then I demonstrate how to cook two or three types of recipes. During each demonstration students must listen, watch, and write, producing a short explanation of the ingredients and cooking methods. Finally, students will, according to their own written recipes, practice cooking to see which group produces something that is closest in flavor to that of their teacher's dish.

Following the three cooking exercises, students should be able to fluently explain the names of cooking ingredients and cooking methods. Finally, organize a cooking contest, where student groups each develop a different type of culinary recipe; student groups then prepare the ingredients, and practice cooking in the kitchen, to see which group's arrangement, color and flavor is the best. The purpose of this activity is to give students a comparatively deeper understanding of Chinese foods, cooking methods, and flavors. However, if the school does not have kitchen facilities, the teacher might show a video simulation exercise: ask the students to choose a recipe for a dish, and video tape the preparation in the teacher's own kitchen; then have students prepare a complete commentary on the food ingredients and cooking steps. Students all really enjoy these types of activities, which can lead to surprising and creative performances.

In terms of teaching proper manners for guests visiting Chinese family homes and the symbolic meanings of foods and eating customs, I usually like students to write their own short skits (the contents of the skit should integrate the new words and sentences in this unit). Students divide into groups, chose characters to perform the dialogue, and by performing the dialogue, students quickly understand and learn how to act as polite guests. Of course, in arranging these performances, they should be as realistic as possible, including appropriate styles of dress for their characters. At the same time I also find a short reading to accompany this dealing with Chinese ceremonies of food and drink, so students will have a more complete understanding of seating arrangements when dining, and the use of foods, drinking customs, and proper manners between hosts and guests.

Chinese views about medicinal foods and comparisons with western medicine provide a further expansion of learning contents. For this part of the discussion, I make simple graphic materials for reading comprehension to provide a basic introduction and understanding. The textbook edited by Liu Xun, *New Practical Chinese* (Vol. 4, lesson 49), features a dialogue on treating a headache. The teacher can use the accompanying CD-ROM to allow students to see and understand the methods of Chinese and western medicine and different views about the human body. A Chinese doctor can be invited to the classroom to do a demonstration on the four principles of looking, smelling, asking, and feeling the pulse in Chinese medicine. The doctor can also introduce students to some common medicinal plants and do a simple comparison of the color, appearance, taste and function of Chinese and western medicinal ingredients. If the teacher is able to bring in some foods commonly used by Chinese in normal life to promote health and have students see and taste them, it will enhance student understanding of Chinese therapeutic foods. The assigned projects for this unit will have produced a set of questions based on a range of classroom contents, allowing students to draw on these questions and search for materials to write a survey of the diversity of western and Chinese medicine and compare their similarities and differences. Each student's ability is different, so for students with stronger abilities, beyond the basic requirements of answering questions for this report, you can encourage them to pursue a deeper level of reflection and allow students to use descriptive examples to support their argument.

I recommend the following idioms/proverbs dealing with food and drink for this unit:饥肠辘辘;众口难调;无米之炊;食之无味;弃之可惜;因噎废食;药补不如食补;心急吃不了热豆腐;肉包子打狗——一去不回;早吃饱,午吃好,晚吃少。Teachers can select from these to complement their teaching. 一瓢饮 from the *Confucian Analects*, says that the way people eat expresses their attitudes toward life. As supplementary teaching materials for 7th and 8th grade, these foster an understanding of the concept of food in people's lives.

Unit Topic Three: Chinese Festivals

In speaking of China's traditional festivals and contemporary holidays, regardless of the age level, the curriculum should definitely involve creative and celebratory activities. Consequently, we can match the timing of festivals with course teaching content, but should not make lessons too long because once the festival is past, the celebratory atmosphere does not remain.

As part of the celebration of traditional holidays each year, teachers plan many of the same activities: for example at Chinese New Year students write spring couplets, make dumplings, cut window decorations, read New Year stories, and perform New Year dances; for the Dragon Boat Festival or Autumn Festival students may make glutinous rice cakes or bake moon cakes and recount the origins and legends of the festivals. However, students in 7th and 8th grades are still not tired of this and still very much enjoy these fun activities, so they should be continued. Many of the preparations that were formerly done by the teacher can now be handed over for the students to organize: for example, editing the program, planning activities and rehearsals, arranging the stage, making stage props, and posting fliers.

We should also bring contemporary holidays into the class curriculum at appropriate times such as Teachers Day, National Day, Children's Day, Ghost Festival, Qing Ming Festival, Labor Day, and Temple Festivals as well as western holidays like Halloween, Thanksgiving, Christmas, and National Day. This is the best way to study everyday culture. Students in 7th and 8th grades are already familiar with the origins and celebrations of traditional festivals, so I propose that the main points of study in this unit focus on the Chinese lunar calendar/almanac; understanding festival taboos; symbolic meanings of and geographic climatic influences on traditional foods; the impact of festivals on people's daily lives, and differences between traditional festivals in former and modern times.

By using traditional legends as a way into the topic, for example the Cowherd and Weaving Maid story from the 7th month, 7th day of the lunar year, students understand that the lunar calendar and western calendar are not the same. Students can also be taught practical ways to read the lunar calendar to differentiate auspicious and inauspicious dates and understand how Chinese people use the lunar calendar to arrange significant events in their lives. Students will be very interested in this type of subject matter, and one might even allow students to imitate the design of the lunar calendar to create a new calendar system for the future, to help them understand how Chinese people use the lunar calendar to select days to conduct their affairs.

In speaking of Chinese festival taboos, the teacher can first divide students into groups to collect materials and illustrations of different festival taboos. During class time, discuss and make a list of the festival taboos of different countries and discuss their underlying origins. Afterwards, gather and arrange all of the information in a poster display. Divide students into groups and have them suggest how conflicts have arisen from cultural taboos, and ask them to propose solutions to avoid these conflicts. Have students discuss examples from real life news events to help arouse in them a sympathetic response to understanding the background and cultural reasons behind taboos and to learn to respect different types of etiquette and follow local customs.

Food is an important part of traditional festivals, so as a part of every festival activity teachers have students make traditional tasty delicacies. I think that 7th and 8th grade students can study the materials for making these traditional foods at a deeper level, recognizing the effects of regional climates and understanding their symbolic meanings. The teacher can first bring in some grains, fruits, and vegetables from different regions to show to the class and ask students to identify their seasonal and regional growth patterns. Then display a large scale geographic climatic map; have students consider reasons why different places produce different crops; and have students explain the influences of geography and climate on food production. After they have reached this stage of understanding, the teacher can select traditional holiday foods from a Chinese and American festival that correspond to a climate chart (prepare this before the lesson) and have students talk about the relevance of climate on the choice of ingredients in traditional dishes, while at the same time studying the historical origins of the two festivals. For example, why are turkeys and pumpkins selected as foods for Thanksgiving? Why are dumplings and preserved meats something that should not be neglected for Chinese New Year? Students can use this sort of topic to discuss the mutual relationships between food, climate, and the environment, as well as the meanings and expectations that local people have toward festival foods. Afterwards, allow students to chose a country for their own personal project; ask them to make a large map and for each region use words and illustrations to display the elevation, climate, distinctive features, primary crops, and festival foods and significance.

What are the major influences of festivals on people's lives? I think that this topic can be approached by first asking about the festivals that are favorites among students, talking about their personal expectations for festivals, and their most unforgettable holiday memories. Then imagine people's lives if these festivals disappeared. Divide students into groups to construct posters that display "A Future without Holidays". Students can use various methods and materials to make the poster, and after completion each group will explain the significance of their poster in front of the class. This allows students a kind of reverse reflection. Students cannot imagine a situation where one day there would really be no Christmas or Thanksgiving holiday; in the course of discussion, they will slowly discover their feelings and appreciation for the great significance of holidays. Later, they can reflect on their feelings of loss in life, while recognizing the significance of holidays in everyone's individual life. These activities, in addition to stimulating students' abilities for creative expression, will also increase student interest and enthusiasm for discussion.

With the space between people shortened by technological progress, festival activities from different regions have begun to mutually influence each other. For example, China currently has also begun to celebrate Christmas with parties and Valentine's Day with chocolate. These festivals did not exist in China in the past, but influenced by western trends, they are slowly developing into new Chinese holidays. In order to help students understand the development of mutual influences between East and West, the teacher can first have the students list various forms of modern communication; discuss common areas of language, customs, and fashion; then add the similarities and differences in holiday celebrations and reflect on the reasons for this. Arrange a "Before and after" cut and paste competition by having students divide into groups, with each group cutting out different pictures that represent popular culture in different periods of time: for example clothing, popular songs, celebrities, and common items. The comparative results of this activity teach students that, along with increased access to information and international exchange, people who live in different parts of the world have also become to some degree assimilated in clothing styles, hairstyles, and music. As China has been affected by western culture, so Chinese people have gradually begun to celebrate western holidays.

How has the celebration of traditional holidays changed over time and why? I recommend that teachers take students outside of the classroom into their own community for this activity. Using a questionnaire that the students have designed, go to the local Chinatown (Chinese association, Chinese social services, old folks home) and interview elderly people from different generations about how they celebrated traditional holidays when they were young. From this, students can compare the changes that have taken place and their reasons, and write a simple report. Students will not only have a chance to communicate with local Chinese people, but can also experience immersing themselves in a different cultural environment.

Unit Topic Four: Geography and Travel

Travel is a very practical yet interesting unit theme. The key points for 7th and 8th grade students should be to study how to read maps, understand geographical locations and coordinates, and distinguish between differences in time and space. At the same time, this emphasizes training students in how to deal with common situations and problems that occur while traveling.

Before this unit begins, I ask students to bring five souvenirs to class and explain the name of each item, what type of item it is, where it is from, what it reminds them of, and something about the pleasures of travel. I then ask students to use a map to find several countries where they have traveled, learn to use the lines of latitude and longitude to record their position, and write their geographic location including the neighboring countries on four sides along with the names of the oceans; then have students find China's geographic location on the world map.

Afterwards, the teacher can guide students into the topic of travel in China. What should one know before beginning travel? First, have students look up the weather forecast on a Chinese website to understand climatic conditions in that place and how to dress appropriately. For this exercise, have students divide into groups and discuss the content of the websites. After the students have finished, have each group pick a Chinese city and go online to read about its climate; then have them pretend to be a meteorologist and give the weather report for the upcoming week; and finally have them give suggestions for appropriate activities to do in that weather. The purpose of this exercise is to have students practice using Chinese websites, and comprehend reading local news. Then give students a classification chart and ask students to go on the Internet to search for information: for example, the currency exchange rate, whether or not a visa is needed, the time it takes to obtain a visa, cost of a visa, time differences, luggage and customs rules, language, taboos a traveler should know about, etc. Students should study the idea of "When in Rome, do as the Romans do", so that aside from packing basic material needs, travelers should also have a familiarity with the local social customs. Finally, ask the students to use the information they have gathered to make a detailed list for traveling in China.

Teachers can further have students create a travel advertisement to allow students to practice their speaking skills. First, display a Chinese travel website to enable students to understand how to introduce the different features (seasonal characteristics, history and culture, festival activities, local cuisine, local customs, etc.) of travel destinations. Using a city as an example, divide students into groups and put each group in charge of explaining a feature. After the students have an overall understanding, ask students to go on the computer and complete the following steps: 1) choose a major city in China; 2) give the geographical location; 3) explain the climate and seasons; 4) list five travel destinations ; 5) list well-known local restaurants or food; 6) explain social customs and holidays; and 7) match each description with pictures. After all the information is gathered, have the students plan a weeklong vacation in that city. One object of this activity is to allow students to practice their ability to organize materials. After planning their trip, students should use the original pictures they collected to create an advertisement (map/scenic spots) in imitation of a travel agent to present and explain the local characteristics, history, and the value of traveling to their site. Afterwards, have each person vote for the most appealing travel destination. The standards for voting are based on whether the travel plans are complete and whether the information on cultural history and scenic places is adequate. After each student has finished their report on their individual travel advertisement board, based on the final votes, have students summarize the discussion and list on the white board the main reasons why a destination is worth visiting

In the resulting discussion of these activities, the teacher can guide students to extend their discussion: "How does traveling affect your understanding of the country you travel to?" Of course if there are supplementary films to view, this unit will be even more interesting. I have shown the film *Chinese Moon* ("中国月亮") and had students record the differences in Chinese and American cultures while watching. This film portrays the story of an American in China. The characters in the film are amusing, and it deeply reflects humorous misunderstandings toward local Chinese customs and living circumstances. Teachers can use this as reference material (the first section where the main character is living in the US has parts that are not that useful for classroom teaching). After watching this video, the teacher can organize a simple question and answer game, and can talk about the similarities and differences in the range of locations where Chinese language is used.

Because the 8th grade graduation trip for my school goes to China, I have my students practice filling in entry forms during class, answering entry questions, and reading airplane and bus schedules.

Recommended idioms for this unit include: 跋山涉水,扶老携幼,呼朋引伴,风餐露宿,美不胜收,乐不思蜀,流连忘返. I also recommend "枫桥夜泊", a Tang poem dealing with the moods of travel.

Unit Topic Five: History, Politics and Religion

When talking about the topics of history, government, and religion, where students often lack interest and motivation, it is important that Chinese written narratives are well focused and not too long. I've discovered that Chinese history books often lack explanations with colorful illustrations. In addition, because the conflicts triggered by religion and politics are tangled and complicated, it is not easy to understand and difficult to arouse student interest in reading. The average student has little patience or willingness to focus on things not directly related to his/her own life, unless they are personal hobbies. Thus, the teacher must abandon traditional rote learning and recitation teaching methods and as much as possible use the contents of students' modern lives and connecting topics to enter this curriculum. Moreover, teachers in this unit must avoid expressing personal points of view; they must faithfully present the actual historical materials. To direct student understanding and reflection, the goal of teaching the students should be to develop their international perspectives and objective understanding.

The learning goals for 7th and 8th grade students are to understand the origins of Chinese civilization; the important historical dynasties; the affects of traditional social class divisions on contemporary people; the role of religion in daily life; and relationships between China and the rest of the world. The contents of study for this unit are many and varied, so teachers may chose their own focus in making their plans, and the subject can be further divided into several smaller units. Also, the contents of this unit are biased towards informational culture, so approaching this topic through every day, practical, interesting things is both a challenge and something that is not easily accomplished. However, I think that you can begin with a familiar story, movie, or novel to stimulate student interest. For example, *Hua Mulan*, the Disney animated film dealing with the war between China and other countries, the importance of the Great Wall, and the degree of submission of Chinese people to the emperor has a lot to offer. Select excerpts from the film for students to watch, gradually leading into the study topic contents. This is a film produced by the west, so much of the dialogue and etiquette follow western styles of expression, and this presents a good opportunity for students to learn about cultural misunderstanding.

After enjoying the movie, the teacher can assign homework for students to gather information, draw a map of China during Mulan's dynastic period and indicate the territorial boundaries of that time. Then show a distribution map of the national minorities, enabling students to understand the different residences of the Han and nomadic peoples; then trace this back to the birthplace of Han Chinese civilization. Give students a puzzle map of China and ask them to complete the puzzle in small groups in a limited period, then ask students to find the names of China's two great rivers on the map, and guess which river basin was the cradle of Chinese civilization. Why? Students in each group will have an opportunity to express their views. The most important point of this activity is to allow students to reflect and express viewpoints, and the teacher should not comment on the accuracy of the views expressed. As result of this process of debate, students will be able to remember that the Yellow River is the cradle of Chinese civilization and achieve the learning objectives.

Chinese dynastic history is diverse, making it impossible for students to understand and remember the history of each dynasty. I think that teachers might wish to begin with a questionnaire "What you know about Chinese history" that asks students to write what they know of Chinese dynasties, emperors, historical conflicts, and stories. The teacher can select from this something that most students show interest in. Have students divide into groups, assign each group a dynastic period, and have them present the cultural history of that dynasty through all kinds of clippings, operas, drama, and drawings. As each group presents in turn, students in the other groups must record on a study sheet (which the teacher has prepared in advance) the most important points of each group's report. This activity allows students to decide their own favorite way to express historical understandings and learn from each other. Before this event, the teacher should plan at least two hours of class time for students to search for materials on the computer. In this way, the classroom teacher can keep track of the directions of student research and provide advice at any time. Teachers should also provide some relevant web pages so that students do not waste too much time. Alternatively, you can take the students to the school library to search for necessary materials; training students to use different types of resources is also an important type of learning.

In approaching the topic of the traditional Chinese social order and contemporary influences, the teacher can first design a card game similar to the American one called "Revolution". Switch the king, queen, tenant farmers, and slaves to the positions of officials, farmers, artisans, and merchants and have the students divide into groups to play the different positions they are familiar with. After the game, ask students, based on their understanding of each occupation's importance, to once again arrange these positions in order of priority and to explain their reasons. At this time the Chinese imperial examination system can be brought into the discussion, and students can debate the positive and negative aspects of this system. Next, provide students with an extract from the real life schooling of Chinese students, to help students understand the differences between Chinese and American schools in class time, course subjects, school clothing, school and classroom etiquette, and rules and regulations. Students can also read a story about academic pressure and discuss why Chinese people value education so highly. A Singapore film, titled "*I not Stupid*" ("小孩不笨"), describes in great detail the academic pressures placed on children in Chinese families by their schools and their parents. Students can understand through this film that for Chinese, the ultimate value of education has to do with parents' expectations for the future development of their children. This also demonstrates the impact of the traditional concepts of social class on modern life.

In terms of changes in Chinese political structures, students should first know about the pattern of political control by the emperors, before they are able to understand differences in governmental administration. A good warm up activity to attract student interest is to show an episode from the movie "*The Last Emperor*", especially the part about the life of the little emperor in the palace. Students are all very curious to know about all kinds of things in the Chinese court. After the movie, play the game of "Acting as the emperor". Use a version of Chinese divination sticks to decide who will become emperor. The person who is chosen emperor can propose three new laws to govern the country, with the other students acting as different classes of people and expressing personal opinions about these new laws. By engaging in this activity, students can consider the impact of the emperor on people's lives, and the different perspectives of the emperor and the masses.

In order to enhance student understanding of the many aspects of the influence of one person imperial rule on the lives of the masses, the stories of Yang Guifei and Wu Zetian with anecdotes from the imperial palace provide entertaining lessons, especially when using pictures to accompany the story. Of course, as the teacher tells the story it is important to understand the key points, pose questions to the students from time to time, or ask students to dramatize part of the story line; this allows students and teacher a process of continuous interaction in listening to the story, in order to maintain student interest in learning and deepen their impression of the topic.

After this, ask students to make a comparison with the American form of government, to list the advantages and disadvantages of "single person rule" with "multi-party government" and drawing on the contents of this list to write out and support their own point of view. In terms of the differences between multi-party government and single-party government, the teacher can have students divide and simulate a multi-party and single-party government conference, to vote on matters, and let students experience the different results of single-party and multi-party influences. Because 8th grade students at my school visit our state capital's legislative assembly every year for first hand learning about the process of assembly discussions, students have a deeper understanding of multi-party government from this practical demonstration. I recommend that teachers arrange for off campus real life experience activities to enhance student learning and achieve "twice the effect with half the effort" (事半功倍).

In talking about religion, the story "*Journey to the West*" will certainly stimulate student interest. Buddhism's ideas about the virtuous life and the concepts of good and evil are all displayed in the lives of the characters in this story. Students can learn the basic concepts of Buddhism from "*Journey to the West*" and can begin to understand the binding moral influence of religious faith on people's lives. Students come from different cultural backgrounds and have grown up in different environments, so certainly they will have different religious beliefs. The teacher can have students divide into groups according to their religious faiths and take turns explaining to the class their religious teachings. They can share some religious images, music, or materials, and further explain the required rituals and restrictions in daily life. Such sharing can help students develop respect for different religions, while at the same time learning to understand the cultural influences of religion and its significance in individual lives.

Prior to the 20th century, what types of exchange relationships did China have with other countries? How did this affect China? We can play a computer search competition: 1) The teacher makes a list asking for the origins of fruit and vegetable sources and have students compete in searching for when they were introduced to China: for example corn, walnuts, pomegranates, spinach, carrots, grapes, parsley, watermelon, figs, peppers, eggplant, and green beans; 2) Ask the students to find out which Chinese technologies spread to Central Asia, Western Asia and Europe; 3) When did Buddhism, Christianity, and Islam spread to China? Through this game the students will learn the time periods of exchanges between China and other countries. In addition you can add short reading selections on Marco Polo, Xuan Zang, Genghis Khan, and Zheng He as after school reading assignments. During class have students take turns presenting an overview of the contents and their impressions of the readings they have chosen (directing them toward their views of the relationships between China and other countries). At the same time have students pose questions to each other, and in this way not only enrich their knowledge level, but also promote student reflections on their understanding of the material.

I suggest that the teacher find some books in the library on the Han Dynasty Silk Road as well as history books on the golden age of the Tang Dynasty. Usually the images used to present history in English books are very plentiful; in the past I have used images of business transactions in the Tang Dynasty Chang'an city to enable students to discover the clothing, materials, and hairstyles of buyers and sellers from different areas, and to guide students to reflect on the mutual influences arising from exchange activities. In another assignment, I arrange for students to borrow library books and ask them to search for images and historical records of China's exchanges with the world prior to the 20th century and bring to the classroom to show. I ask students to report on the contents of their readings and have other students take notes while listening to these reports. I then ask the students to combine their notes together to draw up a timetable and to write an article on the impact on China of the exchange relations between China and other countries. The hope for this project is that students do self-directed reading, listen to reports of other studies, put together the key points of these contents, and then, according to their levels of personal understanding, freely present their views.

History is, in fact, alive. As long as teachers can continuously plan for innovative changes in curriculum design and learning activities; use more diverse kinds of materials to compliment activities; simultaneously grasp the direction of student interest in the topic; and have sensitivity toward the everyday things in student life, then history lessons will not be dull.

The idioms, proverbs, and poetry excerpts recommended for this unit should be selected by teachers to match the different emphases on teaching contents and materials, please refer to the master thematic table.

Unit Topic Six: Friends, Fun, Fashions and Fads

The learning objectives for the thematic unit "Friends, Fun, Fashions and Fads" aim for student understanding of the Chinese cultural views of friendship and how this affects people lives; learning how to build friendly relationships with friends; and how fashion influences social values and relationships.

As 7th and 8th grade students grow older, their self-awareness is gradually increasing and they tend to speak their minds on everything; their psychological state can be both sensitive and subtle. I consider 7th grade as a period where personal style is taking shape; by 8th grade their self-image and character have emerged. In terms of selecting friends, social interactions at school are a major prerequisite. In other words, their success in social relationships depends on whether or not they are welcomed or worshipped at school. At this time the selection criteria for friends often depends on whether they are "cool" so that "cool friends" become more important than so called good or helpful friends.

How can we best teach this subject without arousing student sensitivities, especially for those without many friends or students who are often teased by others? I recommend that you can first have students divide into collaborative groups in order to create four cartoons on the subject "What is a Friend?". Use cartoons to represent dealings between friends. Each group shares its results with the rest of the class and after sharing, ask students to write on a card three adjectives describing the meaning of friend. The teacher pastes the adjectives written by students on a previously prepared wall board for everyone to share. Then, have the students listen to a song sung by Zhou Huajian ("*Friends*"), and ask students to write down the lyrics while listening. Divide students into groups where they read their lyrics aloud and other students help them to correct their errors. Then replay the song and have students sing along with the lyrics. Then have students write down three situations where friends are most needed; students take turns reading out the situations they have selected, and the teacher takes the cards they have written and attaches them to the wall board.

After this activity, students should have a basic view of the definition of friend, so now there is no harm in playing the game "Who is your friend?" Choose a student to go to the front of the stage, and have the teacher ask the student a few questions about their personal hobbies. At the same time the other students write down answers and see who has written the same responses as the student on the stage. The game can provide active interaction between students. Next, play a music video of South Korean, Ahn Jae Wook, singing "*Friends*" Several short stories are included along with the songs in the video. After students watch, using his performance techniques and with the background music of "*Friends*" have them divide into groups and produce a five-minute video story. Prior to production, the teacher can pose some questions to have students consider how to demonstrate their ideas through the video. For example: How do you choose a friend? What can friends do for you? How do you express your concern for a friend? How do you maintain friendship between friends? What sorts of fun activities create feelings between friends? The students have freedom of expression to complete their video. Afterwards they share with the whole class and while sharing they elaborate on their definitions of friendship, as well as making personal recommendations for relationships between friends. Schools without video equipment may require students to combine photos and text to present a story and display the contents.

  Teachers can share their own experiences of making friends when they were growing up as a way of introducing students to the topic of mutual influences. In due course, go into the restrictions that Chinese place on their sons' and daughters' choices of friends and places of activities: for example, selecting friends from the perspective that "proximity to cinnabar makes you red, pitch makes you black" (近朱者赤,近墨者黑); taboos about situations where friends can travel together; patterns of association and behavior between males and females; clothing styles, etc. The teacher designs a questionnaire and asks the students to interview their parents or another teacher at school. Through these interviews they will understand how people of different generations define the concept of friendship, dating methods, and forms of emotional expression, as well as how they choose situations for social interaction. Take the results of these interviews and compare them with the present generation to make a Power Point presentation. Arrange a homework assignment asking students to read the short essay *"Mozi Passing Through the Dye Workshop"* and write an essay on how friends affect your life.

  In terms of fashion, students can talk endlessly about this topic, whether it is hair, clothes, movies, novels, music, dance, make-up, etc. I have found that in teaching lessons about geography and history, students are very curious about the portraits of historical figures and their clothing styles. Students are even fond of copying the clothing and hairstyles of different dynasties and discussing the standards of beauty and ugliness in society at that time. So I suggest that teachers might have students arrange a "fashion era" image collection project; have students do a computer search of popular clothing, hairstyles, music, and slang in China during the 70s, 80s, 90s, and today. Cut and paste the images and text to make a "Past and present" chart, then insert textual explanations in between the images. In keeping with the mood of study in this unit, a friendly fashion show is also not a bad idea. Afterwards ask students to collect materials and divide into groups to perform a short skit on fashions and their affects on interpersonal relationships. Lastly, have a class discussion on how fashion brands reflect social values. Before this discussion students must prepare data on actual events to support and explain their views.

Recommended idioms for this unit include:一诺千金;莫逆之交;志同道合;生死之交;手足之情;义无反顾;忘恩负义;见义勇为;近朱者赤,近墨者黑. Ancient story of friendship about Guan Zhong and Bao Shuga (管仲,鲍叔牙).

Unit Topic Seven: Creative Arts and Sciences

In approaching the subject of Chinese arts, you certainly cannot ignore the traditional Chinese festival folk arts such as paper cuts, window flowers, fragrant pouches, shadow puppets, storytelling, local opera, etc. During the units organized around traditional festivals, I believe that students from 1st through 7th and 8th grades have the opportunity each year to enjoy making arts and crafts, and of course will review the meanings of these festivals. Therefore, in the 7th and 8th grade art and science thematic units, I propose to focus in 7th grade on teaching the art of Chinese calligraphy, painting and music, so that students can gradually strengthen their abilities of both comprehension and artistic appreciation. In 8th grade students will learn once again about China's four great inventions and the evolution of writing, language and technology.

In the past I liked to approach the topic of artistic appreciation of paintings by introducing students to the pleasurable viewing of landscape and flower paintings and explaining the different methods of meticulous and free hand drawing. Students would then have actual practice in using the brush for ink and wash paintings, and from this practice activity learn to distinguish different styles of painting. Afterwards, students would show the contents of their paintings and explain their feelings and opinions. Then, students would be encouraged to bring to class and share a Chinese painting that they especially like, and talk about why it is their favorite and how it makes them feel. Following this, the teacher would show examples of famous western paintings and ask students to discuss and explain the similarities and differences between the two styles.

The contents of this unit can introduce the four ancient Chinese philosophers: Confucius, Mencius, Laozi, and Zhuangzi and their advocates to help students have a basic understanding of the approaches towards life of Chinese scholars. Taiwanese cartoonist Cai Zhizhong has produced a cartoon CD of the sayings of Laozi, Confucius, Mencius, etc. using short stories to illustrate the ideas advocated by each thinker, which students find very easy to understand. The teacher can select short extracts from several theories as supplementary teaching explanation.

Before connecting to the appreciation of Chinese painting, the teacher should first discuss with students western ideas of realistic painting and abstract painting; then ask students to discuss the differences with Chinese landscape painting. This activity first lets students notice the degree to which realistic paintings represent reality; that abstract art represents an individual's imaginative ability and free creative expression, and that Chinese landscape painting is in between realistic and abstract styles, conveying a type of artistic mood. Through this sequence of cognitive learning, it is easier to guide students to experience the ideas behind traditional Chinese painting. You might as well invite students to try Chinese painting, to use natural landscapes, birds, and flowers to present their own personal characteristics, emotions, or ideas. Through this type of activity, students can somewhat experience the emotions of Chinese painting. Finally, have students view the Chinese paintings they have produced and say something about the artistic conception of their painting. The purpose of this activity is to encourage students to try to express the experience and ideas of making art, so you don't want to comment on what is right and wrong about student works.

Trying to figure out the creative concept of artists is very challenging for 7th and 8th grade students who live in a carefree environment and have no experience of the frustrations and psychological course of an artist's life, so their appreciation of art lies for the most part in the rendering of surface colors and lines. Therefore, the learning objectives should focus on student understanding and basic awareness of the differences in Chinese and western artistic expression.

How to appreciate the differences between western and Chinese music? For this unit I first prepare a world map and six different Asian and western musical genres. As students listen to the music they are asked to describe their personal impressions of the rhythm and style of the musical composition; to guess which country it comes from; and to place a label on the map. After enjoying the music, students take turns explaining their individual guesses and descriptions of the music. The teacher sums up the student answers and records them one by one on a whiteboard map. Finally, everyone listens once more to each musical piece and the answers are announced. The following discussion analyzes the differences in the musical instruments used in the songs. The teacher uses slides to show the various sorts and varieties of musical instruments, allowing students to practice distinguishing the different types of Asian and western musical instruments. Students are asked to imitate the sounds of the different musical instruments; of course for unfamiliar instruments, students can only do an imaginative simulation. Students then are divided into two groups of Asian and western instruments for a musical concert; each student represents one instrument and they simulate performing a song. This activity is very amusing and creates a lively classroom mood.

In order to deepen student impressions of the special characteristics of Chinese music, taking students to enjoy a local traditional Chinese musical performance is an excellent extra curricula activity; drawing on the theme of Chinese instruments and traditional music, visit local musicians. For a homework assignment, I ask students to read a short historical story, then let students freely select their favorite music or song to make connections and match the plot development and mood of the story. Students must listen to a variety of Chinese music, be familiar with the special characteristics of their music and copy an excerpt to a CD that is not more than five minutes long; students can also design cover pages for their CD. When this is finished, students play the music from their CD and orally explain the phases of the plot and why they selected this music. This project is rather challenging and requires more time, but students become especially absorbed in the process of designing their own CD; as a result, at the time of their final broadcast in the classroom, they have a great sense of accomplishment.

After gaining a basic understanding of Chinese music, you can ask students to enjoy a European opera and a Chinese Beijing opera. After this, have students divide into groups to make a comparison of styles of performance and singing skills and individually write the conclusions of their discussion on a large character poster. After this, show images of types of facial make-up in Beijing opera and study the different types of facial make-up for different characters. Also, have students research the meanings of the frequently used red, black, blue and white colors in Beijing opera make-up. Then ask students, based on the meaning of these colors, to draw an opera mask creatively matching colors. When the face masks are complete, students divide into groups and wearing masks perform a short play either in the style of western opera or Beijing opera. The learning goal is to raise student interest in Chinese opera and awareness of types of facial make-up in Beijing opera.

Middle school students all have their own favorite music which represents their personal style and taste. Have students share their favorite music with the class, taking turns playing and listening to music, and let students who like to dance accompany the music with their dance movements. After sharing, the teacher can play a few popular Chinese songs and have students listen to whether Chinese popular music has similarities with western popular music and similar dance movements. Have students select English and Chinese popular songs for comparison and explain their personal discoveries of similar points. This is a warm up activity; starting first with students sharing their favorite music, after stimulating their interest, you can proceed to enter into the study of Chinese folk music.

For this curricular unit I will ask students to go on the Internet and listen to several ethnic folksongs, then have students select their favorite song and report on the materials they've collected: where the folksong is from, the song's meaning, the special features of the music, how it differs from popular music, and why they like it. By having the students select their own materials, most students will actively complete this, and at the same time cultivate an interest in Chinese music.

Finally, you can organize a "music quiz" and give awards for answers, having students compare who has the most extensive musical knowledge. Before doing this activity, the teacher must spend some time to pick out in advance all kinds of music: for example, traditional music, folk music, classical music, and songs as well as different kinds of dance videos. During the course of the game in the classroom, the teacher first gives each student a small white board, then plays selected music or video. After the students listen and appreciate the music, pose the questions (the questions must be designed to match the focus of the unit) and ask students to answer the questions within a specified time on their small white board. When the time has ended, students cannot change their answers; each correct answer gets a certain number of points, with points based on the relative difficulty of the question. After the quiz is completed, the teacher can award small prizes to students with the top five scores. In addition, don't forget to give the rest of the students some chocolate to encourage their participation. Even though they are in 7th and 8th grade, students still need constant encouragement; especially after a competitive game, small prizes are a good way of encouraging them.

In talking about the evolution of Chinese characters, students in grades five and six will have received a basic introduction to changes in Chinese characters and different styles of writing. The teacher can start with a few warm up review activities. Begin with a game that assembles *chengyu* (four character phrases); prepare cards using a few different scripts (semi-cursive, grass, clerical) with a single character on each card and write all of the *chengyu* on the white board. Students divide into groups according to the *chengyu* listed on the white board, search out the characters for each *chengyu* and piece them together to form a phrase; see which group finishes first; afterwards students read aloud together the *chengyu* for their group, and one by one they explain the meaning of the *chengyu*. Then collect the character cards and put them in a paper box; students take turns taking out a character card and saying the name of the script and the dynasty in which that scrip appeared.

To enhance the students' interest in learning Chinese characters, I recommend that the teacher bring in another activity; prepare three paper posters, have students divide into three groups and individually write all of the characters they have learned on the posters. When this is complete, the teacher introduces the difference between pictograms, combined ideograms, and phonograms. Take the three posters and give them to different groups of students and have students classify the groups of characters as pictograms, combined ideograms, and phonograms, then record this on a table in their notebooks. In addition, you can arrange a group assignment; have students divide into groups and imitating the form of a Chinese calligraphy scroll, draw an original Chinese character and changes in shape with time period. Each group discusses their design and allocates the work of gathering resources. This project, in addition to improving student understanding of Chinese characters also nurtures student abilities to work in groups. Taking students to the local Chinatown to do a rubbing of a stone tablet is another very pleasurable extra curricular activity to extend learning. In addition, enjoying animated cartoons about Chinese characters on websites can increase the relaxed atmosphere of study in the classroom. I recommend two websites for teacher reference and use: character animation,① and stories of characters②.

Once students have a certain degree of knowledge and understanding about the evolution of Chinese characters, arrange for a homework assignment that asks students to use Power Point for an oral report that integrates their knowledge of the development of Chinese characters with the evolution of the western alphabet, giving students the opportunity for mutual comparisons with their own culture. In addition, the teacher can display Chinese books, newspapers, and magazines from different regions; have students personally discover the differences between complex and simplified characters, and the vertical and horizontal styles of writing forms, and explain the reasons behind the different reading styles. Students ought to understand that in modern countries that use Chinese writing, there are regional differences between the use of complex and simplified characters. The teacher can in due course explain the changes in the Chinese phonetic systems and the different phonetic systems used in books. Then have students use two different phonetic systems to write a short passage, and try out the vertical and horizontal styles of writing. From this writing experience students will gain a deep understanding of the different permutations in ways to read Chinese. Finally, to connect this to the different reading styles in Chinese and western languages, ask the students to make a simple descriptive table with a list of matching images and symbols for interpretation.

Following studies of China's four great inventions in the 3rd through 6th grades, 7th and 8th grade students can generally explain how the compass promoted the development of the sailing industry; how gunpowder was used in military affairs; how printing technology was used to disseminate knowledge, and the contribution of the invention of

---

① http://v.youku.com/v_show/id_XMTg1MTgxMDA=.html
② http://v.youku.com/v_show/id_XMTAwMTQ1OTk2.html

paper making to humanity. Therefore, I focus on the influence of the four great inventions on modern life, talking about them in terms of food, clothing, shelter, and transportation in our daily lives.

To begin with, I first display four large posters with a large round circle in the middle and each of the four inventions (gunpowder, printing, paper, compass) written in one of the circles. Around the large circle I draw small circles; I give the posters to four different groups of students, and ask students to brainstorm and discuss how things in modern life relate to these inventions, writing the names of things in the smaller circles surrounding the larger one. While the students are brainstorming, the teacher can provide examples of food, clothing, and shelter to lead the students into a broader level of thinking. For example, in addition to the development of the maritime industry, what direct relationship does the compass have on travel in our daily lives? Taking a plane, driving a car, taking a boat, asking directions, climbing a mountain... these are activities where you need to differentiate directions. Our dependence on food, clothing, and shelter pushes students through reflective discussion to discover the indirect and direct influences of the four great inventions on their own daily lives.

When speaking about the role of technological development in modern life, the content can be all inclusive. I think that a good way to enter this topic is through the communication devises that students just can't live without, for example, email, phone texts, video, and Facebook. What are the benefits of these technological conveniences? Why? Students are very enthusiastic about these topics, so after everyone shares their opinion, ask students to suggest common communication issues from Internet events that arise through social interaction; investigate the causes that triggered this event and the potential danger from online exchanges and make a report. Students of this age are very quick to master newly popular things, especially the application of new technology. Now almost every student knows how to use the iPhone, iPad and every new type of communication tool on the Internet. But they are still unable to differentiate the truthfulness of the sources of information or be alert to the dangers of disseminating information on the Internet. Consequently, teachers ought to in due course instruct students how to recognize the reliability of Internet information and make use of safe rules for Internet communication.

What is the position of technology in China? This is a large and complex question, so we can take as our focus how technological development in China has promoted rapid economic development and the changing impact of this on cultural life. Students can begin by studying this from the four levels of food, clothing, dwelling, and transportation to understand the importance of technology in economic development. The teacher can ask students to collect images of life in 1990s China and China today, to create a display board comparing "before" and "after" and when this is complete hold a small descriptive presentation in the classroom where each student takes a turn to explain changes and their effects in the contents of the images. I think images really stimulate students' reflections and leave a profound impression. In the process of displaying what they have clipped and pasted, students are especially interested in sharing the fascinating images they have found.

Next, have the students watch the video "*The Future Life of Humankind in 2015*"[1] and write down four changes using examples from this film. Presenting a short play is an activity that most students are happy to participate in, so invite students to take the topic "*Our Future Technological World*" and conceive of performing a short skit; after mutual observation reflect on how these kinds of forms of technology change our culture.

These are my personal recommendations for teaching activities. Teachers can modify and supplement these suggestions to match the needs, interests, and capabilities of their own students. By bringing together relevant idioms and proverbs as supplemental instruction, they can create an even richer and more interesting curriculum.

---

[1] http://www.secretchina.com/news/12/07/19/459934.html

Unit Topic Eight: Expressing Emotions and Feelings

The teaching objectives for 7th and 8th students in this unit are understanding cultural backgrounds in learning proper etiquette in responses to social interaction; promoting the management of individual moods; and appropriate patterns for expressing emotions in life. Patterns of emotional expression vary in relation to cultural background, so, for example, in the design of the 7th grade curriculum I start with individual displays of delight, anger, grief, and happiness; then enter into a discussion of student views of school regulations to trigger student emotional displays; then turn to talking about family relations and learning to understand different patterns of parental treatment; and finally link this topic to forms of emotional expression between males and females. Using the famous traditional Chinese story *"Butterfly Lovers"*, we enter into an investigation of Chinese and western cultural differences and a comparison of styles of expression. In 8th grade, teaching focuses on "Discovering cultural differences in family relations and emotional expressions" and "Chinese people's social attitudes and interpersonal etiquette". The extended range of this content is broader than in 7th grade.

Speaking about "emotions" is an awkward topic for students of 7th and 8th grade age level. Students enjoy using an adult attitude to express the maturity of their own emotions and feelings, but in talking about the topic of relationships between males and females can be sensitive and childish. Students still have a curious state of mind; for most students, this is the age of first love.

In order to prevent student oversensitivity in this unit, the teacher can first approach the topic through school life. For instance, the students can discuss their opinions of school regulations or problems that commonly arise in student relationships, etc. In order to limit the scope of the discussion, the teacher can prepare a questionnaire about managing emotions, allow students to interview each other, and tabulate the results of the interviews. While discussing, the student will also learn vocabulary and sentence patterns regarding emotions. Finally, ask students to select a problematic circumstance from the questionnaire that matches the interview results and design a cartoon image that demonstrates and shares their point of view. Using this small activity as a warm up can increase student interest in learning the content of the next phase.

Following this, we can use this topic to talk about the differences in emotional expression between two different generations. Students can freely express their opinions and ideas about their relationship with their parents; then, have students design a 10—15 question survey to interview their parents as homework. Before students design their questions, first have students practice interviewing the teacher; at the same time you can propose revisions of the students' questions. (The following questions can be used as a reference: What demands did your parents have for your studies at school? Did you think these were fair? In what ways did your parents encourage you to study? Did you like this? When you could not achieve according to your parents' demands, what was your parents' emotional response? When you made mistakes as a child, how were you punished? After your parents punished you, did they explain why? During everyday life with your parents, what types of etiquette did you need to pay attention to? What were family rules? Why? After this task is complete have students divide into groups and make a summary comparison of the results of their questionnaires, create a small skit to perform in the classroom. As other groups watch their performance, they need to take notes. Then ask each group of students to work together to make a Power Point that explains the different emotional expressions in their parents and their own generation and their reasons. Because students have a stereotypical view of their parents, this exercise can help students discover and understand the relationships between themselves and their parents. The family television show "*Families with Children*"（家有儿女）is a very good supplementary audiovisual teaching material; students can learn about the structures of modern Chinese families, differences in parental discipline of children, as well as modern family values. I also personally recommend that teachers use as reading material Zhu Ziqing's literary work "*Rearview*"（背影）which can give students a very profound experience of parental hearts.

The next discussion focuses on differences in emotional expression between men and women. The teacher can use the question "who do you idolize" to lead a discussion about viewpoints of the opposite sex. Students learn how to describe the appearance and distinctive features (of their idols) and explain their charm; then they can vote to select the most liked person and after this summarize their favorite accepted standards. Prepare two groups to create posters for current Chinese and western idols and have students vote to select two widely-liked idols from each group. Then have students play the "Idol match" game and talk about what criteria they used to match their idols. Afterward, use this topic to lead into the subject of the appropriate age for men and women to date and have a simple discussion.

How do males and females express mutual love for each other? I believe that students can quickly speak out about all kinds of ways and for the most part these methods are very direct. I ask students to avoid using the direct vocabulary like "love" and "like" and write a sentence on a card that expresses emotions towards someone they like in an indirect and implicit manner. The cards are collected in a small box; students divide into two groups and each group assigns a student to take a card out of the box. The two students take turns reading aloud the sentence from the card. Using a show of hands, students vote on which sentence show the most appropriate subtle expression. This activity is very interesting; when sharing each student's creative text, there is repeated laughter, creating a high level of student participation.

Next, have students bring in an English love poem and ask students to translate this into Chinese. The process of translation is not just about learning words and expressing things through different sentence patterns; students also have the opportunity to compare and contrast with their own native language while also experiencing the emotions of the verse. After this practice, the teacher can have students create their own love poem. Require students to write a first draft; the teacher reviews this and makes suggestions; the students revise and complete their work and are asked to type this and attach an appropriate image to their final manuscript. Although this educational activity takes a somewhat longer time, after students have completed this assignment, they feel very proud of their accomplishment, making this a very worthwhile activity for teacher's reference. Also, to enhance student reading abilities and to confirm the results of student learning, the teacher can select a modern love poem and use written exam questions to test their comprehension.

In addition, using supplementary films to increase student understanding of Chinese cultural background takes them a step forward in understanding the meanings behind certain patterns of emotional expression. The film "*Chinese Moon*" ("中国月亮") provides very suitable supplementary audiovisual teaching material. This film, which contains many amusing situations that arise due to differences in Chinese and American styles of behavior, is very entertaining. The teacher can select a few segments of the film for students to watch and discuss, increasing students' knowledge and respect for Chinese peoples lives and culture. However, I recommend that teachers omit the beginning section about the life of the male lead in America and select sections of the film that are more appropriate.

A final unit activity is to read the story of "*Liang Shanbo and Zhu Yingtai*"; after reading in the classroom, divide into groups and draw the major plot lines on a poster board; then go on stage to display the main images and report a brief synopsis of the story. I recommend that the teacher accompany this with listening to the film music from "*Liang Zhu*" to let students experience the changing moods and emotions in the story's plot. For example, you can play different sections of music and have students guess what part of the story it comes from and what emotions are being expressed. Ask students to simulate matching music to perform that section of the story.

The general assessment for this project is a group creative project. Divide students into groups and using the outline of the story "*Liang Shanbo and Zhu Yingtai*" merge Chinese and American cultural customs and patterns of expression to change the development of the plot and the final outcome. The space for creative development here is both broad and free, so students can use their own level of understanding of the story to integrate different cultural patterns of emotional expression rendered through drama. This is the ultimate learning objective for the educational theme of this unit.

Unit Plan Example: Expressing Emotions and Feelings (Grade 7, 4 weeks)

Essential Questions	Focus Questions
1. What is emotion? 2. How do we express our feelings? 3. How and why do people express emotions in different ways? 4. How do expressions of emotion affect social relationships?	1. Where do people's emotions come from? 2. What do you think is the appropriate way to express happiness? 3. What are the different ways of expressing emotions? 4. How do emotions affect our behavior? 5. What kind of factors affect the different expression of individual emotions? 6. What do you think are the differences in the ways that Chinese and Western people express emotions? Why? 7. How do you express emotions differently with family members and with friends? Why? 8. How do males and females express emotions in different ways? How can inappropriate emotional expressions lead to misunderstandings? 9. When you are with friends from different cultural backgrounds, have you ever encountered interesting situations or misunderstandings due to different ways of expressing emotions? Please explain. 10. How do you solve the misunderstandings that arise with friends from different cultures?

Functional Outcome/Skills

• Students are able to use correct words and phrases to communicate information, ideas and opinions about emotion in ways that are comprehensible to a native speaker.

• Students are able to give examples and explain the special characteristics and cultural background behind emotional expressions of Chinese children.

• Students are able to compare and contrast emotional expressions, including those between Americans and Chinese.

• Students can use Chinese to communicate both within and outside of class.

Assessment

a) Formative Assessment

• Report on results of questionnaire on how moods are managed (Oral: word and sentence pattern use/grammar).

• Design written questionnaire to interview parents (Writing: word and sentence patterns/grammar).

• Love letter/poem: read and answer questions (Content understanding).

• Create love letters (Writing: word and sentence pattern use/grammar).

• Answer questions about the story "*Liang Shanbo and Zhu Yingtai*" (Content understanding).

• Description of film synopsis (Oral: word and sentence pattern use/grammar).

b) Summative Assessment (Group Projects)

• PowerPoint report: Explain reasons for different emotional expressions in two different generations (parents and students).

• Compile a script: Merging Chinese and American practices and styles of cultural expression; change plot development and conclusion

• Dramatic performance: Through dramatic performance, students display their creative plots.

Weekly Plans

Week One	
Teaching Objectives	• Students are able to use vocabulary and sentence patterns related to emotions to explain their feelings
Lesson Contents	• Personal views of school rules • Understanding the emotional expressions of the parental generation
Materials	• Scenario questionnaire, paper sheets with tabular spaces, sheets of paper to post on the wall • *"Families with Children"*①
Learning Exercises	• Interview each other using scenario questionnaire. • Drawing on interview results, present a creative cartoon image. • Have a class discussion sharing views and opinions about school regulations. • Design an emotional expressions questionnaire for parents and interview parents. • Groups perform skits that compare their different interview results. • Watch the short video *"Families with Children"* to enhance students' understanding of the different emotional expressions in Chinese families. • Read Zhu Ziqing's *"Rear View"*
Formative Assessments	Oral report on interview results, design parental questionnaire, dramatic performances

---

① Refer to the website: http://dianshiju.cntv.cn/city/jiayouernv/videopage/index.shtml; http://www.tudou.com/programs/view/dgegzIgzGXA/

Week Two	
Teaching Objectives	• Students understand different ways of expressing affection between men and women • Students can express personal feelings in appropriate ways
Lesson Contents	• Setting standards for idol/celebrity worship and ways of expressing degrees of liking • Expressing emotions in different ways with people of the same sex and different sex • Expressing positive and negative emotions with the opposite sex • Recognizing cultural backgrounds in dealing with emotional misunderstandings
Materials	• Pictures of American and Chinese celebrities, voting list, cards • Movie: "China Moon"
Learning Exercises	• Vote for idols, discuss personal idol standards—teacher prepares two groups of current Chinese and American stars and singers so that students can select by vote the two top idols. • Divide into groups and discuss different male and female student norms and requirements for idols. • Idol matching game—this activity not only reveals student standards towards boyfriends/girlfriends, but also through this relaxed and interesting game it is easy to begin to discuss the topic of appropriate ages for male and female dating. • "In a word"—give each student a card, ask students to avoid using the direct vocabulary like "love" and "like" and write a sentence on a card that expresses emotions towards someone they like in an indirect and implicit manner. Collect the cards in a small box and divide students into

(Continued)

	Week Two
	two groups; each group assigns a student to choose a card, go on stage, and read the card aloud. Using a show of hands, students vote on which sentence shows the most appropriate subtle expression. Continue to have two people choose cards and compare to the end of all of the cards, then take the chosen cards and post them on the bulletin board for student reference and enjoyment. • Watch the movie *"China Moon"* and discuss the reasons for Chinese and Western misunderstandings and suggest suitable ways to respond.
Formative Assessment	Oral report: compare male and female emotional expressions and standards for love in different circumstances

	Week Three
Teaching Objectives	• Students understand and can explain the reading material—examples of love letters and love poems • Students can express feelings toward the opposite sex in writing
Lesson Contents	• Sharing English love poems • Reading love poetry • Writing a love poem
Materials	• Sample love letters[1] • Love poem: Zheng Chouyu *"Mistaken"*[2]

---

[1] Refer to the website: http://www.yiding8.com/qsdq/2007－3－9/QingShuFanLi-1－4-bmow0141.htm

[2] Refer to the website: http://blog.sina.com.cn/s/blog_4e0711140100bytm.html

(Continued)

	Week Three
	• Handicraft materials, Chinese composition paper
Learning Exercises	• Students bring a favorite English love poem, translate into Chinese, and share. • Create a love poem; study different styles of expression in Chinese and English. • Divide students into groups to work on reading comprehension of a Chinese style love letter. Allow students to express their understandings of the material in different ways; for example, students can do this through pictures, songs, three dimensional figures, stage props, short skits, music, movement, etc. • Write a love letter: during the writing process the teacher should provide assistance and watch carefully that the students use appropriate phrases and sentence patterns.
Formative Assessment	• Poem reading comprehension test • Write a love letter

	Week Four
Teaching Objectives	• Students understand the influence of Chinese and Western cultural backgrounds on emotional expressions • Students can compare cultural differences in writing romance scripts
Lesson Contents	• Story of "Liang Shanbo and Zhu Yingtai"

(Continued)

	Week Four
Materials	• DVD: "*Liang Shanbo and Zhu Yingtai*" • Reading materials: "*Liang Shanbo and Zhu Yingtai*" (读故事学汉语——北京语言大学出版社) • Violin concerto music: "*Liang Shanbo and Zhu Yingtai*"[①] • Movie questions, sheets of paper to post on the wall, writing paper
Learning Exercises	• Read "*Liang Shanbo and Zhu Yingtai*" story, raise questions about understanding of story contents. • After reading is finished, ask students to write comprehension questions. • Play a section of the music from "*Liang Shanbo and Zhu Yingtai*"; ask students to imagine plot development and dialogue in the performance of the story. • Group Creation: Divide into groups and discuss the allocation of roles, background of the story, and the general plot development to rearrange the story "*Liang Shanbo and Zhu Yingtai*".
Formative Assessments	Story reading comprehension questionnaire, short musical dramatic performance
Final Assessment	Dramatic script, dramatic performance

Teaching Suggestions

Designing unit questions: Guiding questions for the themes of this unit should be based on the contents of the teaching materials. In order to improve student interest in learning, when designing questions use basic what, who, why, and how questions as much as possible to

---

[①] http://www.youtube.com/watch? v=5Egmjy8BbME

connect teaching contents and processes. For reference, here is a sample list of questions for themes in this unit:

1. What do you like to do when you are feeling happy? With whom?
2. What do you do when you are feeling unhappy? Why?
3. Which school regulations do you feel are unreasonable? Why?
4. What demands do your parents place on you at home? Do you think they are fair? Why?
5. Who can you talk to about personal matters? Why?
6. How do you choose your friends?
7. What do you like to do when you are together with your friends? Why?
8. If your friend says something in public that makes you uncomfortable, what can you do? Why?
9. When you and your friends have differences of opinion and argue, what should you do?
10. When you don't agree with what your parents say, how do you express your views?
11. When you are unhappy, how do your attitudes differ with your family and friends? Why?
12. How do you let your family members know that you love and care for them?
13. How do you express your feelings to your boyfriend/girlfriend? Please clarify with an example.
14. What do you think are the differences in the ways that males and females express their emotions? Why?
15. Why are Chinese emotional expressions between males and females different from emotional expressions between American males and females?

16. When you are with friends from different cultural backgrounds have you ever encountered interesting situations or misunderstandings because of different styles of expression? Please explain.
17. How do you resolve misunderstandings due to cultural differences between friends?

Vocabulary and Sentence Patterns: These should draw from the educational reading materials prepared by the teacher according to the course design and related themes and can increase or decrease in relation to the language levels of the students. The following are some examples of vocabulary and sentence patterns related to this unit:

◆ **Vocabulary**
紧张、担心、丢脸、烦恼、伤心、抱歉、惊讶、尴尬、害羞、内向、外向、活泼、谈恋爱、失恋、心情、压力、自由、约定、约会、暗示、直接、含蓄、婉转、来往、表达、觉得、建议、应该、理会、了解、比较、合得来/合不来、含蓄、开放、冲突、理解、体谅、代沟、观点、角度、立场

◆ **Sentence Patterns**
万一……该怎么办；对……有兴趣；为了……而……；如果……可以……；不但……反而……；由于……造成……；不仅……而且……

◆ **Idioms**
七上八下；不知所措；男女授受不亲；一见如故；一刀两断；日有所思,夜有所梦

Whyte

Chapter Seven Ongoing Challenges: Materials, Real World Assessments, Teacher Training

The previous chapters have described numerous creative approaches to integrating language and culture instruction at different grade levels. Once again, however, we wish to emphasize that these suggestions and the Master Thematic Table offer suggestions for a curricular framework that will need to be constructed independently by each specific program. As teachers, curriculum specialists, and others embark on this endeavor, they need to pay attention to several key issues that serve as the focus for this final chapter, namely: instructional materials, student assessments, and teacher training.

Engaging Materials

Identifying and assembling appropriate, engaging materials requires both sustained effort and creativity. Previous chapters have featured numerous examples of resources (including texts, songs, film clips, games, internet sites, etc.) that support the style of student-centered, thematic instruction which we advocate. Unlike an older approach to teaching foreign language, where the selection of appropriate texts and supplementary materials dictates lesson topics, this model requires that curricular design begin with a series of thematic (essential and focus) questions that in turn inform the choice of materials used to address these questions and engage student interest. ① Given the inevitable diversity of such topics and their related materials, certain criteria must guide the selection of instructional resources.

One obvious objective, of course, is to identify age appropriate materials that connect with student interests. Keep in mind that topics which might appeal to Chinese students (and parents) in mainland China, Hong Kong or Taiwan will not necessarily appeal to American students, who come from a diverse array of ethnic and linguistic backgrounds. ② Chinese teachers with more limited experience in American classrooms might find it useful to consult the topics and lessons used in the English based curriculum, both as a way to gauge expected levels of student comprehension and as suggestions for possible topics that can be mirrored in both the English and the Chinese curriculum to reinforce student learning. By third grade, the school, district, or state mandated social studies standards should also serve as a guide in selecting appropriate topics and materials related to geography, history, politics, and broader global issues. ③ Remember also that students at the same grade level are not uniform in interests and abilities; topics and related materials need to appeal to the often diverse passions and life experiences of both boys and girls and to students with a range of different aptitudes and learning styles. Thus, teachers should not expect that all students will be equally engaged in every topic and lesson, but should consciously select a range of texts and design a range of learning activities that can eventually connect at some point with each and all of their students.

---

① We are following here, in general, the model developed by Wiggens and McTighe (2005) in *Understanding by Design*.

② Chinese language classes in the United State integrate students from ethnic Chinese, mixed Asian, and non-Asian families. Also, ethnic Chinese students may come from families who speak Cantonese (or other Chinese dialects), Mandarin, or English at home and can also include adoptees being raised by non-Chinese parents.

③ See, for example, *the Oregon Social Studies Standards*: www.ode.state.or.us.

Beyond student interests and general cognitive abilities, teachers also need to pay close attention to the requirements of foreign language pedagogy in selecting instructional materials. Lessons on different topics need to draw upon and repeat vocabulary and grammatical structures from previous lessons if students are to master communication skills in a cumulative and sustained way. Because language and culture learning are iterative processes, model lessons on single culture topics, no matter how appealing, are only useful if they are integrated into a set of connecting lessons, all of which are linked to a broader set of carefully articulated grade level linguistic and cultural goals.① The selection of Chinese language and culture materials must always keep this in mind.

What then, are our suggestions for locating and using specific materials and resources? Language textbooks and authentic materials might be considered at two extreme ends of a continuum of possible resources, each with their advantages and disadvantages. Well conceived Chinese language texts that have been developed for younger students systematically present and review vocabulary and linguistic structures, but typically lack an integrated approach to Chinese culture (Li Yu 2009) and usually have diminishing appeal for upper primary and middle school students. Teachers might wish to consult textbooks as they set language goals and may find selective lessons useful for their students, but we generally do not advocate adopting textbooks as the main form of classroom instruction. By contrast, authentic materials (aural and written forms of communication produced by and for people within a particular culture, such as announcements, newspapers, catalogues, music, TV shows, maps, train schedules, poetry, Internet

---

① See, for example, the sample lessons in the chapter "Standards for Chinese Language Learning" included in *Standards for Foreign Language Learning: Preparing for the 21ˢᵗ Century* (1996:159—198). Although the topics and suggested teaching strategies are carefully constructed, if taught as stand alone units without subsequent repetition and reinforcement, student learning outcomes would quickly fade.

sites, etc.) are both culturally rich and excitingly realistic. Authentic materials challenge students to transfer their classroom acquired knowledge and skills to real Chinese contexts and create opportunities for practicing use of their second language in flexible ways. ① Field trips to local Chinese communities obviously provide one source of authentic engagement and should be carefully integrated into the curriculum where available. More commonly, however, the major connection to a wide range of authentic Chinese language materials comes through the Internet, as described with numerous examples in preceding chapters. Some language specialists advocate giving primacy to authentic materials in foreign language instruction, but this approach has limitations, especially for K—8 students. With the exception of Chinese language websites developed for younger children, most authentic materials from Chinese Internet sources are aimed at adult interests and activities. Even with child friendly Chinese sites and materials, the gap between native and second language abilities can make them difficult for American students to use. With certain exceptions, such as some illustrated story books, language based authentic materials work best with students in grades 4—8. ② For younger students, authentic visual and tactile materials can enrich classroom lessons, but teachers need to use other types of instructional materials to systematically build the language skills that will eventually enable students to connect to a wider array of authentic language-based resources. In all cases, teachers need to carefully consider whether authentic materials are appropriate for their students' developmental and linguistic abilities. Also, in order to discourage direct student access to inappropriate Internetsites, teachers should be prepared to extract materials for student use where necessary.

---

① To quote Jennifer Eddy in her CEC workshop (2010): "Using a language appropriately in a given culture requires high adaptability, tolerance of new situations, dealing with incomplete information and problem solving without cues." Authentic materials offer one way for teachers to integrate these types of experiences into classroom instruction.

② Even illustrated story books, if they are written to be read by Chinese parents to their children, can feature vocabulary that is much too complex for young second language learners.

教汉语,教文化:美国幼儿园至八年级汉语及中国文化课程设计

In addition to Internet based Chinese language and culture learning sites, an expanding array of Chinese books and magazines aimed at younger students are available through bookstores in major cities in the US and Asia. Online catalogues and websites (such as China Sprout and Cheng & Tsui) offer a wide range of colorful story books, games, music, videos, maps, and other reference materials that teachers will find useful. It is important to have a variety of resources available for student use not only in classroom exercises, but as supplementary materials that students will be assigned to read outside of class. Students learning to read English in American primary schools are typically expected to practice reading for at least 20 minutes each day outside of class, and there should be a similar expectation with Chinese. Teachers and schools will need to make these reading materials available to students, paying close attention to matching texts with student reading levels and interests. Many teachers in the schools that I researched kept a selection of such books in their classrooms, where they were able to monitor what students read and periodically assess student comprehension of these materials. I would recommend a similar model, with school budgets including funding for these types of classroom resources. School libraries will also want to build a collection of age and language appropriate Chinese materials to entice further student reading and exploration in their second language. Because there are a wide range of levels in Chinese children's books, rating the relative difficulty of books available in the library or classroom collections can help students select materials that match their interests and abilities. ①

---

① For example, the Chinese International School in Hong Kong had small booklets that rated the level of difficulty for all Chinese books available in the school library. These booklets were used to recommend appropriate supplementary readings to students at different grade levels.

Real World Assessment

People of my generation tend to think of assessment in terms of report cards and final grades. There are, however, many different types of assessment whose goals include not only the demonstration of student mastery of standards, but also the provision of important feedback for teachers as they continually adjust instructional formats and pace for specific classes of students. In fact, the purposes of assessment are multiple: evaluations can be used to monitor student progress, clarify learning expectations, motivate student performance, further educate students, communicate outcomes, document results, and evaluate program content (Blaz 2001: 6—8). Regular testing of students in foreign language classrooms on the four skills of listening, speaking, reading and writing is a long established practice, but more recent assessment protocols have increasingly shifted from old-style static pencil and paper type exams to a more dynamic performative based approach, as exemplified by the Integrated Performance Assessment, or IPA.① Assessment tasks in this model are integrated into daily instruction and circulate through interpretive tasks (using a variety of written, aural, and visual materials), interpersonal tasks (where students exchange information and ideas in dyads or small groups), and presentational tasks (which feature oral or written presentations, either individually or in groups). Many examples of such performative tasks have been offered in previous chapters with the implicit understanding that observations of student performance will provide teachers with ongoing assessments of student progress, which will in turn shape decisions about subsequent teaching strategies.

In model units on the theme of Emotion at the end of each chapter,

---

① Developed by ACTFL with the support of a US Department of Education Grant in 1997, the IPA aims to provide students with ongoing feedback on performance both "to improve learner performance as well as to strengthen instructional practices" (Adair-Hauck et. al. 2006: 363).

Tien Whyte and Li-Ling Cheng have also provided examples of more explicit types of student evaluation, phrased in terms of formative and summative assessments. In general, formative assessments are incorporated into instructional practices and provide ongoing feedback to both teachers and students on their progress towards meeting learning goals. Summative assessments provide an opportunity to measure what students know at a particular point in time, often at the end of a unit, a semester, or even the end of the year. As Garrison and Ehringhaus observe "in a balanced assessment system, both summative and formative assessments are an integral part of information gathering. Depend too much on one or the other and the reality of student achievement in your classroom becomes unclear (2001)."

Evaluating student performance on assessments where tasks lack clearly demarcated right and wrong answers (unlike traditional multiple choice or fill-in-the-blank exams) requires the careful development of rubrics that outline and list criteria for scoring student achievement. Both Blaz (2001) and Sandrock (2011) provide numerous examples of how to develop performance assessment tasks and rubrics for evaluating foreign language competency. Similar approaches should be developed for assessment tasks and scoring rubrics that focus more specifically on cultural behaviors and cultural understandings. In a chapter on testing cultural competence, Bartz and Vermett argue that "while a language and its culture interact, the assessment of cultural proficiency should focus as narrowly and as clearly as possible on measuring the cultural component of an interaction (1996)." These authors list and describe 16 types of evaluation for cultural competence that range from portfolio assessment; to more specific tests of student responses to cultural scenarios and cross-cultural conflict situations; to questioning students about the significance of key facts and events. Although these examples were developed for French foreign language students, many of the ideas proposed in this chapter could be productively adapted to evaluating both the short term and long term progress of cultural understanding and knowledge among K—8 Mandarin students.

Finally, students should be actively involved in the assessment process, both as assessors of their own learning and in providing feedback to teachers on the positive and negative features of their lessons. Although this style of assessment can require extra time and flexibility from both teacher and students, it is essential to perform if we hope to better understand what works and doesn't work for our students individually and for the program at large.

Teacher Training

Although ongoing teacher training is an expected and well established component of K—8 education in the US, the model of instruction that we propose requires particular attention to specific areas of teacher preparation. At present, numerous workshops, conferences, and teacher training classes offer instruction in how to teach Chinese language to foreign students, but often do not distinguish between student age levels (frequently assuming an older learner) and tend to focus largely on linguistic issues. Programs that chose to adopt the framework proposed by our project will need to assist teachers in adapting to new instructional styles; guide teachers to understand and teach about Chinese culture in new ways; and support teachers as they work in teams to develop age-appropriate curriculum that builds from one grade to the next.

The majority of K—8 Chinese language teachers in American schools have been raised and educated in the Chinese settings of mainland China, Taiwan, and Hong Kong, where classroom lessons usually follow mandated textbooks and instructional styles are more teacher focused. Their teacher training in the US will have encouraged a more student-centered approach, an objective that Chinese language teachers continue to seek to refine (Ning 2009). Participation in summer workshops such as STARTALK, where foreign language teachers are trained in active student learning strategies, can further reinforce the shift in focus from teacher to student centered instruction.

Interacting with other teachers at such workshops also provides opportunities for teachers to share successful teaching strategies and materials from their own classroom experiences.

Learning how to introduce and incorporate Chinese culture into language lessons presents additional challenges. Most immigrant Chinese teachers initially equate Chinese culture with the kinds of historic, literary, and artistic culture that they learned in school (*wenhua*), and need to be encouraged to conceive of culture also in terms of daily customs and practices (*fengsu xiguan*). Like many other foreign language teachers, they have not been educated to think in self-conscious ways about the relationship between cultural perspectives, practices, and products (Schulz 2007). Immigrant teachers may also find it difficult to recognize and teach about features of Chinese behavioral culture that they unconsciously take for granted. Our team of teachers discovered that working together and brainstorming about topics linked to behavioral culture pushed us to think about these aspects of culture in new ways. I would also recommend that teachers consult books that focus on issues of cross-cultural communication such as *Doing Culture* (Davis 2001) or *Writing and Culture* (Deng and Liu 1989). These authors present numerous examples of the implicit types of cultural differences that can easily lead to cross-cultural misunderstandings. Additionally, books that instruct students in the contextual use of language such as *When to Say What* (Feng and Liao 2008) or *The Way We Communicate* (Kuo 2009) can provide Chinese teachers with useful strategies for teaching culturally engaged forms of communication.

The reality of Chinese cultural diversity and the need to avoid overly stereotypical approaches to Chinese culture is another important issue. It is easy to equate daily culture with our own experiences, and some immigrant teachers may know comparatively little about the diversity of Chinese ways of life in different Chinese communities or among people of different socioeconomic classes. Teachers need to be supported in learning more about Chinese communities and customs outside of their own native birthplace, either through personal reading and research or perhaps by bringing diverse groups of Chinese teachers together to compare and contrast perspectives and experiences. It is also useful for teachers to cultivate some understanding of the diverse Chinese communities outside of mainland China, Taiwan and Hong Kong, such as those in Southeast Asia, Europe, North America and elsewhere. This type of information is increasingly available through books or on the Internet, and I would also highly recommend a set of DVDs produced in 2005 that documents Chinatowns throughout the world, both for teacher education and as possible resource material for middle school students.

Final Thoughts

This project has been a long voyage of discovery for myself and members of our team. My initial desire to infuse Chinese culture into K—8 Mandarin language instruction combined theoretical (anthropological, linguistic) and practical concerns (about retaining enthusiasm and motivation for studying Mandarin among upper primary and middle school students). First hand research of multiple K—8 Mandarin bilingual programs revealed both a general acknowledgement of the importance of culture for language instruction and a range of approaches to teaching culture, which varied with the linguistic and cultural backgrounds of students, families, and school settings, as well as the private or public structure of the schools themselves. What was missing, however, was a conscious and consistent integration of cultural themes and topics with progressive language instruction: in short, teaching language through culture and culture through language. The curricular model developed by our team and presented in this volume aims to do precisely that.

We believe that our project represents an important first step in articulating an innovative curricular approach toward K—8 Mandarin instruction that combines and emphasizes the following important principles:

- Instructional goals and methods that carefully match student cognitive and emotional levels.

• Topics and learning activities that connect to a variety of different student experiences and interests.

• Cultural themes that reappear and are further developed and expanded at each grade level.

• Instruction that integrates language and culture, giving students the intellectual and emotional skills to flexibly apply what they have learned in their ongoing interactions with Chinese peoples and cultures in diverse contexts.

Our ultimate goal, of course, is to see this model adopted and implemented in actual schools with K—8 Mandarin programs, with expectations for further refinement and development. It is this hope that has spurred our publication, and we look forward to sharing in the continued creation and implementation of innovative approaches to teaching Mandarin to younger students.

Carstens

附录
Appendix

文化主题总表
MASTER THEMATIC TABLE

Essential Questions 核心问题	Focus Questions 焦点问题	Behavioral Culture 行为文化	Informational Culture 信息文化
Family 家庭(K—2) 1) Why is filial piety so important? 为什么中国人如此重视孝道？(K—8) 2) How do family rules apply to social behavior? 家庭教育对个人社交行为有什么影响？(K—8) 3) How and why do males and females play different roles in Chinese families? 男性和女性在中国家庭的地位和职责有何不同？为什么有这些区别？(K—8)	1. What is filial piety? 什么是孝顺？ 2. How should you interact with and get along with your parents and brothers and sisters? 你平时怎样和父母、兄弟姐妹相处？ 3. How do you behave as a polite child? 如何做一个有礼貌的孩子？	* Father is affectionate and son is dutiful; show love and respect between brothers; family order in age and generation 父慈子孝，兄友弟恭，长幼有序 * Be obedient to parents 听父母的话 * Respect elders and care for the young; greeting elders in a proper manner 敬老爱幼，用恰当的方式跟长辈、长者打招呼	* Forms of address for family members 家庭成员的称谓（如爷爷、奶奶、外公、外婆、伯伯、叔叔、姑姑、舅舅、阿姨、哥哥、姐姐、弟弟、妹妹等） * Idioms 成语：母子连心、虎父无犬子、孟母三迁 * Tang poem 唐诗：李白《静夜思》
Family 家庭(3—4) 1) How and why are families important? 家庭有什么重要性？为什么？(K—8) 2) Why does Chinese have so many terms for family members?	1. Why is your family important to you? 对你来说，家庭的重要性是什么？为什么？ 2. Who are the members of your family? How do	* Benevolent father, filial son; love and respect between brothers; family order in age and generation 父慈子孝，兄友弟恭，长幼有序	* Roles of family members 家庭的成员及其角色（长幼有序） * Different family forms and combinations 不同的家庭形态和组合方式

(续表)

Essential Questions 核心问题	Focus Questions 焦点问题	Behavioral Culture 行为文化	Informational Culture 信息文化
中国家庭中为什么对家庭成员有这么多不同的称谓？(3—6) 3) How and why do males and females play different roles in Chinese families? 男性和女性在中国家庭的地位和职责有何不同，为什么有这些区别？(K—8) 4) Why is filial piety so important? 为什么中国人如此重视孝道？(K—8) 5) To what extent do family rules guide social behavior? 家庭教育对个人社交行为有什么影响？(K—8)	you address them and what does this say about your relationship with them? 你的家庭中有哪些人？你怎么称呼他们？家人的称谓和彼此之间的角色有什么关系？ 3. What sort of tasks do you do for your family? Is it the same for boys and girls? 你的家庭义务是什么？儿子和女儿的家庭义务一样吗？ 4. How and why do you show filial piety to your parents? 你怎么孝顺父母？为什么？ 5. What are the rules for behavior in your family? How is this different from the rules at school? 你家里有哪些规矩？家里的规矩和学校里的规矩有什么不同？	* Ways of expressing gratitude towards father and mother 如何回报父母养育之恩 * Establish and maintain forms of good citizenship 建立并维护良好社区公民的形象 * Traditional division of labor: men on the outside and women on the inside "男主外、女主内"的传统分工方式	* Idioms 成语：羔羊跪乳、乌鸦反哺 * Tang Poem 唐诗：贺知章《回乡偶书》 * Children's songs 儿歌：《可爱的家》

(续表)

Essential Questions 核心问题	Focus Questions 焦点问题	Behavioral Culture 行为文化	Informational Culture 信息文化
Family 家庭(5—6) 1) How and why are families important? 家庭有什么重要性？为什么？(K—8) 2) Why does Chinese have so many terms for family members? 为什么中国家庭中有这么多不同的称谓？(3—6) 3) How have Chinese families changed over time? 随着时代的改变，中国家庭有什么样的变化？(5—8) 4) How and why do males and females play different roles in Chinese families? 男性和女性在中国家庭中的地位和角色有何不同？为什么？(K—8) 5) Why is family honor so important? 为什么名声和荣誉对中国家庭很重要？(5—8)	1. Who lives together in a traditional Chinese extended family? 传统的几代同堂的大家庭中有哪些成员？ 2. Whose responsibility is it to take care of aging parents? 谁照顾年老的父母？ 3. What is the responsibility of each member in the family? 每个家庭成员的职责是什么？ 4. What do people do so that they do not disgrace their family? Or does it matter? What honorable things can children do for their family? 怎样才能不让家人"没面子"？儿童的哪些行为会让家人"脸上有光"？ 5. What are some famous stories about filial piety and what	* Traditional family roles：older sister like mother, older brother like father; senior males are responsible for the care of elderly parents 长姐如母，长兄如父；长子的职责：照顾年老的父母 * Norms for female deportment：sit and stand properly, no loud laughter. 女人的仪态规范：坐有坐姿、站有站姿，不宜高声大笑 * Family views in rural households are more traditional and conservative 农村家庭的家庭观念较保守、传统	* Forms of address in large multigenerational families 多代大家庭的成员称谓 * Traditional views：of the three types of unfilial behavior, not giving birth to the next generation is the most serious 传统观念：不孝有三，无后为大 * Traditional preference for male over female; modern emphasis on gender equality 重男轻女的传统，男女平等的现代理念 * Traditionally, males take charge of outside affairs, females take charge of domestic affairs; today men and women both have outside employment "男主外，女主内"的传统；男女共同上班的现状 * The concept of face 中国人的"面子"

(续表)

Essential Questions 核心问题	Focus Questions 焦点问题	Behavioral Culture 行为文化	Informational Culture 信息文化
6) Why is filial piety so important? 为什么中国人如此重视孝道？(K—8) 7) How and why are Chinese families similar and different from each other? 中国家庭之间有什么异同？为什么会有这些异同？(5—8) 8) To what extent do family rules guide social behaviors? 家庭教育对个人社交行为有什么影响？(K—8)	do they teach people? 中国有哪些著名的孝道故事？这些故事的含义是什么？ 6. How do Chinese families living in the city differ from families in a rural region? 城市家庭与农村家庭有什么不一样？		* Mulan takes her father's place in military service 木兰代父从军 * Twenty-four stories of filial piety 二十四孝故事 * Family composition: differences in family responsibilities in urban and rural families 家庭组成方式及家庭成员的职责因是城市家庭或农村家庭而有所不同 * Idioms/proverbs 成语/谚语：大家闺秀；小家碧玉；老吾老以及人之老，幼吾幼以及人之幼；家家有本难念的经 * Tang poem 唐诗：贺知章《回乡偶书》 * Essay 文章：朱自清《背影》

(续表)

Essential Questions 核心问题	Focus Questions 焦点问题	Behavioral Culture 行为文化	Informational Culture 信息文化
Family 家庭(7—8) 1) How and why are families important? 家庭有什么重要性? 为什么? (K—8) 2) How have Chinese families changed over time? 随着时代的改变,中国家庭有什么样的变化? (5—8) 3) How and why do males and females play different roles in Chinese families? 男性和女性在中国家庭中的地位和职责有何不同? 为什么有这样的区别? (K—8) 4) Why is family honor so important? 为什么中国家庭的名声和荣誉那么重要? (5—8) 5) How and why are Chinese families similar and different from each other? 中国家庭之间有什么异同? 为什么会有这些异同? (5—8)	1. What influence do family affairs have on individuals? 家人之间的关系对个人的生活有哪些影响? 2. What are typical family rules? Who decides? Why? 一般家庭有哪些家规? 家规由谁制定? 为什么? 3. What sorts of pressures do children face from their families and at school? 孩子在家庭和学校中常面对哪些压力? 4. What do you think about parents who appear inflexible? 你认为"刻板"的父母是什么样的父母? 5. Do Western countries have problems with male and female inequality? How do you deal with male and female inequality	* Roles and positions of family members: senior male rights and responsibilities: traditional family authority, care for parents, continue ancestral sacrifices. Senior female roles: take care of household affairs 家庭角色关系:长男的权责为传承家族权威、奉养父母、延续香火,长女应照顾家庭生活所需 * Family rules 家规 * Respect elders, love children 尊老爱幼 * School records represent achievement and are linked to family honor 学习成绩代表成就,与父母的"面子"密切相关 * Rules between parents and children 子女与父母间的规矩、礼仪	* Of the three types of unfilial behavior, not giving birth to the next generation is the most serious 不孝有三,无后为大 * Favoring males over females/male female equality 重男轻女观念/男女平等 * Males take charge of outside affairs, females take charge of domestic affairs 男主外,女主内 * The importance of "face" 面子的重要性 * Different household responsibilities for boys and girls 男孩与女孩在家里承担的不同义务 * Parental expectations and demands for their children 中国父母对儿女的期望与要求 * Three generation household 三代同堂

(续表)

Essential Questions 核心问题	Focus Questions 焦点问题	Behavioral Culture 行为文化	Informational Culture 信息文化
	life? 西方国家有没有男女不平等的问题？你怎么看待实际生活中男女不平等的现象？ 6. What sort of daily expectations do Chinese parents have for their children? How is this different from the expectations of Western parents? 中国人在生活中对孩子有哪些期望？和西方家庭对孩子的期望有哪些差别？ 7. What are the different understandings of "face" from Chinese and Western points of view? "面子"在中、西方的观念里有什么不同？ 8. What is the one child policy and why is this important? 什么是"计划生育"？它为什么重要？		* Comparison of Chinese and Western families 中西家庭对比 * One child policy "计划生育"政策 * Idioms/proverbs 成语/谚语：饮水思源；光宗耀祖；家有一老，如有一宝；打在儿身，痛在娘心 * Tang poem 唐诗：孟郊《游子吟》

（续表）

Essential Questions 核心问题	Focus Questions 焦点问题	Behavioral Culture 行为文化	Informational Culture 信息文化
Food and Chinese Medicine 食物与中药（K—2） 1) What do Chinese people usually eat and why? 中国人常吃哪些食物？为什么？（K—8） 2) How is food prepared, served and shared in different settings? 在不同的场合，用餐礼仪和食物的摆设形式有什么不同？（K—8） 3) How is food used to express good wishes and social relationships? 中国人如何选择食物来祈福、进行人情往来？（K—8）	1. Do Chinese use knife and fork, too? If not, what utensils do they use? 中国人用刀叉吃饭吗？中国人用什么吃饭？ 2. Can you use chopsticks? 你知道怎么拿筷子吗？你会用筷子吃饭吗？ 3. Have you ever eaten Chinese food? What kind of Chinese food do you like? 你有没有吃过中国食物？你喜欢哪些中国食物？	* Eating styles 取食方式 * Seating order 就坐次序 * Placement of bowls and chopsticks 碗筷摆放方式 * Etiquette and taboos about chopstick use 使用筷子的礼仪和禁忌	* Utensils used in eating Chinese food 中餐餐具 * Basic Chinese food names 常见中国食物名称 * Traditional style Chinese breakfast 中国传统早餐 * Tang poem 唐诗:李绅《悯农》
Food and Chinese Medicine 食物与中药（3—4） 1) What do Chinese people usually eat and why? 中国人常吃哪些食物？为什么？（K—8）	1. What do you usually eat for your three daily meals? What are the special characteristics of these foods? 你每天三餐吃什么？菜色有什么特点？	* Etiquette and taboos about chopstick use 使用筷子的礼仪和禁忌 * Dining etiquette 进餐礼仪 * Meal patterns at home and in	* Relationship between good eating habits and health; using foods to maintain good health 良好的饮食习惯和健康的关系;食物属性和身体保养的关系

(续表)

Essential Questions 核心问题	Focus Questions 焦点问题	Behavioral Culture 行为文化	Informational Culture 信息文化
2) How is food prepared, served and shared in different settings? 在不同的场合,用餐礼仪和食物的摆设形式有什么不同?(K—8) 3) How is food used to express good wishes and social relationships? 中国人如何选择食物来祈福、进行人情往来?(K—8)	2. Have you eaten at a Chinese restaurant? What is the difference between eating at a restaurant and eating at home? 你去过中国餐馆吗?在中国餐馆和在一般餐馆用餐有什么不同? 3. What type of food and drink does your family offer to guests? Why? 你家有聚会时,用什么食物招待客人?为什么?	restaurants: traditional and contemporary 在家和在餐馆的进餐方式;传统方式(圆桌、合菜)和现代方式(桌子形状不限,西餐或中餐用餐形式)	* Traditional Chinese meals: breakfast, lunch and dinner 传统的中国三餐;早餐可含烧饼、油条、米浆、稀饭、蛋饼等。午餐和晚餐多为米饭和面食、蔬菜和肉类菜、各式家常菜、点心和汤类等 * Tea and food as part of Chinese leisure lifestyle 饮茶、食物与中国人的休闲和社交生活的关系 * Idioms 成语:病从口入、望梅止渴、丰衣足食、巧妇难为无米之炊 * Children's songs 儿歌;喜鹊叫,客人到;客人来家,姐姐泡茶;茶冷,买饼;饼香,买糖;糖甜,买面;面上一块鸡,客人吃了笑嘻嘻

(续表)

Essential Questions 核心问题	Focus Questions 焦点问题	Behavioral Culture 行为文化	Informational Culture 信息文化
Food and Chinese Medicine 食物与中药(5—6) 1) What do Chinese people usually eat and why? 中国人常吃哪些食物? 为什么? (K—8) 2) How is food prepared, served and shared in different settings? 在不同的场合,用餐礼仪和食物的摆放有什么不同? (K—8) 3) How is food used to express good wishes and social relationships? 中国人如何选择食物来祈福、进行人情往来? (K—8) 4) How do Chinese define a healthful diet? 饮食和中国人的养生之道有什么关系? (5—8) 5) How does Chinese medicine promote balance in the human body? 中药如何调理体质? (5—8)	1. How is breakfast different for Chinese people living in the south and in the north? 中国南方人和北方人的早餐有什么不同? 2. What do children eat and drink while at school? 学生在学校时吃些什么? 喝些什么? 3. What are the methods used in Chinese cooking? 中国菜怎么做? 有哪些烹调方式? 4. What are the differences in how food is served at home, street eatery, fast food restaurant or at a formal banquet? 在家、在路边摊、在快餐店和在宴会中吃饭有什么不同? 5. What is a typical healthful meal in a Chinese household? 吃什么、怎样吃才	* Seating order, host's seat 就座次序,主位 * How to refuse food politely 如何谢绝布菜 * The importance of buying fresh food; Chinese people prefer to buy and eat whole chickens and whole fish "新鲜"的重要性;中国人喜欢购买、食用全鸡全鱼 * The order in which food is served 上菜程序 * Using utensils properly 公筷母匙 * Bargaining behavior in traditional Chinese markets 传统市场中的讨价还价行为 * Inviting guests: implied meanings and objectives: face, friendship, connections 请客的内涵意义与实质目的:面子、人情、关系	* The basics of hot and cold foods in relation to health 体质和食物的"温热寒凉"的关系 * Origins of medicinal foods: curing with drugs not as good as medicinal foods 药食同源,药补不如食补 * Medicinal food categories 食疗/药膳食品的分类 * Food symbolism 食物的象征意义 * Relations between religious beliefs and food 宗教信仰和饮食的关系 * Food as the center of life 民以食为天 * Comparison between traditional markets and modern super-markets 传统市场/超级市场的对比 * Comparison between Chinese and Western food

(续表)

Essential Questions 核心问题	Focus Questions 焦点问题	Behavioral Culture 行为文化	Informational Culture 信息文化
	能实现"健康饮食"的目的？ 6. Where do Chinese people get their raw ingredients for cooking? 中国人在哪儿买菜？ 7. What are traditional Chinese medicinal foods and how do they help Chinese people stay healthy? 中国有哪些常见的传统药膳食物？它们的作用是什么？	* Hospitality: prefer to have nothing left 待客之道：宁剩勿少 * Western style banquet: friendship more important than food. Chinese style banquet: food is most important 西式宴会：交谊重于食物；中式宴会：食物交谊并重 * Eating at the night market, night market street stalls 吃夜市、逛路边摊 * Using food for mutual restraint 食物相克的观念 * American fast food in China 美国的速食文化在中国	and drink: Chinese vegetarian food 中西饮食的比较：中国的"蔬食" * Comparison of Chinese and Western styles of cooking 中、西方烹饪方式的比较 * You are what you eat 吃什么补什么 * Idioms 成语：山珍海味、饥不择食 * Tang poem 唐诗：李绅《悯农》（二首）
Food and Chinese Medicine 食物与中药(7—8) 1) What do Chinese people usually eat and why? 中国人常吃哪些食物？为什么？（K—8） 2) How is food prepared, served and shared in different	1. What famous Chinese foods are you familiar with? What are the different cooking methods of Chinese and American food? Does this affect how they taste? 你知道哪些有名的中国菜？美国和中国的烹饪方	* Seating order at special family meals 家庭聚餐就坐次序，主位 * Polite behavior between host and guest 主客之间的应对礼节（领进、用餐、赞美、告别） * Proper human relationships	* Special seasonal foods 应季食物 * Hot and cold food beliefs 食物的"冷""热" * Ideas about healthy foods 健康饮食观念 * Cooking ingredients 烹饪材料

(续表)

Essential Questions 核心问题	Focus Questions 焦点问题	Behavioral Culture 行为文化	Informational Culture 信息文化
settings? 在不同的场合，用餐礼仪和食物的摆设形式有什么不同？(K—8) 3) How is food used to express good wishes and social relationships? 中国人如何选择食物来祈福、进行人情往来？(K—8) 4) How do Chinese define a healthful diet? 饮食和中国人的养生之道有什么关系？(5—8) 5) How does Chinese medicine promote balance in the human body? 中药如何调理体质？(5—8)	法有什么不同？这些方法如何影响味道？ 2. What are the differences in seating order at meals for Chinese and American families? Can you explain this? 中、西方家庭用餐的座位安排方式有什么不同？为什么？ 3. In caring for guests who you have invited for a meal, are there any special forms of etiquette and proper ways of speaking? 在家招待客人吃饭时，有没有什么特别的礼节和用语？ 4. What are Chinese and Western standards for healthy food? 中、西方对于健康饮食的标准是什么？ 5. What is the difference between Chinese and Western medicine? 中药和西药有什么不同？	(inviting guests and giving gifts) 人情（请客/送礼） * Chinese meal customs（soup is the last course, tea and fruit at the end, snacks）中国人的饮食习惯（汤最后喝，饭后喝茶、吃水果/点心）	* Food preparation methods 中国常见烹饪方式 * Common Chinese medicines 常见中药名 * Chinese medical treatments and Western medical treatments 中医治本，西医治标 * Idioms and proverbs 成语/谚语；饥肠辘辘；众口难调；无米之炊；食之无味，弃之可惜；因噎废食；暴饮暴食；药补不如食补；心急吃不了热豆腐；肉包子打狗——一去不回；早吃饱，午吃好，晚吃少 * Confucian sayings from "The Analects" "一瓢饮"（出自《论语·雍也》：子曰："贤哉！回也。一箪食，一瓢饮，在陋巷。人不堪其忧，回也不改其乐。贤哉！回也。"）

（续表）

Essential Questions 核心问题	Focus Questions 焦点问题	Behavioral Culture 行为文化	Informational Culture 信息文化
Chinese Festivals 节庆活动(K—2) 1) How and why do Chinese people celebrate traditional festivals and holidays? 中国人如何庆祝传统节日？(K—8) 2) How and why do Chinese celebrate contemporary festivals and holidays? 中国人如何庆祝非传统节日？(K—8)	1. Do Chinese and Americans celebrate the same holidays? 中国人过的节日和美国一样吗？ 2. What Chinese holidays do you know? 你知道哪些中国节日？ 3. Do you know any stories that relate to holidays? 你知道哪些和节日有关的故事？ 4. What holiday do you think is the most interesting? Why? 你觉得哪一个节日最有意思？为什么？	* New Year activities: lucky sayings, red envelopes, spring couplets, firecrackers, New Year greetings, new clothing 新年吉祥话、压岁钱、贴春联、放鞭炮、拜年、穿新衣 * New Year taboos 新年禁忌 * New Year's Eve preparations 除夕之前的过节准备 * Yuan Xiao: Lantern riddles, making lanterns 元宵节：猜灯谜、做灯笼 * Duan Wu: Dragon boatraces, sticky rice cakes, fragrant pouches 端午节：赛龙舟、包粽子、做香包 * Autumn Festival: Admiring the moon, eating moon cakes 中秋节：赏月、吃月饼	* Origins and traditions of Chinese festivals 节日的由来和传统 * Festival myths and stories 有关节日的神话故事 * Idioms 成语：恭喜发财、万事如意、步步高升、童言无忌、岁岁平安、花好月圆

(续表)

Essential Questions 核心问题	Focus Questions 焦点问题	Behavioral Culture 行为文化	Informational Culture 信息文化
Chinese Festivals 节庆活动(3—4) 1) How and why do Chinese people celebrate traditional festivals and holidays? 中国人如何庆祝传统节日？(K—8) 2) How and why do Chinese celebrate contemporary festivals and holidays? 中国人如何庆祝非传统节日？(K—8) 3) How do Chinese celebrations compare with celebrations in the US? 中国人和美国人庆祝节日的方式有什么不同？(3—8)	1. What are traditional Chinese festivals, what is their significance, and how are they celebrated? 中国的传统节日有哪些？他们怎么进行庆祝？这些节日的意义是什么？ 2. What are the similarities and differences between Chinese holidays and American holidays? 中国节庆、假日和美国节庆、假日有什么异同？	* Autumn Festival: Eat moon cakes and fruit, admire the moon, gather together as a family 中秋节：吃月饼和水果、赏月、家人团圆 * Chinese New Year: Get rid of the old and bring in the new, New Year's Eve dinner, welcome New Year, exchange red envelopes 中国新年(春节)：除旧布新、吃年夜饭、守岁、拜年、给红包 * Yuan Xiao: Hang lanterns, eat dumplings, lantern riddles, folk performances 元宵节：提灯笼、吃元宵、猜灯谜、民俗表演 * Qing Ming: Sweep tombs, worship ancestors, spring hikes, fly kites 清明节：扫墓、祭祀祖先、踏青、放风筝 * Dragon Boat Festival: dragon boat	* Autumn Festival significance: Story of Chang'e, celebrate harvest, family and friends get together 中秋节的意义：嫦娥的故事，庆祝秋收，家人朋友聚会 * Chinese New Year significance and customs: Story of Nian, the lunar calendar and how it compares with the Western calendar 中国人过新年的意义和风俗：年的故事，西历和农历的基本差异，简单的农历观念 * Compare Chinese autumn festival and American Thanksgiving 中国中秋节和美国感恩节的异同 * Compare Chinese and American New Year celebrations 中国新年和美国新年的异同 * Yuan Xiao significance: Making

(续表)

Essential Questions 核心问题	Focus Questions 焦点问题	Behavioral Culture 行为文化	Informational Culture 信息文化
		races, eat zongzi (sticky rice cakes), hang special grasses, wear fragrant pouches 端午节:龙舟竞赛、吃粽子、喝雄黄酒、悬挂艾草、佩带香包 * Seven Fairies Festival (Chinese lover's day) 七巧节(中国情人节) * Teachers' Day: Confucian temples, hairs of wisdom, gratitude for teachers' kindness 教师节:孔庙祭奠、拔智慧毛、感谢师恩 * National Day: parades, review the troops, fireworks 国庆节:游行、阅兵、看烟火 * Chinese Ghost Festival: Ghost worship, snatching offerings. American Halloween: travel and costumes 中国鬼节(农历七月十五):敬神拜鬼、抢孤;美国万圣节:游	lanterns, lantern riddles, dumplings, temple festivals 元宵节:简易的灯笼制作,什么是猜灯谜,如何做元宵,简单的庙会介绍 * Significance of Qing Ming: Tang Poems 清明节:杜牧《清明》 * Dragon Boat Festival significance: story of Qu Yuan, customs, zongzi, fragrant pouches 端午节:屈原的故事,端午节的风俗,粽子的制作,香包的制作 * Seven Fairies Festival significance: Cowherd and weaving maid; comparison between traditional Chinese lovers' day, and Western Valentine's day 七巧节:牛郎织女的故事,中国传统情人节和西洋情人节的异同

(续表)

Essential Questions 核心问题	Focus Questions 焦点问题	Behavioral Culture 行为文化	Informational Culture 信息文化
		行、装扮 * Christmas: home for the holidays, church gatherings, exchanging gifts 圣诞节:回家过节、教堂聚会、互赠礼物	* Meaning of Teachers' Day: simple introduction to Confucius. Confucius advocated educating everyone; students should respect their teachers and work hard at their studies 教师节:简单介绍孔子(孔子主张人人都有接受育的权力,学生要尊敬老师、努力学习) * National Day 国庆节 * Compare Halloween and Chinese Ghost Festival 万圣节和中国鬼节的相同和不同 * Compare American Christmas and Chinese New Year celebrations 美国圣诞节和中国新年的比较 * Idioms/proverbs 成语/谚语:光阴似箭;日月如梭;月圆人圆;一年之计在于春,一日之计在于晨 * Tang Poems

(续表)

Essential Questions 核心问题	Focus Questions 焦点问题	Behavioral Culture 行为文化	Informational Culture 信息文化
			唐诗：春节——王安石《元日》；清明节——杜牧《清明》；中秋节——李白《古朗月行》
Chinese Festivals 节庆活动（5—6） 1）How and why do Chinese people organize activities by different calendars? 中国人如何根据不同的历法来安排活动？(5—8) 2）How and why do Chinese people celebrate traditional festivals and holidays? 中国人如何庆祝传统节日？(K—8) 3）How and why do Chinese celebrate contemporary festivals and holidays? 中国人如何庆祝非传统节日？(K—8)	1. What is the difference between the Chinese and Western calendars? 中国历法和西方历法有什么不同？ 2. What are the origins of Chinese traditional festivals? 中国传统节日的由来是什么？ 3. How do Chinese children celebrate traditional festivals? 中国儿童在过节时做些什么？ 4. Are there differences in how Chinese people from different regions celebrate the traditional festivals? 庆祝传统节日的方式是否有地方性区别？ 5. Do you see Western influence on some Chinese recent	* Holiday rituals, activities, taboos, superstitions 节日的庆祝仪式、活动、忌讳、迷信 * Chinese people consult the almanac to seek luck and avoid calamities 中国人看黄历行事：趋吉避凶 * Vegetarian food for 15th/first day of the month 初一十五吃素	* Chinese calendar/leap month 中国历法/闰月 * Twenty-four solar periods 二十四节气 * The origins of Chinese traditional holidays, legendary stories, and celebratory practices 中国传统节日的由来、传奇故事及庆祝方式 * Children's festival roles and responsibilities 儿童在节庆中的角色、职责 * Regional festival celebrations 节日庆祝方式的地域性 * Mutual cultural influences on Chinese and Western holiday celebrations 中西文化交流后中西节日的相互影响 * Idioms/proverbs 成语/谚语：张灯结彩、喜气洋洋、

(续表)

Essential Questions 核心问题	Focus Questions 焦点问题	Behavioral Culture 行为文化	Informational Culture 信息文化
	celebrations? How have things changed? 有哪些中国人庆祝的现代节日受到了西方节日的影响？庆祝方式有什么不同？		月到中秋分外明、千里共婵娟 * Depictions of Chinese festivals in ancient poetry 古诗词：春节——王安石《元日》；元宵节——元好问《京都元夕》；清明节——杜牧《清明》；中秋节——李白《静夜思》；重阳节——王维《九月九日忆山东兄弟》 * Modern song depicting winter 描绘冬日的现代歌谣：《九九歌》
Chinese Festivals 节庆活动(7—8) 1) How and why do Chinese people organize activities by different calendars? 中国人如何根据不同的历法来安排活动？(5—8) 2) How and why do Chinese people celebrate traditional festivals and holidays? 中国人如何庆祝传	1. How did Chinese holidays originate? Why are they celebrated in these ways? 节日是怎么来的？为什么有庆祝活动？ 2. How do holidays relate to the seasons? Why? 哪些节庆和季节有关系？为什么？ 3. What special meanings do holidays	* Chinese student teacher relations 中国师生关系 * Holiday rituals and activities 节庆礼仪与活动 * Traditional holiday foods 节庆传统食物 * Responding to taboos 应对禁忌	* Holidays：Teachers' Day, Autumn Festival, National Day, Halloween/Ghost Festival, Christmas/twelfth month, New Year/Spring Festival, Yuan Xiao, Valentines Day, temple fair, Ching Ming, Labor Day, Duan Wu Festival 节日：教师节、中

(续表)

Essential Questions 核心问题	Focus Questions 焦点问题	Behavioral Culture 行为文化	Informational Culture 信息文化
统节日？(K—8) 3) How and why do Chinese celebrate contemporary festivals and holidays? 中国人如何庆祝非传统节日？(K—8) 4) How do Chinese celebrations compare with celebrations in the US? 中国人和美国人庆祝节日的方式有什么不同？(3—8)	hold for Chinese people? How is this different from Western people? 庆祝节日对中国人有什么重要意义？这与西方有何差别？ 4. What Western holidays do Chinese people celebrate? Why? 中国人庆祝哪些西方节日？为什么？ 5. How has the celebration of traditional holidays changed over time? 从以前到现在，传统节日的庆祝方式和活动有什么样的改变？		秋节、国庆、万圣节/中元节、圣诞节/腊月、新年/春节、元宵节、情人节、庙会、清明节、劳动节、端午节 * Similarities and differences between traditional Chinese and Western holidays 中西传统节日的意义异同 * Chinese lunar calendar 中国农历 * Selected Tang and Song dynasty poems about autumn 有关秋天的诗词：苏轼《水调歌头》（明月几时有）；李白《子夜秋歌》；杜牧《秋夕》；李煜《虞美人》；辛弃疾《丑奴儿·书博山道中》
Geography and Travel 地理与旅游 (K—2) 1) How do people express time? 人们如何表示时间？(K—6) 2) How do we ask and explain directions?	1. Do you know how to tell time? 你会表示时间吗？ 2. How do you travel to school? 你每天怎么到学校？ 3. What things do you see in the classroom	* Walking, riding a bicycle, taking a car, bus, train, or airplane 走路、坐车、骑自行车、坐公共汽车、坐火车、坐飞机	* Maps: seven continents, four oceans, America, China 地图：七大洲四大洋；中国、美国 * Putting things in order 物品放置位置

(续表)

Essential Questions 核心问题	Focus Questions 焦点问题	Behavioral Culture 行为文化	Informational Culture 信息文化
如何询问和说明方向？(K—4) 3) How do people travel to different places? 我们用哪些方法到不同的地方旅游？(K—4)	and where are they? 教室里有哪些东西？都放在哪儿？ 4. What sorts of things are found on different sides of your house? 你家的周围有些什么？ 5. Have you ever traveled to China? Where is China? 你去过中国吗？中国在哪儿？		* Directions 方向 * Home/school location 家庭/学校的位置 * Calendar/time 日期/时间 * Idioms 成语：走马观花、人山人海、景色如画、一路顺风、一路平安 * Poem 诗歌：邵康节《山村咏怀》
Geography and Travel 地理与旅游 (3—4) 1) How do people express time? 人们如何表示时间？(K—6) 2) How do we ask and give directions? 我们如何问路、指路？(K—4) 3) How can we use maps to understand people in different times and places? 如何使用地图来了解不同时空里的人？(3—8) 4) What can travel in China teach you	1. Do you know how to ask and tell time? 你知道怎么看时间吗？ 2. How do you tell directions and give directions when at school and on the street? 在学校或街上，你怎么认路、指路？ 3. Do you know how to use a map? 你会用地图吗？ 4. Can you use a map to explain the locations of the US and China? Is it the same time of the day in China	* Polite greetings in public 在公共场合打招呼 * Chinese customs of telling time 中国人表达时间的习惯 * Telephone etiquette 电话礼仪 * Proper manners in taking public transportation, such as taking seats on a bus 搭乘公共交通工具的礼貌，例如坐公车时的礼让行为 * How to write a simple text message	* Using maps and compasses 地图、指南针的功能 * Using a globe 地球仪的使用 * Traveling to famous cities in China：Beijing, Shanghai, Xi'an, Hong Kong, Taipei 著名的中国旅游地：北京、上海、西安、香港、台北 * Types of public transportation 大众运输工具的种类 * Tools to measure time 计时工具 * Chinatowns 中

(续表)

Essential Questions 核心问题	Focus Questions 焦点问题	Behavioral Culture 行为文化	Informational Culture 信息文化
about Chinese history, culture, and customs? 到中国旅游能学习到哪些有关文化、历史和当地风俗的知识？(3—8) 5) How do people travel to different places? 人们如何到不同的地方旅游？(K—4) 6) Where in the world is Chinese commonly spoken? 哪些国家/区域使用中文？(3—8)	and the US? Why? 你能用地图说明中国和美国的位置吗？中国和美国的时间相同吗？为什么？ 4. Where would you like to travel in China? What would you like to know when you travel to China? 你想去中国的哪些地方旅游？去中国旅游时，你想知道关于中国的什么内容？ 5. Do you know what kind of transport you would take to go from the US to China? 你知道从美国到中国可以使用哪些交通工具吗？ 6. Does your city have a Chinatown? Have you visited Chinatown? 你住的城市有中国城吗？你去过中国城吗？	如何写留言 * Types of transportation while traveling in China 在中国旅游时使用的交通工具	国城 * Idioms/proverbs 成语/谚语：百闻不如一见；读万卷书，行万里路 * Tang Poem 唐诗：王之涣《登鹳雀楼》

(续表)

Essential Questions 核心问题	Focus Questions 焦点问题	Behavioral Culture 行为文化	Informational Culture 信息文化
Geography and Travel 地理与旅游 (5—6) 1) How do people express time? 人们如何表示时间？(K—6) 2) How can we use maps to understand people in different times and places? 如何使用地图来了解不同时空里的人？(3—8) 3) What can travel in China teach you about Chinese history, culture, and customs? 到中国旅游能学习到哪些有关文化、历史或当地风俗的知识？(3—8) 4) Where in the world is Chinese commonly spoken? 哪些国家/区域使用中文？(3—8)	1. Why are there different time zones? 为什么会有不同的时区？ 2. How can you tell time if you do not use a watch or clock? 没有时钟时，你怎么知道时间？ 3. What places in China would be good for learning about Chinese history? 到中国的哪些地方可以学习中国历史？ 4. Can you use regular maps or satellite maps to help with your travel plans? 你会使用地图或卫星地图来安排旅行路线吗？ 5. How do you keep in touch with your family during travel? 旅行中如何和家人联系？ 6. What obstacles might you encounter during travel? 旅行中可能会遇到的困难有哪些？	* Travel clothing that follows local customs 服装的入乡随俗 * Behavior taboos 行为忌讳 * Bargaining 讨价还价 * Toilet/bathroom customs 厕所文化 * Night markets 夜市 * Reading a transportation time schedule 看交通时刻表 * How to buy a train ticket; how to take different forms of transportation 如何买火车票？如何搭乘交通工具？ * Using the information counter 找寻及使用咨询台 * Filling out entry forms, immunizations 入关表格填写、防疫 * Using email, SMS/text messages, postcards 电子邮件、短信/简讯、明信片的使用	* Time conversion between the US and China 中美时差换算 * Exchange rates 汇率 * Traditional methods of telling time：sundial, heavenly stems and earthly branches 传统计时方式：日晷、天干地支 * Internet and satellite maps 使用卫星地图、网络地图 * Weather maps 气象图的使用 * China's geography：silk road, terracotta warriors 中国地理：丝绸之路、兵马俑 * Major cities and famous scenic and historical sites in China：Beijing, Shanghai, Xian, Guangzhou, Hong Kong, Taipei 101, Great Wall 中国主要城市及风景、古迹：北京、上海、西安、广州、香港、台北101大楼、长城

(续表)

Essential Questions 核心问题	Focus Questions 焦点问题	Behavioral Culture 行为文化	Informational Culture 信息文化
	7. Where and with whom can you use Mandarin Chinese? Where in China do people use languages other than Mandarin Chinese? 你和哪些人在哪些地方用普通话沟通？中国哪些地方不使用普通话？		* Minority regions, customs, language 少数民族居住地区、生活习惯、语言 * Overseas Chinese and Chinatowns 海外华人与中国城 * Idioms/proverbs 成语/谚语：读万卷书，行万里路；百闻不如一见；四海之内皆兄弟；走马观花；井底之蛙 * Ancient poem 古诗词：马致远《天净沙·秋思》
Geography and Travel 地理与旅游(7—8) 1) How can we use maps to understand people in different times and places? 如何使用地图来了解在不同时间和空间里的人？(3—8) 2) What can travel in China teach you about Chinese history, culture, and customs? 到中国旅游能学习到哪些有关文化、历史或当代风俗的知识？(3—8)	1. What do the coordinates on maps tell us? 地图上的地理位置坐标告诉我们哪些信息？ 2. How are people's lives affected by different geographic locations? 不同地理位置对当地人的生活有什么样的影响？ 3. What sorts of cultural differences do Westerners encounter when they travel to China?	* Following local customs when traveling: food, clothing, speaking, behavior, attitude, rules, taboos 入乡随俗：食物、服装、语言、行为、态度、规范、禁忌 * How to order, eat, and pay for food in a restaurant 餐馆点餐、用餐及付费方式 * Regional shopping patterns: bargaining 购物方式：讨价还价	* Famous Chinese places: Forbidden City, Tianan Men, Summer Palace, Great Wall, Silk Road, Terracotta Warriors 中国著名景点：紫禁城、天安门、颐和园、长城、丝绸之路、兵马俑 * Time differences, foreign exchange, visas 时差、汇率、签证 * Weather maps 气象图

(续表)

Essential Questions 核心问题	Focus Questions 焦点问题	Behavioral Culture 行为文化	Informational Culture 信息文化
3) Where is the world the Chinese language commonly spoken? 哪些国家/地区使用中文？(3—8)	What is the most difficult to endure? 西方人到中国旅行时会面临哪些文化差异？哪些是最不容易克服的？ 4. What can your travels teach you about Chinese history, culture and customs? 你怎么在旅行中了解中国历史、文化和当地的风俗习惯？ 5. Do you know where Chinese language is spoken? How does Chinese language change from place to place? 你知道哪些国家或地区使用汉语？在不同国家或地区中的汉语有什么相同与不同的地方吗？	* How to take local transportation 如何搭乘交通工具 * Filling out entry forms 入境表格填写 * Customs inspections questions and responses 入关检查问题应对 * Reading airplane, train, bus schedules 读飞机/火车/公车时刻表 * Buying tickets 买票 * Checking local weather on the internet 上网查询当地天气预报	* Morning markets, night markets 早市、夜市 * Morning exercise in public parks 公园晨练 * City street divisions and names 城市街道划分和街名 * Differences between urban and rural lifestyles 城乡生活差异 * Chinese minorities 少数民族 * Overseas Chinese 海外华人 * Important cities：Beijing, Xian, Shanghai, Guangzhou, Taipei 主要城市：北京、西安、上海、广州、台北 * Places where Chinese language is used：Mainland, Hong Kong, Taiwan of China and singapore, Chinatowns... 汉语使用区：中国内地、香港、台湾地区、新加坡及海外

(续表)

Essential Questions 核心问题	Focus Questions 焦点问题	Behavioral Culture 行为文化	Informational Culture 信息文化
			世界各地的"中国城",等等 * Idioms 成语:跋山涉水、扶老携幼、呼朋引伴、风餐露宿、美不胜收、乐不思蜀、流连忘返、天涯海角。 * Tang Poem 唐诗:张继《枫桥夜泊》
History, Politics and Religion 历史、政治与宗教(K—2) 1) Why does Chinese society generally attach such importance to education? 为什么中国社会极度重视教育?(K—8)	1. Why do we go to school? 为什么要上学? 2. How do you show respect to your teachers? How do you treat your friends? 你怎么尊敬老师?怎么与朋友相处? 3. What are classroom rules? 教室里有哪些规矩? 4. Who was Confucius? 孔子是谁?	* School dress code in China 中国学校的服装规定 * Etiquette between Chinese teachers and students 中国学生与老师之间的礼仪(行礼问好) * Etiquette for entering and leaving the classroom 上下课礼仪	* Occupations: police, teacher, principal, postal worker, fire fighter, librarian, business person, cook 职业:警察、老师、校长、邮差、消防员、图书馆员、商人、厨师 * Relations between teachers and students 师生关系 * The story of Confucius 孔子的故事 * Idioms 成语:光阴似箭、有教无类、努力不懈、勤学苦练 * Poetry excerpts 诗句节选:一日为师,终身为父;少壮不努力,老大徒

(续表)

Essential Questions 核心问题	Focus Questions 焦点问题	Behavioral Culture 行为文化	Informational Culture 信息文化
			伤悲；一寸光阴一寸金,寸金难买寸光阴
History, Politics and Religion 历史、政治与宗教(3—4) 1) How was China governed prior to the 20th century? 二十世纪以前,中国处于什么样的统治之下?(3—8) 2) Why does Chinese society generally attach such importance to education? 为什么中国社会极度重视教育?(K—8) 3) How do religious beliefs and practices affect people's daily lives? 宗教信仰如何影响人们的日常生活?(3—8) 4) What connections did China have with the rest of the world prior to the 20th century? 二十世纪之前,中国和世界其他地区有哪些联系与交流?(3—8)	1. What stories are told about the Great Wall of China? 关于中国长城有哪些故事? 2. Why do many Chinese students attach special importance to their studies? 为什么许多中国学生特别重视学习? 3. What do Chinese do when they go to (Chinese) temples? How are these temples different from churches? 中国人去寺庙做什么? 寺庙和教堂有什么不同? 4. What stories are told of the famous Chinese monkey "Monkey King"? 中国著名的猴子"美猴王"有哪些故事?	* Chinese people work hard in school and use scholarly achievement to establish family honor 中国人努力读书、求取功名,以建立家族荣誉 * Chinese spiritual beliefs and temple practices: Burn incense and worship deities; make a wish, change luck, drive out demons, pray for peace 中国人的心灵信仰与寺庙功能：烧香拜神、许愿还愿、改运驱邪、求平安	* Emperor Qin Shi and the Great Wall 秦始皇与长城 * Stories about the mother of Mencius 孟母三迁的故事 * Comparisons between Chinese temples and American churches 中国寺庙和美国教堂的比较 * The Story of Monkey King "美猴王"的故事 * Idioms/proverbs 成语/谚语：仁民爱物、苛政猛于虎、慈悲为怀、好学不倦 * Tang poem 唐诗：贾岛《寻隐者不遇》

(续表)

Essential Questions 核心问题	Focus Questions 焦点问题	Behavioral Culture 行为文化	Informational Culture 信息文化
History, Politics and Religion 历史、政治与宗教(5—6) 1) How was China governed prior to the 20th century? 二十世纪前,中国处于什么样的统治之下？(3—8) 2) Why does Chinese society generally attach such importance to education? 为什么中国社会极度重视教育？(K—8) 3) How does religion affect people's daily life? 宗教信仰如何影响人们的日常生活？(3—8) 4) Why and how did Chinese people settle in America? 中国人是怎么移民到美国的？(5—8) 5) How has China been governed since 1949? 1949年后,中国政府的管理形态是怎样的？(5—8)	1. What is the legacy of China's first emperor? 秦始皇对中国的贡献和影响有哪些？ 2. Why do Chinese students take their studies so seriously? 为什么中国学生特别在意在校的学习表现？ 3. Do people in China practice the same religion as mine? 在中国有和你一样的宗教信仰吗？ 4. Why did Chinese people immigrate to US? Who were the earliest immigrants? 中国人是怎么移民到美国的？最早移民到美国的中国人是哪些人？ 5. What historical events have made Chinese people feel pride or shame? 有哪些历史事件让中国人感到光荣或没有面子？	* Student/teacher relations: teacher for a day, father for life; teachers expound wisdom 师生关系：一日为师,终身为父；师者,传道授业解惑者也 * Temple worship practices and functions 祭拜礼仪/寺庙功能 * Making requests from deities, throwing the divination blocks 求神还愿：卜卦、掷筊 * Taoist and Buddhist beliefs do not conflict 道佛同信不冲突 * Typical views of overseas Chinese 对海外华人的一般看法 * After school supplementary classes 课后补习 * School entrance exams 升学考试 * Middle school students in regular	* Famous historical Chinese and their contributions: Qin Shi, Mulan, Empress Wu, Xuan Zang, Genghis Khan, Zheng He 具代表性的中国历史人物及其事迹：秦始皇、花木兰、武则天、玄奘、成吉思汗、郑和 * Silk Road, Dunhuang Caves and Carvings 丝绸之路, 敦煌石窟 * Chinese immigration history/Chinatowns 中国移民史/中国城 * Imperial examinations/school entrance exams 科举考试/升学考试 * Modern Chinese history: Opium war, foreign forces occupy Beijing(1900), Sino-Japanese war 中国近代史：鸦片战争、八国联军侵华战争、中日战争 * Important religious beliefs: Taoism and

(续表)

Essential Questions 核心问题	Focus Questions 焦点问题	Behavioral Culture 行为文化	Informational Culture 信息文化
6) What connections did China have with the rest of the world prior to the 20th century? 二十世纪之前，中国和世界其他地区有哪些联系与交流？(3—8)	6. What is the Silk Road? How has the Silk Road influenced Western countries? 什么是丝绸之路？丝绸之路对西方国家有什么影响？	schools and boarding schools 中学生走读/住校	Buddhism 主要宗教信仰：道教、佛教 * Idioms/proverbs 成语/谚语：书中自有颜如玉，书中自有黄金屋；做一天和尚撞一天钟；万般皆下品，唯有读书高；开卷有益 * Ancient poem 古诗词：孟郊《登科后》
History, Politics and Religion 历史、政治与宗教 (7—8) 1) How was China governed prior to the 20th century? 二十世纪前，中国的政治形态是怎样的？(3—8) 2) Why does Chinese society generally attach such importance to education? 为什么中国社会极度重视教育？(K—8) 3) How does religion effect people's daily life? 宗教信仰如何影响人们的日常生活？(3—8) 4) What is the	1. Where did Chinese civilization originate? When did it begin? 中国文明起源于何处、何时？ 2. During China's dynastic history, what emperors are recognized for their great achievements/contributions? What did they do? 中国的历史朝代中，有哪些皇帝被认为是对中国有贡献的？他们都做了些什么？ 3. Why is education so important to society? 教育对社会有什么样的重要性？ 4. What influence do the perspectives	* High school and college competitive entrance exams 高中、大学升学考试 * Value knowledge and education/do not value physical activities 重视知识教育/不重视体能活动 * Importance of supplementary classes 补习班的重要性 * Worshipping ancestors and deities 祭拜祖先、神祇	* Origins of Chinese civilization 中国文明发源地 * China's important dynastic periods 中国重要历史朝代 * Traditional and moderns concepts of social class 传统社会阶级观念/现代观念 * Chinese religions 中国的宗教 * Change from government by emperor to government by political party 从传统皇帝统制到政府党派统制的改变 * Government administration in China 中国政府的管理形态

(续表)

Essential Questions 核心问题	Focus Questions 焦点问题	Behavioral Culture 行为文化	Informational Culture 信息文化
difference between the mainland, Hong Kong, Taiwan in China and Singapore? 中国内地、香港、台湾地区、新加坡之间有什么不同之处？(7—8) 5) How has China been governed since 1949? 1949年后，中国政府的管理形态是怎样的？(5—8) 6) What connections did China have with rest of world prior to the 20th century? 二十世纪之前，中国和世界其他地区有哪些联系与交流？(3—8)	of China's traditional four class system have on people's lives today? 传统中国的"士、农、工、商"社会阶层观念对现代人的生活有什么样的影响？ 5. What are the most important Chinese religions? When did they begin? 中国有哪些重要的宗教？起源于何时？ 6. What are the main differences between the Chinese mainland, Hong Kong, Taiwan and Singapore? 你认为中国内地、香港、台湾地区、新加坡之间的差别在哪儿？ 7. How did China's political system change from rule by the emperor to rule by political party? What are the main differences? 中国的政治管理方式是怎么从皇帝		* Pre-20th century exchanges and influences between China and the rest of the world 中国二十世纪前与世界的交流及其影响 * Imperial exams/school entrance exams 科举考试/升学考试 * History of overseas immigration 海外移民史 * Mao Zedong 毛泽东 * Communism 共产主义 * Historical stories: Mulan, Zheng He, Xuan Zang, Monkey, Marco Polo, Genghis Khan, Empress Wu, Yang Guifei 有关历史人物故事：花木兰代父从军，郑和下西洋，玄奘取经，马可·波罗，成吉思汗，武则天，杨贵妃 * Taoism and Buddhism 道教与佛教

（续表）

Essential Questions 核心问题	Focus Questions 焦点问题	Behavioral Culture 行为文化	Informational Culture 信息文化
	管理改变到政府管理的？这两种管理方式有什么差别？ 8. What sorts of relations did China have with other countries prior to the 20th century? How did this influence China? 二十世纪之前，中国和世界其他地区有哪些联系与交流？这对中国有什么影响？		* Idioms/Proverbs 成语/谚语：功成名就；学以致用；勤能补拙；学海无涯；书中自有黄金屋；善有善报，恶有恶报；放下屠刀，立地成佛；回头是岸 * Poetry collection 集句诗：山外青山楼外楼，强中自有强中手。黑发不知勤学早，白首方悔读书迟。
Friends, Fun, Fashions and Fads 朋友、娱乐与时尚（K—2） 1）What does it mean to be a friend? 朋友的意义是什么？(K—8) 2) How do people express friendship and friendliness? 如何表达友谊和友好？(K—8) 3) How do people have fun? 如何寻找生活乐趣？(K—8)	1. How do you make friends? 你怎么交朋友？ 2. What activities do you enjoy sharing with friends? 你喜欢和朋友一起做些什么游戏？ 3. What do you like to do when you are not in school? 你平常不上课的时候，喜欢做什么？玩什么？	* Origami, paper cuts, pull bells, kick the shuttlecock, play tops, play chess 折纸、剪纸、扯铃（抖空竹）、踢毽子、打陀螺、下棋（跳棋） * Playing at a friend's house, attending a friend's birthday party 去朋友家玩，参加朋友的生日派对	* Traditional fun activities：origami, paper cuts, pull bells shuttlecock, kites, tops, clay figures, chess 传统游戏：折纸、剪纸、扯铃（抖空竹）、踢毽子、放风筝、打陀螺、捏面人、下跳棋、下象棋 * Contemporary fun activities：electronic games, card games, television, cartoons 现代游戏：电子游戏、扑克牌、电视节目、动画片 * Fables 寓言故事：狐假虎威、鹬蚌相争、狮子与老鼠

(续表)

Essential Questions 核心问题	Focus Questions 焦点问题	Behavioral Culture 行为文化	Informational Culture 信息文化
			* Idioms 成语：一言为定、情同手足、将心比心、和睦相处、相亲相爱、不分彼此
Friends, Fun, Fashions and Fads 朋友、娱乐与时尚(3—4) 1) What does it mean to be a friend? 朋友的意义是什么？(K—8) 2) How do people express friendship and friendliness? 如何表达友谊和友好？(K—8) 3) How do people have fun? 如何寻找生活乐趣？(K—8) 4) How do fashions reflect social values and social relationships? 流行时尚如何反映社会价值观和社交关系？(K—8)	1. Who can be a friend? 什么人可以做朋友？ 2. How do you express friendship? How can you be good to your friends? 你认为什么是友情的表现？向朋友示好的方式有哪些？ 3. What sorts of things do you enjoy doing with your friends? Why? 和朋友在一起时你们都喜欢做些什么活动？为什么？ 4. What are the differences in things that you and your friends prefer? Why? 你和你的朋友有什么不同的喜好吗？为什么？	* Male and female differences in body language to express friendship 男女表达友情的肢体语言差异 * Ways that Chinese children maintain friendship 中国儿童维系友谊的方式 * Children's social and leisure activities 儿童的社交与休闲活动 * Ways that children acknowledge each other 儿童认同彼此的方式 * Wearing school uniforms 校服的穿着 * Pop culture 大众流行文化	* Chinese historical stories of friendship 关于友情的中国历史故事 * Chinese folk toys, games 中国的民间玩具、游戏 * Comparative treatment of pets in the US and China 中美对待宠物的异同 * Idioms/proverbs：成语/谚语：近朱者赤，近墨者黑；耳濡目染；一见如故；平易近人；形影不离

(续表)

Essential Questions 核心问题	Focus Questions 焦点问题	Behavioral Culture 行为文化	Informational Culture 信息文化
Friends, Fun, Fashions and Fads 朋友、娱乐与时尚 (5—6) 1) What does it mean to be a friend? 朋友的意义是什么? (K—8) 2) How do people express friendship and friendliness? 如何表达友谊和友好? (K—8) 3) How do people have fun? 如何寻找生活乐趣? (K—8) 4) How do fashions reflect social values and social relationships? 流行时尚如何反映社会价值观和社交关系? (K—8) 5) What do fads say about people? 时尚潮流可传达什么样的信息? (5—8)	1. Is an acquaintance a friend? What sorts of behaviors are acceptable and unacceptable between friends? 熟人就是朋友吗? 朋友间有哪些该或不该有的行为? 2. What SMS codes do Chinese children use? 中国儿童也用短信吗? 在他们的短信中会使用哪些缩略代码? 3. How do Chinese children use technology in their daily life? 中国儿童如何把科技运用到生活里? 4. What are considered cool gifts to give to your Chinese friends? 送什么礼物给中国朋友比较合适? 5. Where do Chinese children hang out with their friends? What are the activities Chinese children like to do when they are with their friends?	* Cell phones, text messages 手机,手机短信 * Acceptable body contact between same sex friends 同性朋友之间身体碰触的可接受度 * What do you give as gifts and when and how do you open them? 送礼和收礼的礼仪 * Selecting clothing styles, colors 服装质地/样式/颜色选择 * Clothing and appearance standards 服装和仪容的标准 * Acceptance and stereotypes of tattoos and dyed hair 刺青/纹身/染发的被接受程度和刻板印象 * Popular phrases, slang 流行语/俚语 * Worshipping movie stars, artists, idols of the opposite sex 对明星/艺人/异性偶像的崇拜	* Famous historical stories of friendship 著名友情故事,如桃园三结义 * Three friends of winter 岁寒三友 * Television/movies 电视/电影分级 * Social activities of young adolescents: what do they like to do, where do they like to do it, what is currently popular? 儿童/青少年的社交与休闲生活:他们爱做什么? 在哪儿做? 现在流行什么? * Parental attitudes towards their children's selection of friends 近朱者赤,近墨者黑:父母左右儿女择友 * Social networking 社交网络:Face book 和QQ * Cartoons, animation, karaoke 漫画、动画、卡拉OK * Brands 品牌 * Clothing styles:

(续表)

Essential Questions 核心问题	Focus Questions 焦点问题	Behavioral Culture 行为文化	Informational Culture 信息文化
	中国儿童和他们的朋友在一块儿时会去哪儿？做什么？ 6. How do Chinese children dress? Do they like popular American fashion brands? 中国儿童如何打扮自己？他们也喜欢美国服饰品牌吗？		traditional/minorities/contemporary 服装类型：传统服装、少数民族服装、现代服饰 * Idioms/proverbs 成语/谚语：八拜之交；有福同享，有难同当；风雨同舟；海内存知己，天涯若比邻；君子之交淡如水，小人之交甜如蜜；情同手足 * Song 歌曲：李叔同《送别》
Friends Fun, Fashions and Fads 朋友、娱乐与时尚 (7—8) 1) What does it mean to be a friend? 朋友的意义是什么？(K—8) 2) How do people express friendship and friendliness? 如何表达友谊和友好？(K—8) 3) How do people have fun? 如何寻找生活乐趣？(K—8) 4) How do fashions reflect social values and social relationships? 流行时尚如何反映社会	1. How do you choose your friends? What can friends do for you? 你如何选择朋友？你认为"朋友"可以为你做什么？ 2. How do you express friendship and friendliness to others? 对他人表示友好的方式有哪些？ 3. How do you maintain friendships? 如何维系朋友之间的友好关系？ 4. What things do you enjoy doing with your friends? 你和	* Same sex expressions of intimacy 同性之间的亲密接触 * Leisure activities and amusements for adolescents 青少年的休闲活动与乐趣 * Age restrictions on drinking alcohol 饮酒的年龄限制 * Internet café 网吧 * Female dress taboos 女性穿着禁忌 * Worshipping boy/girl friend, brand names 崇拜对象/品牌 * Social relations and dating; active/	* Three friends of winter 岁寒三友 * Television/movies 电视/电影分级 * Traditional, minorities, contemporary clothing styles 服饰类型：传统服装、少数民族服装、现代服饰 * Chinese favorite brand names and social relations 中国人喜爱的名牌与社交关系 * Chinese popular expressions 中国现代流行语 * Traditional and contemporary views

（续表）

Essential Questions 核心问题	Focus Questions 焦点问题	Behavioral Culture 行为文化	Informational Culture 信息文化
价值观和社交关系？（K—8） 5) What do fads say about people? 时尚潮流可传达什么样的信息？（5—8）	朋友在一起时，最喜爱的活动有哪些？为什么？ 6. What special activities do friends from different cultural backgrounds enjoy doing? 不同文化背景的朋友是否有特别的活动爱好？ 7. Can wearing popular name brand clothing affect social relationships? 穿着名牌服饰会影响人际关系吗？如何影响？ 8. Where do popular expressions come from? What special meanings are conveyed? 流行语是怎么来的？有什么特别的意义？ 9. What Chinese popular expressions and slang terms do you know and how can you use them? 你知道哪些中国流行语和俚语？怎么用？	passive 异性交往关系：主动/被动 * Popular expressions/slang 流行语/俚语 * Comparative psychology 比较心态	about contacts between men and women 中国人关于男女交往的传统观念/现代观念 * Differences in Chinese and Western views about male and female contacts 中、西方男女交往的观念差别 * Historic stories of friendship 体现友情的历史故事：管鲍之交（管仲与鲍叔牙） * Idioms 成语：一诺千金；莫逆之交；志同道合；生死之交；患难之交；手足之情；义无反顾；忘恩负义；见义勇为；近朱者赤，近墨者黑 * Confucian sayings 《论语》："益者三友……友直、友谅、友多闻，益矣。"

(续表)

Essential Questions 核心问题	Focus Questions 焦点问题	Behavioral Culture 行为文化	Informational Culture 信息文化
Creative Arts and Sciences 艺术与科学创造(K—2) 1) How do folk arts play a part in Chinese daily life? 民俗艺术与中国人的生活有什么样的关系？(K—6) 2) How is Chinese music different from Western music? 中国乐曲与西方音乐有何不同？(K—8) 3) How did Chinese written language develop over time? 中国文字是如何演变的？(K—8) 4) What makes Chinese language so different from Western language? 中国语言和西方语言为什么有如此大的区别？(K—8)	1. What do Chinese kids do in their leisure time? 中国孩子下课后喜欢做什么？学什么？ 2. What Chinese songs have you sung? 你唱过哪些中文歌？ 3. What Chinese poems have you studied? 你学过哪些中国诗？ 4. How many kinds of Chinese instruments are there? What do they sound like? 你知道哪些中国乐器？它们的声音听起来像什么？ 5. What is a "character"? How are Chinese characters different from the alphabet? What is a "pictograph"? Is there a cursive form in Chinese writing? 什么是"字"？中国字是怎么来的？中国字和字母有什么差别？中国字也有草体吗？	* Children's talent shows 儿童才艺展示 * Reciting Tang poetry, singing songs 背诵唐诗、演唱儿歌	* Parental expectations for children in studying and showing off their talents 父母对孩子学习才艺、表现才艺的期望

(续表)

Essential Questions 核心问题	Focus Questions 焦点问题	Behavioral Culture 行为文化	Informational Culture 信息文化
	6. How is Chinese writing different from English writing? 中国字的写法和英文的写法有什么不一样?		
Creative Arts and Sciences 艺术与科学创造(3—4) 1) How did China's four great inventions influence world civilization? 中国的四大发明如何影响世界文明? (3—8) 2) How do folk arts influence Chinese daily life? 民俗艺术如何影响中国人的生活? (K—6) 3) How is Chinese music different from western music? 中国乐曲和西方音乐有何不同? (K—8) 4) How did Chinese written language develop over time? 中国文字是如何演变的? (K—8) 5) How is Chinese	1. What are the four great Chinese inventions? 什么是中国的四大发明? 2. What kinds of Chinese handicrafts are commonly used in Chinese celebrations? 中国节庆中常用到哪些民俗手工艺品? 3. On festival and other special days, what types of music do Chinese play, and what songs do they sing? 中国人在节庆或其他特殊的日子里,会演奏些什么音乐或唱些什么歌曲? 4. Do all Chinese characters imitate natural forms? 中国字都是模仿物体形象而造的吗?	* Practicing calligraphy and Chinese painting: meditation, cultivating patience and perseverance 练习书法/国画:静心、培养耐性及恒心	* Stories about the four great Chinese inventions 有关中国四大发明的故事 * Simple introduction to Chinese folk arts and handicrafts: origami, paper cuts, kite making, Chinese knots 简易民族手工艺:中国剪纸、折纸、风筝制作、中国结 * Chinese songs and ballads 中国儿歌/民谣 * Comparisons between traditional and modern musical instruments 传统乐器和现代乐器的比较 * Beijing opera, traditional shadow plays and puppet shows 京剧脸谱、传统皮影戏和布袋戏 * Interesting

(续表)

Essential Questions 核心问题	Focus Questions 焦点问题	Behavioral Culture 行为文化	Informational Culture 信息文化
language different from Western language? 中国语言和西方语言为什么有如此大的区别？(K—8)	5．What is a tone? When you speak Mandarin if the tone is not correct, what will happen? 什么是声调？说普通话时如果声调不正确，会有什么后果？		joint ideograms （3rd grade) 有趣的会意字（三年级学生） * Interesting phonograms (4th grade) 有趣的形声字（四年级学生） * The basic tones and structures of Chinese characters: radicals 声调、汉字的基本造字结构（部首偏旁） * Familiar children's song, poetry, tongue twisters, Tang poems 耳熟能详的儿歌、绕口令、唐诗 * Idioms/proverbs: 成语/谚语：画饼充饥；画龙点睛；画蛇添足；诗中有画，画中有诗；对牛弹琴 * Tang poem 唐诗：白居易《琵琶行》

(续表)

Essential Questions 核心问题	Focus Questions 焦点问题	Behavioral Culture 行为文化	Informational Culture 信息文化
Creative Arts and Sciences 艺术与科学创造（5—6） 1) How did China's four great inventions change the world? 中国四大发明如何影响世界？（3—8） 2) How do Chinese arts reflect Chinese thought? 中国艺术如何反映中国人的思维方式？（5—8） 3) How do folk arts play a part in Chinese daily life? 民俗艺术与中国人的生活有什么样的关系？（K—6） 4) How is Chinese music different from Western music? 中国乐曲与西方音乐有何不同？（K—8） 5) How did Chinese written language develop over time? 中国文字是如何演变的？（K—8） 6) What makes Chinese language so different from	1. What were the four great inventions and what was their influence? 四大发明的由来和影响分别是什么？ 2. What types of Chinese arts do Chinese children learn at school? 中国学生在校会学习哪些中国艺术？ 3. What are some famous Chinese folk arts and artists? 中国有哪些有名的民俗艺术？你知道哪些有名的中国艺术家？ 4. How is Chinese music used in daily life? 中国音乐在日常生活中有哪些用途？ 5. What is the difference between Chinese traditional music and Western music? 中国传统乐团和西洋交响乐团有什么分别？ 6. What are the differences in Chinese	* Spring couplets, spring flowers, household decorative arts: construction and meaning 春联、窗花、家中艺术饰品摆设的含义 * Children's achievements in art and music bring honor to their parents 儿女学习艺术、音乐的成就会给父母带来荣耀	* Origins/influences of the four great inventions 四大发明的由来及影响 * Other famous Chinese inventions 四大发明之外的其他中国发明 * Technological development in China today and its reflections in daily life 科技发展在中国日常生活中的体现及影响 * Art education in Chinese schools life 中国学校及生活中的艺术教育 * Famous collections in the National Palace Museum 故宫博物院中的著名收藏品：《清明上河图》、肉形石、翠玉白菜 * Famous child artists and their works 著名的儿童艺术家及其作品 * Famous Chinese paintings 著名的国画作品：徐悲鸿《八骏图》

(续表)

Essential Questions 核心问题	Focus Questions 焦点问题	Behavioral Culture 行为文化	Informational Culture 信息文化
western language? 中国语言和西方语言为什么有如此大的区别？(K—8) 7) What role does technology play in China? 科技在今日中国扮演着什么样的角色？(5—8)	phonetic systems? 汉语有哪些拼音系统？ 7. How has Chinese written script changed over time? 中国文字是怎么演变的？ 8. How have Chinese technological developments influenced you? 中国的科技发展对你有什么影响？		* Comparison between famous Chinese operas and American Broadway plays 著名的中国戏曲与美国百老汇剧的比较 * Folk art activities and festival celebrations 民俗艺术活动与节庆的关系 * Creation of the Chinese writing system 中国文字的造字方法 * Idioms 成语：诗中有画，画中有诗；诗情画意 * Ancient poem 古诗词：刘长卿《听弹琴》
Creative Arts and Sciences 艺术与科学创造（7—8） 1) How did China's four great inventions change the world? 中国四大发明如何影响世界？(3—8) 2) How do Chinese arts reflect Chinese thought? 中国艺术如何反映中国人的思维方式？(5—8) 3) How is Chinese	1. How do you think that modern life has been affected by the four great Chinese inventions? 你认为现代生活中哪些事物的进步与发展受到了中国四大发明的影响？ 2. What sorts of artistic influences and history have been shared between China and the West?	* Use of stamps/chops in daily life 印章在生活中的应用 * Chinese painting materials, using the brush 国画材料、毛笔的使用 * Cultivating moral and emotional restraint 修身养性的生活观 * Correspondence 书信往来	* China's four great inventions and their modern influences 中国四大发明及其对现代的影响 * China's four major thinkers 中国四大思想家的主张 * Appreciation of works of past and present famous Chinese calligraphers and painters 中国书

(续表)

Essential Questions 核心问题	Focus Questions 焦点问题	Behavioral Culture 行为文化	Informational Culture 信息文化
music different from Western music? 中国乐曲与西方音乐有何不同？（K—8） 4）How did Chinese written language develop over time? 中国文字是如何演变的？（K—8） 5）What makes Chinese language so different from Western language? 中国语言和西方语言为什么有如此大的区别？（K—8） 6）What role does technology play in China today? 科技在今日中国扮演着什么样的角色？（5—8）	中国和西方国家曾经有过什么样的艺术交流？ 3．What do you know about Chinese art? Do you think that art can change peoples' situations? In what ways? 你了解哪些中国艺术？你认为艺术能改变人的性格吗？如何改变？ 4．What do you think is the biggest difference between Chinese paintings and western paintings? 你认为中国画和西方绘画最大的不同点是什么？ 5．Can you compare western musical instruments and melodies with Chinese musical instruments and melodies? 哪些西方乐器的音调与中国乐器的相似？ 6．Can you identify some famous American classical music, folk music, and contemporary		法/国画及古今名家及作品欣赏 * Famous contemporary artists：Bei Yuming, Ma Youyou 现代艺术名人：贝聿铭、马友友 * Drama, music：Beijing opera, Huangmei melody 戏剧、音乐：京剧、黄梅戏 * Chinese opera and American opera make up 中国戏剧脸谱/美国歌剧的化妆 * Chinese folk dances/modern popular music 中国民族舞蹈/现代流行音乐 * Chinese traditional musical instruments 中国传统乐器 * Chinese gardens, architecture 中国园林/建筑 * Carving, porcelain, embroidery, chess 雕刻、陶瓷、丝绸、棋艺 * Literature, poetry 文学、诗词

(续表)

Essential Questions 核心问题	Focus Questions 焦点问题	Behavioral Culture 行为文化	Informational Culture 信息文化
	popular music? 你能说出一些美国古典音乐、民族音乐和经典流行音乐作品的名称吗？ 7. Do China and America have similar modern dance styles? 中国与美国有没有共同流行的舞蹈形式？ 8. Is Beijing opera's style of singing and acting similar to Western opera? 京剧的唱法和表演方式和西方戏剧有没有相同点？ 9. Does American theatre use similar styles of make up (as Chinese opera)? 美国戏剧中有没有类似脸谱的化妆方法？ 10. Do Chinese and American theatrical plays use similar types of stories? 中国和美国有没有相似的戏剧故事？ 11. How did Chinese writing change over time? Was this similar to changes in Western style writing systems?		* Creation and evolution of written language 文字的创造与演变 * Comparison of Chinese and Western painting, theatre, music scores, writing, popular music 中西绘画、戏剧、乐曲、文字、流行乐的对比 * Idioms 成语：一唱一和、异口同声、弦外之音、曲高和寡、自吹自擂、雅俗共赏、充耳不闻、靡靡之音、四面楚歌、有声有色、余音绕梁、震耳欲聋

(续表)

Essential Questions 核心问题	Focus Questions 焦点问题	Behavioral Culture 行为文化	Informational Culture 信息文化
	中国文字是如何演变的？这与西方文字的演变过程相同吗？ 12. What are the differences between Chinese and Western styles of reading? 中西方的文字阅读方式有什么样的差异？ 13. What is the place of technological development in China today? 科技发展在今日中国占有什么样的地位？		
Expressing Emotions and Feelings 情绪与情感表达(K—2) 1) What is emotion? 什么是情绪？(K—8) 2) How do we express our feelings? 我们如何表达个人情感？(K—8) 3) How do emotional expressions affect social relationships? 情感的表达方式如何影响人际关系？(K—8)	1. What is the difference between feeling happy, angry, sad and scared? 高兴、生气、伤心、害怕的感觉有什么不同？ 2. What kinds of things make you happy, angry, sad and scared? Why? 什么样的事情会让你高兴、生气、伤心或害怕？为什么？ 3. What do you do when you are happy, angry, sad or scared?	* Ways of expressing emotions 情绪表达方式 * Learning to control upsetting emotions 学习控制情绪 * Understanding the causes of emotions 了解情绪产生的原因 * Understanding how emotions influence relationships with friends 情绪会如何影响朋友关系	* Facial expression chart 面部表情图 * Nursery rhymes 童谣：高兴的时候拍拍手，生气的时候跺跺脚，伤心的时候眼泪流，害怕的时候会发抖 * Fables 寓言故事：东郭先生与狼/中山狼、螳螂之勇、老虎与刺猬 * Idioms 成语：唉声叹气、泪流满面、大惊小怪、兴奋不已、欢天喜地、得意洋洋

(续表)

Essential Questions 核心问题	Focus Questions 焦点问题	Behavioral Culture 行为文化	Informational Culture 信息文化
	当你高兴、生气、伤心或者害怕时会做什么？ 4. How do your friends recognize that you are angry? 你怎么让你的朋友知道你生气了？ 5. What causes you to argue or fight with your friends? How do you get along with friends? 我们为什么会和朋友吵架？该怎么和朋友和好？	* Learning to care for others 学习关怀他人 * Learning how to treat friends well 学习与朋友和好	
Expressing Emotions and Feelings 情绪与情感表达(3—4) 1) What are emotions and feelings? 什么是情感/情绪？(K—8) 2) How do we express our feelings? 我们如何表达情感？(K—8) 3) How and why do people express emotions in so many ways? 造成情感及情绪表达多样性的	1. Can you describe your personal feelings? 你能描述自己的情感吗？ 2. In addition to facial expressions, what other clues can help us understand our own or other people's feelings? 除了表情，还有哪些线索可以帮助我们了解自己或别人的情感？ 3. How do you express different types of	* Non-verbal emotional expressions such as facial expressions, eye contact, gestures, manner of speaking and body movements 表情、眼神、手势、语气和动作等非语言情绪表达方式 * Using appropriate emotional expressions to improve interpersonal relations 用适当的情绪表达方式来增进	* Chinese society is more tolerant and accepting of children's emotional behavior, because they are still young 中国社会对儿童的情绪表达有较高的接纳、包容度，因为他们年纪小 * Chinese people regard modesty as a virtue and do not easily accept people who are proud and arrogant 中国人视

(续表)

Essential Questions 核心问题	Focus Questions 焦点问题	Behavioral Culture 行为文化	Informational Culture 信息文化
原因是什么？(3—8) 4) How do emotional expressions affect social relationships? 情感的表达方式如何影响人际关系？(K—8)	emotions? How is this similar and different from the ways that others express these emotions? 你如何表达不同的情感？你和别人的表达方式有何不同？为什么？ 4. What are the effects of inappropriate emotional expressions? 情绪表达方式不当时会有什么影响？	人际关系 * Ways to respond when being praised 被赞美时的回应方式 * Chinese people do not often visibly show their delight does not mean they do not have emotions 中国人不常喜形于色 * You are more likely to express your inner feelings in more intimate relationships 关系亲密时，更容易进行内在情绪的表达	谦虚为美德，不容易接受自视较高、骄傲的人 * Chinese generally do not emphasize the individual，but consider the public/nation more important 中国人较不注重"小我"，凡事以"大我"为前提 * Idioms/proverbs 成语/谚语：喜上眉梢、喜气洋洋、喜极而泣、怒发冲冠、怒气冲冲、乐极生悲、乐不思蜀 * Tang poem 唐诗：张继《枫桥夜泊》
Expressing Emotions and Feelings 情绪与情感表达(5—6) 1) What are emotions and feelings? 什么是情感、情绪？(K—8) 2) How do we express our feelings? 我们如何表达情感？(K—8) 3) How and why do people express emotions in so many	1. Why do we have emotions? 人为什么会有情绪？ 2. How do you express your emotions? 你常用什么方式来表达情绪？ 3. What approach do you use for understanding other people's emotions? 你常用什么方法来了解	* Face, connections, etiquette 面子、关系、客气 * Chinese people believe that emotions are a personal matter and rarely seek professional counseling 中国人认为情绪处理是个人的事情，很少进行专业咨询 * Boys do not cry	* Basic emotions (joy, anger, fear, sorrow) and more complex emotions 基本情绪（喜怒哀惧）与多重复杂情绪 * Body language to expression emotions 表达情绪的肢体语言 * Sources of negative emotions: bullying, conflict with family

(续表)

Essential Questions 核心问题	Focus Questions 焦点问题	Behavioral Culture 行为文化	Informational Culture 信息文化
ways? 造成情感及情绪表达多样性的原因是什么？(3—8) 4) How do emotional expressions affect social relationships? 情感的表达方式如何影响人际关系？(K—8)	别人的心情？ 4. How do your emotional expressions change when interacting with different people or in different places? 对不同的人，或在不同的场合里，你的情感表达方式会有哪些不同？ 5. How do boys and girls express emotions in different ways? 男孩女孩表达情感的方式有哪些异同？ 6. How does culture shape different emotional expressions? 情感的表达方式有哪些文化差异？	easily 男儿有泪不轻弹 * Chinese people are more likely to use facial expressions than words in communicating emotions 中国人很少通过言语直接表达，多利用表情、脸色来表达或感知情绪	and friends, academic stress 负面情绪的来源：欺凌、与家人朋友的冲突、课业压力 * Methods of controlling emotions 调控情绪的方法 * Cultural differences in emotional expression 情绪表达的文化差异 * Poetry, calligraphy and painting as mediums of emotional expression 诗歌等表达情感的手段 * Emoticons 表情符号 * Idiom 成语（参考课程计划） * Tang poems 唐诗：李白《春夜洛城闻笛》，骆宾王《咏鹅》
Expressing Emotions and Feelings 情绪与情感表达(7—8) 1) What is emotion? 什么是情绪？(K—8) 2) How do we express our feelings? 我们如何表达个人	1. Where do people's emotions come from? What are the different ways of expressing emotions? 人的情绪是怎么产生的？心情的表达方式有哪些？	* Ways of expressing emotions within the family 面对家人时的情感表达方式 * Ways of expressing emotions between friends 朋友之间的情感表达方式	* Emotion related vocabulary 与情绪相关的词汇 * Chinese style letter writing 中式书信的写法 * Liang Shanbo and Zhu Yingtai 梁山伯与祝英台

(续表)

Essential Questions 核心问题	Focus Questions 焦点问题	Behavioral Culture 行为文化	Informational Culture 信息文化
情感？（K—8） 3) How and why do people express emotions in different ways? 人如何以不同的方式来表达情感？为什么？（3—8） 4) How do emotional expressions affect social relationships? 情感的表达方式如何影响人际关系？（K—8）	2. What do you think is the appropriate way to express happiness? 你认为用什么方式表达个人的喜怒哀乐是恰当的？ 3. How do emotions affect our behavior? 行为的表现与心情有什么对关系？ 4. What do you think are the differences in the ways that Chinese and Western people express emotions? Why? 你认为中国人的情绪表达方式与西方人有什么样的差别？为什么？ 5. How do you express emotions differently with family members and with friends? Why? 面对家人和朋友时，你的情绪表达方式有什么差异？为什么？ 6. How do males and females express emotions in different	* Gender differences in emotional and physical expression 男女的情感表达差异和肢体语言差别 * Be perfunctory (go through the motions), be evasive: expressions of refusal (let's think about it; let's study it) 敷衍、搪塞：拒绝的说法（可以考虑考虑，再研究研究） * Criticism: hinting at shortcomings (…but…/hopefully) 批评：以正面说法来暗示对方的缺点（……但是……/希望……） * Chinese people do not speak out, do not show visible pleasure, do not praise their family members in front of others, follow rules when accepting gifts 中国人不明言、不喜形于色，不在众人之前夸赞自家人，接受礼	* Attitudes towards life: showing modesty, being reserved, exercising self-restraint 生活态度：谦虚、含蓄、自持 * Cultural misunderstandings in modes of expression 表达中的"文化误解" * Idioms 成语：六亲不认；满面春风；惊魂未定；急不择言；七上八下；不知所措；愁眉苦脸；男女授受不亲；一见如故；一刀两断；无声胜有声；日有所思，夜有所梦；一切尽在不言中 * Love poems 情诗：柳永《凤栖梧》；秦观《鹊桥仙》；李白《三五七言》；元好问《摸鱼儿》

Master Thematic Table 429

(续表)

Essential Questions 核心问题	Focus Questions 焦点问题	Behavioral Culture 行为文化	Informational Culture 信息文化
	ways? How can inappropriate emotional expressions lead to misunderstandings? 你认为男性和女性表达情感的方式哪些异同？不恰当的方式会引起什么样的误会？ 7. When you are with friends from different cultural backgrounds, have you ever encountered interesting situations or misunderstandings cue to different ways of expressing emotions? Please explain. 你和来自不同文化背景的朋友在一起时，是否曾经因为表达方式不同而发生过有趣的事情或误会？ 8. How do you solve the misunderstandings that arise with friends from different cultures? 你怎么解决朋友之间因文化差异而造成的误会？	物的习惯表达方式 * Chinese views of social activities: males are active, females passive 中国人社交生活观念：男人主动，女人被动	

参考文献
References

Adair-Hauck, et. al., 2006. The Integrated Performance Assessment (IPA): Connecting Assessment to Instruction and Learning. Foreign Language Annals 39 (3): 359—382.

Anon., 2006. Beyond Festivals and Food: How Chinese Culture is Taught at CAIS. CAIS Connections Newsletter. Fall/Winter 2005—2006.

Bartz, Walter and Rosalie Vermette, 1996. Testing Cultural Competence. In Alan J. Singerman, ed. Acquiring Cross-Cultural Competence: Four Stages for Students of French. Lincolnwood, IL: National Textbook Company. Pp. 75—84.

Blaz, Deborah, 2011. A collection of performance tasks and rubrics: foreign language. Larchmont, NY: Eye on Education.

Bonin, Therese, 1982. Teaching Culture in Beginning Language Classes. Journal of the Chinese Language Teachers Association 17(3): 33—48.

Carstens, Sharon A., 2008. Conceptualizing and Teaching Chinese Culture in K—8 Mandarin Bilingual Programs. Journal of the Chinese Language Teachers Association 43 (3): 25—64.

Chiang Hsun (蒋勋), 2009, The Beauty of Chinese Calligraphy (汉字书法之美). Guilin: Guangxi Normal University Press.

Christensen, Matthew and J. PaulWarnick, 2006. Performed Culture: An Approach to East Asian Language Pedagogy. Columbus, OH: Ohio State University, National East Asian Languages Resource Center.

Davis, Linell, 2001. Doing Culture: Cross-Cultural Communication in Action. Beijing: Foreign Language Teaching and Research Press.

Deng Yan Chang and Liu Run Qing, 1989. Writing and Culture. Beijing: Foreign Language Teaching and Research Press.

Eddy, Jennifer, 2010. Theme and Variation: Composing Thematic Units and Performance Assessments. Pre-Conference Workshop, Chinese Education Conference, Chinese American International School Institute. San Francisco, April 9—11.

Falsgraf, Carl Douglas, 1994. Language and Culture at a Japanese Immersion School. Ph. D. Dissertation, University of Oregon.

Feng Shengli, Liao Haohsiang, and Wang Qiuyu, 2008. When to Say What. Beijing: The Commercial Press.

Garrison, Catherine and Michael Ehringhaus, n. d. Formative and Summative Assessments in the Classroom. National Middle School Association Website. www. nmsa. org/publications/webexclusive/assessment/tabid/1120/default. aspx (accessed 4/18/2011).

Griffiths, Carol, 2008. Age and Good Language Learners. In Carol Griffiths, ed. Lessons from Good Language Learners. Cambridge: Cambridge University Press. Pp. 35—48.

Hammerly, Hector, 1982. Synthesis in Second Language Teaching: An Introduction to Languistics. Blaine, WA: Second Language Publications.

Heusinkveld, Paula R., ed., 1997. Pathways to Culture: Readings on Teaching Culture in the Foreign Language Class. Yarmouth, ME: Intercultural Press Inc.

K—12 Chinese Standards Project, 1998. http://www. intac. com/%7Equick/chart1. htm (accessed 7/25/2003).

Klafehn, Jennifer and Pretta M. Banerjee and Chi-Yue Chiu, 2008. Navigating Cultures: The Role of Metacognitive Cultural Intelligence. In Soon Ang and Linn Van Dyne, (eds.) Handbook of Cultural Intelligence: Theory, Measurement, and Applications. Amonk, NY: ME Sharpe. Pp. 318—331.

Kuo, Cynthia, 2009. The Way We Communicate, Vols. I&II. Beijing: Sinolingua.

Kramsch, Claire, 1993. Context and Culture in Language Teaching. Oxford: Oxford University Press.

Lange, Dale and R. Michael Paige, eds., 2003. Culture as the Core: Perspectives on Culture in Second Language Learning. Greenwich, CN: Information Age Publishing.

Langford, Peter, 1989. Children's Thinking and Learning in the Elementary School. Lancaster PA: Technomic Publishing Co. Inc.

Language Learning Difficulty. Foreign Language Web. http://www. foreignlanguagesweb. com/essentials/difficulty-1. htm (Aaccessed Jan. 12, 2013).

Li Yuan (李湲), 2006. Childlike Innocence (童言无忌. 北京). Beijing: Foreign Languages Press.

Liu Changyue; Wang Jiyan; Li Jirui; Jia Yan, et. al. (刘长乐,王纪言,李吉瑞,贾赝,编导),2005. Tangrenjie (唐人街), Chinatown. Phoenix Satellite TV (凤凰卫视); Shantou Ocean Audio Visual Publishing, Tianyi Audiovisual Product Corporation. (汕头海洋音像出版社;天艺音像制品有限公司发行).

Liu Lixin (刘立新), 2010. Families with Children (家有儿女). Shanghai: Shanghai

World Book Publishing Co.

Liu Xun (刘珣), 2002. New Practical Chinese Reader (新实用汉语课本). Beijing: Beijing Language and Culture University Press.

Munoz, Carmen, 2006. The Effects of Age on Foreign Language Learning: The BAF Project. In Carmen Munoz, ed. Age and the Rate of Foreign Language Learning. Clevedon: Multilingual Matters Ltd. Pp. 1—40.

Myers, Dan, 2000. Teaching Culture with Key Words in Chinese as a Foreign Language: The State of the Field. Journal of the Chinese Language Teachers Association 35(3): 1—28.

Ning, Cynthia, 2009. Focusing on the Learner in the Chinese Language Classroom: Moving from "Talking the Talk" to "Walking the Walk." In Michael Everson and Yun Xiao, eds. Teaching Chinese as a Foreign Language: Theories and Applications. Boston: Cheng & Tsui Company. Pp. 35—60.

Office of Chinese Language Council International (OCLCI), 2009. International Curriculum for Chinese Language Education. Beijing: Foreign Language Teaching aand Research Press.

Paige, R. Michael et. al., 1999. Culture Learning in Language Education: A Review of the Literature. In M. Paige, D. Lange & Y. Yershova, eds. Culture as Core: Integrating Culture into the Language Curriculum. CARLA Working Paper Series #15. Minneapolis, MN: University of Minnesota. Pp. 1—72.

Phillips, J. K., 2003. National Standards for Foreign Language Learning: Culture, the Driving Force. In D. Lange and R. M. Paige, eds. Culture as the Core: Perspectives on Culture in Second Language Learning. Greenwich, CN: Information Age Publishing. Pp. 161—171.

Riekehof, Lottie, L., 1987. The Joy of Signing: the illustrated guide for mastering sign language and the manual alphabet. 2nd ed. Springfield, MO: Gospel Publishing House.

Risager, Karen, 2006. Language and Culture: Global Flows and Local Complexity. Clevedon: Multilingual Matters Ltd.

Sandrock, Paul, 2011. The Keys to Assessing Language Performance: Teacher's Manual. Alexandria, VA: American Council on the Teaching of Foreign Languages.

Schulz, Renate A., 2007. The Challenge of Assessing Cultural Understanding in the Context of Foreign Language Instruction. Foreign Language Annals 40 (1): 9—26.

Shu Yibing (舒一兵), 2011. A Comparative Guide to Chinese and American Culture

（中美国别文化教程）. Beijing: Peking University Press.

Standards for Foreign Language Learning: Preparing for the 21st Century, 1996. ERIC Clearinghouse.

Standards for Foreign Language Learning in the 21st Century, 1999. Lawrence, KS: Allen Press.

Tang, Yanfang, 2006. Beyond Behavior: Goals of Cultural Learning in the Second Language Classroom. The Modern Language Journal 90 (1): 86—99.

Teng, Chunhong, 2001. Bridging the Gap between Language and Culture: Integrating the PanGu Cartoon Video Program into Chinese Instruction. Journal of the Chinese Language Teachers Association 36 (2): 43—54.

Tragant, Elsa, 2006. Language Learning Motivation and Age. In Carmen Munoz, ed. Age and the Rate of Foreign Language Learning. Clevedon: Multilingual Matters Ltd. Pp. 237—267.

Walker, Galal and Mari Noda, 2000. Remembering the Future: Compiling Knowledge of Another Culture. In D. Birchbichler, ed. Reflecting on the past to shape the future. Pp. 187—212. Lincolnwood, IL: National Textbook Company. Pp. 187—212.

Wiggins, Grant and Jay McTighe, 2005. Understanding by Design (3rd ed.) Alexandria, VA: Association for Supervision and Curriculum Development.

Xing, Janet Zhiqun, 2006. Teaching and Learning Chinese as a Foreign Language: ae: a pedagogical grammar. Hong Kong: Hong Kong University Press.

Yang Jingzhen（杨景震）, 1998. 中国传统节日风俗的形成及其特征（The Characteristics and Forms of China's Traditional Festivals and Customs）中华文化论坛（Chinese Culture Forum）No. 3:32—36.

Yu, Li, 2009. Where is Culture: Culture Instruction and the Foreign Language Textbook. Journal of the Chinese Language Teachers Association 44 (3): 73—108.

Zhou Yanzhuo, shu Yibing（周彦卓,舒一兵）, 2010. *Games for Learning Chinese*（游戏学中文）. Beijing: Beijing Language and Cultrue University Press.